Canadian Cataloguing in Publication Data
Main entry under title:

Literary experiences: volume 1

Includes index.
ISBN 0-13-064528-1 (bound) ISBN 0-13-537762-5 (pbk.)

1. Canadian literature (English) - 20th
century.* 2. English literature. 3. English
literature - 20th century. 4. American literature.
5. American literature - 20th century.
I. Oster, John Edward. II. Iveson, Margaret L.,
1948-   . III. McClay, Jill Kedersha, 1952-   .

PN6014.L57 1989   808'.0427   C88-094955-4

Prentice-Hall, Inc., Englewood Cliffs, *New Jersey*
Prentice-Hall International, Inc., *London*
Prentice-Hall of Australia, Pty., Ltd., *Sydney*
Prentice-Hall of India Pvt., Ltd., *New Delhi*
Prentice-Hall of Japan, Inc., *Tokyo*
Prentice-Hall of Southest Asia (PTE) Ltd., *Singapore*
Editora Prentice-Hall do Brasil Ltda., *Rio de Janeiro*
Prentice-Hall Hispanoamericana, S.A., *Mexico*

ISBN 0-13-064528-1

Acquiring Editors: Dorothy Greenaway and David Steele
Project Editors: Paula Pettitt and MaryBeth Leatherdale
Production Editors: Ian Chunn and Lavinia Inbar
Production: Lois Enns
Design: David Peden
Composition: CompuScreen Typesetting
Cover photo: Robert Bourdeau
                1973
                Neg. N° 73-810-57
                8″ x 10″ (20.3 x 25.4 cm) Print

                Quebec, Canada
                Courtesy: Jane Corkin Gallery, Toronto

Printed and bound in Canada by Gagné Printing
1 2 3 4 5 6 GP 98 97 96 95 94 93

Literary Experiences

Volume One

Stories Poems Essays Plays

John E. Oster
Margaret L. Iveson
Jill Kedersha McClay

PRENTICE-HALL CANADA INC. SCARBOROUGH, ONTARIO

Table of Contents

UNIT ONE: THE REAL YOU

UNIT TWO: TRAVELLING THROUGH

UNIT THREE: NO MAN IS AN ISLAND

UNIT FOUR: WHAT I BELIEVE

Acknowledgments

No literary anthology is solely the work of its editors. The authors whose works are included here really began the process by creating literature which inspires us in our work with students. The students and teachers who responded to early drafts of the manuscript offered interesting and useful suggestions, many of which were incorporated into the final version of the book. Dorothy Greenaway and David Steele have provided assistance and support throughout this project. Also at Prentice-Hall, editors Paula Pettitt, MaryBeth Leatherdale and Lavinia Inbar carefully read and edited the drafts. Our families have read and responded to selections as well as encouraged and supported our efforts on this project as well as in our work more generally. Earl Buxton's example continues to influence the direction of our thinking about literature. Our thanks to you all.

John E. Oster

Margaret L. Iveson

Jill Kedersha McClay

To the Student

This book contains a wide variety of poems, stories, plays, and essays for your enjoyment. The selections will give you an opportunity to share the thoughts and feelings of writers from different times and many countries. It is important to realize, however, that literature also helps us to understand our own thoughts and feelings. To appreciate literature fully the reader must be receptive to what the author is saying through the content and form of the literary work. As we become more experienced in reading literature, we become aware of how the author's technique and style influence our response to the work. We should also be aware that our own past experiences influence the way we respond to what we read.

A number of writers have found very interesting ways of describing the relationship between readers and writers. In the following short poem, the Saskatchewan poet Robert Currie vividly illustrates the way in which the impact of a poem depends on a reader as well as a writer.

> My poems
> are slim bombs
> craving explosion
> Their fuses lie
> dark on the page
> awaiting your arrival with a light.

Similarly, the American novelist John Updike once stated in a radio interview, "When I create a mountain I create it out of all the mountains *you* have ever seen; when I create a woman I create her out of all the women *you* have ever known." Currie and Updike are just two of many modern writers who feel that the reader is as important as the writer in the literary experience. Alden Nowlan, in fact, in the following poem, "An Exchange of Gifts," claims that poems are rewritten every time someone reads them.

> As long as you read this poem
> I will be writing it.
> I am writing it here and now
> Before your eyes,
> Although you can't see me.
> Perhaps you'll dismiss this
> As a verbal trick,
> The joke is you're wrong;
> The real trick
> Is your pretending
> This is something
> Fixed and solid,
> External to us both.
> I tell you better:
> I will keep on
> Writing this poem for you
> Even after I'm dead.

These authors are suggesting that your own thoughts, feelings, and experiences affect your response to literature.

The poems, plays, stories, and essays in this anthology are arranged according to themes that have interested many people over the years. You will probably find that many of these works in some way touch your own life. You are invited, through reading, thinking, talking, and writing about your response to these selections, to share in the creative experience which the authors began.

UNIT 1

THE REAL YOU

Much of literature, like much of life, is an exploration of identity. In our daily conversation, we define our own identity through telling the stories of our lives and by commenting on the identities of others. The sense we have of who we are is influenced by our self-perception and by the perceptions of others. It is also influenced by the roles we play in life, the people with whom we associate, and the groups to which we belong. It is affected by our relationships with our environment and by the experiences we encounter.

Yet in most people there are certain consistent qualities that will remain the same regardless of circumstances. The question "Who am I?" is one which recurs throughout life, but is perhaps especially important to young adults faced with decisions that will affect the course of their lives.

Writers, too, are fascinated by who and what people are, and by the incidents or circumstances which may have shaped their characters and personalities. Works in this section explore some aspects of personal, group, and cultural identity, and the struggles of individuals to attain, understand, and maintain their identity. Reading selections such as these may help us reflect on our own identity and increase our understanding of other people.

Eighteen

Maria Banus

(translated by Willis Barnstone and Matei Calinescu)

Wet streets. It has rained drops big as silver coins,
gold in the sun.
My mind charges the world like a bull.
Today I am eighteen.

The good rain batters me with crazy thoughts.
Look. Drops are warm and slow
as when I was in a carriage, pinned tight
in diapers, drenched and unchanged for an hour.

Yes, it rained as tomorrow, in the past, always.
The heart scrapes through time, is one heart.
My temples beat stronger than temples of time.

Like a common bum I think of drinking life,
but I am burnt, even by the hot stream of its juices.
I am eighteen.

The Game of Our Lives

Peter Gzowski

I N the winters of my boyhood, my life centred on a hockey rink in Dickson Park, across the road and down the hill from my parents' duplex apartment. The rink lay on a low stretch of the park, between the baseball diamond and a low, grey building used to exhibit farmers' wares during the fall fair. Even before freeze-up, workmen would set up boards around the rink's space, and the boards would stand there through the last days of autumn, pale against the darkening grass, waiting for the season to begin. Metal light standards sprouted along their edges. With the first frost, the workmen would begin to flood, so that well before Christmas we could skate, and each day after school and all day on weekends, until spring softened the ice, we would give our lives to our game.

Weekends were the best. I would wake early Saturday morning, and pad down the hall to the sunny kitchen at the back of the apartment, careful not to wake my parents. I would slither down the back stairs for the milk, reaching one goose-pimply arm out to clutch the cold bottles, from which, as often as not, the frozen golden Guernsey cream had pushed the tops. Then upstairs again for cereal with brown sugar and, if I felt leisurely, a piece of toast. Into my clothes: warm corduroy trousers, a plaid shirt and heavy sweater, thick woollen socks. Down the stairs again, where my skates and outer clothing had steamed overnight on the radiator. I would lace on the skates, stretching out my leg with each eyehole to get the laces tight enough to stop the circulation. A good pair of laces could be pulled tight enough to be looped around the ankles twice and tied in a double bow in front. Stand on the linoleum to get the feel. Up on the toes. Good. Then into coat and toque, ear-muffs if the day was cream-popping cold, then on with the mittens—wool, unfortunately, with a hope of hockey gloves for Christmas—and out across the squeaky snow.

If I was lucky, I would get to the rink before anyone else. Then, I could move around by myself, revelling in the clean air and the early light, and the untrammelled freedom I would feel as my body swayed with the rhythm of my strides. My hockey stick was an extension of my body, swinging back and forth in front of me as I moved. Counter-clockwise I went at first, moving on the right wing along the boards and down along the end, making ever longer strides as I built up speed, digging in with the pushing foot, hearing the *rask, rask* as I glided into each step. Around the corners, crossing the right leg over the left, leaning into the turn, building up momentum for the straightaway, then harder even down the boards, bent at the waist, getting my shoulders into it. Head down, with the stick held horizontal in front. Dig, dig, then turn again, my body warming as I moved. Now some turns the other way. Kitty-corner across the diagonal of the rink, swerving around rough patches, skates biting into the good ice, bumping ratch-et-quick across the choppy islands. Tighter turns now, smaller circles, raising the outer leg to swing with centrifugal force. Back onto the long stretch of open ice, glass smooth, its surface cleared by the overnight winds, exulting with jumps and hops, scissoring in the air, heading breakneck toward the boards to stop in a spray of snow and stand laughing and panting in the morning sun.

Dickson park was in Galt, a small industrial city in southwestern Ontario, long since swallowed up (though not in spirit) by the municipality of Cambridge. But the rink where I spent so much of my boyhood could have been at Eighty-sixth Street in Edmonton, or on the mill-pond of Richibucto, New Brunswick, or in the parish schoolyard of Sainte-Justine-de-Dorchester, Quebec, where Roch Carrier set a classic short story that translated my experience into French. Swapping memories in later years, I would sometimes imagine one great outdoor hockey game, stretching from just inside the Rockies to the shores of the Atlantic, detouring only around the too temperate climate of a few of the bigger cities. Or, perhaps, a hundred thousand simultaneous games, all overlapping as our own used to overlap at Dickson Park, kept separate only by the carved initials, inlaid in snow, on our pucks.

There were, to be sure, regional variations. In the west, a rule provided that if a frozen puck shattered against whatever was serving as a goalpost, the destiny of the biggest portion would determine if a goal had been scored. Western kids often wore what they called "garbage mitts"—padded for heavy duty by city workers—instead of hockey gloves; Maritimers used their father's work gauntlets, with heavy leather up the wrists. But the essential rules were the same everywhere: no goal-sucking, no raising, unless whoever's younger brother was stuck in goal was also foolish enough to wear shin-pads, no long shots, no throwing your stick to stop a breakaway. We began our games the same way, by choosing up sides, and we played the same infinite hours, and kept the same infinite scores. The initials on our pucks were in fact superfluous, for we knew how to stick-handle and keep track of our own game without looking down; we had learned it playing keepaway, where you held your head up or lost the puck forever. Wherever we played, we knew the same pleasures: the thrill of carrying the puck at top speed, cradling it with your stick pushed out like a probing lance; the satisfaction of a well-executed pass, the joy of slipping past a defenceman to go in on the open goal.

Our best sticks were made of rock elm, but since they cost as much as $1.25 each, we settled for grey ash or ordinary elm, and wrapped them thick in tar tape; when the tar tape wore through at the bottom and made moth's wings on the blades, we taped them with adhesive tape from our families' medicine chests, and the sticks lasted all winter. We would wear them down to what we all called toothpicks, then use them through the spring for road hockey. On the rinks, we secured our shin pads with rings from our mothers' sealers, or strips cut from inner tubes, and the agony of a puck that caught us just under the kneecap—worse even than the searing ache of frozen feet —was as common to all our experiences as was winter itself.

I sometimes wonder if the fervour with which we pursued our game moulded us more than we realized. In 1976, in *The International Review of Sports Sociology*, a Canadian named Howard L. Nixon wrote of "those who are consumed by this passion," and concluded that "the culture of hockey will profoundly affect their values, attitudes, and behaviour . . . as they mature." I think, for example, of the way we looked on girls, with their white skates and their hours on the nearby—but separate—"pleasure rink," or of those few of our own sex who chose not to play hockey at all, and were branded forever as outsiders. And I wonder if those attitudes, formed on the rinks and rivers and sloughs, have not stayed with us into our marriages and our boardrooms.

I know that it was in hockey that we found our heroes. We collected their images on Beehive Golden Corn Syrup cards and tore their history from the pages of newspapers and magazines we delivered. Sometimes we touched them. In Galt, Syl Apps, the captain of the Maple Leafs, addressed our hockey banquet and gave out advice I can still recite—"shoot low and on the stick side." We watched an awkward Gordie Howe make his first shy (and illegal, since he was a transfer from Saskatchewan) forays into junior hockey, with the Galt Red Wings. And one memorable summer afternoon, Marty Pavelich and Harry Lumley, two Junior Red Wings who would later go to Detroit—and who played on the same team as Lee Fogolin's father—tossed a gang of us, squealing, into Willow Lake. We could, all of us, recite the line-ups of our favourite teams, and on Saturday nights, we huddled by our radios to hear Foster Hewitt limn their skills. For their skills were our skills; in our dreams, and sometimes alone on the evening ice, we would score over and over again the winning goal in overtime of the Stanley Cup's deciding game, and in our own scratchy voices we would hail the astonishing debut of the lanky rookie from Edmonton or Richibucto or Galt.

The boys I played hockey with have gone on, the more successful of them, to run newspapers and department stores, to become chemists and lawyers. But there is not one who would not have been a hockey player if he could have been. As we matured, we chose other heroes, and even in the days of our boyhood there may have been those among us who dreamed of other futures. But all of us dreamed of hockey glory. Later, when Elvis Presley sang or Pierre Trudeau made his way through adoring throngs, we envied and admired them. But when Bobby Hull wheeled down the wing, his sweater bulging in the wind, we were there with him. We understood; we knew what it felt like. All that separated us from our true heroes was that they were better at something we all had done. They belonged to us, as no other kind of hero ever could, at once more celebrated and more approachable because of what we shared. They were *of* us, playing the game of our lives.

Red Dress—1946

Alice Munro

MY mother was making me a dress. All through the month of November I would come from school and find her in the kitchen, surrounded by cut-up red velvet and scraps of tissue-paper pattern. She worked at an old treadle machine pushed up against the window to get the light, and also to let her look out, past the stubble fields and bare vegetable garden, to see who went by on the road. There was seldom anybody to see.

The red velvet material was hard to work with, it pulled, and the style my mother had chosen was not easy either. She was not really a good sewer. She liked to make things; that is different. Whenever she could she tried to skip basting and pressing and she took no pride in the fine points of tailoring, the finishing of buttonholes and the overcasting of seams as, for instance, my aunt and my grandmother did. Unlike them she started off with an inspiration, a brave and dazzling idea; from that moment on, her pleasure ran downhill. In the first place she could never find a pattern to suit her. It was no wonder; there were no patterns made to match the ideas that blossomed in her head. She had made me, at various times when I was younger, a flowered organdie dress with a high Victorian neckline edged in scratchy lace, with a poke bonnet to match; a Scottish plaid outfit with a velvet jacket and tam; an embroidered peasant blouse worn with a full red skirt and black laced bodice. I had worn these clothes with docility, even pleasure, in the days when I was unaware of the world's opinion. Now, grown wiser, I wished for dresses like those my friend Lonnie had, bought at Beale's store.

I had to try it on. Sometimes Lonnie came home from school with me and she would sit on the couch watching. I was embarrassed by the way my mother crept around me, her knees creaking, her breath coming heavily. She muttered to herself. Around the house she wore no corset or stockings, she wore wedge-heeled shoes and ankle socks; her legs were marked with lumps of blue-green veins. I thought her squatting position shameless, even obscene; I tried to keep talking to Lonnie so that her attention would be taken away from my mother as much as possible. Lonnie wore the composed, polite, appreciative expression that was her disguise in the presence of grownups. She laughed at them and was a ferocious mimic, and they never knew.

My mother pulled me about, and pricked me with pins. She made me turn around, she made me walk away, she made me stand still. "What do you think of it, Lonnie?" she said around the pins in her mouth.

"It's beautiful," said Lonnie, in her mild, sincere way. Lonnie's own mother was dead. She lived with her father who never noticed her, and this, in my eyes, made her seem both vulnerable and privileged.

"It *will* be, if I can ever manage the fit," my mother said. "Ah, well," she said theatrically, getting to her feet with a woeful creaking and sighing, "I doubt if she appreciates it." She enraged me, talking like this to Lonnie, as if Lonnie were grown up and I were still a child. "Stand still," she said, hauling the pinned and basted dress over my head. My head was muffled in velvet, my body exposed in an old cotton school slip. I felt like a great raw lump, clumsy and goose-pimpled. I wished I was like Lonnie, light-boned, pale and thin; she had been a Blue Baby.

"Well nobody ever made me a dress when I was going to high school," my mother said. "I made my own, or I did without." I was afraid she was going to start again on the story of her walking seven miles to town and finding a job waiting on tables in a boarding-house, so that she could go to high school. All the stories of my mother's life which had once interested me had begun to seem melodramatic, irrelevant, and tiresome.

"One time I had a dress given to me," she said. "It was a cream-coloured cashmere wool with royal blue piping down the front and lovely mother-of-pearl buttons. I wonder what ever became of it?"

When we got free Lonnie and I went upstairs to my room. It was cold, but we stayed there. We talked about the boys in our class, going up and down the rows and saying, "Do you like him? Well, do you half-like him? Do you *hate* him? Would you go out with him if he asked you?" Nobody had asked us. We were thirteen, and we had been going to high school for two months. We did questionnaires in magazines, to find out whether we had personality and whether we would be popular. We read articles on how to make up our faces to accentuate our good points and how to carry on a conversation on the first date and what to do when a boy tried to go too far. Also we read articles on frigidity of the menopause, abortion and why husbands seek satisfaction away from home. When we were not doing school work, we were occupied most of the time with the garnering, passing on and discussing of sexual information. We had made a pact to tell each other everything. But one thing I did not tell was about this dance, the high school Christmas Dance for which my mother was making me a dress. It was that I did not want to go.

At high school I was never comfortable for a minute. I did not know about Lonnie. Before an exam, she got icy hands and palpitations, but I was close to despair at all times. When I was asked a question in class, any simple little question at all, my voice was apt to come out squeaky, or else hoarse and trembling. When I had to go to the blackboard I was sure— even at a time of the month when this could not be true—that I had blood on my skirt. My hands became slippery with sweat when they were required to work the blackboard compass. I could not hit the ball in volleyball; being called upon to per- form an action in front of others made all my reflexes come undone. I hated Business Practice because you had to rule pages for an account book, using a straight pen, and when the teacher looked over my shoulder all the delicate lines wobbled and ran together. I hated Science; we perched on stools under harsh lights behind tables of unfamiliar, fragile equipment, and were taught by the principal of the school, a man with a cold, self-relishing voice—he read the Scriptures every morning—and a great talent for inflicting humiliation. I hated English because the boys played bingo at the back of the room while the teacher, a stout, gentle girl, slightly cross-eyed, read Wordsworth at the front. She threatened them, she begged them, her face red and her voice as unreliable as mine. They offered burlesqued apologies and when she started to read again they took up rapt postures, made swooning faces, crossed their eyes, flung their hands over their hearts. Sometimes she would burst into tears, there was no help for it, she had to run out into the hall. Then the boys made loud mooing noises; our hungry laughter—oh, mine too—pursued her. There was a carnival atmosphere of brutality in the room at such times, scaring weak and suspect people like me.

But what was really going on in the school was not Business Practice and Science and English, there was something else that gave life its urgency and brightness. That old building, with its rock-walled clammy basements and black cloakrooms and pictures of dead royalties and lost explorers, was full of the tension and excitement of sexual competition, and in this, in spite of daydreams of vast successes, I had premonitions of total defeat. Something had to happen, to keep me from that dance.

With December came snow, and I had an idea. Formerly I had considered falling off my bicycle and spraining my ankle and I had tried to manage this, as I rode home along the hard-frozen, deeply rutted country roads. But it was too difficult. However, my throat and bronchial tubes were supposed to be weak; why not expose them? I started getting out of bed at night and opening my window a little. I knelt down and let the wind, sometimes stinging with snow, rush in around my bared throat. I took off my pajama top. I said to myself the words "blue with cold" and as I knelt there, my eyes shut, I pictured my chest and throat turning blue, the cold, greyed blue of veins under the skin. I stayed until I could not stand it any more, and then I took a handful of snow from the windowsill and smeared it all over my chest, before I buttoned my pajamas. It would melt against the flannelette and I would be sleeping in wet clothes, which was supposed to be the worst thing of all. In the morning, the moment I woke up, I cleared my throat, testing for soreness, coughed experimentally, hopefully, touched my forehead to see if I had fever. It was no good. Every morning, including the day of the dance, I rose defeated, and in perfect health.

The day of the dance I did my hair up in steel curlers. I had never done this before, because my hair was naturally curly, but today I wanted the protection of all possible female rituals. I lay on the couch in the kitchen, reading *The Last Days of Pompeii*, and wishing I was there. My mother, never satisfied, was sewing a white lace collar on the dress; she had decided it was too grown-up looking. I watched the hours. It was one of the shortest days of the year. Above the couch, on the wallpaper, were old games of Xs and Os, old drawings and scribblings my brother and I had done when we were sick with bronchitis. I looked at them and longed to be back safe behind the boundaries of childhood.

When I took out the curlers my hair, both naturally and artificially stimulated, sprang out in an exuberant glossy bush. I wet it, I combed it, beat it with the brush and tugged it down along my cheeks. I applied face powder, which stood out chalkily on my hot face. My mother got out her Ashes of Roses Cologne, which she never used, and let me splash it over my arms. Then she zipped up the dress and turned me around to the mirror. The dress was princess style, very tight in the midriff. I saw how my breasts, in their new stiff brassiere, jutted out surprisingly, with mature authority, under the childish frills of the collar.

"Well I wish I could take a picture," my mother said. "I am really, genuinely proud of that fit. And you might say thank you for it."

"Thank you," I said.

The first thing Lonnie said when I opened the door to her was, "Jesus, what did you do to your hair?"

"I did it up."

"You look like a Zulu. Oh, don't worry. Get me a comb and I'll do the front in a roll. It'll look all right. It'll even make you look older."

I sat in front of the mirror and Lonnie stood behind me, fixing my hair. My mother seemed unable to leave us. I wished she would. She watched the roll take shape and said, "You're a wonder, Lonnie. You should take up hairdressing."

"That's a thought," Lonnie said. She had on a pale blue crepe dress, with a peplum and bow; it was much more grown-up than mine even without the collar. Her hair had come out as sleek as the girl's on the bobby-pin card. I had always thought secretly that Lonnie could not be pretty because she had crooked teeth, but now I saw that crooked teeth or not, her stylish dress and smooth hair made me look a little like a golliwog, stuffed into red velvet, wide-eyed, wild-haired, with a suggestion of delirium.

My mother followed us to the door and called out into the dark, "Au reservoir!" This was a traditional farewell of Lonnie's and mine; it sounded foolish and desolate coming from her, and I was so angry with her for using it that I did not reply. It was only Lonnie who called back cheerfully, encouragingly, "Good night!"

The gymnasium smelled of pine and cedar. Red and green bells of fluted paper hung from the basketball hoops; the high barred windows were hidden by green boughs. Everybody in the upper grades seemed to have come in couples. Some of the Grade Twelve and Thirteen girls had brought boy friends who had already graduated, who were young businessmen around the town. These young men smoked in the gymnasium, nobody could stop them, they were free. The girls stood beside them, resting their hands casually on male sleeves, their faces bored, aloof and beautiful. I longed to be like that. They behaved as if only they—the older ones—were really at the dance, as if the rest of us, whom they moved among and peered around, were, if not invisible, inanimate; when the first dance was announced—a Paul Jones—they moved out languidly, smiling at each other as if they had been asked to take part in some half-forgotten childish game. Holding hands and shivering, crowding up together, Lonnie and I and the other Grade Nine girls followed.

I didn't dare look at the outer circle as it passed me, for fear I should see some unmannerly hurrying-up. When the music stopped I stayed where I was, and half-raising my eyes I saw a boy named Mason Williams coming reluctantly towards me. Barely touching my waist and my fingers, he began to dance with me. My legs were hollow, my arm trembled from the shoulder, I could not have spoken. This Mason Williams was one of the heroes of the school; he played basketball and hockey and walked the halls with an air of royal sullenness and barbaric contempt. To have to dance with a nonentity like me was as offensive to him as having to memorize Shakespeare. I felt this as keenly as he did and imagined that he was exchanging looks of dismay with his friends. He steered me, stumbling, to the edge of the floor. He took his hand from my waist and dropped my arm.

"See you," he said. He walked away.

It took me a minute or two to realize what had happened and that he was not coming back. I went and stood by the wall alone. The Physical Education teacher, dancing past energetically in the arms of a Grade Ten boy, gave me an inquisitive look. She was the only teacher in the school who made use of the words social adjustment, and I was afraid that if she had seen, or if she found out, she might make some horribly public attempt to make Mason finish out the dance with me. I myself was not angry or surprised at Mason; I accepted his position, and mine, in the world of school and I saw that what he had done was the realistic thing to do. He was a Natural Hero, not a Student Council type of hero bound for success beyond the school; one of those would have danced with me courteously and patronizingly and left me feeling no better off. Still, I hoped not many people had seen. I hated people seeing. I began to bite the skin on my thumb.

When the music stopped I joined the surge of girls to the end of the gymnasium. Pretend it didn't happen, I said to myself. Pretend this is the beginning, now.

The band began to play again. There was movement in the dense crowd at our end of the floor, it thinned rapidly. Boys came over, girls went out to dance. Lonnie went. The girl on the other side of me went. Nobody asked me. I remembered a magazine article Lonnie and I had read, which said *Be gay! Let the boys see your eyes sparkle, let them hear laughter in your voice! Simple, obvious, but how many girls forget!* It was true, I had forgotten. My eyebrows were drawn together with tension, I must look scared and ugly. I took a deep breath and tried to loosen my face. I smiled. But I felt absurd, smiling at no one. And I observed that girls on the dance floor, popular girls, were not smiling; many of them had sleepy, sulky faces and never smiled at all.

Girls were still going out to the floor. Some, despairing, went with each other. But most went with boys. Fat girls, girls with pimples, a poor girl who didn't own a good dress and had to wear a skirt and sweater to the dance; they were claimed, they danced away. Why take them and not me? Why everybody else and not me? I have a red velvet dress, I did my hair in curlers, I used a deodorant and put on cologne. *Pray*, I thought. I couldn't close my eyes but I said over and over again in my mind, *Please, me, please*, and I locked my fingers behind my back in a sign more potent than crossing, the same secret sign Lonnie and I used not to be sent to the blackboard in Math.

It did not work. What I had been afraid of was true. I was going to be left. There was something mysterious the matter with me, something that could not be put right like bad breath or overlooked like pimples, and everybody knew it, and I knew it; I had known it all along. But I had not known it for sure, I had hoped to be mistaken. Certainty rose inside me like sickness. I hurried past one or two girls who were also left and went into the girls' washroom. I hid myself in a cubicle.

That was where I stayed. Between dances girls came in and went out quickly. There were plenty of cubicles; nobody noticed that I was not a temporary occupant. During the dances, I listened to the music which I liked but had no part of any more. For I was not going to try any more. I only wanted to hide in here, get out without seeing anybody, get home.

One time after the music started somebody stayed behind. She was taking a long time running the water, washing her hands, combing her hair. She was going to think it funny that I stayed in so long. I had better go out and wash my hands, and maybe while I was washing them she would leave.

It was Mary Fortune. I knew her by name, because she was an officer of the Girls' Athletic Society and she was on the Honour Roll and she was always organizing things. She had something to do with organizing this dance; she had been around to all the classrooms asking for volunteers to do the decorations. She was in Grade Eleven or Twelve.

"Nice and cool in here," she said. "I came in to get cooled off. I get so hot."

She was still combing her hair when I finished my hands. "Do you like the band?" she said.

"It's all right." I didn't really know what to say. I was surprised at her, an older girl, taking this time to talk to me.

"I don't. I can't stand it. I hate dancing when I don't like the band. Listen. They're so choppy. I'd just as soon not dance as dance to that."

I combed my hair. She leaned against a basin, watching me.

"I don't want to dance and don't particularly want to stay in here. Let's go and have a cigarette."

"Where?"

"Come on, I'll show you."

At the end of the washroom there was a door. It was unlocked and led into a dark closet full of mops and pails. She had me hold the door open, to get the washroom light, until she found the knob of another door. This door opened into darkness.

"I can't turn on the light or somebody might see," she said. "It's the janitor's room." I reflected that athletes always seemed to know more than the rest of us about the school as a building; they knew where things were kept and they were always coming out of unauthorized doors with a bold, preoccupied air. "Watch out where you're going," she said. "Over at the far end there's some stairs. They go up to a closet on the second floor. The door's locked at the top, but there's like a partition between the stairs and the room. So if we sit on the steps, even if by chance someone did come in here, they wouldn't see us."

"Wouldn't they smell smoke?" I said.

"Oh, well. Live dangerously."

There was a high window over the stairs which gave us a little light. Mary Fortune had cigarettes and matches in her purse. I had not smoked before except the cigarettes Lonnie and I made ourselves, using papers and tobacco stolen from her father; they came apart in the middle. These were much better.

"The only reason I even came tonight," Mary Fortune said, "is because I am responsible for the decorations and I wanted to see, you know, how it looked once people got in there and everything. Otherwise why bother? I'm not boy-crazy."

In the light from the high window I could see her narrow, scornful face, her dark skin pitted with acne, her teeth pushed together at the front, making her look adult and commanding.

"Most girls are. Haven't you noticed that? The greatest collection of boy-crazy girls you could imagine is right here in this school."

I was grateful for her attention, her company and her cigarette. I said I thought so too.

"Like this afternoon. This afternoon I was trying to get them to hang the bells and junk. They just get up on the ladders and fool around with boys. They don't care if it ever gets decorated. It's just an excuse. That's the only aim they have in life, fooling around with boys. As far as I'm concerned, they're idiots."

We talked about teachers, and things at school. She said she wanted to be a physical education teacher and she would have to go to college for that, but her parents did not have enough money. She said she planned to work her own way through, she wanted to be independent anyway, she would work in the cafeteria and in the summer she would do farm work, like picking tobacco. Listening to her, I felt the acute phase of my unhappiness passing. Here was someone who had suffered the same defeat as I had—I saw that—but she was full of energy and self-respect. She had thought of other things to do. She would pick tobacco.

We stayed there talking and smoking during the long pause in the music, when, outside, they were having doughnuts and coffee. When the music started again Mary said, "Look, do we have to hang around here any longer? Let's get our coats and go. We can go down to Lee's and have a hot chocolate and talk in comfort, why not?"

We felt our way across the janitor's room, carrying ashes and cigarette butts in our hands. In the closet, we stopped and listened to make sure there was nobody in the washroom. We came back into the light and threw the ashes into the toilet. We had to go out and cut across the dance-floor to the cloak-room, which was beside the outside door.

A dance was just beginning. "Go round the edge of the

floor," Mary said. "Nobody'll notice us."

I followed her. I didn't look at anybody. I didn't look for Lonnie. Lonnie was probably not going to be my friend any more, not as much as before anyway. She was what Mary would call boy-crazy.

I found that I was not so frightened, now that I had made up my mind to leave the dance behind. I was not waiting for anybody to choose me. I had my own plans. I did not have to smile or make signs for luck. It did not matter to me. I was on my way to have a hot chocolate, with my friend.

A boy said something to me. He was in my way. I thought he must be telling me that I had dropped something or that I couldn't go that way or that the cloakroom was locked. I didn't understand that he was asking me to dance until he said it over again. It was Raymond Bolting from our class, whom I had never talked to in my life. He thought I meant yes. He put his hand on my waist and almost without meaning to, I began to dance.

We moved to the middle of the floor. I was dancing. My legs had forgotten to tremble and my hands to sweat. I was dancing with a boy who had asked me. Nobody told him to, he didn't have to, he just asked me. Was it possible, could I believe it, was there nothing the matter with me after all?

I thought that I ought to tell him there was a mistake, that I was just leaving, I was going to have a hot chocolate with my girl friend. But I did not say anything. My face was making certain delicate adjustments, achieving with no effort at all the grave absent-minded look of those who were chosen, those who danced. This was the face that Mary Fortune saw, when she looked out of the cloakroom door, her scarf already around her head. I made a weak waving motion with the hand that lay on the boy's shoulder, indicating that I apologized, that I didn't know what had happened and also that it was no use waiting for me. Then I turned my head away, and when I looked again she was gone.

Raymond Bolting took me home and Harold Simons took Lonnie home. We all walked together as far as Lonnie's corner. The boys were having an argument about a hockey game, which Lonnie and I could not follow. Then we separated into couples and Raymond continued with me the conversation he had been having with Harold. He did not seem to notice that he was now talking to me instead. Once or twice I said, "Well I don't know I didn't see that game," but after a while I decided just to say "H'm hmm," and that seemed to be all that was necessary.

One other thing he said was, "I didn't realize you lived such a long ways out." And he sniffled. The cold was making my nose run a little too, and I worked my fingers through the candy wrappers in my coat pocket until I found a shabby Kleenex. I didn't know whether I ought to offer it to him or not, but he sniffled so loudly that I finally said, "I just have this one Kleenex, it probably isn't even clean, it probably has ink on it. But if I was to tear it in half we'd each have something."

"Thanks," he said. "I sure could use it."

It was a good thing, I thought, that I had done that, for at my gate, when I said, "Well, good night," and after he said, "Oh, yeah. Good night," he leaned towards me and kissed me, briefly, with the air of one who knew his job when he saw it, on the corner of my mouth. Then he turned back to town, never knowing he had been my rescuer, that he had brought me from Mary Fortune's territory into the ordinary world.

I went around the house to the back door, thinking, I have been to a dance and a boy has walked me home and kissed me. It was all true. My life was possible. I went past the kitchen window and I saw my mother. She was sitting with her feet on the open oven door, drinking tea out of a cup without a saucer. She was just sitting and waiting for me to come home and tell her everything that had happened. And I would not do it, I never would. But when I saw the waiting kitchen, and my mother in her faded, fuzzy Paisley kimono, with her sleepy but doggedly expectant face, I understood what a mysterious and oppressive obligation I had, to be happy, and how I had almost failed it, and would be likely to fail it, every time, and she would not know.

A Boy I Knew

E. B. WHITE

I am quite sure that the character I'm least likely to forget is a boy I grew up with and nowadays see little of. I keep thinking about him. Once in a while I catch sight of him—down a lane, or just coming out of a men's washroom. Sometimes I will be gazing absently at my own son, now nine years old, and there in his stead this other boy will be, blindingly familiar yet wholly dreamlike and unapproachable. Although he enjoys a somewhat doubtful corporality, and occurs only occasionally, like a stitch in the side, without him I should indeed be lost. He is the boy that once was me.

The most memorable character in any man's life, and often the most inspiring, is the lad that once he was. I certainly can never forget him, and, at rare intervals when his trail crosses mine, the conjunction fills me with elation. Once, quite a while ago, I wrote a few verses which I put away in a folder to ripen. With the reader's kind permission I will exhume these lines now, because they explain briefly what I am getting at:

> In the sudden mirror in the hall
> I saw not my own self at all,
> I saw a most familiar face:
> My father stood there in my place,
> Returning, in the hall lamp's glare,
> My own surprised and watery stare.
> In thirty years my son shall see
> Not himself standing there, but me.

This bitter substitution, or transmigration, one generation with another, must be an experience which has disturbed men from the beginning of time. There comes a moment when you discover yourself in your father's shoes, saying his say, putting on his act, even looking as he looked; and in that moment everything is changed, because if you are your father, then your son must be you. Or something like that—it's never quite clear. But anyway you begin to think of this early or original self as someone apart, a separate character, not someone you once were but someone you once knew.

I remember once taking an overnight journey with my son in a Pullman compartment. He slept in the lower berth, handy to the instrument panel containing fan and light controls; I slept in the upper. Early in the morning I awoke and from my vantage point looked down. My boy had raised the shade a few inches and was ingesting the moving world. In that instant I encountered my unforgettable former self: it seemed as though it were I who was down there in the lower berth looking out of the train window just as the sky was growing light, absorbing the incredible wonder of fields, houses, bakery trucks, and before-breakfast world, tasting the sweetness and scariness of things seen and only half understood—the train penetrating the morning, the child penetrating the meaning of the morning and of the future. To this child the future was always like a high pasture, a little frightening, full of herds of steers and of intimations of wider prospects, of trysts with fate, of vague passionate culminations and the nearness to sky and to groves, of juniper smells and sweet-fern in a broiling noon sun. The future was one devil of a fine place, but it was a long while on the way.

This boy (I mean the one I can't forget) had a good effect on me. He was a cyclist and an early riser. Although grotesque in action, he was of noble design. He lived a life of enchantment; virtually everything he saw and heard was being seen and heard by him for the first time, so he gave it his whole attention. He took advantage of any slight elevation of ground or of spirit, and if there was a fence going his way, he mounted it and escaped the commonplace by a matter of four feet. I discovered in his company the satisfactions of life's interminable quest; he was always looking for something that had no name and no whereabouts, and not finding it. He either knew instinctively or he soon found out that seeking was more instructive than finding, that journeys were more rewarding than destinations. (I picked up a little of that from him, and have found it of some use.)

He was saddled with an unusual number of worries, it seems to me, but faith underlay them—a faith nourished by the natural world rather than by the supernatural or the spiritual. There was a lake, and at the water's edge a granite rock upholstered with lichen. This was his pew, and the sermon went on forever.

He traveled light, so that he was always ready for a change of pace or of direction and was in a position to explore any opportunity and become a part of any situation, unhampered. He spent an appalling amount of time in a semidormant state on curbstones, pier-heads, moles, stringpieces, carriage blocks, and porch steps, absorbing the anecdotes, logic and technique of artisans. He would travel miles to oversee a new piece of construction.

I remember this boy with affection, and feel no embarrassment in idealizing him. He himself was an idealist of shocking proportions. He had a fine capacity for melancholy and the gift of sadness. I never knew anybody on whose spirit the weather had such a devastating effect. A shift of wind, or of mood, could wither him. There would be times when a dismal sky conspired with a forlorn side street to create a moment of such profound bitterness that the world's accumulated sorrow seemed to gather in a solid lump in his heart. The appearance of a coasting hill softening in a thaw, the look of backyards along the railroad tracks on hot afternoons, the faces of people in trolley cars on Sunday—these could and did engulf him in a vast wave of depression. He dreaded Sunday afternoon because it had been deliberately written in a minor key.

He dreaded Sunday also because it was the day he spent worrying about going back to school on Monday. School was consistently frightening, not so much in realization as in anticipation. He went to school for sixteen years and was uneasy and full of dread the entire time—sixteen years of worrying that he would be called upon to speak a piece in the assembly hall. It was an amazing test of human fortitude. Every term was a nightmare of suspense.

The fear he had of making a public appearance on a platform seemed to find a perverse compensation, for he made frequent voluntary appearances in natural amphitheaters before hostile audiences, addressing himself to squalls and thunderstorms, rain and darkness, alone in rented canoes. His survival is something of a mystery, as he was neither very expert nor very strong. Fighting natural disturbances was the only sort of fighting he enjoyed. He would run five blocks to escape a boy who was after him, but he would stand up to any amount of punishment from the elements. He swam from the rocks of Hunter's Island, often at night, making his way there alone and afraid along the rough, dark trail from the end of the bridge (where the house was where they sold pie) up the hill and through the silent woods and across the marsh to the rocks. He hated bathing beaches and the smell of bathhouses, and would go to any amount of trouble to avoid the pollution of undressing in a stall.

This boy felt for animals a kinship he never felt for people. Against considerable opposition and with woefully inadequate equipment, he managed to provide himself with animals, so that he would never be without something to tend. He kept pigeons, dogs, snakes, polliwogs, turtles, rabbits, lizards, singing birds, chameleons, caterpillars and mice. The total number of hours he spent just standing watching animals, or refilling their water pans, would be impossible to estimate; and it would be hard to say what he got out of it. In spring he felt a sympathetic vibration with earth's renascence, and set a hen. He always seemed to be under some strange compulsion to assist the processes of incubation and germination, as though without him they might fail and the earth grow old and die. To him a miracle was essentially egg-shaped. (It occurs to me that his faith in animals has been justified by events of recent years: animals, by comparison with men, seem to have been conducting themselves with poise and dignity.)

In love he was unexcelled. His whole existence was a poem of tender and heroic adoration. He harbored delusions of perfection, and with consummate skill managed to weave the opposite sex into them, while keeping his distance. His search for beauty was always vaguely identified with his search for the ideal of love, and took him into districts which he would otherwise never have visited. Though I seldom see him these days, when I do I notice he still wears that grave inquiring expression as he peers into the faces of passers-by, convinced that some day he will find there the answer to his insistent question.

As I say, I feel no embarrassment in describing this character, because there is nothing personal in it—I have rather lost track of him and he has escaped me and is just a strange haunting memory, like the memory of love. I do not consider him in any way unusual or special; he was quite ordinary and had all the standard defects. They seem unimportant. It was his splendor that matters—the unforgettable splendor. No wonder I feel queer when I run into him. I guess all men do.

I Spy

Graham Greene

C HARLIE STOWE waited until he heard his mother snore before he got out of bed. Even then he moved with caution and tiptoed to the window. The front of the house was irregular, so that it was possible to see a light burning in his mother's room. But now all the windows were dark. A searchlight passed across the sky, lighting the banks of cloud and probing the dark deep spaces between, seeking enemy airships. The wind blew from the sea, and Charlie Stowe could hear behind his mother's snores the beating of the waves. A draught through the cracks in the window-frame stirred his nightshirt. Charlie Stowe was frightened.

But the thought of the tobacconist's shop which his father kept down a dozen wooden stairs drew him on. He was twelve years old, and already boys at the Country School mocked him because he had never smoked a cigarette. The packets were piled twelve deep below, Gold Flake and Players, De Reszke, Abdulla, Woodbines, and the little shop lay under a thin haze of stale smoke which would completely disguise his crime. That it was a crime to steal some of his father's stock Charlie Stowe had no doubt, but he did not love his father; his father was unreal to him, a wraith, pale, thin, and indefinite, who noticed him only spasmodically and left even punishment to his mother. For his mother he felt a passionate demonstrative love; her large boisterous presence and her noisy charity filled the world for him; from her speech he judged her the friend of everyone, from the rector's wife to the "dear Queen", except the "Huns", the monsters who lurked in Zeppelins in the clouds. But his father's affection and dislike were as indefinite as his movements. To-night he had said he would be in Norwich, and yet you never knew. Charlie Stowe had no sense of safety as he crept down the wooden stairs. When they creaked he clenched his fingers on the collar of his nightshirt.

At the bottom of the stairs he came out quite suddenly into the little shop. It was too dark to see his way, and he did not dare touch the switch. For half a minute he sat in despair on the bottom step with his chin cupped in his hands. Then the regular movement of the searchlight was reflected through an upper window and the boy had time to fix in memory the pile of cigarettes, the counter, and the small hole under it. The footsteps of a policeman on the pavement made him grab the first packet to his hand and dive for the hole. A light shone along the floor and a hand tried the door, then the footsteps passed on, and Charlie cowered in the darkness.

At last he got his courage back by telling himself in his curiously adult way that if he were caught now there was nothing to be done about it, and he might as well have his smoke. He put a cigarette in his mouth and then remembered that he had no matches. For a while he dared not move. Three times the searchlight lit the shop, while he muttered taunts and encouragements. "May as well be hung for a sheep," "Cowardy, cowardy custard," grown-up and childish exhortations oddly mixed.

But as he moved he heard footfalls in the street, the sound of several men walking rapidly. Charlie Stowe was old enough to feel surprise that anybody was about. The footsteps came nearer, stopped; a key was turned in the shop door, a voice said: "Let him in," and then he heard his father, "If you wouldn't mind being quiet, gentlemen. I don't want to wake up the family." There was a note unfamiliar to Charlie in the undecided voice. A torch flashed and the electric globe burst into blue light. The boy held his breath; he wondered whether his father would hear his heart beating, and he clutched his nightshirt tightly and prayed, "O God, don't let me be caught." Through a crack in the counter he could see his father where he stood, one hand held to his high stiff collar, between two men in bowler hats and belted mackintoshes. They were strangers.

"Have a cigarette," his father said in a voice dry as a biscuit. One of the men shook his head. "It wouldn't do, not when we are on duty. Thank you all the same." He spoke gently, but without kindness; Charlie Stowe thought his father must be ill.

"Mind if I put a few in my pocket?" Mr. Stowe asked, and when the man nodded he lifted a pile of Gold Flake and Players from a shelf and caressed the packets with the tips of his fingers.

"Well," he said, "there's nothing to be done about it, and I may as well have my smokes." For a moment Charlie Stowe feared discovery, his father stared round the shop so thoroughly; he might have been seeing it for the first time. "It's a good little business," he said, "for those that like it. The wife will sell out, I suppose. Else the neighbours'll be wrecking it. Well, you want to be off. A stitch in time. I'll get my coat."

"One of us'll come with you, if you don't mind," said the stranger gently.

"You needn't trouble. It's on the peg here. There, I'm all ready."

The other man said in an embarrassed way: "Don't you want to speak to your wife?" The thin voice was decided, "Not me. Never do to-day what you can put off till to-morrow. She'll have her chance later, won't she?"

"Yes, yes," one of the strangers said and he became very cheerful and encouraging. "Don't you worry too much. While there's life . . ." and suddenly his father tried to laugh.

When the door had closed Charlie Stowe tiptoed upstairs and got into bed. He wondered why his father had left the house again so late at night and who the strangers were. Surprise and awe kept him for a little while awake. It was as if a familiar photograph had stepped from the frame to reproach him with neglect. He remembered how his father had held tight to his collar and fortified himself with proverbs, and he thought for the first time that, while his mother was boisterous and kindly, his father was very like himself, doing things in the dark which frightened him. It would have pleased him to go down to his father and tell him that he loved him, but he could hear through the window the quick steps going away. He was alone in the house with his mother, and he fell asleep.

X

Lois Gould

Once upon a time, a Baby named X was born.
It was named X so that nobody could tell whether it
was a boy or a girl.

Its parents could tell, of course, but they couldn't tell anybody else. They couldn't even tell Baby X—at least not until
much, much later.

You see, it was all part of a very important Secret Scientific
Xperiment known officially as Project Baby X.

This Xperiment was going to cost Xactly 23 billion dollars
and 72 cents. Which might seem like a lot for one Baby, even
if it was an important Secret Scientific Xperimental Baby.

But when you remember the cost of strained carrots, stuffed
bunnies, booster shots, 28 shiny quarters from the tooth fairy
. . . you begin to see how it adds up.

Long before Baby X was born, the smartest scientists had to
work out the secret details of the Xperiment, and to write the
Official Instruction Manual, in secret code, for Baby X's
parents, whoever they were.

These parents had to be selected very carefully. Thousands
of people volunteered to take thousands of tests, with
thousands of tricky questions.

Almost everybody failed because, it turned out, almost everybody wanted a boy or a girl, and not a Baby X at all.

Also, almost everybody thought a Baby X would be more
trouble than a boy or a girl. (They were right, too.)

There were families with grandparents named Milton and

Agatha, who wanted the baby named Milton or Agatha instead of X, even if it was an X.

There were aunts who wanted to knit tiny dresses and uncles who wanted to send tiny baseball mitts.

Worst of all, there were families with other children who couldn't be trusted to keep a Secret. Not if they knew the Secret was worth 23 billion dollars and 72 cents—and all you had to do was take one little peek at Baby X in the bathtub to know what it was.

Finally, the scientists found the Joneses, who really wanted to raise an X more than any other kind of baby—no matter how much trouble it was.

The Joneses promised to take turns holding X, feeding X, and singing X to sleep.

And they promised never to hire any baby-sitters. The scientists knew that a baby-sitter would probably peek at X in the bathtub, too.

The day the Joneses brought their baby home, lots of friends and relatives came to see it. And the first thing they asked was what kind of a baby X was.

When the Joneses said, "It's an X!" nobody knew what to say.

They couldn't say, "Look at her cute little dimples!"

On the other hand, they couldn't say, "Look at his husky little biceps!"

And they didn't feel right about saying just plain "kitchy-coo."

The relatives all felt embarrassed about having an X in the family.

"People will think there's something wrong with it!" they whispered.

"Nonsense!" the Joneses said cheerfully. "What could possibly be wrong with this perfectly adorable X?"

Clearly, nothing at all was wrong. Nevertheless, the cousins who had sent a tiny football helmet would not come and visit any more. And the neighbors who sent a pink-flowered romper suit pulled their shades down when the Joneses passed their house.

The *Official Instruction Manual* had warned the new parents that this would happen, so they didn't fret about it.

Besides, they were too busy learning how to bring up Baby X.

Ms. and Mr. Jones had to be Xtra careful. If they kept bouncing it up in the air and saying how strong and active it was, they'd be treating it more like a boy than an X. But if all they did was cuddle it and kiss it and tell it how sweet and dainty it was, they'd be treating it more like a girl than an X.

On page 1654 of the *Official Instruction Manual*, the scientists prescribed: "plenty of bouncing and plenty of cuddling, *both*. X ought to be strong and sweet and active. Forget about *dainty* altogether."

There were other problems, too. Toys, for instance. And clothes. On his first shopping trip, Mr. Jones told the store clerk, "I need some things for a new baby." The clerk smiled and said, "Well, now, is it a boy or a girl?" "It's an X," Mr. Jones said, smiling back. But the clerk got all red in the face and said huffily, "In *that* case, I'm afraid I can't help you, sir."

Mr. Jones wandered the aisles trying to find what X needed. But everything was in sections marked BOYS or GIRLS: "Boys' Pajamas" and "Girls' Underwear" and "Boys' Fire Engines" and "Girls' Housekeeping Sets." Mr. Jones went home without buying anything for X.

That night he and Ms. Jones consulted page 2326 of the *Official Instruction Manual*. It said firmly: "Buy plenty of everything!"

So they bought all kinds of toys. A boy doll that made pee-pee and cried "Pa-Pa." And a girl doll that talked in three languages and said, "I am the Pres-i-dent of Gen-er-al Mo-tors."

They bought a storybook about a brave princess who rescued a handsome prince from his tower, and another one about a sister and brother who grew up to be a baseball star and a ballet star, and you had to guess which.

The head scientists of Project Baby X checked all their purchases and told them to keep up the good work. They also reminded the Joneses to see page 4629 of the *Manual* where it said. "Never make Baby X feel *embarrassed* or *ashamed* about what it wants to play with. And if X gets dirty climbing rocks, never say, 'Nice little Xes don't get dirty climbing rocks.'"

Likewise, it said. "If X falls down and cries, never say, 'Brave little Xes don't cry.' Because, of course, nice little Xes *do* get dirty, and brave little Xes *do* cry. No matter how dirty

X gets, or how hard it cries, don't worry. It's all part of the Xperiment."

Whenever the Joneses pushed Baby X's stroller in the park, smiling strangers would come over and coo: "Is that a boy or a girl?" The Joneses would smile back and say, "It's an X." The strangers would stop smiling then and often snarl something nasty—as if the Joneses had said something nasty to them.

Once a little girl grabbed X's shovel in the sandbox, and zonked X on the head with it. "Now, now, Tracy," the mother began to scold, "little girls mustn't hit little—" and she turned to ask X, "Are you a little boy or a little girl, dear?"

Mr. Jones, who was sitting near the sandbox, held his breath and crossed his fingers.

X smiled politely, even though X's head had never been zonked so hard in its life. "I'm a little X," said X.

"You're a *what?*" the lady exclaimed angrily. "You're a little b-r-a-t, you mean!"

"But little girls mustn't hit little Xes, either!" said X, retrieving the shovel with another polite smile. "What good's hitting, anyway?"

X's father finally X-haled, uncrossed his fingers, and grinned.

And at their next secret Project Baby X meeting, the scientists grinned, too. Baby X was doing fine.

But then it was time for X to start school. The Joneses were really worried about this, because school was even more full of rules for boys and girls, and there were no rules for Xes.

Teachers would tell boys to form a line, and girls to form another line.

There would be boys' games and girls' games, and boys' secrets and girls' secrets.

The school library would have a list of recommended books for girls, and a different list for boys.

There would even be a bathroom marked BOYS and another one marked GIRLS.

Pretty soon boys and girls would hardly talk to each other. What would happen to poor little X?

The Joneses spent weeks consulting their *Instruction Manual*.

There were 249 and one-half pages of advice under "First Day of School." Then they were all summoned to an Urgent

Xtra Special Conference with the smart scientists of Project Baby X.

The scientists had to make sure that X's mother had taught X how to throw and catch a ball properly, and that X's father had been sure to teach X what to serve at a doll's tea party.

X had to know how to shoot marbles and jump rope and, most of all, what to say when the Other Children asked whether X was a Boy or a Girl.

Finally, X was ready.

X's teacher had promised that the class could line up alphabetically, instead of forming separate lines for boys and girls. And X had permission to use the principal's bathroom, because it wasn't marked anything except BATHROOM. But nobody could help X with the biggest problem of all—Other Children.

Nobody in X's class had ever known an X. Nobody had even heard grown-ups say, "Some of my best friends are Xes."

What would other children think? Would they make Xist jokes? Or would they make friends?

You couldn't tell what X was by its clothes. Overalls don't even button right to left, like girls' clothes, or left to right, like boys' clothes.

And did X have a girl's short haircut or a boy's long haircut?

As for the games X liked, either X played ball very well for a girl, or else played house very well for a boy.

The children tried to find out by asking X tricky questions, like, "Who's your favorite sports star?" X had two favorite sports stars: a girl jockey named Robyn Smith and a boy archery champion named Robin Hood.

Then they asked, "What's your favorite TV show?" And X said: "Lassie," which stars a girl dog played by a boy dog.

When X said its favorite toy was a doll, everyone decided that X must be a girl. But then X said the doll was really a robot, and that X had computerized it, and that it was programmed to bake fudge and then clean up the kitchen.

After X told them that, they gave up guessing what X was. All they knew was they'd sure like to see X's doll.

After school, X wanted to play with the other children. "How about shooting baskets in the gym?" X asked the girls.

But all they did was make faces and giggle behind X's back.

"Boy, is *he* weird," whispered Jim to Joe.

"How about weaving some baskets in the arts and crafts room?" X asked the boys. But they all made faces and giggled behind X's back, too.

"Boy, is *she* weird," whispered Susie to Peggy.

That night, Ms. and Mr. Jones asked X how things had gone at school. X tried to smile, but there were two big tears in its eyes. "The lessons are okay," X began, "but . . ."

"But?" said Ms. Jones.

"The Other Children hate me," X whispered.

"Hate you?" said Mr. Jones.

X nodded, which made the two big tears roll down and splash on its overalls.

Once more, the Joneses reached for their *Instruction Manual*. Under "Other Children," it said:

"What did you Xpect? Other Children have to obey silly boy-girl rules, because their parents taught them to. Lucky X —you don't have rules at all! All you have to do is be yourself.

"P.S. We're not saying it'll be easy."

X liked being itself. But X cried a lot that night. So X's father held X tight, and cried a little, too. X's mother cheered them up with an Xciting story about an enchanted prince called Sleeping Handsome, who woke up when Princess Charming kissed him.

The next morning, they all felt much better, and little X went back to school with a brave smile and a clean pair of red and white checked overalls.

There was a seven-letter-word spelling bee in class that day. And a seven-lap boys' relay race in the gym. And a seven-layer-cake baking contest in the girls' kitchen corner.

X won the spelling bee. X also won the relay race.

And X almost won the baking contest, Xcept it forgot to light the oven. (Remember, nobody's perfect.)

One of the Other Children noticed something else, too. He said: "X doesn't care about winning. X just thinks it's fun playing boys' stuff and girl's stuff."

"Come to think of it," said another one of the Other Children, "X is having twice as much fun as we are!"

After school that day, the girl who beat X in the baking

contest gave X a big slice of her winning cake.

And the boy X beat in the relay race asked X to race him home.

From then on, some really funny things began to happen.

Susie, who sat next to X, refused to wear pink dresses to school any more. She wanted red and white checked overalls— just like X's.

Overalls, she told her parents, were better for climbing monkey bars.

Then Jim, the class football nut, started wheeling his little sister's doll carriage around the football field.

He'd put on his entire football uniform, except for the helmet.

Then he'd put the helmet *in* the carriage, lovingly tucked under an old set of shoulder pads.

Then he'd jog around the field, pushing the carriage and singing "Rockabye Baby" to his helmet.

He said X did the same thing, so it must be okay. After all, X was now the team's star quarterback.

Susie's parents were horrified by her behavior, and Jim's parents were worried sick about his.

But the worst came when the twins, Joe and Peggy, decided to share everything with each other.

Peggy used Joe's hockey skates, and his microscope, and took half his newspaper route.

Joe used Peggy's needlepoint kit, and her cookbooks, and took two of her three baby-sitting jobs.

Peggy ran the lawn mower, and Joe ran the vacuum cleaner.

Their parents weren't one bit pleased with Peggy's science experiments, or with Joe's terrific needlepoint pillows.

They didn't care that Peggy mowed the lawn better, and that Joe vacuumed the carpet better.

In fact, they were furious. It's all that little X's fault, they agreed. X doesn't know what it is . . . or what it's supposed to be! So X wants to mix everybody *else* up, too!

Peggy and Joe were forbidden to play with X any more. So was Susie, and then Jim, and then *all* the Other Children.

But it was too late: the Other Children stayed mixed-up and happy and free, and refused to go back to the way they'd been before X.

Finally, the parents held an emergency meeting to discuss "The X Problem."

They sent a report to the principal stating that X was a "bad influence," and demanding immediate action.

The Joneses, they said, should be *forced* to tell whether X was a boy or a girl. And X should be *forced* to behave like whichever it was.

If the Joneses refused to tell, the parents said, then X must take an Xamination. An Impartial Team of Xperts would Xtract the secret. Then X would start obeying all the old rules. Or else.

And if X turned out to be some kind of mixed-up misfit, then X must be Xpelled from school. Immediately! So that no little Xes would ever come to school again.

The principal was very upset. X, a bad influence? A mixed-up misfit? But X was a Xcellent student! X set a fine Xample! X was Xtraordinary!

X was president of the student council. X had won first prize in the art show, honorable mention in the science fair, and six events on field day, including the potato race.

Nevertheless, insisted the parents, X is a Problem Child. X is the Biggest Problem Child we have ever seen!

So the principal reluctantly notified X's parents and the Joneses reported this to the Project X scientists, who referred them to page 85769 of the *Instruction Manual*. "Sooner or later," it said, "X will have to be Xamined by an Impartial Team of Xperts.

"This may be the only way any of us will know for sure whether X is mixed up—or everyone else is."

At Xactly 9 o'clock the next day, X reported to the school health office. The principal, along with a committee from the Parents' Association, X's teacher, X's classmates, and Ms. and Mr. Jones, waited in the hall outside.

Inside, the Xperts had set up their famous testing machine: the Superpsychiamedicosocioculturometer.

Nobody knew Xactly how the machine worked, but everybody knew that this examination would reveal Xactly what everyone wanted to know about X, but were afraid to ask.

It was terribly quiet in the hall. Almost spooky. They could hear very strange noises from the room.

There were buzzes.

And a beep or two.

And several bells.

An occasional light flashed under the door. Was it an X ray?

Through it all, you could hear the Xperts' voices, asking questions, and X's voice, answering answers.

I wouldn't like to be in X's overalls right now, the children thought.

At last, the door opened. Everyone crowded around to hear the results. X didn't look any different; in fact, X was smiling. But the Impartial Team of Xperts looked terrible. They looked as if they were crying!

"What happened?" everyone began shouting.

"*Sssh*," ssshed the principal. "The Xperts are trying to speak."

Wiping his eyes and clearing his throat, one Xpert began: "In our opinion," he whispered—you could tell he must be very upset—"in our opinion, young X here—"

"Yes? Yes?" shouted a parent.

"Young X," said the other Xpert, frowning, "is just about the *least* mixed-up child we've ever Xamined!" Xclaimed the two Xperts, together. Behind the closed door, the Superpsychiamedicosocioculturometer made a noise like a contented hum.

"Yay for X!" yelled one of the children. And then the others began yelling, too. Clapping and cheering and jumping up and down.

"*SSSH!*" SSShed the principal, but nobody did.

The Parents' Committee was angry and bewildered. How *could* X have passed the whole Xamination?

Didn't X have an *identity* problem? Wasn't X mixed up at *all*? Wasn't X *any* kind of a misfit?

How could it *not* be, when it didn't even *know* what it was?

"Don't you see?" asked the Xperts. "X isn't one bit mixed up! As for being a misfit—ridiculous! X knows perfectly well what it is! Don't you, X?" The Xperts winked. X winked back.

"But what *is* X?" shrieked Peggy and Joe's parents. "*We* still want to know what it is!"

"Ah, yes," said the Xperts, winking again. "Well, don't

worry. You'll all know one of these days. And you won't need us to tell you."

"What? What do they mean?" Jim's parents grumbled suspiciously.

Susie and Peggy and Joe all answered at once. "They mean that by the time it matters which sex X is, it won't be a secret any more!"

With that, the Xperts reached out to hug Ms. and Mr. Jones. "If we ever have an X of our own," they whispered, "we sure hope you'll lend us your instruction manual."

Needless to say, the Joneses were very happy. The Project Baby X scientists were rather pleased, too. So were Susie, Jim, Peggy, Joe, and all the Other Children. Even the parents promised not to make any trouble.

Later that day, all X's friends put on their red and white checked overalls and went over to see X.

They found X in the backyard, playing with a very tiny baby that none of them had ever seen before.

The baby was wearing very tiny red and white checked overalls.

"How do you like our new baby?" X asked the Other Children proudly.

"It's got cute dimples," said Jim. "It's got husky biceps, too," said Susie.

"What kind of baby is it?" asked Joe and Peggy.

X frowned at them. "Can't you tell?" Then X broke into a big, mischievous grin. *"It's a Y!"*

Unfolding as They Should

June Callwood

ADOLESCENCE is a psychiatric disorder only when
the victim is not a teenager. In a 31-year-old, for
instance, a state of adolescence is called a nervous
breakdown. When a man of 45 has adolescence, the condition
is described as the male climacteric, or mid-life crisis. In older
people, adolescence is identified either as a search for meaning
or as self-indulgence, depending upon the eye of the beholder.

Teenagers, however, are not similarly perceived as people in
pain. When they become messy, irrational, depressed, testy,
narcissistic and stalled, they are not given mood-brighteners or
a leave of absence or something cuddly to take to bed. They
are advised instead to knock it off and take out the garbage.

The reason teenagers have such a long and wretched adolescence is that they are too young for it. In the first place, they
don't have adequate vocabularies to discuss it. If they could be
articulate about loneliness or their need for identity or even
about what pimples do to their self-image, they could enlist
sympathy and support in their affliction.

But their language and insights are inadequate, scarcely better than the wisdom of Grade 6. They behave among adults
like prisoners in enemy hands, giving nothing but their name,
rank and serial number; torture won't make them tell where
the cavalry is hiding.

The truth is, they don't have a cavalry. The only known cure
for severe adolescence is a human support system, rooters;

plus some acknowledged talents and skills, enough to keep self-esteem out of the infirmary; and a sense of humour, because humour makes misery tolerable.

The age group newly arisen from childhood rarely has discovered that it has any talent or skills at all. Besides, it is surrounded by non-fans. Accordingly, teenagers laugh a lot but seldom have a good time.

Their messages tend to be non-verbal and revolting. To indicate despair, they slouch. When they feel too tight or so loose that discomposure seems to be setting in, they drink, drive too fast, try drugs, steal something or test out the sporty new genitalia. Occasionally they kill someone, most frequently themselves.

They are so alarming to view that most adults would rather not. This is known as the generation gap.

Some families, however, have such a relatively tranquil time that they wonder if something is wrong. There are thousands of parents of teenagers who don't live with their stomach nerves in a knot, and there are thousands of teenagers who are unfolding as they should, sensible, truthful, independent and appreciative.

To prove it, we found four. Maxine Sidran, a researcher, asked around about all-right teenagers: not the brain banks who do calculus to entertain themselves or the gutsy quarterbacks or the concert hall prodigies, but the teenager down the block who gives the general appearance of being in one piece, the likable one, the thoughtful one.

She asked her own friends if they knew a stick-out kid, which led her to Diane Morrison. A Y counsellor recommended Christopher Prendergast. The Big Brothers knew Nat Hall. And the neighbors were high on Scott Crowley. For tactical convenience only, the selections were all made in the Toronto area.

The teenagers themselves turned out to be distinct individuals, each one totally unlike any of the others. But they had two notable qualities in common: a value system that kept them out of trouble, and affectionate respect for their parents.

The parents had more marked similarities. In the first place, they were intact individuals, reliable, responsible, logical, coherent people who can connect with others. The most distinctive feature in them all was steadiness. Without exception, they said what they meant and they meant what they said.

Further, in every family there was consistency and structure. The four teenagers had known from birth what the rules of the house were, and why; and also that they were not subject to whims. Discipline was administered rarely. Something in the household harmony and expectations seemed to work against maverick moods. When discipline was used—and all parents employed a mixture of grounding plus "a talk"—there was clear provocation; parental behaviour therefore was not inexplicable to a youngster.

In all four households the common clashes of messy rooms, lateness for meals, loutish manners or taking off without permission almost never occurred. The parents were unable to explain why their teenagers were so cooperative; it seemed to happen by itself.

In every family, however, attention was paid. Teenagers could ask for suspension or adjustment of the rules and expect consideration. Parents—even when there was only one—spent time with their children, buckets of it. The housekeeping mothers adjusted their outside activities in order to be at home after school. The mothers and fathers with paid jobs put extra emphasis on the quality of their limited time with their families.

In all four families, the teenagers liked the adults, really liked them. With only minor complaints, they saw them as doing a good job of raising them, and thought of their homes as desirable places to be.

And in every family the adults just happened to have an unshakable conviction that their teenager is a wonderful kid. Not perfect, but without any question wonderful. O happy days.

Christopher Prendergast is 15, which is nowhere. He is too young for almost all important independent activity and too old for almost all supervision. He is waiting the year out in the state of gloomy patience common to those in his predicament. Meanwhile he is getting himself in balance. He is willing to take the consequences of a fearless stating of his views, but the price for losing his temper is too high: he wants to control it better.

The concern that dominates his private life is that he doesn't see in himself any excellence, and excellence is what he wants to possess. He once made a list of his goals: astronaut, neurosurgeon, politician, psychiatrist, psychologist. Lately he's been crossing them off one by one; his present school grades are influencing his options.

He's bright enough, and so mature he's out of kilter with most of his age group, but his marks are only average. He says of himself that he appears to be medium all over. He has no special skills, he's a fair hockey player but no star, and he has only the normal number of unexamined friendships, examined hangups, concerns about his skin, arguments with his mother and loneliness.

"I have a definite fear of a 9-to-5 life," he comments, his big 5-foot-10 frame sprawled on a sofa, one Adidas on the coffee table. "I want to be outstanding, but all the things I want to get into cost money, or else I should have started when I was 5."

That was about when his parents split up. There were five children in the family, the oldest 8 and the youngest a baby. They live with their mother, Starr Prendergast, who waited until the youngest was 4 and then enrolled herself in teachers' college. She teaches Grade 6, and is a breezy, sensible, worried, all-systems-open woman, doing her best with the oldest son, Christopher's brother, who is acting out, and Christopher, who is acting in. It is a demonstration of her practical approach to problems that last year she joined a Y group, Communication for Parents of Adolescents. She needed information and guidance and she was not above asking for it; the bumps that began with puberty had been a jolt.

"My picture of raising kids was that they didn't make waves," she explains with amusement. "They did the right thing, grew up, graduated, and that was that. My biggest surprise was the change they go through around 12 or 13 when they think they know everything and you know nothing.

"I'm learning a lot. I'm learning they don't fall into a mold. As kids get older parents have to learn to compromise. And that's a shock."

She's no quitter and she *tries*; her children know it. When she's angry she blows her stack and they are free to yell back—

and do. And when she's made a mistake, she admits it and suffers their delight. It's a noisy, chaotic, sturdy household, full of warmth, humour and flare-ups. It is, most notably, an honest one.

She says Christopher is the child who most resembles her own style; he looks only mildly skeptical at this. Most of their collisions occur around their mutual proclivity to speak their minds. They used to have fiery encounters but now he deals with her in a style he's developed recently, which is to debate the issue with his considerable powers of cold analysis and then leave the scene before he spoils the effect by getting mad.

His older brother, only 15 months his senior, has a venturesome nature that perhaps has shaped Christopher's more conservative tendencies. Chris is a non-smoker and he's not interested in drugs or alcohol, which are endemic in his age group; he picks his friends among those with similar views.

He's a reliable person. If he is going to be later than he promised, he calls home. He believes in promise-keeping.

For all his concern about being medium and about his temper, he is a rock; you could tie a ship to him. He is amazed that most teenagers worry so much about the opinions of others that they live submerged. "I'm not like that," he says. "I'll say what I think no matter what. I have to live with myself and that's all that matters. I know I have to improve but right now I'm exactly the way I want to be at this age."

He seems to be moody after he's made a mistake. He explains that he's thinking it over, trying to figure how it happened, preparing his responses so it won't happen again. It's the hardest work of all, growing. He goes about the chore the way his mother goes about hers: if it's got to be done, do it.

Starr Prendergast says that no matter how her children turn out she isn't going to *mea culpa* herself to death. "I'm doing my best, I'm setting the best example I know how, and I know what my values are. I hope they take the right direction and make it."

They're both doing their best. It's something to see.

Stan and Dorothy Crowley have been married for 24 years. One child is 20, a woman in college. There are two other girls, one 11 and one 9. And there is Scott, who is 14 and is beginning to believe in his own miracle.

He's been an apprehensive child, uncomfortable with outsiders, unhappy at being compelled to go to Cubs, easily hurt by slurs about his colour. Lately he's been developing some hide and some sureness. Sarcasm, for instance, sometimes works against bigots, but if he has to fight, he can. Also he's finding Scouts a pleasure. His sisters don't bug him as much as they used to. Being 14 feels good, feels like things are going to be all right.

The Crowleys' philosophy of childraising emphasizes activity. Scott, for instance, takes piano lessons and must practise for one hour every day, like it or not; and he never likes it. He's joined a canoe club, takes odd jobs (such as delivering catalogues) in order to pay for a 10-speed bike, volunteered last August to help at the Olympiad for disabled athletes, plays football, chess, baseball.

In addition to school and homework, which give him no trouble, he's spending a lot of time with his father. On Saturday mornings they go together to the basketball league his father helped launch because there was a recreational vacuum in the community. They bowl together and Scott drives with him to Ontario colleges, where his father is an intercollegiate basketball and football referee.

The Crowleys are motivated towards packing the schedule only in part because they believe a child whose life is taken up with supervised, constructive activities is not likely to be drawn into the self-destructive adrenalin-high pursuits that are alluring to idle, bored youngsters. Their more important objective is to prepare their children for the intricacies of adult life. They feel that school and the suburbs provide a healthy but limited range of muscles for the obstacle race ahead.

"We want him to meet all kinds of people, see all kinds of places," Stan Crowley explains. "A lot of people just have a narrow channel while they're young. When they get out in the big world, it's scary."

Accordingly, the Crowleys subscribe to a variety of periodicals and keep abreast of the less sane world outside their walls. They've driven their children to Washington, D.C., to show them ghettos and to Prince Edward Island to show them green hills.

The hidden agenda is to armour the Crowley children with

sufficient poise and accomplishment to weatherproof them against the adversities ahead of them as members of society's most visible minority. The techniques don't come in an instruction kit; they are homemade, individually tailored.

"You can talk about prejudice all your life to your children but it won't prepare them for the moment when it hits," Stan Crowley comments.

It hit Scott and all his sisters around Grades 5 and 6. The unsettling effects of pubescence seem to find an outlet in a vicious pecking at selected targets, the children who are different. Scott came home day after day in shock and pain. His mother said gently, "Stand up for yourself."

Eventually he learned to fight back, first with his fists and now with his quick wit. That recess slaughter of his dignity took the heart out of him for a long time. It is only recently that he has been able to trust his peers enough to have friends among them or to value himself enough to undertake anything independent of loyal family support.

Self-control plays a large part in the Crowley household. Scott is required to show respect not only to all adults but also to his sisters, though the younger two are sometimes a trial. When he's furious, he's obliged to keep it under wraps. He retires to his bedroom where he'd like to slam the door, but doesn't dare. Instead, he punches his bed. Hard.

The Crowleys used to administer spankings when their children were younger but discipline now is verbal, rather heated when Dorothy is offended by her children's behaviour, and likely to be a trenchant resolve-making lecture when Stanley is taking them to task.

The family has never tolerated lazing around, or not coming in at night as soon as the street lights flick on, or forgetting the chores, or being rude, or being messy. All the children are accustomed to the rules; they have been there forever, just as they have always been able to count on their mother to be in her spotless home, or their father to sell insurance house to house and dress them handsomely. It is the foundation of their lives—and unshakable.

Scott is a stocky boy, 5-foot-3 and 107 pounds. He's bright, amused, cautious and emerging. He's going to be an astronaut or a pilot. There's no limit to what he's going to do. That's what life at the Crowleys is all about.

Diane Morrison is almost 15 and she's in that suspended stage of growth just before the bobsled hits the chute and nothing can be stopped. She's taken the Donny Osmond pictures off her bedroom wall and replaced them with something neutral—animals. She's announced that she's going to be a vet. She's washing her hair a lot, keeping her crushes and her complexities to herself, biding her time.

She lives in a picture-book family. Look, look, says mother. Here comes father. Here comes Dick. Here comes Jane. See Spot run.

She's Jane. Dick is her brother, David, 18 months older, an assured, articulate, gregarious person. Mother is Ann Morrison, a former nurse, friendly and sensible. Father is Stu Morrison, news editor with a radio station. The part of Spot is played by a black and white short-haired cat named Lovey. They all live in a suburban split-level with ivy growing over the bricks.

But they all are very real. When Stu loses his temper, he yells. When Diane's feelings are hurt, she's morose for hours. And Lovey kills birds.

The household operates with effortless pleasantness. The family has a seamless quality, each member of it enfolded by all the others. It is, however, an illusion, an airy-looking structure that floats on steel pilings. A sense of order was built in long ago; there was routine in the babies' lives, when bedtimes and mealtimes didn't vary much and no meant no, and responsibility in the parents, who shaped their choices around the priority of stability and didn't say no too often.

As a consequence, Ann and Stu Morrison take it for granted that Diane will report home after school promptly or else telephone her whereabouts, that she will be punctual on all occasions, that she will ask permission before making plans, that she will observe the curfew, which usually is 9 o'clock, that her room will be kept reasonably tidy and her bed made.

For her part, Diane is aware that she has space to move. If she wants to go to a school dance there will be a family discussion about it around the dinner table. She'll be consulted about the curfew. When she's feeling grumpy, there is accommodation to her mood. She goes outside with her cat and smooths herself out by weeding her flower patch. Her parents understand that; they wait for her to come around at her own speed and appreciate her when she's made it.

An example of the Morrison style of controlled freedom happened when Diane was in Grade 6. She was attracted to a group of fast-moving, relatively unsupervised classmates who were in the habit of sampling their parents' liquor and beer supplies after school. A teacher drew Ann Morrison aside and said she was worried about the company Diane was keeping.

Ann replied stoutly, "*I'm* not."

It was her hunch that Diane was curious to see how other children lived, children who weren't snuggled under parental wings. The Morrisons conferred and decided to let their daughter explore, within limits: she was forbidden to go into any of her new friends' houses.

Still, it was a nervous winter all around. Once the vice-principal caught Diane smoking in the school. She was so upset by the encounter that she never tried it again. And in the spring she was bored with her crowd. She's in Grade 10 now and many of her friends share her aversion to cigarettes, drugs and alcohol.

She's a tiny person, 4-foot-11½ and 90 pounds. Her father, who was small himself at her age, says it influences personality, makes her chippy, made him chippy. She's defended herself against all comers on this subject: she maintains that it doesn't bother her at all, in fact it's an advantage because "everyone likes short people."

When she was younger she was a bubbling, confident gang leader. That strident scrappy person has withdrawn. The present Diane Morrison is neat, careful, somewhat opaque with people she doesn't trust. She's in a holding pattern right now and betrays the currents within only in an occasional testiness that her father, in particular, finds exasperating.

There is already a family legend about the most spectacular of their clashes. One time she prevailed upon him to play checkers with her, though he detests games. It was an edgy match that she ended abruptly by standing up and deliberately knocking the table over, then fleeing to her room. Her father followed in such a fury that when he attempted to punch the flimsy door open, he put his fist through it.

The Morrisons now find that incident hilarious, and especially the consternation all four felt when it happened. It requires a notable amount of safety and strength for a family to enjoy telling that story and know it is in the context of life-long love and respect.

Diane Morrison has so much certainty about her own safety that even when she was experiencing weeks of nightmares after watching a film in Grade 2 about a burning house, in her dreams she always escaped. And she always had with her the two objects she cared most about then—an Ookpik and her cat. And her family always escaped. In fact, nothing important burned in her nightmare.

That's safety. That much safeness will last approximately forever, and she knows it.

Nat Hall has covered some uneven ground in his 19 years. His parents separated when he was a baby and he hasn't seen his father since. His mother has held a full-time job since he was born. And while he is intelligent, he failed repeatedly in school and dropped out at 16.

It's a combination of stresses that is more than some young people can bear: it makes them fragile and desperate. Nat Hall, however, is not a case history, he's a pleasure. He's perceptive, astute, relaxed, genial, open and appreciative: a find.

When he was younger he felt the absence of his father. He didn't seem to know anyone else in the world who didn't have one. His mother contacted the Big Brother movement, which provided him with a pal. They went bowling one day, a Big Brothers outing, and Nat returned to describe how the place was packed with kids. His mother told him, "Nat, every one of those kids has no father. Every one." After that he felt less conspicuous and less anxious, anxious to be ordinary.

He remained a sensitive child, the kind to cringe from a raised voice. He still can't abide being yelled at. When he was in Grade 3 the family moved and he attended a strange school where it was his bad luck to have a teacher given to roaring when angry, occasionally clouting the side of a pupil's head. He never stopped being afraid of her. He failed that year.

He stayed in school for the obligatory eight years more, a trial to teachers who were baffled that he could be so articulate and yet score such appalling marks. He was never tested for a learning disability. He was miserable and discouraged and humiliated for a long time and then he gave up trying. He left in Grade 9.

That's what went wrong for Nat Hall. What went right is his mother, Dixie Hall, and her mother, called Nanny. Dixie Hall set the standards for her son, laying down a routine of chores and considerations derived from what she calls "the old school." When he misbehaved she would sit him down for an earnest talk, explaining why it was wrong and concluding with, "Do you understand?" He sees his grandmother as a contemporary, always staunchly on his side, and unflappable.

He's a lanky 6-foot-3, 155 pounds, deft with his hands, detached and philosophical about his adversities. Despite her disappointment at his school record, Dixie Hall says, "There have been many days when I couldn't be a prouder mom."

She cites as examples Nat's empathy for people in pain. Once when he was about 11 he witnessed a teacher making malicious asides to a black child. The child broke down and wept. Nat got up, found the head of the school and reported it. "That took a lot of courage," Dixie Hall says. "That's what Nat is like."

Nat comments drily, "There are a lot of stupid people like that in the world. It didn't really make any difference."

"Yes it did," his mother flares. "Every bit helps." He grins at her fondly. They are both right.

Dixie Hall is a fighter. She has worked almost all her adult life and despite a skimpy salary in the beginning, she was frugal enough to be able to buy the house she shares with her mother and son. She's now an office manager and Nat works in a garage.

He says he lives at home because it's cheaper, but that isn't it. The fact is he cares deeply for his mother and grandmother. If they're 10 minutes late coming back from a cottage weekend, he starts to feel alarm. He gets his car ready to begin looking for them. They've had their differences, and still do, but because they genuinely like each other it always gets sorted out.

The Big Brother movement matched Nat perfectly with a college professor who has become one of his closest friends.

He patterns himself on people like that, men he admires. He's known some good ones.

Some of his peers have tried everything: drugs, brawls, crime, booze, macho sex. Something holds him back, he's not sure what. "I get a feeling in my stomach that says no," he explains.

No one pushes him around on that account. He tells someone leaning on his car to quit it. The other says, "Yeah, you want to make something of it?" and Nat says simply, "No." He stands loose and quiet and after a moment there's no one leaning on the car.

The car is how Nat Hall got back his pride. During those mortifying years in a classroom, Nat was working weekends and saving his money to buy it. It still represents his peace of mind. He is always puttering with it, making it perfect. He would love to tear the engine down himself but he would need to consult a book to do it, so he won't. He still can't face a situation even remotely like school.

That's his only problem now, getting back his confidence. He's working on it and some day he'll fix it.

He can fix anything. Ask Dixie. Ask anyone.

Memoirs of a Non-Prom Queen

Ellen Willis

T HERE'S a book out called *Is There Life after High School?* It's a fairly silly book, maybe because the subject matter is the kind that only hurts when you think. Its thesis—that most people never get over the social triumphs or humiliations of high school—is not novel. Still, I read it with the respectful attention a serious hypochondriac accords the lowliest "dear doctor" column. I don't know about most people, but for me, forgiving my parents for real and imagined derelictions has been easy compared to forgiving myself for being a teenage reject.

Victims of high school trauma—which seems to have afflicted a disproportionate number of writers, including Ralph Keyes, the author of this book—tend to embrace the ugly duckling myth of adolescent social relations: the "innies" (Keyes's term) are good-looking, athletic mediocrities who will never amount to much, while the "outies" are intelligent, sensitive individuals who will do great things in an effort to make up for their early defeats. Keyes is partial to this myth. He has fun with celebrity anecdotes: Kurt Vonnegut receiving a body-building course as a "gag prize" at a dance; Frank Zappa yelling "expletive" at a cheerleader; Mike Nichols,[1] as a nightclub

---

[1] Vonnegut, American novelist, author of *Cat's Cradle* (1963); *God Bless You, Mr. Rosewater* (1964); *Slaughterhouse-Five* (1969); and *Breakfast of Champions* (1973). Zappa was the leader of the rock music group, Mothers of Invention. Nichols is a former night club and television comedian, now a film and stage director.

comedian, insulting a fan—an erstwhile overbearing classmate turned used-car salesman. In contrast, the ex-prom queens and kings he interviews slink through life, hiding their pasts lest someone call them "dumb jock" or "cheerleader type," perpetually wondering what to do for an encore.

If only it were that simple. There may really be high schools where life approximates an Archie comic, but even in the Fifties, my large (5000 students), semisuburban (Queens, New York), heterogeneous high school was not one of them. The students' social life was fragmented along ethnic and class lines; there was no universally recognized, schoolwide social hierarchy. Being an athlete or a cheerleader or a student officer didn't mean much. Belonging to an illegal sorority or fraternity meant more, at least in some circles, but many socially active students chose not to join. The most popular kids were not necessarily the best looking or the best dressed or the most snobbish or the least studious. In retrospect, it seems to me that they were popular for much more honorable reasons. They were attuned to other people, aware of subtle social nuances. They projected an inviting sexual warmth. Far from being slavish followers of fashion, they were self-confident enough to set fashions. They suggested, initiated, led. Above all—this was their main appeal for me—they knew how to have a good time.

True, it was not particularly sophisticated enjoyment—dancing, pizza eating, hand holding in the lunchroom, the usual. I had friends—precocious intellectuals and bohemians—who were consciously alienated from what they saw as all that teenage crap. Part of me identified with them, yet I badly wanted what they rejected. Their seriousness engaged my mind, but my romantic and sexual fantasies, and my emotions generally, were obsessively fixed on the parties and dances I wasn't invited to, the boys I never dated. I suppose what says it best is that my "serious" friends hated rock & roll; I loved it.

If I can't rationalize my social ineptitude as intellectual rebellion, neither can I blame it on political consciousness. Feminism has inspired a variation of the ugly duckling myth in which high school wallflower becomes feminist heroine, suffering because she has too much integrity to suck up to boys by playing a phony feminine role. There is a tempting grain of truth in this idea. Certainly the self-absorption, anxiety and physical and social awkwardness that made me a difficult teenager were not unrelated to my ambivalent awareness of women's oppression. I couldn't charm boys because I feared and resented them and their power over my life; I couldn't be sexy because I saw sex as a mine field of conflicting, confusing rules that gave them every advantage. I had no sense of what might make me attractive, a lack I'm sure involved unconscious resistance to the game girls were supposed to play (particularly all the rigmarole surrounding clothes, hair and cosmetics); I was a clumsy dancer because I could never follow the boy's lead.

Yet ultimately this rationale misses the point. As I've learned from comparing notes with lots of women, the popular girls were in fact much more in touch with the reality of the female condition than I was. They knew exactly what they had to do for the rewards they wanted, while I did a lot of what feminist organizers call denying the awful truth. I was a bit schizy. Desperate to win the game but unwilling to learn it or even face my feelings about it, I couldn't really play, except in fantasy; paradoxically, I was consumed by it much more thoroughly than the girls who played and played well. Knowing what they wanted and how to get it, they preserved their sense of self, however compromised, while I lost mine. Which is why they were not simply better game players but genuinely more likable than I.

The ugly duckling myth is sentimental. It may soothe the memory of social rejection, but it falsifies the experience, evades its cruelty and uselessness. High school permanently damaged my self-esteem. I learned what it meant to be impotent; what it meant to be invisible. None of this improved my character, spurred my ambition, or gave me a deeper understanding of life. I know people who were popular in high school who later became serious intellectuals, radicals, artists, even journalists. I regret not being one of those people. To see my failure as morally or politically superior to their success would be to indulge in a version of the Laingian[2] fallacy—that because a destructive society drives people crazy, there is something dishonorable about managing to stay sane.

[2] R.D. Laing, the Scottish psychiatrist, argues that personality division is a predictable result of modern life.

Me as My Grandmother

Rosemary Aubert

Sometimes
I look up quickly
and see for an instant
her face
in my mirror,
random tightness
turns my mouth
into a facsimile of hers,
eyes caught oddly
in the glass
make me
into her
looking at me.

Now that she's dead,
I understand
that it is right
that I should age
and wrinkle into her.
It brings her back,
it puts me into
the cycle of family.
We look at all time
with just that
one same face.

Mother

Nagase Kiyoko
translated by Kenneth Rexroth and Ikuko Atsumi

I am always aware of my mother,
ominous, threatening,
a pain in the depths of my consciousness.
My mother is like a shell,
so easily broken.
Yet the fact that I was born
bearing my mother's shadow
cannot be changed.
She is like a cherished, bitter dream
my nerves cannot forget
even after I awake.
She prevents all freedom of movement.
If I move she quickly breaks,
and the splinters stab me.

My Stepmother, Myself

Garrison Keillor

R ECENTLY in Weeseville, Pennsylvania, a woman
was dismissed from her job as a human-resources
coordinator and driven over a cliff by an angry mob
of villagers carrying flaming torches and hurling sharp rocks
after they learned that she was married to a man who had custody of his three children by a previous marriage.

In California, soon after her marriage to a prince (her first
marriage, his seventh), a woman named Sharon Mittel was
shut up in a dungeon under the provisions of that state's Cruel
and Unnatural Parent Act, which allows the immediate im-
prisonment of a stepparent upon the complaint of a stepchild.
The prince's oldest daughter accused Sharon of slapping her.
She was later freed after an appeal to a king, but she now faces
a long series of tests to prove her innocence, such as finding a
tree of pure gold and a seedless grapefruit. She also must answer some riddles.

Are these merely two isolated incidents? Or are they, as a
new and exhaustive report on stepmothers clearly points out,
fairly indicative?

"The myth of the evil stepmother is still with us," the report concludes. "Stepmothers are still associated with the
words *cruel* and *wicked*, which has made them easy targets for
torture and banishment as well as severely limiting their employment, particularly in the so-called 'caring' professions such

as nursing, social work, and education. The myth that stepmothers use poisons and potions has virtually barred them from the food and drug industries. In general, stepmothers are not only underpaid and underemployed but also feared and despised."

How cruel is the typical stepmother?

Not very, according to the report, which examines many cases of alleged cruelty and finds almost all of them untrue. "The media have jumped on every little misunderstanding, and have blown it up to outlandish proportions," the report finds. Recently, three stepdaughters whose relationships with their stepmothers are well known agreed to speak out and set the record straight. Because each has suffered from publicity in the past and is trying to lead as normal a life as possible under the circumstances, only first names will be used.

SNOW

The story the press told was that I was in a life-threatening situation as a child and that the primary causal factor was my stepmother's envy. I can see now that there were other factors, and that *I* didn't give *her* much reinforcement—but anyway, the story was that I escaped from her and was taken in by dwarves and she found me and poisoned me with an apple and I was dead and the prince fell in love with me and brought me back to life and we got married, et cetera, et cetera. And this is what *I* believed right up to the day I walked out on him. I felt like I owed my life to Jeff because he had begged the dwarves for my body and carried it away and so the apple was shaken loose from my throat. That's why I married him. Out of gratitude.

As I look back on it, I can see that that was a very poor basis for a relationship. I was traumatized, I had been lying in a coffin under glass for *years*, and I got up and married the first guy I laid eyes on. The big prince. My hero.

Now I can see how sick our marriage was. He was always begging me to lie still and close my eyes and hold my breath. He could only relate to me as a dead person. He couldn't accept me as a living woman with needs and desires of my own. It is terribly hard for a woman to come to terms with the fact that her husband is a necrophiliac, because, of course, when it all starts, you aren't aware of what's going on—you're dead.

In trying to come to terms with myself, I've had to come to terms with my stepmother and her envy of my beauty, which made our relationship so destructive. She was a victim of the male attitude that prizes youth over maturity when it comes to women. Men can't dominate the mature woman, so they equate youth with beauty. In fact, she *was* beautiful, but the mirror (which, of course, reflected that male attitude) presented her with a poor self-image and turned her against me.

But the press never wrote the truth about that.

Or about the dwarves. All I can say is that they should have been named Dopey, Sleepy, Slimy, Sleazy, Dirty, Disgusting, and Sexist. The fact is that I *knew* the apple was poisoned. For me, it was the only way out.

GRETEL

When Hansel and I negotiated the sale of book rights to Grimm Bros., he and I retained the right of final approval of the manuscript and agreed to split the proceeds fifty-fifty. We shook hands on it and I thought the deal was set, but then his lawyers put me under a spell, and when I woke up, they had rewritten the contract and the book too! I couldn't believe it! Not only did the new contract cut me out (under the terms, I was to get ten shiny baubles out of the first fortune the book earned and three trinkets for each additional fortune) but the book was pure fiction.

Suddenly he was portrayed as the strong and resourceful one, a regular little knight, and I came off as a weak sister. Dad was shown as a loving father who was talked into abandoning us in the forest by Gladys, our "wicked" stepmother.

Nothing could be further from the truth.

My brother was a basket case from the moment the birds ate his bread crumbs. He lay down in a heap and whimpered, and I had to slap him a couple times *hard* to make him walk. Now the little wiener makes himself out to be the hero who kept telling me, "Don't cry, Gretel." Ha! The only crying I did was from sheer exhaustion carrying him on my back.

As for Dad, he was no bleeding heart. He was very much into that whole woodcutter/peasant/yeoman scene—cockfighting, bullbaiting, going to the village on Saturday to get drunk and watch a garroting or a boiling—don't kid yourself, Gladys couldn't send us to our *rooms* without his say-so. The truth is that he was in favor of the forest idea from the word go.

What I can't understand is why they had to lie about it. Many, *many* parents left their children in the forest in those days. It was nothing unusual.

Nowadays, we tend to forget that famine can be a very difficult experience for a family. For many parents, ditching the kids was not only a solution, it was an act of faith. They believed that ravens would bring morsels of food in their beaks, or that wolves would take care of the kids, or a frog would, or that the fairies would step in. Dwarves, a hermit, a band of pilgrims, a kindly shepherd, *somebody*. And they were right.

And that is why I was never seriously worried for one single moment while we were there. Deep down, I always knew we would make it.

I don't mean to say that it wasn't a trying experience, an *emotional* experience. It was. And yet there isn't a single documented case of a child left in the forest who suffered any lasting damage. You look at those children today and you will find they are better people for having gone through it. Except for my brother, that is. The little jerk. He and my father live in luxurious manors with beautiful tapestries and banners and ballrooms, and I live above an alchemist's shop in a tiny garret they call a condo. As for Gladys, she was kicked out without so much as a property settlement. She didn't even get half of the hut. I guess she is the one who suffered most. Her and the witch.

I often think about the witch—I ask myself, Why did I give her the shove? After all, it wasn't me she was after.

I guess that, back then, I wasn't prepared to understand her type of militance. I couldn't see that she was fattening up Hansel in order to make a very radical statement. If only I had. Not that I necessarily would have joined her in making that statement, but I would have seen that from her point of view it had validity and meaning.

And I would have seen that Gladys, in proposing the forest as a viable alternative, was offering me independence at a very early age.

I wish I had been able to thank her.

CINDERELLA

A woman in my position does not find it easy to "come out of the palace," so to speak, and to provide intimate details of her personal life. I do so only because I believe it is time to put the Cinderella myth to rest once and for all—the myth that one can escape housework by marrying a prince.

The truth is that I am busier than ever. Supervising a large household staff—cooks, maids, footmen, pages, ladies-in-waiting, minstrels and troubadours, a bard or two—is just plain hard work. Often I find myself longing for the "good old days" when my stepmother made me sweep the hearth.

We see each other almost every day—she comes up here and we play tennis or I go down there for lunch—and we often reminisce and laugh about our little disagreements. She is one of my best friends. Other people treat me like royalty but she treats me like a real person. My husband won't let me touch a broom, but I go to her house and she puts me to work! I love it. I tell her, "Mother, you're the only one who yells at me. Don't ever stop." And I mean it. Anger is real. It's honest.

Honesty is a rare commodity in a palace, and that is why so many "fairy-tale" marriages end up on the rocks. You wouldn't believe the amount of fawning and flattering that goes on! Between the courtiers bowing and scraping and the suppliants and petitioners wheedling and whining, and the scheming of bishops and barons, not to mention the sorcery and witchcraft, the atmosphere is such that it's terribly hard for a man and a woman to establish a loving, trusting, sharing type of relationship.

It's true that we lived happily ever after, but believe me, we have had to work at it!

Jewish Christmas

Fredelle Bruser Maynard

C HRISTMAS, when I was young, was the season of
bitterness. Lights beckoned and tinsel shone, store
windows glowed with mysterious promise, but I knew
the brilliance was not for me. Being Jewish, I had long grown
accustomed to isolation and difference. Difference was in my
bones and blood, and in the pattern of my separate life. My
parents were conspicuously unlike other children's parents in
our predominantly Norwegian community. Where my schoolmates were surrounded by blond giants appropriate to a village called Birch Hills, my family suggested still the Russian
plains from which they had emigrated years before. My handsome father was a big man, but big without any suggestion of
physical strength or agility; one could not imagine him at the
wheel of a tractor. In a town that was all wheat and cattle, he
seemed the one man wholly devoted to urban pursuits: he
operated a general store. Instead of the native costume—
overalls and mackinaws—he wore city suits and pearl-grey
spats. In winter he was splendid in a plushy chinchilla coat
with velvet collar, his black curly hair an extension of the high
Astrakhan hat which he had brought from the Ukraine. I was
proud of his good looks, and yet uneasy about their distinctly
oriental flavor.

My mother's difference was of another sort. Her beauty was
not so much foreign as timeless. My friends had slender young

Scandinavian mothers, light of foot and blue of eye; my mother was short and heavyset, but with a face of classic proportions. Years later I found her in the portraits of Ingres and Corot—face a delicate oval, brown velvet eyes, brown silk hair centrally parted and drawn back in a lustrous coil—but in those days I saw only that she too was different. As for my grandparents, they were utterly unlike the benevolent, apple-cheeked characters who presided over happy families in my favorite stories. (Evidently all those happy families were gentile.) My grandmother had no fringed shawl, no steel-rimmed glasses. (She read, if at all, with the help of a magnifying glass from Woolworth's.) Ignorant, apparently, of her natural role as gentle occupant of the rocking chair, she was ignorant too of the world outside her apartment in remote Winnipeg. She had brought Odessa with her, and—on my rare visits—she smiled lovingly, uncomprehendingly, across an ocean of time and space. Even more unreal was my grandfather, a black cap and a long beard bent over the Talmud. I felt for him a kind of amused tenderness, but I was glad that my schoolmates could not see him.

At home we spoke another language—Yiddish or Russian—and ate rich foods whose spicy odors bore no resemblance to the neighbors' cooking. We did not go to church or belong to clubs or, it seemed, take any meaningful part in the life of the town. Our social roots went, not down into the foreign soil on which fate had deposited us, but outwards, in delicate, sensitive connections, to other Jewish families in other lonely prairie towns. Sundays, they congregated around our table, these strangers who were brothers; I saw that they too ate knishes and spoke with faintly foreign voices, but I could not feel for them or for their silent swarthy children the kinship I knew I owed to all those who had been, like us, both chosen and abandoned.

All year I walked in the shadow of difference; but at Christmas above all, I tasted it sour on my tongue. There was no room at the tree. "You have Hanukkah," my father reminded me. "That is *our* holiday." I knew the story, of course—how, over two thousand years ago, my people had triumphed over the enemies of their faith, and how a single jar of holy oil had miraculously burned eight days and nights in the temple of the Lord. I thought of my father lighting each night another candle in the *menorah*, my mother and I beside him as he recited the ancient prayer: "Blessed art Thou, O Lord our God, ruler of the universe, who has sanctified us by thy commandments and commanded us to kindle the light of Hanukkah." Yes, we had our miracle too. But how could it stand against the glamor of Christmas? What was *gelt*, the traditional gift coins, to a sled packed with surprises? What was Judas Maccabaeus the liberator compared with the Christ child in the manger? To my sense of exclusion was added a sense of shame. "You *killed* Christ!" said the boys on the playground. "*You* killed him!" I knew none of the facts behind this awful accusation, but I was afraid to ask. I was even afraid to raise my voice in the chorus of "Come All Ye Faithful" lest I be struck down for my unfaithfulness by my own God, the wrathful Jehovah. With all the passion of my child's heart I longed for a younger, more compassionate deity with flowing robe and silken hair. Reluctant conscript to a doomed army, I longed to change sides. I longed for Christmas.

Although my father was in all things else the soul of indulgence, in this one matter he stood firm as Moses. "You cannot have a tree, *herzele*. You shouldn't even want to sing the carols. You are a Jew." I turned the words over in my mind and on my tongue. What was it, to be a Jew in Birch Hills, Saskatchewan? Though my father spoke of Jewishness as a special distinction, as far as I could see it was an inheritance without a kingdom, a check on a bank that had failed. Being Jewish was mostly not doing things other people did—not eating pork, not going to Sunday school, not entering, even playfully, into childhood romances, because the only boys around were *goyishe* boys. I remember, when I was five or six, falling in love with Edward Prince of Wales. Of the many arguments with which Mama might have dampened my ardor, she chose surely the most extraordinary. "You can't marry him. He isn't Jewish." And of course, finally, definitely, most crushing of all, being Jewish meant not celebrating Christ's birth. My parents allowed me to attend Christmas parties, but they made it clear that I must receive no gifts. How I envied the white and gold Norwegians! Their Lutheran church was not glamorous, but it was less frighteningly strange than the synagogue I had visited in Winnipeg, and in the Lutheran church, each December, joy came upon the midnight clear.

It was the Lutheran church and its annual concert which brought me closest to Christmas. Here there was always a tree, a jolly Santa Claus, and a program of songs and recitations. As the town's most accomplished elocutionist, I was regularly invited to perform. Usually my offering was comic or purely secular—*Santa's Mistake, The Night Before Christmas*, a scene from *A Christmas Carol*. But I had also memorized for such occasions a sweetly pious narrative about the housewife who, blindly absorbed in cleaning her house for the Lord's arrival, turns away a beggar and finds she has rebuffed the Savior himself. Oddly enough, my recital of this vitally un-Jewish material gave my parents no pain. My father, indeed, kept in his safe-deposit box along with other valuables a letter in which the Lutheran minister spoke gratefully of my last Christmas performance. "Through her great gift, your little Freidele has led many to Jesus." Though Papa seemed untroubled by considerations of whether this was a proper role for a Jewish child, reciting *The Visit* made me profoundly uneasy. And I suppose it was this feeling, combined with a natural disinclination to stand unbidden at the feast, which led me, the year I was seven, to rebel.

We were baking in the steamy kitchen, my mother and I— or rather she was baking while I watched, fascinated as always, the miracle of the strudel. First, the warm ball of dough, no larger than my mother's hand. Slap, punch, bang—again and again she lifted the dough and smacked it down on the board. Then came the moment I loved. Over the kitchen table, obliterating its patterned oilcloth, came a damask cloth; and over this in turn a cloud of flour. Beside it stood my mother, her hair bound in muslin, her hands and arms powdered with flour. She paused a moment. Then, like a dancer about to execute a particularly difficult pirouette, she tossed the dough high in the air, catching it with a little stretching motion and tossing again until the ball was ball no longer but an almost transparent rectangle. The studel was as large as the tablecloth now. *"Unter Freidele's vigele Ligt eyn groys veys tsigele,"* she sang. "Under Freidele's little bed A white goat lays his silken

head." *Tsigele iz geforen handlen Rozinkes mit mandlen....* "
For some reason that song, with its gay fantastic images of the
white goat shopping for raisins and almonds, always made me
sad. But then my father swung open the storm door and stood,
stamping and jingling his galoshes buckles, on the icy mat.

"Boris, look how you track in the snow!"

Already flakes and stars were turning into muddy puddles.
Still booted and icy-cheeked he swept us up—a kiss on the
back of Mama's neck, the only spot not dedicated to strudel,
and a hug for me.

"You know what? I have just now seen the preacher. Rev-
erend Pederson, he wants you should recite at the Christmas
concert."

I bent over the bowl of almonds and snapped the nut-
cracker.

"I should tell him it's all right, you'll speak a piece?"

No answer.

"Sweetheart—dear one—you'll do it?"

Suddenly the words burst out. "No, Papa! I don't want to!"

My father was astonished. "But why not? What is it with
you?"

"I hate those concerts!" All at once my grievances swarmed
up in an angry cloud. "I never have any fun! And everybody
else gets presents and Santa Claus never calls out 'Freidele
Bruser'! They all know I'm Jewish!"

Papa was incredulous. "But, little daughter, always you've
had a good time! Presents! What presents? A bag of candy, an
orange? Tell me, is there a child in town with such toys as you
have? What should you want with Santa Claus?"

It was true. My friends had tin tea sets and dolls with saw-
dust bodies and crude Celluloid smiles. I had an Eaton Beauty
with real hair and delicate jointed body, two French dolls with
rosy bisque faces and—new this last Hanukkah—Rachel, my
baby doll. She was the marvel of the town: exquisite china
head, overlarge and shaped like a real infant's, tiny wrinkled
hands, legs convincingly bowed. I had a lace and taffeta doll
bassinet, a handmade cradle, a full set of rattan doll furniture,
a teddy bear from Germany and real porcelain dishes from
England. What *did* I want with Santa Claus? I didn't know, I
burst into tears.

Papa was frantic now. What was fame and the applause of the Lutherans compared to his child's tears? Still bundled in his overcoat he knelt on the kitchen floor and hugged me to him, rocking and crooning. "Don't cry, my child, don't cry. You don't want to go, you don't have to. I tell them you have a sore throat, you can't come."

"Boris, wait. Listen to me." For the first time since my outburst, Mama spoke. She laid down the rolling pin, draped the strudel dough delicately over the table, and wiped her hands on her apron. "What kind of a fuss? You go or you don't go, it's not such a big thing. But so close to Christmas you shouldn't let them down. The one time we sit with them in the church and such joy you give them. Freidele, look at me...." I snuffed loudly and obeyed, not without some satisfaction in the thought of the pathetic picture I made. "Go this one time, for my sake. You'll see, it won't be so bad. And if you don't like it—pfffff, no more! All right? Now, come help with the raisins."

On the night of the concert we gathered in the kitchen again, this time for the ritual of the bath. Papa set up the big tin tub on chairs next to the black iron stove. Then, while he heated pails of water and sloshed them into the tub, Mama set out my clothes. Everything about this moment contrived to make me feel pampered, special. I was lifted in and out of the steamy water, patted dry with thick towels, powdered from neck to toes with Mama's best scented talcum. Then came my "reciting outfit." My friends in Birch Hills had party dresses mail-ordered from Eaton's—crackly taffeta or shiny rayon satin weighted with lace or flounces, and worn with long white stockings drawn up over long woolen underwear. My dress was Mama's own composition, a poem in palest peach crepe de chine created from remnants of her bridal trousseau. Simple and flounceless, it fell from my shoulders in a myriad of tiny pleats no wider than my thumbnail; on the low-slung sash hung a cluster of silk rosebuds. Regulation drop-seat underwear being unthinkable under such a costume, Mama had devised a snug little apricot chemise which made me, in a world of wool, feel excitingly naked.

When at last I stood on the church dais, the Christmas tree glittering and shimmering behind me, it was with the familiar feeling of strangeness. I looked out over the audience-congregation, grateful for the myopia that made faces indistinguishable, and began:

> A letter came on Christmas morn
> In which the Lord did say
> "Behold my star shines in the east
> And I shall come today.
> Make bright thy hearth. . . ."

The words tripped on without thought or effort. I knew by heart every nuance and gesture, down to the modest curtsey and the properly solemn pace with which I returned to my seat. There I huddled into the lining of Papa's coat, hardly hearing the "Beautiful, beautiful!" which accompanied his hug. For this was the dreaded moment. All around me, children twitched and whispered. Santa had come.

"Olaf Swenson!" Olaf tripped over a row of booted feet, leapt down the aisle and embraced an enormous package. "Ellen Njaa! Fern Dahl! Peter Bjorkstrom!" There was a regular procession now, all jubilant. Everywhere in the hall children laughed, shouted, rejoiced with their friends. "What'd you get?" "Look at mine!" In the seat next to me, Gunnar Olsen ripped through layers of tissue: "I got it! I got it" His little sister wrestled with the contents of a red net stocking. A tin whistle rolled to my feet and I turned away, ignoring her breathless efforts to retrieve it.

And then—suddenly, incredibly, the miracle came. "Freidele Bruser!" For me, too, the star had shone. I looked up at my mother. A mistake surely. But she smiled and urged me to my feet. "Go on, look, he calls you!" It was true, Santa was actually coming to meet me. My gift, I saw, was not wrapped—and it could be no mistake. It was a doll, a doll just like Rachel, but dressed in christening gown and cap. "Oh Mama, look! He's brought me a doll! A twin for Rachel! She's just the right size for Rachel's clothes. I can take them both for walks in the carriage. They can have matching outfits. . . ." I was in an ecstasy of plans.

Mama did not seem to be listening. She lifted the hem of

the gown. "How do you like her dress? Look, see the petti-coat?"

"They're beautiful!" I hugged the doll rapturously. "Oh Mama, I *love* her! I'm going to call her Ingrid. Ingrid and Rachel...."

During the long walk home Mama was strangely quiet. Usually I held my parents' hands and swung between them. But now I stepped carefully, clutching Ingrid.

"You had a good time, yes?" Papa's breath frosted the night.

"Mmmmmmm." I rubbed my warm cheek against Ingrid's cold one. "It was just like a real Christmas. I got the best present of anybody. Look, Papa—did you see Ingrid's funny little cross face? It's just like Rachel's. I can't wait to get her home and see them side by side in the crib."

In the front hall, I shook the snow from Ingrid's lace bonnet. "A hot cup cocoa maybe?" Papa was already taking the milk from the icebox. "No, no, I want to get the twins ready for bed!" I broke from my mother's embrace. The stairs seemed longer than usual. In my arms Ingrid was cold and still, a snow princess. I could dress her in Rachel's flannel gown, that would be the thing.... The dolls and animals watched glassy-eyed as I knelt by the cradle. It rocked at my touch, oddly light. I flung back the blankets. Empty. Of course.

Sitting on the cold floor, the doll heavy in my lap, I wept for Christmas. Nothing had changed then, after all. For Jews there was no Santa Claus; I understood that. But my parents.... *Why* had they dressed Rachel?

From the kitchen below came the mingled aromas of hot chocolate and buttery popcorn. My mother called softly. "Let them call," I said to Ingrid-Rachel. "I don't care!" The face of the Christmas doll was round and blank under her cap; her dress was wet with my tears. Brushing them away, I heard my father enter the room. He made no move to touch me or lift me up. I turned and saw his face tender and sad like that of a Chagall violinist. "Mama worked every night on the clothes," he said. "Yesterday even, knitting booties."

Stiff-fingered, trembling, I plucked at the sleeve of the christening gown. It was indeed a miracle—a wisp of batiste but as richly overlaid with embroidery as a coronation robe. For the first time I examined Rachel's new clothes—the lace insets and lace overlays, the French knots and scalloped edges, the rows of hemstitching through which tiny ribbons ran like fairy silk. The petticoat was tucked and pleated. Even the little diaper showed an edge of hand crochet. There were booties and mittens and a ravishing cap.

"Freidele, dear one, my heart," my father whispered. "We did not think. We could not know. Mama dressed Rachel in the new clothes, you should be happy with the others. We so much love you."

Outside my window, where the Christmas snow lay deep and crisp and even, I heard the shouts of neighbors returning from the concert. "Joy to the world!" they sang,

> Let earth receive her King!
> Let every heart prepare Him room
> And heaven and nature sing . . .

It seemed to me, at that moment, that I too was a part of the song. I wrapped Rachel warmly in her shawl and took my father's hand.

Woodtick

Joy Kogawa

The spring day the teen on his bike slanted his caucasian eyes
At my eight year old beautiful daughter
And taunted gibberish
I was eight years old and the Japs were
Enemies of Canada and the big white boys
And their golden haired sisters who
Lived in the ghost town of Slocan
Were walking together, crowding me
Off the path of the mountain, me running
Into the forest to escape
Into the pine brown and green lush dark
And getting lost and fearing woodticks
Which burrowed into your scalp beneath
Thick black hair follicles and could only be
Dug out by a doctor with hot needles—
Fearing sudden slips caused by melting snow
And steep ravines and the thick silence of
Steaming woods and cobwebs, so listening
For the guiding sound of their laughter
To lead me back to the path and
Following from a safe distance unseen
Till near the foot of the mountain
Then running past faster than their laughter
Home, vowing never to go again to the mountain
Alone—and Deidre whispers to walk faster
Though I tell her there are no
Woodticks in Saskatoon.

Cowboys and Indians

Basil Johnston

HOLLYWOOD grew fast and big. By the 1930s there were many studios employing many actors in the production of many motion pictures. Within the same few years as the studios got bigger, techniques improved; as techniques improved so did the quality of acting; and as acting got better, so did the range and variety of themes enlarge. And of course viewers' tastes became more refined and discriminating, requiring of Hollywood and the studios more authenticity and less artificiality in their productions.

And the studios were willing to oblige.

It was decided by the producer and director of a major studio planning a western picture with either Hoot Gibson, Tom Mix, or Ken Maynard as the principal star, to hire real Indians to take part in the production. With real Indians the advantages were obvious. Besides lending authenticity to the motion picture, Indians represented a substantial saving. Their natural pigmentation would reduce expenses in cosmetics and make-up artistics; their natural horsemanship would save time and expenses usually incurred in training greenhorns to ride; their possession of herds of ponies would save time and outlay in the rental and feeding of horses; and their natural talent for art would obviate the need for anthropologists to act as consultants in authenticating Indian art and design. The only expense to be incurred was the fee of $2.00 per day for movie extras.

Management calculated that 500 Indians along with 500

horses were needed for no more than two days to shoot an attack upon a wagon-train. The producer and the director also decided that there would be substantial savings by establishing the location of the filming near an Indian reservation somewhere in the west.

Inquiries, preliminary and cursory, made of historians and the Bureau of Indian Affairs in Washington indicated that the Crow Indians of Montana, having retained their traditions and still owning large herds of horses, would be best suited for a motion picture of the kind planned by the studio. Besides, the terrain in the area was genuine honest-to-goodness Indian country, excellent for camera work.

Negotiations with the Bureau of Indian Affairs for permission to treat with the Crows for their services as actors and for the provision of horses began at once. Permission was granted by Washington; and the Crows were more than willing to take part.

Crew and cast arrived by train in Billings, Montana. Anxious to get started and to finish shooting the siege of a wagon-train in as short a time as possible, the producer and director sent a limousine to the reservation to fetch the chief.

Over a meal with the chief and his retinue of councillors and hangers-on, the producer, portly and bald, beneath a cloud of smoke produced by a fat cigar, informed the chief that it was a great privilege to work with the Crows and that it was an honour and a distinction for his studio to set precedent in the entire industry by being the first to use real, live, honest-to-goodness Indians in a motion picture. For the Crows, it would mean fame and national recognition . . . and money . . . $2.00 a day for those taking part; $1.00 per day for those providing horses; and $1.00 per day for those providing art work and the loan of teepees.

An interpreter translated for the chief.

The producer smiled and blew a cloud of smoke out of the side of his mouth. The Crow responded 'How! How! How!'

'It shouldn't take long chief, three or four days . . . no more. A day to get ready and two or three to film the scene. We don't want to interfere too much in your affairs, you've probably got a lot to do and . . . we are working under a pretty tight schedule.'

The interpreter relayed this information to the chief.

'Now chief. We want 500 warriors; 500 horses; bows and arrows and . . . maybe fifty or so rifles . . . feathers, head-dresses, buckskin jackets, and . . . buckskin leggings . . . and four or five people who can paint designs on horses and put make-up on warriors.' The producer continued, 'The scene itself will be easy. The warriors will attack the wagon-train at daybreak. It shouldn't take more than half an hour. Very easy, really don't need any rehearsals. My colleague will tell you what to do. Probably the easiest two bucks you'll ever make . . . cash, as soon as the scene's shot. Can you get all this stuff by tomorrow night, chief?' And the producer flicked ashes from his fat cigar.

The interpreter prattling in Crow to his chief and councillors pounded the table, slashed the air, shrugged his shoulders to emphasize his message to his listeners, who looked dumbfounded. Nevertheless they injected a 'How! How!' frequently enough into the discourse to intimate some understanding.

The chief said something.

'How many horses?'

'500, the producer might even settle for 450.'

The interpreter addressed his chief who shook his head grunting 'How!'

'Ain't got 500 horses,' the interpreter said sadly.

'450?'

'Ain't dat many on de reservation.'

'300?'

'No, not dat many: not like long time ago.'

'Well! How many have you got?' the producer asked, his face pinching into worried lines and his voice losing its cheer and vitality.

'Maybe 10 . . . 20 . . . an' not very good dem.'

'Keeee . . . rice . . . !' And the producer bit a chunk of cigar, crushing the other end in the ashtray. 'Are there any horses around here?'

'Yeah. Ranchers and farmers got dem.'

To his assistant, the producer instructed 'Get 500 horses by tomorrow evening. We have to shoot that scene next morning with the Indians charging down the slope.'

The interpreter whispered to his chief who shook his head.

'Say, mister,' the interpreter addressed the producer, 'how about saddles?'

'Saddles!' the word erupted.

'Yeah, saddles.'

There was a moment of cosmic silence. 'Saddles!' the producer repeated mouthing the word in disbelief. 'What do you mean ... saddles! You're all going to ride bare-back. This film is going to be authentic ... who ever heard of Indians riding on saddles ... supposed to be the finest horsemen in the world.'

The interpreter stiffened in fright at the thought that he might be one of the warriors to ride bare-back, and he hung his head.

'Don't know how to ride ... us. Forgot how ... long time ago ... Need saddles ... might fall off an' git hurt ... us.'

'This is incredible! ... unbelievable! ... no horses! ... can't ride!' ... the producer gasped as he sank into the chair. 'Keeeeee-rice.'

Hope waning from his brow and voice, the producer tried 'You still got bows an' arrows?'

The interpreter slouched even lower 'No! Got none of dem t'ings, us.'

'Buckskin outfits?'

'No,' another shameful shrug.

'Moccasins?'

'Some,' a little brighter.

'Head-dresses?'

'Maybe two, three—very old dem.'

'Teepees?'

'No more—live in houses us.'

'Anyone know Indian designs ... you know—war paint for warriors ... and horses?'

'Don't t'ink so ... everybody forgot.'

The producer groaned. 'This is astounding ... I can't believe it ... No horses ... can't ride ... no teepees ... no buckskin ... no ... no moccasins ... no ... no head-dresses ... and ... probably not even loin-cloths ...' and he was quivering. 'It boggles the mind.'

'What do we do?' the director asked.

For several moments the producer assessed the circumstances, and possessing an analytical mind he stated what needed to be done.

'With all our crew and cast here, and with our wagon-train and cannon and horses, we can't very well go back now. We'll have to train these Indians to ride. Now ... Adams,' the producer's assistant, 'I want you to get on the line right away. Get a guy who knows something about Indians, from the Bureau of Indian Affairs. I want you to get maybe a dozen chiefs' outfits; and 500 loin-cloths, bows an' arrows for everyone, about a dozen head-dresses and moccasins ... everything we need to make these Indians ... *Indians*. Is that clear? And get those horses by tomorrow night.'

'Yes sir!'

'In the meantime, I'll call the studio office for more money. Let's get movin'.'

The assistant went out.

'How long we gotta stay in this miserable God-forsaken cow-town? Ken Maynard inquired.

'Coupla weeks ... maybe.'

Ken Maynard groaned.

'Now!' directing his cigar at the interpreter and his remarks to the chief, the producer said, 'Tell the chief to get 500 young men to learn to ride bare-back; an' to learn fast.'

The interpreter apprised his chief of the message. The chief responded.

'He say $2.00 a day!'

'Keeee-rice! Tell him, okay!'

Two mornings later, 500 horses borrowed and rented from the local ranchers were delivered to the Indian reservation. 500 Crows began practising the art of horsemanship at once, and in earnest. And while it is true that many Crows shied away from the horses, just as many horses shied away from the Crows, so that there was much anxious circling of horses around Indians and Indians around horses, pulling and jerking midst the clamour of pleas 'Whoa! Whoa! Steady there Nellie! Easy there!' all in Crow; and the horses perhaps because they were unfamiliar with Crow refusing to 'whoa.' Eventually, horses and Crows overcame their mutual distrust and suspicions and animosities to enable the Indians to mount their beasts.

There were of course some casualties, a few broken legs, sprained ankles, cracked ribs, and bruised behinds suffered by the novices on the first day. But by the third day most of the young men, while not accomplished equestrians, were able to ride passably well; that is, they fell off their mounts less often.

With the arrival of the equipment, bows and arrows, head-dresses, moccasins, loin-cloths, shipped by express from Washington, one day was set aside for the Crow warriors to practise shooting arrows from bows, first from a standing position and then from horseback. There were a few more casualties but nothing serious.

Along with the equipment came twelve make-up artists accompanied by an anthropologist to advise the artists in war-paint designs and to instruct the Crow in war-whooping. Twelve immense pavilions were erected, outside of each bill boards bearing symbols and markings representative of warrior war-paint and horse-paint designs. Each Indian having selected the design that best suited his taste and his horse entered a pavilion where he and his steed were painted, emerging at the other end of the massive tent looking very fierce and ready for war.

The movie moguls decided that they would film the siege of the wagon-train at 5 a.m. regardless of the readiness of the Indians. 'So what if a few Red-skins fall off their horses ... be more realistic.'

As planned and according to script ten Crows, dressed in white buckskin heavily beaded and wearing war-bonnets to represent leadership, along with 450 warriors wearing only loin-cloths and armed with bows and arrows were assembled in a shallow depression unseen from the wagon-train. The horses pawed the ground and snorted and whinnied, while the director, producer, assorted assistants, and camera-men waited for the sun to cast its beams upon the wagon-train. When that critical moment occurred, signalled by an assistant with a wave of an arm, the director shouted 'Action! Cameras roll!'

450 Indians on 450 horses erupted over the lip of the valley a 'hoopin' an' a hollerin', their savage war-cries splitting the air while 1800 hooves thundered down the slope, shaking the earth. Wagon-train passengers spilled out of covered-wagons, splashed up from blankets, seized rifles, yelling 'Injuns! In-

juns!' and hurled themselves behind boxes and crates and barrels and began firing. At one end of the valley, Ken Maynard
on his white charger waited for his cue; at the other end fifty
cavalrymen waited to charge to the rescue. Bang! Bang! Bang!
The Crows, a 'hoopin' an' a hollerin' were riding round and
round the wagon-train, firing their arrows into the covered
wagon and into boxes and crates and barrels. Bang! Bang!
Bang! Round and round rode the Crows.

'Cut! Cut! Cut!' everyone was shouting. 'Cut! Cut! Cut! everyone was waving his arms. Cut! Cut! Cut! 450 Crows, yelling
whoa! whoa! whoa! brought their steeds to a halt.

The director, also on a horse, was livid with rage. He almost
choked. 'Somebody's gotta die; when you're shot, you fall off
your horse and die. Don't you understand?'

The Indians nodded and grunted 'How! How!'

The director in disgust rode off leaving the cast and crew to
repair 3000 to 4000 punctures and perforations inflicted by arrows on the canvas of the covered wagons. Six members of the
cast suffering injuries from stray arrows needed medical attention. The Indians, with the arrows they had recovered, retired
to the reservation to mend their weapons.

Just before sun-up next day there was a final admonition.
'Get it done right this time!' The warriors responded 'How!
How!'

At the hand signal, 'Action! Cameras roll!' were uttered.

450 Indians on 450 horses boiled over the lip of the valley, a
'hoopin an' a hollerin', their savage war cries rending the
peace, while 1800 hooves pounded down the slope convulsing
the ground. Wagon-train patrons scurried out of covered
wagons, sprang from blankets, seized their rifles, yelling 'Injuns! Injuns!' and dove behind boxes and crates and barrels
and began firing. Bang! Bang! Bang!

Seventy-five of the Crows, a 'hoopin' an' a hollerin' fell off
their horses. Bang! Bang! Bang! 200 more Crows, a 'hoopin'
an' a hollerin' spun off their mounts. Bang! Bang! Bang! The
rest pitched off their steeds who fled in all directions.

'Cut! Cut! Cut!' everyone was shouting. 450 Crows
suspended their moanin' an' a groanin' an' a rollin' on the
ground, even though many had sustained real injuries, to listen
to and to watch the director.

There was a torrent of curses, sulphuric glares, which eventually subsided into mutterings, the gist of which was relayed by the interpreter to the chiefs and warriors 'that not everyone should have fallen off his horse.' To this the chief replied $2.00.

The scene was re-enacted the next day without incident. After the shooting there were hand-shakes all around; the expressions of admiration tendered by Ken Maynard to the Crows for the speed with which they had developed horsemanship, remarking that 'it must be in-bred.'

Crew and cast were celebrating over wine and whiskey, cheese and crackers, when the film editor summoned the director. 'Come here and look at these,' he said, thrusting a magnifying glass to his superior. The director held the film strip against the light; he applied the magnifying glass to the stills.

'Sun-glasses! Keeee-rice ... sun-glasses ... those damned Indians. Keeee-rice ... what next ...'

When told, the producer kicked a chair after hurling a bottle into a corner: for close to ten minutes he cursed Indians. But it was useless, the scene had to be shot again.

Horses and Indians had to be recalled and reassembled for retakes for which the good chief demanded $2.00 for his people. It took another week before the wagon-train siege was filmed to the satisfaction of the producer and his director. In the interim there were two days of rain, one filming aborted by several Crows wearing watches, an extra filming of a prairie fire ignited by Ken Maynard that miscarried because several Crow warriors, supposedly dead, moved to avoid getting burned during a critical segment of the filming. When the first real epic of 'Cowboys and Indians' was finally done, the Crows were jubilant, indebted to their chief for the prosperity and lasting renown that he exacted during difficult times. The producer and director, cast and crew, departed in disquiet over having exceeded their budget.

But whatever doubts the producer and the director might have entertained were more than vindicated by reviews of the film in which the horsemanship of the Crow was acclaimed and the genius of the producer for his vision and for his foresight in using Indians in motion pictures.

Elephants

Patrick Lane

The cracked cedar bunkhouse
hangs behind me like a grey pueblo
in the sundown where I sit
to carve an elephant
from a hunk of brown soap
for the Indian boy who lives
in the village a mile back
in the bush.

The alcoholic truck-driver
and the cat-skinner sit beside me
with their eyes closed
all of us waiting out the last hour
until we go back on the grade

and I try to forget the forever
clank   clank   clank
across the grade
pounding stones and earth to powder
for hours in mosquito darkness
of the endless cold mountain night.

The elephant takes form—
my knife caresses smooth soap
scaling off curls of brown

which the boy saves to take home
to his mother in the village

Finished, I hand the carving to him
and he looks at the image of the great
beast for a long time
then sets it on dry cedar
and looks up at me:
                    What's an elephant?
he asks
so I tell him of the elephants
and their jungles. The story
of the elephant graveyard
which no one has ever found
and how the silent
animals of the rain forest
go away to die somewhere
in the limberlost of distances
and he smiles

tells me of his father's
graveyard where his people have been
buried for years. So far back
no one remembers when it started
and I ask him where the graveyard is
and he tells me it is gone
now where no one will ever find it
buried under the grade of the new
highway.

God Is Not a Fish Inspector

W. D. Valgardson

Although Emma made no noise as she descended, Fusi Bergman knew his daughter was watching him from the bottom of the stairs.

"God will punish you," she promised in a low, intense voice.

"Render unto Caesar what is Caesar's," he snapped. "God's not a fish inspector. He doesn't work for the government."

By the light of the front ring of the kitchen stove, he had been drinking a cup of coffee mixed half and half with whisky. Now, he shifted in his captain's chair so as to partly face the stairs. Though he was unable to make out more than the white blur of Emma's nightgown, after living with her for 48 years he knew exactly how she would look if he turned on the light.

She was tall and big boned with the square, pugnacious face of a bulldog. Every inch of her head would be crammed with metal curlers and her angular body hidden by a plain white cotton shift that hung from her broad shoulders like a tent. Whenever she was angry with him, she always stood rigid and white lipped, her hands clenched at her sides.

"You prevaricate," she warned. "You will not be able to prevaricate at the gates of Heaven."

He drained his cup, sighed, and pulled on his jacket. As he opened the door, Fusi said, "He made fish to catch. There is no place in the Bible where it says you can't catch fish when you are three score and ten."

"You'll be the ruin of us," she hissed as he closed the door on her.

She was aggressive and overbearing, but he knew her too well to be impressed. Behind her forcefulness, there was always that trace of self-pity nurtured in plain women who go unmarried until they think they have been passed by. Even if they eventually found a husband, the self-pity returned to change their determination into a whine. Still, he was glad to have the door between them.

This morning, as every morning, he had wakened at three. Years before, he had trained himself to get up at that time and now, in spite of his age, he never woke more than five minutes after the hour. He was proud of his early rising for he felt it showed he was not, like many of his contemporaries, relentlessly sliding into the endless blur of senility. Each morning, because he had become reconciled to the idea of dying, he felt, on the instant of his awakening, a spontaneous sense of amazement at being alive. The thought never lasted longer than the brief time between sleep and consciousness, but the good feeling lingered throughout the day.

When Fusi stepped outside, the air was cold and damp. The moon that hung low in the west was pale and fragile and very small. Fifty feet from the house, the breakwater that ran along the rear of his property loomed like the purple spine of some great beast guarding the land from a lake which seemed, in the darkness, to go on forever.

Holding his breath to still the noise of his own breathing, Fusi listened for a cough or the scuff of gravel that would mean someone was close by, watching and waiting, but the only sound was the muted rubbing of his skiff against the piling to which it was moored. Half a mile away where the land was lower, rows of gas boats roped five abreast lined the docks. The short, stubby boats with their high cabins, the grey surface of the docks and the dark water were all tinged purple from the mercury lamps. At the harbour mouth, high on a thin spire, a red light burned like a distant star.

Behind him, he heard the door open and, for a moment, he was afraid Emma might begin to shout, or worse still, turn on the back-door light and alert his enemies, but she did neither.

Above all things, Emma was afraid of scandal, and would do anything to avoid causing an unsavoury rumour to be attached to her own or her husband's name.

Her husband, John Smith, was as bland and inconsequential as his name. Moon faced with wide blue eyes and a small mouth above which sat a carefully trimmed moustache, he was a head shorter than Emma and a good 50 pounds lighter. Six years before, he had been transferred to the Eddyville branch of the Bank of Montreal. His transfer from Calgary to a small town in Manitoba was the bank's way of letting him know that there would be no more promotions. He would stay in Eddyville until he retired.

A year after he arrived, Emma had married him and instead of her moving out, he had moved in. For the last two years, under Emma's prodding, John had been taking a correspondence course in theology so that when he no longer worked at the bank he could be a full-time preacher.

On the evenings when he wasn't balancing the bank's books, he laboured over the multiple-choice questions in the Famous Preacher's course that he received each month from the One True and Only Word of God Church in Mobile, Alabama. Because of a freak in the atmosphere one night while she had been fiddling with the radio, Emma had heard a gospel hour advertising the course and, although neither she nor John had ever been south of Minneapolis and had never heard of the One True and Only Word of God Church before, she took it as a sign and immediately enrolled her husband in it. It cost $500.

John's notes urged him not to wait to answer His Call but to begin ministering to the needy at once for the Judgment Day was always imminent. In anticipation of the end of the world and his need for a congregation once he retired, he and Emma had become zealous missionaries, cramming their Volkswagen with a movie projector, a record-player, films, trays of slides, religious records for every occasion, posters and pamphlets, all bought or rented from the One True and Only Word of God Church. Since the townspeople were obstinately Lutheran, and since John did not want to give offence to any of his bank's customers, he and Emma hunted converts along the grey dirt roads that led past tumble-down farmhouses, the inhabitants of which were never likely to enter a bank.

Fusi did not turn to face his daughter but hurried away because he knew he had no more than an hour and a half until dawn. His legs were fine as he crossed the yard, but by the time he had mounted the steps that led over the breakwater, then climbed down fifteen feet to the shore, his left knee had begun to throb.

Holding his leg rigid to ease the pain, he waded out, loosened the ropes and heaved himself away from the shore. As soon as the boat was in deep water, he took his seat, and set both oars in the oar-locks he had carefully muffled with strips from an old shirt.

For a moment, he rested his hands on his knees, the oars rising like too-small wings from a cumbersome body, then he straightened his arms, dipped the oars cleanly into the water and in one smooth motion pulled his hands toward his chest. The first few strokes were even and graceful but then as a speck of pain like a grain of sand formed in his shoulder, the sweep of his left oar became shorter than his right. Each time he leaned against the oars, the pain grew until it was, in his mind, a bent shingle-nail twisted and turned in his shoulder socket.

With the exertion, a ball of gas formed in his stomach, making him uncomfortable. As quickly as a balloon being blown up, it expanded until his lungs and heart were cramped and he couldn't draw in a full breath. Although the air over the lake was cool, sweat ran from his hairline.

At his two-hundredth stroke, he shipped his left oar and pulled a coil of rope with a large hook from under the seat. After checking to see that it was securely tied through the gunwale, he dropped the rope overboard and once more began to row. Normally, he would have had a buoy made from a slender tamarack pole, a block of wood and some lead weights to mark his net, but he no longer had a fishing licence so his net had to be sunk below the surface where it could not be seen by the fish inspectors.

Five more strokes of the oars and the rope went taut. He lifted both oars into the skiff, then, standing in the bow, began to pull. The boat responded sluggishly but gradually it turned and the cork line that lay hidden under two feet of water broke the surface. He grasped the net, freed the hook and began to collect the mesh until the lead line appeared. For once he had been lucky and the hook had caught the net close to one end so there was no need to backtrack.

Hand over hand he pulled, being careful not to let the corks and leads bang against the bow, for on the open water sound carried clearly for miles. In the first two fathoms there was a freshly caught pickerel. As he pulled it toward him, it beat the water with its tail, making light, slapping sounds. His fingers were cramped, but Fusi managed to catch the fish around its soft middle end, and with his other hand, work the mesh free of the gills.

It was then that the pain in his knee forced him to sit. Working from the seat was awkward and cost him precious time, but he had no choice, for the pain had begun to inch up the bone toward his crotch.

He wiped his forehead with his hand and cursed his infirmity. When he was twenty, he had thought nothing of rowing five miles from shore to lift five and six gangs of nets and then, nearly knee deep in fish, row home again. Now, he reflected bitterly, a quarter of a mile and one net were nearly beyond him. Externally, he had changed very little over the years. He was still tall and thin, his arms and legs corded with muscle. His belly was hard. His long face, with its pointed jaw, showed his age the most. That and his hands. His face was lined until it seemed there was nowhere the skin was smooth. His hands were scarred and heavily veined. His hair was grey but it was still thick.

While others were amazed at his condition, he was afraid of the changes that had taken place inside him. It was this invisible deterioration that was gradually shrinking the limits of his endurance.

Even in the darkness, he could see the distant steeple of the Lutheran church and the square bulk of the old folk's home that was directly across from his house. Emma, he thought grimly, would not be satisfied until he was safely trapped in one or carried out of the other.

He hated the old folk's home. He hated the three stories of pale yellow brick with their small, close-set windows. He hated the concrete porch with its five round pillars and the large white buckets of red geraniums. When he saw the men poking at the flowers like a bunch of old women, he pulled his blinds.

The local people who worked in the home were good to the inmates, tenants they called them, but there was no way a man could be a man in there. No whisky. Going to bed at ten. Getting up at eight. Bells for breakfast, coffee and dinner. Bells for everything. He was surprised that they didn't have bells for going to the toilet. Someone watching over you every minute of every day. It was as if, having earned the right to be an adult, you had suddenly, in some inexplicable way, lost it again.

The porch was the worst part of the building. Long and narrow and lined with yellow and red rocking-chairs, it sat ten feet above the ground and the steps were so steep that even those who could get around all right were afraid to try them. Fusi had lived across from the old folk's home for 40 years and he had seen old people, all interchangeable as time erased their identities, shuffling and bickering their way to their deaths. Now, most of those who came out to sleep in the sun and to watch the world with glittering, jealous eyes were people he had known.

He would have none of it. He was not afraid of dying, but he was determined that it would be in his own home. His licence had been taken from him because of his age, but he did not stop. One net was not thirty, but it was one, and a quarter-mile from shore was not five miles, but it was a quarter-mile.

He didn't shuffle and he didn't have to be fed or have a rubber diaper pinned around him each day. If anything, he had become more cunning for, time and again, the inspectors had come and destroyed the illegal nets of other fishermen, even catching and sending them to court to be fined, but they hadn't caught him for four years. Every day of the fishing season, he pitted his wits against theirs and won. At times, they had come close, but their searches had never turned up anything and, once, to his delight, when he was on the verge of being found with freshly caught fish on him, he hid them under a hole in the breakwater and then sat on the edge of the boat, talked about old times, and shared the inspectors' coffee. The memory still brought back a feeling of pleasure and excitement.

As his mind strayed over past events, he drew the boat along the net in fits and starts for his shoulder would not take the strain of steady pulling. Another good-sized fish hung limp as he pulled it to him, but then as he slipped the mesh from its head, it gave a violent shake and flew from his hands. Too stiff and slow to lunge for it, he could do nothing but watch the white flash of its belly before it struck the water and disappeared.

He paused to knead the backs of his hands, then began again. Before he was finished, his breath roared in his ears like the lake in a storm, but there were four more pickerel. With a sigh that was nearly a cry of pain, he let the net drop. Immediately, pulled down by the heavy, rusted anchors at each end, it disappeared. People were like that, he thought. One moment they were here, then they were gone and it was as if they had never been.

Behind the town, the horizon was a pale, hard grey. The silhouette of rooftops and trees might have been cut from a child's purple construction paper.

The urgent need to reach the shore before the sky became any lighter drove Fusi, for he knew that if the inspectors saw him on the water they would catch him as easily as a child. They would take his fish and net, which he did not really mind, for there were more fish in the lake and more nets in his shed, but he couldn't afford to lose his boat. His savings were not enough to buy another.

He put out the oars, only to be unable to close the fingers of his left hand. When he tried to bend his fingers around the handle, his whole arm began to tremble. Unable to do anything else, he leaned forward and pressing his fingers flat to the seat, he began to relentlessly knead them. Alternately, he prayed and cursed, trying with words to delay the sun.

"A few minutes," he whispered through clenched teeth. "Just a few minutes more." But even as he watched, the horizon turned red, then yellow and a sliver of the sun's rim rose above the houses.

Unable to wait any longer, he grabbed his left hand in his

right and forced his fingers around the oar, then braced himself and began to row. Instead of cutting the water cleanly, the left oar skimmed over the surface, twisting the handle in his grip. He tried again, not letting either oar go deep. The skiff moved sluggishly ahead.

Once again, the balloon in his chest swelled and threatened to gag him, making his gorge rise, but he did not dare stop. Again and again, the left oar skipped across the surface so that the bow swung back and forth like a wounded and dying animal trying to shake away its pain. Behind him, the orange sun inched above the sharp angles of the roofs.

When the bow slid across the sand, he dropped the oars, letting them trail in the water. He grasped the gunwale, but as he climbed out, his left leg collapsed and he slid to his knees. Cold water filled his boots and soaked the legs of his trousers. Resting his head against the boat, he breathed noisily through his mouth. He remained there until gradually his breathing eased and the pain in his chest closed like a night flower touched by daylight. When he could stand, he tied the boat to one of the black pilings that was left from a breakwater that had long since been smashed and carried away.

As he collected his catch, he noticed the green fisheries department truck on the dock. He had been right. They were there. Crouching behind his boat, he waited to see if anyone was watching him. It seemed like a miracle that they had not already seen him, but he knew that they had not for if they had, their launch would have raced out of the harbour and swept down upon him.

Bending close to the sand, he limped into the deep shadow at the foot of the breakwater. They might, he knew, be waiting for him at the top of the ladder, but if they were, there was nothing he could do about it. He climbed the ladder and, hearing and seeing nothing, he rested near the top so that when he climbed into sight, he wouldn't need to sit down.

Noone was in the yard. The block was empty. With a sigh of relief, he crossed to the small shed where he kept his equipment and hefted the fish onto the shelf that was nailed to one wall. He filleted his catch with care, leaving none of the translucent flesh on the back-bone or skin. Then, because they were pickerel, he scooped out the cheeks, which he set aside with the roe for his breakfast.

As he carried the offal across the backyard in a bucket, the line of gulls that gathered every morning on the breakwater broke into flight and began to circle overhead. Swinging back the bucket, he flung the guts and heads and skin into the air and the gulls darted down to snatch the red entrails and iridescent heads. In a thrumming of white and grey wings, those who hadn't caught anything descended to the sand to fight for what remained.

Relieved at being rid of the evidence of his fishing—if anyone asked where he got the fillets he would say he had bought them and the other fishermen would lie for him—Fusi squatted and wiped his hands clean on the wet grass.

There was no sign of movement in the house. The blinds were still drawn and the high, narrow house with its steep roof and faded red-brick siding looked deserted. The yard was flat and bare except for the dead trunk of an elm, which was stripped bare of its bark and wind polished to the colour of bone.

He returned to the shed and wrapped the fillets in a sheet of brown waxed paper, then put the roe and the cheeks into the bucket. Neither Emma nor John were up when he came in and washed the bucket and his food, but as he started cooking, Emma appeared in a quilted housecoat covered with large, purple tulips. Her head was a tangle of metal.

"Are you satisfied?" she asked, her voice trembling. "I've had no sleep since you left."

Without turning from the stove, he said, "Leave. Nobody's making you stay."

Indignantly, she answered, "And who would look after you?"

He grimaced and turned over the roe so they would be golden brown on all sides. For two weeks around Christmas he had been sick with the flu and she never let him forget it.

"Honour thy father and mother that thy days may be long upon this earth."

He snorted out loud. What she really wanted to be sure of was that she got the house.

"You don't have to be like this," she said, starting to talk to him as if he was a child. "I only want you to stop because I care about you. All those people who live across the street, they don't. . . ."

"I'm not one of them," he barked.

"You're 70 years old. . . ."

"And I still fish," he replied angrily, cutting her off. "And I still row a boat and lift my nets. That's more than your husband can do and he's just 50." He jerked his breakfast off the stove. Because he knew it would annoy her, he began to eat out of the pan.

"I'm 70," he continued between bites, "and I beat the entire fisheries department. They catch men half my age, but they haven't caught me. Not for four years. And I fish right under their noses." He laughed with glee and laced his coffee with a finger of whisky.

Emma, her lips clamped shut and her hands clenched in fury, marched back up the stairs. In half an hour both she and John came down for their breakfast. Under Emma's glare, John cleared his throat and said, "Emma, that is we, think—" He stopped and fiddled with the knot of his tie. He always wore light grey ties and a light grey suit. "If you don't quit breaking the law, something will have to be done." He stopped and looked beseechingly at his wife, but she narrowed her eyes until little folds of flesh formed beneath them. "Perhaps something like putting you in custody so you'll be saved from yourself."

Fusi was so shocked that for once he could think of nothing to say. Encouraged by his silence, John said, "It will be for your own good."

Before either of them realized what he was up to, Fusi leaned sideways and emptied his cup into his son-in-law's lap.

The coffee was hot. John flung himself backward with a screech, but the back legs of his chair caught on a crack in the linoleum and he tipped over with a crash. In the confusion Fusi stalked upstairs.

In a moment he flung an armload of clothes down. When his daughter rushed to the bottom of the stairs, Fusi flung another armload of clothes at her.

"This is my house," he bellowed. "You're not running it yet."

Emma began grabbing clothes and laying them flat so they wouldn't wrinkle. John, both hands clenched between his legs, hobbled over to stare.

Fusi descended the stairs and they parted to let him by. At the counter, he picked up the package of fish and turning toward them, said, "I want you out of here when I get back or I'll go out on the lake and get caught and tell everyone that you put me up to it."

His fury was so great that once he was outside he had to lean against the house while a spasm of trembling swept over him. When he was composed, he rounded the corner. At one side of the old folk's home there was an enclosed fire escape that curled to the ground like a piece of intestine. He headed for the kitchen door under it.

Fusi had kept on his rubber boots, dark slacks and red turtle-neck sweater, and because he knew that behind the curtains, eyes were watching his every move, he tried to hide the stiffness in his left leg.

Although it was early, Rosie Melysyn was already at work. She always came first, never missing a day. She was a large, good natured widow with grey hair.

"How are you today, Mr. Bergman?" she asked.

"Fine," he replied. "I'm feeling great." He held out the brown paper package. "I thought some of the old people might like some fish." Although he had brought fish for the last four years, he always said the same thing.

Rosie dusted off her hands, took the package and placed it on the counter.

"I'll see someone gets it," she assured him. "Help yourself to some coffee."

As he took the pot from the stove, she asked, "No trouble with the inspectors?"

He always waited for her to ask that. He grinned delightedly, the pain of the morning already becoming a memory. "No trouble. They'll never catch me. I'm up too early. I saw them hanging about, but it didn't do them any good."

"Jimmy Henderson died last night," Rosie offered.

"Jimmy Henderson," Fusi repeated. They had been friends, but he felt no particular sense of loss. Jimmy had been in the home for three years. "I'm not surprised. He wasn't more than

68 but he had given up. You give up, you're going to die. You believe in yourself and you can keep right on going."

Rosie started mixing oatmeal and water.

"You know," he said to her broad back, "I was with Jimmy the first time he got paid. He cut four cords of wood for 60¢ and spent it all on hootch. He kept running up and down the street and flapping his arms, trying to fly. When he passed out, we hid him in the hayloft of the stable so his old man couldn't find him."

Rosie tried to imagine Jimmy Henderson attempting to fly and failed. To her, he was a bent man with a sad face who had to use a walker to get to the dining-room. What she remembered about him best was coming on him unexpectedly and finding him silently crying. He had not seen her and she had quietly backed away.

Fusi was lingering because after he left, there was a long day ahead of him. He would have the house to himself and after checking the vacated room to see that nothing of his had been taken, he would tie his boat properly, sleep for three hours, then eat lunch. In the afternoon he would make a trip to the docks to see what the inspectors were up to and collect information about their movements.

The back door opened with a swish and he felt a cool draft. Both he and Rosie turned to look. He was shocked to see that instead of it being one of the kitchen help, it was Emma. She shut the door and glanced at them both, then at the package of fish.

"What do you want?" he demanded.

"I called the inspectors," she replied, "to tell them you're not responsible for yourself. I told them about the net."

He gave a start, but then was relieved when he remembered they had to actually catch him fishing before they could take the skiff. "So what?" he asked, confident once more.

Quietly, she replied, "You don't have to worry about being caught. They've known about your fishing all along."

Suddenly frightened by her calm certainty, his voice rose as he said, "That's not true."

"They don't care," she repeated. "Inspector McKenzie was the name of the one I talked to. He said you couldn't do any harm with one net. They've been watching you every morning just in case you should get into trouble and need help."

Emma stood there, not moving, her head tipped back, her eyes benevolent.

He turned to Rosie. "She's lying, isn't she? That's not true. They wouldn't do that?"

"Of course, she's lying," Rosie assured him.

He would have rushed outside but Emma was standing in his way. Since he could not get past her, he fled through the swinging doors that led to the dining-room.

As the doors shut, Rosie turned on Emma and said, "You shouldn't have done that." She picked up the package of fish with its carefully folded wrapping. In the artificial light, the package glowed like a piece of amber. She held it cupped in the hollows of her hands. "You had no right."

Emma seemed to grow larger and her eyes shone.

"The Lord's work be done," she said, her right hand partly raised as if she were preparing to give a benediction.

What You See is the Real You

Willard Gaylin

I T was, I believe, the distinguished Nebraska financier Father Edward J. Flanagan[1] who professed to having "never met a bad boy." Having, myself, met a remarkable number of bad boys, it might seem that either our experiences were drastically different or we were using the word "bad" differently. I suspect neither is true, but rather that the Father was appraising the "inner man," while I, in fact, do not acknowledge the existence of inner people.

Since we psychoanalysts have unwittingly contributed to this confusion, let one, at least, attempt a small rectifying effort. Psychoanalytic data—which should be viewed as supplementary information—is, unfortunately, often viewed as alternative (and superior) explanation. This has led to the prevalent tendency to think of the "inner" man as the real man and the outer man as an illusion or pretender.

While psychoanalysis supplies us with an incredibly useful tool for explaining the motives and purposes underlying human behavior, most of this has little bearing on the moral nature of that behavior.

Like roentgenology, psychoanalysis is a fascinating, but relatively new, means of illuminating the person. But few of us are prepared to substitute an X-ray of Grandfather's head for the portrait that hangs in the parlor. The inside of the man

---

[1] (1886–1948), founder of Boys' Town orphanage near Omaha, Nebraska.

represents another view, not a truer one. A man may not always be what he appears to be, but what he appears to be is always a significant part of what he is. A man is the sum total of *all* his behavior. To probe for unconscious determinants of behavior and then define *him* in their terms exclusively, ignoring his overt behavior altogether, is a greater distortion than ignoring the unconscious completely.

Kurt Vonnegut[2] has said, "You are what you pretend to be," which is simply another way of saying, you are what we (all of us) perceive you to be, not what you think you are.

Consider for a moment the case of the 90-year-old man on his deathbed (surely the Talmud[3] must deal with this?) joyous and relieved over the success of his deception. For 90 years he has shielded his evil nature from public observation. For 90 years he has affected courtesy, kindness, and generosity—suppressing all the malice he knew was within him while he calculatedly and artificially substituted grace and charity. All his life he has been fooling the world into believing he was a good man. This "evil" man will, I predict, be welcomed into the Kingdom of Heaven.

Similarly, I will not be told that the young man who earns his pocket money by mugging old ladies is "really" a good boy. Even my generous and expansive definition of goodness will not accommodate that particular form of self-advancement.

It does not count that beneath the rough exterior he has a heart—or, for that matter, an entire innards—of purest gold locked away from human perception. You are for the most part what you seem to be, not what you would wish to be, nor, indeed, what you believe yourself to be.

Spare me, therefore, your good intentions, your inner sensitivities, your unarticulated and unexpressed love. And spare me also those tedious psychohistories which—by exposing the goodness inside the bad man, and the evil in the good—invariably establish a vulgar and perverse egalitarianism, as if the arrangement of what is outside and what inside makes no moral difference.

[2] American novelist, author of *Cat's Cradle* (1963); *God Bless You, Mr. Rosewater* (1964); *Slaughterhouse-Five* (1969); and *Breakfast of Champions* (1973).

[3] Book of orthodox Jewish civil and religious law.

Saint Francis may, in his unconscious, indeed have been compensating for, and denying, destructive, unconscious Oedipal impulses identical to those which Attilla projected and acted on. But the similarity of the unconscious constellations in the two men matters precious little, if it does not distinguish between them.

I do not care to learn that Hitler's heart was in the right place. A knowledge of the unconscious life of the man may be an adjunct to understanding his behavior. It is *not* a substitute for his behavior in describing him.

The inner man is a fantasy. If it helps you to identify with one, by all means, do so; preserve it, cherish it, embrace it, but do not present it to others for evaluation or consideration, for excuse or exculpation, or, for that matter, for punishment or disapproval.

Like any fantasy, it serves your purposes alone. It has no standing in the real world which we share with each other. Those character traits, those attitudes, that behavior—that strange and alien stuff sticking out all over you—*that's the real you!*

The Unknown Citizen

W. H. Auden

*(To JS/07/M/378 This Marble Monument Is Erected by the
State)*

He was found by the Bureau of Statistics to be
One against whom there was no official complaint,
And all the reports on his conduct agree
That, in the modern sense of an old-fashioned word, he was a
    saint,
For in everything he did he served the Greater Community.
Except for the War till the day he retired
He worked in a factory and never got fired,
But satisfied his employers, Fudge Motors Inc.
Yet he wasn't a scab or odd in his views,
For his Union reports that he paid his dues,
(Our report on his Union shows it was sound)
And our Social Psychology workers found
That he was popular with his mates and liked a drink.
The Press are convinced that he bought a paper every day
And that his reactions to advertisements were normal in every
    way.
Policies taken out in his name proved that he was fully
    insured,
And his Health-card shows he was once in hospital but left it
    cured.

Both Producers Research and High-Grade Living declare
He was fully sensible to the advantages of the Installment
    Plan
And had everything necessary to the Modern Man,
A phonograph, a radio, a car and a frigidaire.
Our researchers into Public Opinion are content
That he held the proper opinions for the time of year;
When there was peace, he was for peace; when there was war,
    he went.
He was married and added five children to the population,
Which our Eugenist says was the right number for a parent of
    his generation.
And our teachers report that he never interfered with their
    education.
Was he free? Was he happy? The question is absurd:
Had anything been wrong, we should certainly have heard.

Unto Dust

Herman Charles Bosman

I have noticed that when a young man or woman dies, people get the feeling that there is something beautiful and touching in the event, and that it is different from the death of an old person. In the thought, say, of a girl of twenty sinking into an untimely grave, there is a sweet wistfulness that makes people talk all kinds of romantic words. She died, they say, young, she that was so full of life and so fair. She was a flower that withered before it bloomed, they say, and it all seems so fitting and beautiful that there is a good deal of resentment, at the funeral, over the crude questions that a couple of men in plain clothes from the landdrost's office are asking about cattle-dip.

But when you have grown old, nobody is very much interested in the manner of your dying. Nobody except you yourself, that is. And I think that your past life has got a lot to do with the way you feel when you get near the end of your days. I remember how, when he was lying on his death-bed, Andries Wessels kept on telling us that it was because of the blameless path he had trodden from his earliest years that he could compose himself in peace to lay down his burdens. And I certainly never saw a man breathe his last more tranquilly, seeing that right up to the end he kept on murmuring to us how happy he was, with heavenly hosts and invisible choirs of angels all around him.

Just before he died, he told us that the angels had even become visible. They were medium-sized angels, he said, and they had cloven hoofs and carried forks. It was obvious that Andries Wessels's ideas were getting a bit confused by then, but all the same I never saw a man die in a more hallowed sort of calm.

Once, during the malaria season in the Eastern Transvaal, it seemed to me, when I was in a high fever and like to die, that the whole world was a big burial-ground. I thought it was the earth itself that was a grave-yard, and not just those little fenced-in bits of land dotted with tombstones, in the shade of a Western Province oak tree or by the side of a Transvaal kop-pie. This was a nightmare that worried me a great deal, and so I was very glad, when I recovered from the fever, to think that we Boers had properly marked-out places on our farms for white people to be laid to rest in, in a civilised Christian way, instead of having to be buried just anyhow, along with a dead wild-cat, maybe, or a Bushman with a clay-pot, and things.

When I mentioned this to my friend, Stoffel Oosthuizen, who was in the Low Country with me at the time, he agreed with me wholeheartedly. There were people who talked in a high-flown way of death as the great leveller, he said, and those high-flown people also declared that everyone was made kin by death. He would still like to see those things proved, Stoffel Oosthuizen said. After all, that was one of the reasons why the Boers trekked away into the Transvaal and the Free State, he said, because the British Government wanted to give the vote to any Cape Coloured person walking about with a *kroes* head and big cracks in his feet.

The first time he heard that sort of talk about death coming to all of us alike, and making us all equal, Stoffel Oosthuizen's suspicions were aroused. It sounded like out of a speech made by one of those liberal Cape politicians, he explained.

I found something very comforting in Stoffel Oosthuizen's words.

Then, to illustrate his contention, Stoffel Oosthuizen told me a story of an incident that took place in a bygone Transvaal Kafir War. I don't know whether he told the story incorrectly, or whether it was just that kind of story, but, by the time he had finished, all my uncertainties had, I discovered, come back to me.

"You can go and look at Hans Welman's tombstone any time you are at Nietverdiend," Stoffel Oosthuizen said. "The slab of red sandstone is weathered by now, of course, seeing how long ago it all happened. But the inscription is still legible. I was with Hans Welman on that morning when he fell. Our commando had been ambushed by the kafirs and was retreating. I could do nothing for Hans Welman. Once, when I looked round, I saw a tall kafir bending over him and plunging an assegai into him. Shortly afterwards I saw the kafir stripping the clothes off Hans Welman. A yellow kafir dog was yelping excitedly around his black master. Although I was in grave danger myself, with several dozen kafirs making straight for me on foot through the bush, the fury I felt at the sight of what that tall kafir was doing made me hazard a last shot. Reining in my horse, and taking what aim I could under the circumstances, I pressed the trigger. My luck was in. I saw the kafir fall forward beside the naked body of Hans Welman. Then I set spurs to my horse and galloped off at full speed, with the foremost of my pursuers already almost upon me. The last I saw was that yellow dog bounding up to his master —whom I had wounded mortally, as we were to discover later.

"As you know, that kafir war dragged on for a long time. There were few pitched battles. Mainly, what took place were bush skirmishes, like the one in which Hans Welman lost his life.

"After about six months, quiet of a sort was restored to the Marico and Zoutpansberg districts. Then the day came when I went out, in company of a handful of other burghers, to fetch in the remains of Hans Welman, at his widow's request, for burial in the little cemetery plot on the farm. We took a coffin with us on a Cape cart.

"We located the scene of the skirmish without difficulty. Indeed, Hans Welman had been killed not very far from his own farm, which had been temporarily abandoned, together with the other farms in that part, during the time that the trouble with the kafirs had lasted. We drove up to the spot where I remembered having seen Hans Welman lying dead on the ground, with the tall kafir next to him. From a distance I again saw that yellow dog. He slipped away into the bush at our approach. I could not help feeling that there was something rather stirring about that beast's fidelity, even though it was bestowed on a dead kafir.

"We were now confronted with a queer situation. We found that what was left of Hans Welman and the kafir consisted of little more than pieces of sun-dried flesh and the dismembered fragments of bleached skeletons. The sun and wild animals and birds of prey had done their work. There was a heap of human bones, with here and there leathery strips of blackened flesh. But we could not tell which was the white man and which the kafir. To make it still more confusing, a lot of bones were missing altogether, having no doubt been dragged away by wild animals into their lairs in the bush. Another thing was that Hans Welman and that kafir had been just about the same size."

Stoffel Oosthuizen paused in his narrative, and I let my imagination dwell for a moment on that situation. And I realised just how those Boers must have felt about it: about the thought of bringing the remains of a Transvaal burgher home to his widow for Christian burial, and perhaps having a lot of kafir bones mixed up with the burgher—lying with him in the same tomb on which the mauve petals from the oleander overhead would fall.

"I remember one of our party saying that that was the worst of these kafir wars," Stoffel Oosthuizen continued. "If it had been a war against the English, and part of a dead Englishman had got lifted into that coffin by mistake, it wouldn't have mattered so much," he said.

There seemed to me in this story to be something as strange as the African veld. Stoffel Oosthuizen said that the little party of Boers spent almost a whole afternoon with the remains in order to try to get the white man sorted out from the kafir. By the evening they had laid all they could find of what seemed like Hans Welman's bones in the coffin in the Cape cart. The rest of the bones and flesh they buried on the spot.

Stoffel Oosthuizen added that, no matter what the difference in the colour of their skin had been, it was impossible to say that the kafir's bones were less white than Hans Welman's. Nor was it possible to say that the kafir's sun-dried flesh was any blacker than the white man's. Alive, you couldn't go wrong in distinguishing between a white man and a kafir. Dead, you had great difficulty in telling them apart.

"Naturally, we burghers felt very bitter about this whole affair," Stoffel Oosthuizen said, "and our resentment was something that we couldn't explain, quite. Afterwards, several other men who were there that day told me that they had the same feelings of suppressed anger that I did. They wanted somebody —just once—to make a remark such as 'in death they were not divided'. Then you would have seen an outburst all right. Nobody did say anything like that, however. We all knew better. Two days later a funeral service was conducted in the little cemetery on the Welman farm, and shortly afterwards the sandstone memorial was erected that you can still see there."

That was the story Stoffel Oosthuizen told me after I had recovered from the fever. It was a story that, as I have said, had in it features as strange as the African veld. But it brought me no peace in my broodings after that attack of malaria. Especially when Stoffel Oosthuizen spoke of how he had occasion, one clear night when the stars shone, to pass that quiet graveyard on the Welman farm. Something leapt up from the mound beside the sandstone slab. It gave him quite a turn, Stoffel Oosthuizen said, for the third time—and in that way— to come across that yellow kafir dog.

UNIT 2

TRAVELLING THROUGH

A person's life is composed of a wide variety of encounters—with other people, with nature, with unexpected events, with different cultures, with new challenges. As we progress through our own lives, each of us has different experiences. When we read works of literature, we gain insights into a much broader range of experience than is available to any one individual in his or her lifetime.

The various pieces in this unit all involve individuals experiencing significant incidents, crystallized for us in a literary form. The selections provide an opportunity for the reader to explore a variety of events and experiences—some commonplace and some extraordinary. Ordinary incidents encountered through literature lead us to reflect on the impact of such events in our own lives. Unusual situations which we read about expand our awareness and increase our sensitivity.

"Travelling Through" the literary experiences contained in this section provides an opportunity to learn more about both literature and life.

Star-Gaze Poem

Sandford Lyne

In whatever galaxy,
I believe there must be creatures like ourselves,
dreamers,
savages,
poets,
builders of canoes,
far-scattered eyes moving
against the twinkling darkness of the heavens,
pilgrims
in equivalents of dust,
singers of small laments:
the ones we also know,
so well.

So,
for each such as me
this earth is enough of the possibility of grace.

I step out on my small porch, gaze:

these tiny lights, these beacons, bobbing
so far away in the night
we
cannot hear their bells
marking
the shallows of the universe.

When I Heard the Learn'd Astronomer

Walt Whitman

When I heard the learn'd astronomer,
When the proofs, the figures, were ranged in columns before
   me,
When I was shown the charts and diagrams, to add, divide,
   and measure them,
When I sitting heard the astronomer where he lectured with
   much applause in the lecture-room,
How soon unaccountable I became tired and sick,
Till rising and gliding out I wander'd off by myself,
In the mystical moist night-air, and from time to time,
Look'd up in perfect silence at the stars.

The Veldt

Ray Bradbury

"**G**EORGE, I wish you'd look at the nursery."

"What's wrong with it?"

"I don't know."

"Well, then."

"I just want you to look at it, is all, or call a psychologist in to look at it."

"What would a psychologist want with a nursery?"

"You know very well what he'd want." His wife paused in the middle of the kitchen and watched the stove busy humming to itself, making supper for four.

"It's just that the nursery is different now than it was."

"All right, let's have a look."

They walked down the hall of their soundproofed Happy-life Home, which had cost them thirty thousand dollars installed, this house which clothed and fed and rocked them to sleep and played and sang and was good to them. Their approach sensitized a switch somewhere and the nursery light flicked on when they came within ten feet of it. Similarly, behind them, in the halls, lights went on and off as they left them behind, with a soft automaticity.

"Well," said George Hadley.

They stood on the thatched floor of the nursery. It was forty feet across by forty feet long and thirty feet high; it had cost half again as much as the rest of the house. "But nothing's too good for our children," George had said.

The nursery was silent. It was empty as a jungle glade at hot high noon. The walls were blank and two-dimensional. Now, as George and Lydia Hadley stood in the center of the room, the walls began to purr and recede into crystalline distance, it seemed, and presently an African veldt appeared, in three dimensions; on all sides, in colors reproduced to the final pebble and bit of straw. The ceiling above them became a deep sky with a hot yellow sun.

George Hadley felt the perspiration start on his brow.

"Let's get out of the sun," he said. "This is a little too real. But I don't see anything wrong."

"Wait a moment, you'll see," said his wife.

Now the hidden odorophonics were beginning to blow a wind of odor at the two people in the middle of the baked veldtland. The hot straw smell of lion grass, the cool green smell of the hidden water hole, the great rusty smell of animals, the smell of dust like a red paprika in the hot air. And now the sounds: the thump of distant antelope feet on grassy sod, the papery rustling of vultures. A shadow passed through the sky. The shadow flickered on George Hadley's upturned, sweating face.

"Filthy creatures," he heard his wife say.

"The vultures."

"You see, there are the lions, far over, that way. Now they're on their way to the water hole. They've just been eating," said Lydia. "I don't know what."

"Some animal." George Hadley put his hand up to shield off the burning light from his squinted eyes. "A zebra or a baby giraffe, maybe."

"Are you sure?" His wife sounded peculiarly tense.

"No, it's a little late to be *sure*," he said, amused. "Nothing over there I can see but cleaned bone, and the vultures dropping for what's left."

"Did you hear that scream?" she asked.

"No."

"About a minute ago?"

"Sorry, no."

The lions were coming. And again George Hadley was filled with admiration for the mechanical genius who had conceived this room. A miracle of efficiency selling for an absurdly low price. Every home should have one. Oh, occasionally they frightened you with their clinical accuracy, they startled you, gave you a twinge, but most of the time what fun for everyone, not only your own son and daughter, but for yourself when you felt like a quick jaunt to a foreign land, a quick change of scenery. Well, here it was!

And here were the lions now, fifteen feet away, so real, so feverishly and startlingly real that you could feel the prickling fur on your hand, and your mouth was stuffed with the dusty upholstery smell of their heated pelts, and the yellow of them was in your eyes like the yellow of an exquisite French tapestry, the yellows of lions and summer grass, and the sound of matted lion lungs exhaling on the silent noontide, and the smell of meat from the panting, dripping mouths.

The lions stood looking at George and Lydia Hadley with terrible green-yellow eyes.

"Watch out!" screamed Lydia.

The lions came running at them.

Lydia bolted and ran. Instinctively, George sprang after her. Outside, in the hall, with the door slammed, he was laughing and she was crying and they both stood appalled at the other's reactic

"George!"

"Lydia! Oh, my dear poor sweet Lydia!"

"They almost got us!"

"Walls, Lydia, remember; crystal walls, that's all they are. Oh, they look real, I must admit—Africa in your parlor—but it's all dimensional superactionary, supersensitive color film and mental tape film behind glass screens. It's all odorophonics and sonics, Lydia. Here's my handkerchief."

"I'm afraid." She came to him and put her body against him and cried steadily. "Did you see? Did you *feel*? It's too real."

"Now, Lydia . . ."

"You've got to tell Wendy and Peter not to read any more on Africa."

"Of course—of course." He patted her.

"Promise?"

"Sure."

"And lock the nursery for a few days until I get my nerves settled.'

"You know how difficult Peter is about that. When I punished him a month ago by locking the nursery for even a few hours—the tantrum he threw! And Wendy too. They *live* for the nursery."

"It's got to be locked, that's all there is to it."

"All right." Reluctantly he locked the huge door. "You've been working too hard. You need a rest."

"I don't know—I don't know," she said, blowing her nose, sitting down in a chair that immediately began to rock and comfort her. "Maybe I don't have enough to do. Maybe I have time to think too much. Why don't we shut the whole house off for a few days and take a vacation?"

"You mean you want to fry my eggs for me?"

"Yes." She nodded.

"And darn my socks?"

"Yes." A frantic, water-eyed nodding.

"And sweep the house?"

"Yes, yes—oh, yes!"

"But I thought that's why we bought this house, so we wouldn't have to do anything?"

"That's just it. I feel like I don't belong here. The house is wife and mother now and nursemaid. Can I compete with an African veldt? Can I give a bath and scrub the children as efficiently or quickly as the automatic scrub bath can? I cannot. And it isn't just me. It's you. You've been awfully nervous lately."

"I suppose I have been smoking too much."

"You look as if you don't know what to do with yourself in this house, either. You smoke a little more every morning and drink a little more every afternoon and need a little more sedative every night. You're beginning to feel unnecessary too."

"Am I?" He paused and tried to feel into himself to see what was really there.

"Oh, George!" She looked beyond him, at the nursery door. "Those lions can't get out of there, can they?"

He looked at the door and saw it tremble as if something had jumped against it from the other side.

"Of course not," he said.

At dinner they ate alone, for Wendy and Peter were at a special plastic carnival across town and had televised home to say they'd be late, to go ahead eating. So George Hadley, bemused, sat watching the dining-room table produce warm dishes of food from its mechanical interior.

"We forgot the ketchup," he said.

"Sorry," said a small voice within the table, and ketchup appeared.

As for the nursery, thought George Hadley, it won't hurt for the children to be locked out of it awhile. Too much of anything isn't good for anyone. And it was clearly indicated that the children had been spending a little too much time on Africa. That *sun*. He could feel it on his neck, still, like a hot paw. And the *lions*. And the smell of blood. Remarkable how the nursery caught the telepathic emanations of the children's minds and created life to fill their every desire. The children thought lions, and there were lions. The children thought zebras, and there were zebras. Sun—sun. Giraffes—giraffes. Death and death.

The *last*. He chewed tastelessly on the meat that the table had cut for him. Death thoughts. They were awfully young, Wendy and Peter, for death thoughts. Or, no, you were never too young, really. Long before you knew what death was you were wishing it on someone else. When you were two years old you were shooting people with cap pistols.

But this—the long, hot African veldt—the awful death in the jaws of a lion. And repeated again and again.

"Where are you going?"

He didn't answer Lydia. Preoccupied, he let the lights glow softly on ahead of him, extinguish behind him as he padded to the nursery door. He listened against it. Far away, a lion roared.

He unlocked the door and opened it. Just before he stepped inside, he heard a faraway scream. And then another roar from the lions, which subsided quickly.

He stepped into Africa. How many times in the last year had he opened this door and found Wonderland, Alice, and Mock Turtle, or Aladdin and his Magical Lamp, or Jack Pumpkinhead of Oz, or Dr. Doolittle, or the cow jumping over a very real-appearing moon—all the delightful contraptions of a make-believe world. How often had he seen Pegasus flying in the sky ceiling, or seen fountains of red fireworks, or heard angel voices singing. But now, this yellow hot Africa, this bake oven with murder in the heat. Perhaps Lydia was right. Perhaps they needed a little vacation from the fantasy which was growing a bit too real for ten-year-old children. It was all right to exercise one's mind with gymnastic fantasies, but when the lively child mind settled on *one* pattern ... ? It seemed that, at a distance, for the past month, he had heard lions roaring, and smelled their strong odor seeping as far away as his study door. But, being busy, he had paid it no attention.

George Hadley stood on the African grassland alone. The lions looked up from their feeding, watching him. The only flaw to the illusion was the open door through which he could see his wife, far down the dark hall, like a framed picture, eating her dinner abstractedly.

"Go away," he said to the lions.

They did not go.

He knew the principle of the room exactly. You sent out your thoughts. Whatever you thought would appear.

"Let's have Aladdin and his lamp," he snapped.

The veldtland remained; the lions remained.

"Come on, room! I demand Aladdin!" he said.

Nothing happened. The lions mumbled in their baked pelts.

"Aladdin!"

He went back to dinner. "The fool room's out of order," he said. "It won't respond."

"Or—"

"Or what?"

"Or it *can't* respond," said Lydia, "because the children have thought about Africa and lions and killing so many days that the room's in a rut."

"Could be."

"Or Peter's set it to remain that way."

"*Set* it?"

"He may have got into the machinery and fixed something."

"Peter doesn't know machinery."

"He's a wise one for ten. That I.Q. of his—"

"Nevertheless—"

"Hello, Mom. Hello, Dad."

The Hadleys turned. Wendy and Peter were coming in the front door, cheeks like peppermint candy, eyes like bright blue agate marbles, a smell of ozone on their jumpers from their trip in the helicopter.

"You're just in time for supper," said both parents.

"We're full of strawberry ice cream and hot dogs," said the children, holding hands. "But we'll sit and watch."

"Yes, come tell us about the nursery," said George Hadley.

The brother and sister blinked at him and then at each other. "Nursery?"

"All about Africa and everything," said the father with false joviality.

"I don't understand," said Peter.

"Your mother and I were just traveling through Africa with rod and reel; Tom Swift and his Electric Lion," said George Hadley.

"There's no Africa in the nursery," said Peter simply.

"Oh, come now, Peter. We know better."

"I don't remember any Africa," said Peter to Wendy. "Do you?"

"No."

"Run see and come tell."

She obeyed.

"Wendy, come back here!" said George Hadley, but she was gone. The house lights followed her like a flock of fireflies. Too late, he realized he had forgotten to lock the nursery door after his last inspection.

"Wendy'll look and come tell us," said Peter.

"She doesn't have to tell *me*. I've seen it."

"I'm sure you're mistaken, Father."

"I'm not, Peter. Come along now."

But Wendy was back. "It's not Africa," she said breathlessly.

"We'll see about this," said George Hadley, and they all walked down the hall together and opened the nursery door.

There was a green, lovely forest, a lovely river, a purple mountain, high voices singing, and Rima, lovely and mysterious, lurking in the trees with colorful flights of butterflies, like animated bouquets, lingering in her long hair. The African veldtland was gone. The lions were gone. Only Rima was here now, singing a song so beautiful that it brought tears to your eyes.

George Hadley looked in at the changed scene. "Go to bed," he said to the children.

They opened their mouths.

"You heard me," he said.

They went off to the air closet, where a wind sucked them like brown leaves up the flue to their slumber rooms.

George Hadley walked through the singing glade and picked up something that lay in the corner near where the lions had been. He walked slowly back to his wife.

"What is that?" she asked.

"An old wallet of mine," he said.

He showed it to her. The smell of hot grass was on it and the smell of a lion. There were drops of saliva on it, it had been chewed, and there were blood smears on both sides.

He closed the nursery door and locked it, tight.

In the middle of the night he was still awake and he knew his wife was awake. "Do you think Wendy changed it?" she said at last, in the dark room.

"Of course."

"Made it from a veldt into a forest and put Rima there instead of lions?"

"Yes."

"Why?"

"I don't know. But it's staying locked until I find out."

"How did your wallet get there?"

"I don't know anything," he said, "except that I'm beginning to be sorry we bought that room for the children. If children are neurotic at all, a room like that—"

"It's supposed to help them work off their neuroses in a healthful way."

"I'm starting to wonder." He stared at the ceiling.

"We've given the children everything they ever wanted. Is this our reward—secrecy, disobedience?"

"Who was it said, 'Children are carpets, they should be stepped on occasionally'! We've never lifted a hand. They're insufferable—let's admit it. They come and go when they like; they treat us as if *we* were offspring. They're spoiled and we're spoiled."

"They've been acting funny ever since you forbade them to take the rocket to New York a few months ago."

"They're not old enough to do that alone, I explained."

"Nevertheless, I've noticed they've been decidedly cool toward us since."

"I think I'll have David McClean come tomorrow morning to have a look at Africa."

"But it's not Africa now, it's Green Mansions country and Rima."

"I have a feeling it'll be Africa again before then."

A moment later they heard the screams.

Two screams. Two people screaming from downstairs. And then a roar of lions.

"Wendy and Peter aren't in their rooms," said his wife.

He lay in his bed with his beating heart. "No," he said. "They've broken into the nursery."

"Those screams—they sound familiar."

"Do they?"

"Yes, awfully."

And although their beds tried very hard, the two adults couldn't be rocked to sleep for another hour. A smell of cats was in the night air.

"Father?" said Peter.

"Yes."

Peter looked at his shoes. He never looked at his father any more, nor at his mother. "You aren't going to lock up the nursery for good, are you?"

"That all depends."

"On what?" snapped Peter.

"On you and your sister. If you intersperse this Africa with a little variety—oh, Sweden perhaps, or Denmark or China—"

"I thought we were free to play as we wished."

"You are, within reasonable bounds."

"What's wrong with Africa, Father?"

"Oh, so now you admit you have been conjuring up Africa, do you?"

"I wouldn't want the nursery locked up," said Peter coldly. "Ever."

"Matter of fact, we're thinking of turning the whole house off for about a month. Live sort of a carefree one-for-all existence."

"That sounds dreadful! Would I have to tie my own shoes instead of letting the shoe tier do it? And brush my own teeth and comb my hair and give myself a bath?"

"It would be fun for a change, don't you think?"

"No, it would be horrid. I didn't like it when you took out the picture painter last month."

"That's because I wanted you to learn to paint all by yourself, Son."

"I don't want to do anything but look and listen and smell; what else *is* there to do?"

"All right, go play in Africa."

"Will you shut off the house sometime soon?"

"We're considering it."

"I don't think you'd better consider it any more, Father."

"I won't have any threats from my son!"

"Very well." And Peter strolled off to the nursery.

"Am I on time?" said David McClean.

"Breakfast?" asked George Hadley.

"Thanks, had some. What's the trouble?"

"David, you're a psychologist."

"I should hope so."

"Well, then, have a look at our nursery. You saw it a year ago when you dropped by; did you notice anything peculiar about it then?"

"Can't say I did; the usual violences, a tendency toward a slight paranoia here or there, usual in children because they feel persecuted by parents constantly, but, oh, really nothing."

They walked down the hall. "I locked the nursery up," explained the father, "and the children broke back into it during the night. I let them stay so they could form the patterns for you to see."

There was a terrible screaming from the nursery.

"There it is," said George Hadley. "See what you make of it."

They walked in on the children without rapping.

The screams had faded. The lions were feeding.

"Run outside a moment, children," said George Hadley. "No, don't change the mental combination. Leave the walls as they are. Get!"

With the children gone, the two men stood studying the lions clustered at a distance, eating with great relish whatever it was they had caught.

"I wish I knew what it was," said George Hadley. "Sometimes I can almost see. Do you think if I brought high-powered binoculars here and—"

David McClean laughed dryly. "Hardly." He turned to study all four walls. "How long has this been going on?"

"A little over a month."

"It certainly doesn't *feel* good."

"I want facts, not feelings."

"My dear George, a psychologist never saw a fact in his life. He only hears about feelings; vague things. This doesn't feel good, I tell you. Trust my hunches and my instincts. I have a nose for something bad. This is very bad. My advice to you is to have the whole damn room torn down and your children brought to me every day during the next year for treatment."

"Is it that bad?"

"I'm afraid so. One of the original uses of these nurseries was so that we could study the patterns left on the walls by the child's mind, study at our leisure, and help the child. In this case, however, the room has become a channel toward—destructive thoughts, instead of a release away from them."

"Didn't you sense this before?"

"I sensed only that you had spoiled your children more than most. And now you're letting them down in some way. What way?"

"I wouldn't let them go to New York."

"What else?"

"I've taken a few machines from the house and threatened them, a month ago, with closing up the nursery unless they did their homework. I did close it for a few days to show I meant business."

"Ah, ha!"

"Does that mean anything?"

"Everything. Where before they had a Santa Claus now they have a Scrooge. Children prefer Santas. You've let this room and this house replace you and your wife in your children's affections. This room is their mother and father, far more important in their lives than their real parents. And now you come along and want to shut it off. No wonder there's hatred here. You can feel it coming out of the sky. Feel that sun. George, you'll have to change your life. Like too many others, you've built it around creature comforts. Why, you'd starve tomorrow if something went wrong in your kitchen. You wouldn't know how to tap an egg. Nevertheless, turn everything off. Start new. It'll take time. But we'll make good children out of bad in a year, wait and see."

"But won't the shock be too much for the children, shutting the room up abruptly, for good?"

"I don't want them going any deeper into this, that's all."

The lions were finished with their red feast.

The lions were standing on the edge of the clearing watching the two men.

"Now *I'm* feeling persecuted," said McClean. "Let's get out of here. I never have cared for these damn rooms. Make me nervous."

"The lions look real, don't they?" said George Hadley. "I don't suppose there's any way—

"What?"

"—that they could *become* real?"

"Not that I know."

"Some flaw in the machinery, a tampering or something?"

"No."

They went to the door.

"I don't imagine the room will like being turned off," said the father.

"Nothing ever likes to die—even a room."

"I wonder if it hates me for wanting to switch it off?"

"Paranoia is thick around here today," said David McClean. "You can follow it like a spoor. Hello." He bent and picked up a bloody scarf. "This yours?"

"No." George Hadley's face was rigid. "It belongs to Lydia."

They went to the fuse box together and threw the switch that killed the nursery.

The two children were in hysterics. They screamed and pranced and threw things. They yelled and sobbed and swore and jumped at the furniture.

"You can't do that to the nursery, you can't!"

"Now, children."

The children flung themselves onto a couch, weeping.

"George," said Lydia Hadley, "turn on the nursery, just for a few moments. You can't be so abrupt."

"No."

"You can't be so cruel."

"Lydia, it's off, and it stays off. And the whole damn house dies as of here and now. The more I see of the mess we've put ourselves in, the more it sickens me. We've been contemplating our mechanical, electronic navels for too long. My God, how we need a breath of honest air!"

And he marched about the house turning off the voice clocks, the stoves, the heaters, the shoe shiners, the shoe lacers, the body scrubbers and swabbers and massagers, and every other machine he could put his hand to.

The house was full of dead bodies, it seemed. It felt like a mechanical cemetery. So silent. None of the humming hidden energy of machines waiting to function at the tap of a button.

"Don't let them do it!" wailed Peter at the ceiling, as if he was talking to the house, the nursery. "Don't let Father kill everything." He turned to his father. "Oh, I hate you!"

"Insults won't get you anywhere."

"I wish you were dead!"

"We were, for a long while. Now we're going to really start living. Instead of being handled and massaged, we're going to *live*."

Wendy was still crying and Peter joined her again. "Just a moment, just one moment, just another moment of nursery," they wailed.

"Oh, George," said the wife, "it can't hurt."

"All right—all right, if they'll only just shut up. One minute, mind you, and then off forever."

"Daddy, Daddy, Daddy!" sang the children, smiling with wet faces.

"And then we're going on a vacation. David McClean is coming back in half an hour to help us move out and get to the airport. I'm going to dress. You turn the nursery on for a minute, Lydia, just a minute, mind you."

And the three of them went babbling off while he let himself be vacuumed upstairs through the air flue and set about dressing himself. A minute later Lydia appeared.

"I'll be glad when we get away," she sighed.

"Did you leave them in the nursery?"

"I wanted to dress too. Oh, that horrid Africa. What can they see in it?"

"Well, in five minutes we'll be on our way to Iowa. Lord, how did we ever get in this house? What prompted us to buy a nightmare?"

"Pride, money, foolishness."

"I think we'd better get downstairs before those kids get engrossed with those damn beasts again."

Just then they heard the children calling, "Daddy, Mommy, come quick—quick!"

They went downstairs in the air flue and ran down the hall. The children were nowhere in sight. "Wendy? Peter!"

They ran into the nursery. The veldtland was empty save for the lions waiting, looking at them. "Peter, Wendy?"

The door slammed.

"Wendy, Peter!"

George Hadley and his wife whirled and ran back to the door.

"Open the door!" cried George Hadley, trying the knob. "Why, they've locked it from the outside! Peter!" He beat at the door. "Open up!"

He heard Peter's voice outside, against the door.

"Don't let them switch off the nursery and the house," he was saying.

Mr. and Mrs. George Hadley beat at the door. "Now, don't be ridiculous, children. It's time to go. Mr. McClean'll be here in a minute and . . ."

And then they heard the sounds.

The lions on three sides of them, in the yellow veldt grass, padding through the dry straw, rumbling and roaring in their throats.

The lions.

Mr. Hadley looked at his wife and they turned and looked back at the beasts edging slowly forward, crouching, tails stiff.

Mr. and Mrs. Hadley screamed.

And suddenly they realized why those other screams had sounded familiar.

"Well, here I am," said David McClean in the nursery doorway. "Oh, hello." He stared at the two children seated in the center of the open glade eating a little picnic lunch. Beyond them was the water hole and the yellow veldtland; above was the hot sun. He began to perspire. "Where are your father and mother?"

The children looked up and smiled. "Oh, they'll be here directly."

"Good, we must get going." At a distance Mr. McClean saw the lions fighting and clawing and then quieting down to feed in silence under the shady trees.

He squinted at the lions with his hand up to his eyes.

Now the lions were done feeding. They moved to the water hole to drink.

A shadow flickered over Mr. McClean's hot face. Many shadows flickered. The vultures were dropping down the blazing sky.

"A cup of tea?" asked Wendy in the silence.

In the Dome Car of the 'Canadian'

Sid Marty

The mongoloid boy is astounded
with joy at terrific
white-fanged mountains

The shining makes him cry aloud

Tunnels through stone to him
are mysteries, are happy as the womb
And equally happy to him alone
embraced by folly's equanimity
was his birth in this bright world

He claps his hand over his mouth
and moans with ecstasy
to be swallowed whole again
then borne into the glimmering light

These boats along the Fraser
trailing their glistening sweepers
of logs along the river
are arks of all creation
rocking on the dappled water

Oh passengers, you travellers
may strain your eyes to blindness
but never again you'll see
what he is seeing

As he dances in the aisles, for joy

Pet Teachers

Erika Ritter

I don't want to give you the erroneous impression that my childhood relationships with teachers were always harmonious. Back in Grade Five, for instance, we had a hideous young woman in dowdily pleated skirts and rimless glasses who made a special project of making my life hell, as she'd made hell of my brother's life before me. But perhaps my own particular set of problems with this malevolent soul can be dated from the day that, impatient to answer a question, I waved my arm vigorously in the air in the time-honoured manner of a student signalling eagerness to be called upon.

What I forgot was that the hand at the end of the waving arm had an uncapped fountain pen in it. Within a few moments, the most alarmingly inexplicable Peacock Blue flecks began to appear on the front of my teacher's white Banlon sweater set. Then on her pale perpetually unhappy-looking countenance, and finally on the lenses of her thick rimless glasses.

Even more astounding to report, the longer I continued to thrash my arm in the air seeking her attention, the thicker the spattering of blue spots upon her person.

Needless to say, it took my teacher less time than it took me to figure out the connection between my arm-waving and the flecking of ink on her front, and while I cannot recall my punishment for this unwitting infraction, it was no doubt swift and horrible—as you'd expect from a woman who could fasten shut the mouth of a talker with Scotch tape, compel a gum-chewer to wear the detected wad on the end of her nose, or lock a child who'd neglected his homework outside the school with no coat or mittens while the classroom thermometer showed an outdoor reading of -30 degrees Fahrenheit.

My Grade Five teacher was an imported American, and while I don't mean to imply her imperialistic ways were in any sense characteristic of her countrymen, I can without hesitation connect my own feelings of fervent Canadian cultural nationalism to those endless months so long ago that I spent under her doubtful tutelage.

For one thing, she refused to lead us in "O Canada" in the mornings the way the rest of the teachers did. Instead, she taught us with painstaking meticulousness a new song called "My Country 'Tis of Thee", writing the words out on the blackboard until we had them down by rote. Although, as she pointed out, the tune was the same as "God Save the Queen", I felt sure there was something the matter with this new morning anthem. Not the least of the problem was that it had lines in it about "land of the pilgrims' pride", and I was pretty certain that the pilgrims didn't belong to us.

But when I approached her about this, my teacher's eyes flashed behind their rimless lenses, and she launched into her familiar refrain about how unintelligent Canadian children were, compared to American children. It was a charge I could not, even then, take seriously, not from a woman—an American woman at that—who professed to believe that the name of the Great State of Iowa was pronounced Eye-*Oh*-Ah.

In the end, I did what any indignant Canadian would do. I complained to higher authorities—in this case, my mother, who was horrified to learn I was singing a song about "sweet land of li-ber-tee", when everyone knew that Canada was not the sort of nation to inspire such a jingoistic lyric.

After my mother in turn complained to the principal—a man, incidentally, whose eyebrows met in the middle and who insisted to his Grade Eights that the synonym for "crazy" was pronounced "lun-*at*-tic"—some changes were made to the Grade Five morning regimen. "God Save the Queen" came in as a hasty replacement for "My Country 'Tis of Thee", although it was a long time before any of us, by now massively confused, could remember to end up with "Go-od save the-eh Queen!" instead of "Le-et free-duh-um ring!"

Meanwhile, my teacher's suspicion that *I* had been the one who'd alerted the Thought Police only exacerbated a relationship already made difficult by the inkspots-on-the-glasses episode. And by the time she discovered that I'd also altered a picture in my social studies textbook so that the overseer of ancient Egyptian pyramid construction looked just like her, the rest of my tenure as a Grade Five student was not worth living, to the point that, eventually, expulsion to the frozen schoolyard seemed a positively balmy fate, compared to the deep-freeze I was experiencing inside the classroom.

It was not, in short, the halcyon experiences of earlier grades, when I was petted and pampered by my teachers, who enjoyed my cheerful eagerness. In fact, my sentence to Grade Five provided my first indication that school could be difficult, and relationships with teachers combative and mutually wary. I began to sense, however dimly, the potential of political leverage available to the trouble-maker, the misfit, the brat, and by the time I got to high school and the restrictive atmosphere of a nun-run life, I had begun to assume that the teacher was the enemy, to be outsmarted and, whenever possible, ignored.

A far cry, altogether, from the good old days—arguably the best old days—of Grade Two, where I was one of thirty or so seven-year-olds who made the inexhaustibly delightful acquaintance of Miss Riley. I frankly loved Miss Riley, and I believe that, to this day, I could pick her out in a crowd, with her red-gold hair and her slightly gummy smile, and her merry laugh which, surely, not even the weight of intervening years could have dulled or diminished.

A significant fact—perhaps *the* significant fact—about Miss Riley was that she had come from England, the first person I had ever met from any place east of Winnipeg. How on earth was it that a pretty (I'm *sure* that she was pretty) and vigorous young woman from Britain should take it into her head to teach Grade Two in a pink-brick primary school stuck, like an eraser on a sheet of foolscap, on the snow-swept Canadian prairies of the 1950s? Miss Riley never said, and it certainly never occurred to us, at the age of seven, that bleak employment conditions in Europe or any other sharp exigency could have had something to do with her decision to emigrate. Anyway, Miss Riley seemed like the kind of person who did things on the prompting of no other impulse than curiosity, enthusiasm, and unbridled high spirits.

Unlike the sour-faced shrew lying in wait for us in Grade Five, Miss Riley *liked* Canada. She even liked Saskatchewan. At least she insisted that she did, as a troupe of us trailed her around the snowdrifted playground at recess, vying and jostling to be the lucky two who got to clutch Miss Riley's Albian hands.

Of course, as she gave us clearly to understand, things were very different in England. In England, she said, little boys wore short pants and knee socks, even in the winter, which struck us as hilarious, although, as Miss Riley pointed out, it wasn't nearly so cold there. Or anywhere.

There were many other things about England that made it different. What we called a "pullover", girls in England called "a jumper", and what we called a jumper was known there as a pinafore. You didn't play Follow-the-Leader in England; instead, you followed the Bangalory Man. And spring came in March instead of at the end of May, and a robin was a round and rosy-breasted thing, as opposed to the tall, orange-chested bird that we knew, and schoolchildren over there sang songs like "D'ye Ken John Peel"—which Miss Riley duly taught to us, along with the plot of Gilbert and Sullivan's *Iolanthe*, in which she was playing one of the fairies in a local little-theatre production.

What made it possible to learn so much about England and John Peel and Iolanthe was the fact that Miss Riley didn't adhere much to the curriculum. Nevertheless, she made a point of being eager to help us appreciate what our own culture had to offer as well, even if she was a bit vague sometimes as to what that might be.

In order to induce us to brave the sub-zero weather of a Saskatchewan winter recess, Miss Riley awarded a prize each day to the boy and the girl with the rosiest cheeks. She dug out a song called "Land of the Silver Birch" and made us learn it, even though we protested we'd never once seen "the mighty moose wander at will" anywhere in our town. And when the weather finally warmed up at the end of May, Miss Riley insisted that we go on nature hikes around the gumbo-ridden playground so that we could bring back seeds to germinate on pieces of moistened blotting-paper, and neat-looking bugs to inhabit mason jars in the Nature Corner she had instituted at the back of the classroom.

It was the day that the school janitor—a shrivelled but over-bearing little German man whom the boys whispered about as "Not-zee"—threw out our Nature display that Miss Riley lost her temper. She came into our classroom to find him heaving seeds, blotting-paper, bugs and all into a metal wastebasket, while haranguing a frozen grouping of us girls about "brink-ing zuch mezzy chunk" into the classroom. Her face became as red as her hair, red enough to win any Rosy Cheek Prize go-ing, and she screamed at the janitor in a way that gladdened the hearts of all of us who had been systematically terrorized by him since the first day of Grade One.

But there must have been other irritants than the janitor in Miss Riley's life at our school, despite her perpetually cheerful demeanour. For one thing, our prairie parochialism must have depressed her, in those moments when she found herself missing England most. I remember one day she asked, almost wistfully, whether any of us had been born outside Canada, and one of the boys immediately stuck up his hand to report that his family had come from Estevan.

"Estevan?" You could see Miss Riley brighten with hope, as she contemplated the possibility of some Near Eastern princi-pality, or even a dreary Soviet republic bordering on Lithuania. "Where exactly is Estevan?"

Oh jeez, I thought, what jerks she'll think we are, as I put up *my* hand to let her know that Estevan was close to Wey-burn, which was in turn less than two hours' drive away.

Poor Miss Riley. You could tell that she was made both an-gry and crestfallen by this news, and though she fought to keep these feelings from showing, she virtually snapped at the boy from Estevan, "I said another *country*, not another *town*."

Then there was the time she took it into her head that our Grade Two class should come up with an impromptu enter-tainment for the edification of the rest of the school, and drilled us in some sort of *cloun-et-mime* dance performed to a scratchy record, after which she assembled all the other grades to watch us perform.

It was a complete disaster. Not only were we under-talented and under-rehearsed; none of the other students could comprehend us as clowns and elves and golliwogs, since we had not a single costume or one prop to our names.

When one of the other teachers professed herself as mystified as the students by our pantomime, I heard Miss Riley wail tearfully, "It's meant to be a work of the *imagination*."

Imagination. A sacred concept to Miss Riley, and no doubt the area in which she benefited pupils like me most. A slave to cigarettes, like most teachers of her generation, Miss Riley would long to repair to the staff room for a restorative puff, and quickly learned that the accepted trick was to leave a moderately entertaining student in charge. That student, in our Grade Two class, often turned out to be me.

I could read well enough to march importantly up to the front of the room and prattle speedily through whole chapters of *Black Beauty*, while somewhere off-camera, Miss Riley smoked, and while the rest of the class alternately sighed and cheered, depending upon whether the news for Beauty and his friends Ginger and Merrylegs was bad or good.

My task became more difficult once *Black Beauty* had been laughed and cried to a conclusion; Miss Riley handed me another horsy story about the highwayman Dick Turpin and his courageous mare, Black Bess, before heading off to the staff room, her deck of Sweet Caporal cork-tips peeking from her pocket.

Dick Turpin and Black Bess made a wonderful story; it was only when we came galloping to the end that I got into trouble. It seemed that Dick Turpin had been forced to ride his steed mercilessly to elude a trap set by his enemies, and as we neared the conclusion, Black Bess was winded and close to collapse, while my classmates were on the edge of their chairs.

As I read aloud in an excited treble, my eye went racing ahead to the last paragraph, and I saw some fateful words that indicated the heart of the noble horse was about to burst from her exertions. I couldn't stand it. I clapped the book shut, and started to cry.

"What's the matter?" the rest of the class demanded.

"Black Bess!" I bawled. "She dies!" And immediately the entire class, even the boys, burst into sobs. Poor Miss Riley came hurrying back from the staff room, stale cigarette smoke clinging to her jumper or pullover, to discover her Grade Two class collectively awash with tears.

The wages of imagination were not always so traumatic. Sometimes, when Miss Riley needed a cigarette or had piles of marking to do, she would set me up at the front of the classroom with a piece of chalk in my hand to tell the class an illustrated story. As I recall it, I would have no idea, when I set out, where the story was going to come from, or where it might go. I would merely begin talking, and temporizing by drawing pictures on the blackboard as fast as I could to bring to life the characters I was talking about. Eventually, I guess, I managed to weave a story, cobbled together from fairy tales and TV and whatever else came to mind, that would come to a convenient conclusion whenever Miss Riley's assignments were done.

I never had, before or since, a teacher so encouraging of my enthusiasm for inventing stories on the spot. Nor a group of classmates so appreciative of the efforts I made to beguile them. No wonder the news, at the end of the year, that Miss Riley was leaving our school came as a cruel devastation.

Why she'd chosen—or had it chosen *for* her—to leave, we never found out. Was it as a result of having screamed at the janitor? Or was it because she'd mistakenly addressed the visiting Archbishop as "Mr. Grace" the day he came to our school? Had the failed clown-and-elf pageant inspired anger along with derision in the other teachers? Or was it, perhaps, that Miss Riley's enthusiasm for piercing prairie winters was less unbridled than she'd pretended?

Our class, of course, bought Miss Riley a gift on the last day of school. But my best friend and I, motivated by our superior love, decided to pool our savings to purchase for Miss Riley a present of our own, something worthy of her charms. There was a garish yellow plaster spaniel on sale at Lakeview Hardware, and we bought it, and took it to Miss Riley on the last afternoon, long after everyone else had left the school.

It was scaldingly hot, the way days could suddenly be on the prairies at the end of June. The desks, I remember, reeked of the Lysol we had all been compelled to clean them out with earlier in the day. I found myself dizzy, both from the emotion of the moment, and from the smell.

Of course Miss Riley loved the plaster spaniel (what she called a "figguh" and what we called an "orn-u-ment"). It was exactly what she'd always wanted, she said. I felt thick-tongued and sick-hearted, trying and failing to articulate to her what she'd meant to us, how I'd miss her, how devastating it was going to be to go into Grade Three, where nobody would ever trust me to step up to the front of the class and concoct a story, illustrated in chalk. So, after some desultory chit-chat, my friend and I left Miss Riley—to dispose of the "figguh", I now assume. I went home, flushed and wretched, to bed, where I remained, physically sick with my grief, for several days of the summer vacation.

The weather continued dizzyingly hot. In a vacant lot across the street from our house, construction was in progress, with huge machines droning an accompaniment to my delirium. I dreamed Miss Riley hadn't left after all, but each time I awoke, confused, soaked with sweat and with Caterpillar tractors grinding in my ears, she was still gone. Each time that happened, I would burrow back down into the sheets, to dream about her once more, overwhelmed by the first separation of my entire life.

The separations, of course, have come again and again since, although none, perhaps, with the impact of that first piercing loss. Predictably, I have often wished I might run into Miss Riley again, or even hear news of her whereabouts. Oh, I know she is not Miss Riley any more, probably not even in name. Nor crowned with a mane of curly red-gold hair, nor young and sprightly and defiant of the stodgy ways of a prosaic little pink-brick school stuck on the grey-green lapel of the prairie like some prosaic orn-u-mental pin.

But I still dream that now, if I saw her, I might make her understand how the oxygen of imagination she breathed into our circumscribed lives gave me lasting hope. How much I valued the opportunity she gave me to beguile others by making things up.

And how, in the end, I admired her for daring to be quintessentially, if sometimes erroneously, herself—in an environment that decreed, with dull regularity, that one should always be anything but.

Lagoons, Hanlan's Point

Raymond Souster

Mornings
before the sun's liquid
spilled gradually, flooding
the island's cool cellar,
there was the boat
and the still lagoons,
with the sound of my oars
the only intrusion
over cries of birds
in the marshy shallows,
or the loud thrashing
of the startled crane
rushing the air.

And in one strange
dark, tree-hung entrance,
I followed the sound
of my heart all the way
to the reed-blocked ending,
with the pads of the lily
thick as green-shining film
covering the water.

And in another
where the sun came
to probe the depths
through a shaft of branches,
I saw the skeletons
of brown ships rotting
far below in their burial-ground,
and wondered what strange fish
with what strange colours
swam through these palaces
under the water....

A small boy
with a flat-bottomed punt
and an old pair of oars
moving with wonder
through the antechamber
of a waking world.

A Wreath for Miss Totten

Hortense Calisher

C HILDREN growing up in the country take their images of integrity from the land. The land, with its changes, is always about them, a pervasive truth, and their midget foregrounds are crisscrossed with minute dramas which are the animalcules of a larger vision. But children who grow in a city where there is nothing greater than the people brimming up out of subways, riveting in the streets—these children must take their archetypes where and if they find them.

In P.S. 146, between periods, when the upper grades were shunted through the halls in that important procedure known as "departmental," although most of the teachers stood about chatting relievedly in couples, Miss Totten always stood at the door of her "home room," watching us straightforwardly, alone. As, straggling and muffled, we lined past the other teachers, we often caught snatches of upstairs gossip which we later perverted and enlarged; passing before Miss Totten we deflected only that austere look, bent solely on us.

Perhaps, with the teachers, as with us, she was neither admired nor loathed but simply ignored. Certainly none of us ever fawned on her as we did on the harshly blond and blue-eyed Miss Steele, who never wooed us with a smile but slanged us delightfully in the gym, giving out the exercises in a voice like scuffed gravel. Neither did she obsess us in the way of the Misses Comstock, two liverish, stunted women who could have had nothing so vivid about them as our hatred for them, and though all of us had a raffish hunger for metaphor, we never dubbed Miss Totten with a nickname.

Miss Totten's figure, as she sat tall at her desk or strode angularly in front of us rolling down the long maps over the blackboard, had that instantaneous clarity, one metallic step removed from the real, of the daguerreotype. Her clothes partook of this period too—long, saturnine waists and skirts of a stuff identical with that in a good family umbrella. There was one like it in the umbrella-stand at home—a high black one with a seamed ivory head. The waists enclosed a vestee of dim, but steadfast lace; the skirts grazed narrow boots of that etiolated black leather, venerable with creases, which I knew to be a sign both of respectability and foot trouble. But except for the vestee, all of Miss Totten, too, folded neatly to the dark point on her shoes, and separated from these by her truly extraordinary length, her face presided above, a lined, ocher ellipse. Sometimes, as I watched it on drowsy afternoons, her face floated away altogether and came to rest on the stand at home. Perhaps it was because of this guilty image that I was the only one who noticed Miss Totten's strange preoccupation with "Mooley" Davis.

Most of us in Miss Totten's room had been together as a group since first grade, but we had not seen Mooley since down in second grade, under the elder and more frightening of the two Comstocks. I had forgotten Mooley completely, but when she reappeared I remembered clearly the incident which had given her her name.

That morning, very early in the new term, back in Miss Comstock's, we had lined up on two sides of the classroom for a spelling bee. These were usually a relief to good and bad spellers alike, since it was the only part of our work which resembled a game, and even when one had to miss and sit down, there was a kind of dreamy catharsis in watching the tenseness of those still standing. Miss Comstock always rose for these occasions and came forward between the two lines, standing there in an oppressive close-up in which we could watch the terrifying action of the cords in her spindling gray neck and her slight smile as a boy or a girl was spelled down. As the number of those standing was reduced, the smile grew, exposing the oversize slabs of her teeth, through which the words issued in a voice increasingly unctuous and soft.

On this day the forty of us still shone with the first fall neatness of new clothes, still basked in that delightful anonymity in which neither our names nor our capacities were already part of the dreary foreknowledge of the teacher. The smart and quick had yet to assert themselves with their flying, staccato hands; the uneasy dull, not yet forced into recitations which would make their status clear, still preserved in the small, sinking corners of their hearts a lorn, factitious hope. Both teams were still intact when the word "mule" fell to the lot of a thin colored girl across the room from me, in clothes perky only with starch, her rusty fuzz of hair drawn back in braids so tightly sectioned that her eyes seemed permanently widened.

"Mule," said Miss Comstock, giving out the word. The ranks were still full. She had not yet begun to smile.

The girl looked back at Miss Comstock, soundlessly. All her face seemed drawn backward from the silent, working mouth, as if a strong, pulling hand had taken hold of the braids.

My turn, I calculated, was next. The procedure was to say the word, spell it out, and say it again. I repeated it in my mind: "Mule. M-u-l-e. Mule."

Miss Comstock waited quite a long time. Then she looked around the class, as if asking them to mark well and early this first malfeasance, and her handling of it.

"What's your name?" she said.

"Ull—ee." The word came out in a glottal, molasses voice, hardly articulate, the *l*'s scarcely pronounced.

"Lilly?"

The girl nodded.

"Lilly what?"

"Duh-avis."

"Oh. Lilly Davis. Mmmm. Well, spell 'mule,' Lilly." Miss Comstock trilled out the name beautifully.

The tense brown bladder of the girl's face swelled desperately, then broke at the mouth. "Mool," she said, and stopped. "Mmm—oo—"

The room tittered. Miss Comstock stepped closer.

"*Mule!*"

The girl struggled again. "Mool."

This time we were too near Miss Comstock to dare laughter. Miss Comstock turned to our side. "Who's next?"

I half raised my hand.

"Go on." She wheeled around on Lilly, who was sinking into her seat. "No. Don't sit down."

I lowered my eyelids, hiding Lilly from my sight. "Mule," I said. "M-u-l-e. Mule."

The game continued, words crossing the room uneventfully. Some children survived. Others settled, abashed, into their seats, craning around to watch us. Again the turn came around to Lilly.

Miss Comstock cleared her throat. She had begun to smile.

"Spell it now, Lilly," she said. "Mule."

The long-chinned brown face swung from side to side in an odd writhing movement. Lilly's eyeballs rolled. Then the thick sound from her mouth was lost in the hooting, uncontrollable laughter of the whole class. For there was no doubt about it: the long, coffee-colored face, the whitish glint of the eyeballs, the bucking motion of the head suggested it to us all—a small brown quadruped, horse or mule, crazily stubborn, or at bay.

"Quiet!" said Miss Comstock. And we hushed, although she had not spoken loudly. For the word had smirked out from a wide, flat smile and on the stringy neck beneath there was a creeping, pleasurable flush which made it pink as a young girl's.

That was how Mooley Davis got her name, although we had a chance to use it only for a few weeks, in a taunting singsong when she hung up her coat in the morning, or as she flicked past the little dust-bin of a store where we shed our pennies for nigger-babies and tasteless, mottoed hearts. For after a few weeks, when it became clear that her cringing, mucoused talk was getting worse, she was transferred to the "ungraded" class. This group, made up of the mute, the shambling, and the oddly tall, some of whom were delivered by bus, was housed in a basement part of the school, with a separate entrance which was forbidden us not only by rule but by a lurking distaste of our own.

The year Mooley reappeared in Miss Totten's room, a dispute in the school system had disbanded all the ungraded classes in the city. Here and there, now, in the back seat of a class, there would be some grown-size boy who read haltingly from a primer, fingering the stubble of his slack jaw. Down in 4-A there was a shiny, petted doll of a girl, all crackling hair-bow and nimble wheelchair, over whom the teachers shook their heads feelingly, saying: "Bright as a dollar! Imagine!" as if there were something sinister in the fact that useless legs had not impaired the musculature of a mind. And in our class, in harshly clean, faded dresses which were always a little too infantile for her, her spraying ginger hair cut short now and held by a round comb which circled the back of her head like a snaggletoothed tiara which had slipped, there was this bony, bug-eyed wraith of a girl who raised her hand instead of say-ing "Present!" when Miss Totten said "Lilly Davis?" at roll call, and never spoke at all.

It was Juliet Hoffman, the pace-setter among the girls in the class, who spoke Mooley's nickname first. A jeweller's daughter, Juliet had achieved an eminence even beyond that due her curly profile, embroidered dresses, and prancing, lead-ing-lady ways when, the Christmas before, she had brought as her present to teacher a real diamond ring. It had been a mod-est diamond, to be sure, but undoubtedly real, and set in real gold. Juliet had heralded it for weeks before and we had all seen it—it and the peculiar look on the face of the teacher, a young substitute whom we hardly knew—when she had lifted it from the pile of hankies and fancy notepaper on her desk. The teacher, over the syrupy protests of Mrs. Hoffman, had returned the ring, but its sparkle lingered on, iridescent around Juliet's head.

On our way out at three o'clock that first day with Miss Tot-ten, Juliet nudged at me to wait. Obediently, I waited behind her. Twiddling her bunny muff, she minced over to the clothes closet and confronted the new girl.

"I know you," she said. "Mooley Davis, that's who you are!" A couple of the other children hung back to watch.

"Aren't you? Aren't you Mooley Davis?"

I remember just how Mooley stood there because of the coat she wore. She just stood there holding her coat against her stomach with both hands. It was a coat of some pale, vague tweed, cut the same length as mine. But it wrapped the wrong way over for a girl and the revers, wide ones, came all the way down and ended way below the pressing hands.

"Where you been?" Juliet flipped us all a knowing grin. "You been in ungraded?"

One of Mooley's shoulders inched up so that it almost touched her ear, but beyond that, she did not seem able to move. Her eyes looked at us, wide and fixed. I had the feeling that all of her had retreated far, far back behind the eyes which—large and light, and purposefully empty—had been forced to stay.

My back was to the room, but on the suddenly wooden faces of the others I saw Miss Totten's shadow. Then she loomed thinly over Juliet, her arms, which were crossed at her chest, hiding the one V of white in her garments, so that she looked like an umbrella which had been tightly furled.

"What's *your* name?" she asked, addressing not so much Juliet as the white muff which, I noticed now, was slightly soiled.

"Jooly-ette."

"Hmm. Oh, yes. Juliet Hoffman."

"Jooly-ette, it is." She pouted creamily up at Miss Totten, her glance narrow with the assurance of finger rings to come.

Something flickered in the nexus of yellow wrinkles around Miss Totten's lips. Poking out a bony forefinger, she held it against the muff. "You tell your mother," she said slowly, "that the way she spells it, it's *Juliet*."

Then she dismissed the rest of us but put a delaying hand on Mooley. Turning back to look, I saw that she had knelt down painfully, her skirt-hem graying in the floor dust, and staring absently over Mooley's head she was buttoning up the queerly shaped coat.

After a short, avid flurry of speculation we soon lost interest in Mooley, and in the routine Miss Totten devised for her. At first, during any kind of oral work, Mooley took her place at the blackboard and wrote down her answers, but later, Miss Totten sat her in the front row and gave her a small slate. She grew very quick at answering, particularly in "mental arithmetic" and in the card drills, when Miss Totten held up large Manila cards with significant locations and dates inscribed in her Palmer script, and we went down the rows, snapping back the answers.

Also, Mooley had acquired a protector in Ruby Green, the other Negro girl in the class—a huge, black girl with an arm-flailing, hee-haw way of talking and a rich, contralto singing voice which we had often heard in solo at Assembly. Ruby, boasting of her singing in night clubs on Saturday nights, of a father who had done time, cowed us all with these pungent inklings of the world on the other side of the dividing line of Amsterdam Avenue—that deep, velvet murk of Harlem which she lit for us with the flash of razors, the honky-tonk beat of the "numbahs," and the plangent wails of the mugged. Once, hearing David Hecker, a doctor's son, declare "Mooley has a cleft palate, that's what," Ruby wheeled and put a large hand on his shoulder, holding it there in menacing caress.

"She ain' got no cleff palate, see? She talk sometime, 'roun' home." She glared at us each in turn with such a pug-scowl that we flinched, thinking she was going to spit. Ruby giggled.

"She got no cause to talk, 'roun' here. She just don' need to bother." She lifted her hand from David, spinning him backward, and joined arms with the silent Mooley. "Me neither!" she added, and walked Mooley away, flinging back at us her gaudy, syncopated laugh.

Then one day, lolloping home after three, I suddenly remembered my books and tam, and above all my homework assignment, left in the pocket of my desk at school. I raced back there. The janitor, grumbling, unlocked the side door at which he had been sweeping and let me in. In the mauve, settling light the long maw of the gym held a rank, uneasy stillness. I walked up the spiral metal stairs feeling that I thieved on some part of the school's existence not intended for me. Outside the ambushed quiet of Miss Totten's room I stopped, gathering breath. Then I heard voices, one of them surely Miss Totten's dark, firm tones, the other no more than an arrested gurgle and pause.

I opened the door slowly. Miss Totten and Mooley raised their heads. It was odd, but although Miss Totten sat as usual at her desk, her hands clasped to one side of her hat, lunch-box, and the crinkly boa she wore all spring, and although Mooley was at her own desk in front of a spread copy of our thick reader, I felt the distinct, startled guilt of someone who interrupts an embrace.

"Yes?" said Miss Totten. Her eyes had the drugged look of eyes raised suddenly from close work. I fancied that she reddened slightly, like someone accused.

"I left my books."

Miss Totten nodded, and sat waiting. I walked down the row to my desk and bent over, fumbling for my things, my haunches awkward under the watchfulness behind me. At the door, with my arms full, I stopped, parroting the formula of dismissal.

"Good afternoon, Miss Totten."

"Good afternoon."

I walked home slowly. Miss Totten, when I spoke to her, had seemed to be watching my mouth, almost with enmity. And in front of Mooley there had been no slate.

In class the next morning, as I collected the homework in my capacity as monitor, I lingered a minute at Mooley's desk, expecting some change, perhaps in her notice of me, but there was none. Her paper was the same as usual, written in a neat script quite legible in itself, but in a spidery backhand which just faintly silvered the page, like a communiqué issued out of necessity, but begrudged.

Once more I had a glimpse of Miss Totten and Mooley to-gether, on a day when I had joined the slangy, athletic Miss Steele who was striding capably along in her Ground Grippers on the route I usually took home. Almost at once I had known I was unwelcome, but I trotted desperately in her wake, not knowing how to relieve her of my company. At last a stitch in my side forced me to stop, in front of a corner fishmongers.'

"Folks who want to walk home with me have to step on it!" said Miss Steele. She allotted me one measuring, stone-blue glance, and moved on.

Disposed on the bald white window-stall of the fish store there was a rigidly mounted eel which looked as if only its stuffing prevented it from growing onward, sinuously, from either impersonal end. Beside it were several tawny shells. A finger would have to avoid the spines on them before being able to touch their rosy, pursed throats. As the pain in my side lessened, I raised my head and saw my own face in the window, egg-shaped and sad. I turned away. Miss Totten and Mooley stood on the corner, their backs to me, waiting to cross. A trolley clanged by, then the street was clear, and Miss Totten, looking down, nodded gently into the black boa and took Mooley by the hand. As they passed down the hill to St. Nicholas Avenue and disappeared, Mooley's face, smoothed out and grave, seemed to me, enviably, like the serene, guided faces of the children I had seen walking securely under the restful duennaship of nuns.

Then came the first day of Visiting Week, during which, according to convention, the normal school day would be on display, but for which we had actually been fortified with rapid-fire recitations which were supposed to erupt from us in sequence, like the somersaults which climax acrobatic acts. On this morning, just before we were called to order, Dr. Piatt, the principal, walked in. He was a gentle man, keeping to his office like a snail, and we had never succeeded in making a bogey of him, although we tried. Today he shepherded a group of mothers and two men, officiously dignified, all of whom he seated on some chairs up front at Miss Totten's left. Then he sat down too, looking upon us benignly, his head cocked a little to one side in a way he had, as if he hearkened to some unseen arbiter who whispered constantly to him of how bad children could be, but he benevolently, insistently, continued to disagree.

Miss Totten, alone among the teachers, was usually immune to visitors, but today she strode restlessly in front of us and as she pulled down the maps one of them slipped from her hand and snapped back up with a loud, flapping roar. Fumbling for the rollbook, she sat down and began to call the roll from it, something she usually did without looking at the book and favoring each of us, instead, with a warming nod.

"Arnold Ames?"
"Pres-unt!"
"Mary Bates?"
"Pres-unt!"
"Wanda Becovic?"
"Pres-unt!"
"Sidney Cohen?"
"Pres-unt!"
"L—Lilly Davis?"

It took us a minute to realize that Mooley had not raised her hand. A light, impatient groan rippled over the class. But Mooley, her face uplifted in a blank stare, was looking at Miss Totten. Miss Totten's own lips moved. There seemed to be a cord between her lips and Mooley's. Mooley's lips moved, open.

"Pres-unt!" said Mooley.

The class caught its breath, then righted itself under the sweet, absent smile of the visitors. With flushed, lowered lids, but in a rich full voice, Miss Totten finished calling the roll. Then she rose and came forward with the Manila cards. Each time, she held up the name of a state and we answered with its capital city.

Pennsylvania.
"Harrisburg!" said Arnold Ames.
Illinois.
"Springfield!" said Mary Bates.
Arkansas.
"Little Rock!" said Wanda Becovic.
North Dakota.
"Bismarck!" said Sidney Cohen.
Idaho.
We were afraid to turn our heads.
"Buh . . . Boise!" said Mooley Davis.

After this, we could hardly wait for the turn to come around to Mooley. When Miss Totten, using a pointer against the map, indicated that Mooley was to "bound" the state of North Carolina, we focused on one spot with such attention that the visitors, grinning at each other, shook their heads at such zest. But Dr. Piatt was looking straight at Miss Totten, his lips parted, his head no longer to one side.

"N-north Cal . . . Callina." Just as the deaf gaze at the speaking, Mooley's eyes never left Miss Totten's. Her voice issued, burred here, choked there, but unmistakably a voice. "Bounded by Virginia on the north . . . Tennessee on the west . . . South Callina on the south . . . and on the east . . . and on the east . . ." She bent her head and gripped her desk with her hands. I gripped my own desk, until I saw that she suffered only from the common failing—she had only forgotten. She raised her head.

"And on the east," she said joyously, "and on the east by the Atlannic Ocean."

Later that term Miss Totten died. She had been forty years in the school system, we heard in the eulogy at Assembly. There was no immediate family, and any of us who cared to might pay our respects at the chapel. After this, Mr. Moloney, who usually chose *Whispering* for the dismissal march, played something slow and thrumming which forced us to drag our feet until we reached the door.

Of course none of us went to the chapel, nor did any of us bother to wonder whether Mooley went. Probably she did not. For now that the girl withdrawn for so long behind those rigidly empty eyes had stepped forward into them, they flicked about quite normally, as captious as anyone's.

Once or twice in the days that followed we mentioned Miss Totten, but it was really death that we honored, clicking our tongues like our elders. Passing the umbrella-stand at home, I sometimes thought of Miss Totten, furled forever in her coffin. Then I forgot her too, along with the rest of the class. After all this was only reasonable in a class which had achieved Miss Steele.

But memory, after a time, dispenses its own emphasis, making a *feuilleton* of what we once thought most ponderable, laying its wreath on what we never thought to recall. In the country, the children stumble upon the griffin mask of the mangled pheasant, and they learn; they come upon the murderous love-knot of the mantis, and they surmise. But in the city, although no man looms very large against the sky, he is silhouetted all the more sharply against his fellows. And sometimes the children there, who know so little about the natural world, stumble still upon that unsolicited good which is perhaps only a dislocation in the insensitive rhythm of the natural world. And if they are lucky, memory holds it in waiting. For what they have stumbled upon is their own humanity —their aberration, and their glory. That must be why I find myself wanting to say aloud to someone: "I remember . . . a Miss Elizabeth Totten."

Melvin Arbuckle's
First Course in Shock Therapy

W.O. Mitchell

L AST year like thousands of other former Khar-
toumians, I returned to Khartoum, Saskatchewan, to
help her celebrate her Diamond Jubilee year. In the
Elks' Bar, on the actual anniversary date, September 26, the
Chamber of Commerce held a birthday get-together, and it
was here that Roddy Montgomery, Khartoum's mayor, introduced me to a man whose face had elusive familiarity.

"One of Khartoum's most famous native sons," Roddy said
with an anticipatory smile. "Psychiatrist on the West Coast,
Portland."

I shook hands; I knew that I should remember him from the
litmus years of my prairie childhood. As soon as he spoke I
remembered: Miss Coldtart first, then *Pippa Passes*—then
Melvin Arbuckle.

I was tolled back forty years: Melvin Arbuckle, only son of
Khartoum's electrician, the boy who had successfully frustrated
Miss Coldtart through all our Grade Four reading classes.
Then, and today it seemed, he was unable to say a declarative
sentence; he couldn't manage an exclamatory or imperative
one either. A gentle-spoken and utterly stubborn woman with
cream skin and dyed hair, Miss Coldtart called upon Melvin to
read aloud every day of that school year, hoping against hope
that one of his sentences would not turn up at the end like the
sandal toes of an *Arabian Nights* sultan. The very last day of

Grade Four she had him read *Pippa Passes* line for line after her. He did—interrogatively down to the last "God's in His Heaven?—All's right with the world?"

And forty years later it seemed quite fitting to me that Melvin was a psychiatrist, especially when I recalled Melvin's grandfather who lived with the Arbuckles, a long ropey octogenarian with buttermilk eyes, the sad and equine face of William S. Hart. I liked Melvin's grandfather. He claimed that he had been imprisoned by Louis Riel in Fort Garry when the Red River Rebellion started, that he was a close friend of Scott whom Riel executed in 1870. He said that he was the first man to enter Batoche after it fell, that he'd sat on the jury that condemned Riel to hang in '85. By arithmetic he could have been and done these things, but Melvin said his grandfather was an historical liar.

Melvin's grandfather had another distinction: saliva trouble. He would gather it, shake it back and forth from cheek to cheek, the way you might rattle dice in your hand before making a pass—then spit. He did this every twenty seconds. Also he wandered a great deal, wearing a pyramid peaked hat of RCMP or boy scout issue, the thongs hanging down either cheek, a lumpy knapsack high between his shoulder blades, a peeled and varnished willow root cane in his hand. Since the Arbuckles' house stood an eighth of a mile apart from the eastern edge of Khartoum, it was remarkable that the old man never got lost on the empty prairie flung round three sides. Years of wilderness travel must have drawn him naturally towards habitation; Melvin's after-fours were ruined with the mortification of having to knock on front doors in our end of town, asking people if they'd seen anything of his lost grandfather. All his Saturdays were unforgivably spoiled too, for on these days Melvin's mother went down to the store to help his father, and Melvin had to stay home to see that his grandfather didn't get lost.

No one was ever able to get behind Melvin's grandfather, he sat always in a corner with two walls at his back; this was so in the house or in the Soo Beer Parlor. Melvin's mother had to cut her father's hair, for he refused to sit in Leon's barber chair out in the unprotected centre of the shop. If he met someone on the street and stopped to talk, he would circle uneasily until he had a building wall or a hedge or a fence at his back; sometimes he would have to settle for a tree. He had a very sensible reason for this; they were coming to get him one day, he said. It was never quite clear who was coming to get him one day, but I suspected revengeful friends of the half-breed renegade, Dumont. He may have been an historical liar as Melvin said, but there was no doubting that he was afraid—afraid for his life.

I sincerely believed that someone was after him; nobody could have spent as much time as he did in the Arbuckle privy if somebody weren't after him. From mid-April when the sun had got high and strong to harvest he spent more time out there with four walls closing safe around him than he did in the house. I can hardly recall a visit to Melvin's place that there wasn't blue smoke threading from the diamond cutout in the back-house door. Melvin's grandfather smoked natural leaf Quebec tobacco that scratched with the pepper bitterness of burning willow root. He had the wildest smell of any man I had ever known, compounded of wine and iron tonic, beer, natural leaf, wood smoke, buckskin and horses. I didn't mind it at all.

He was a braggarty sort of old man, his words hurrying out after each other as though he were afraid that if he stopped he wouldn't be permitted to start up again and also as though he knew that no one was paying attention to what he was saying anyway, so that he might just as well settle for getting it *said* as quickly as possible. Even Miss Coldtart would have found many of his expressions colorful: "she couldn't cook guts for a bear"; "spinnin' in the wind like the button on a backhouse door"; "so stubborn she was to drown'd you'd find her body upstream"; "when he was borned they set him on the porch to see if he barked or cried". Even though you felt he was about to embarrass you by spitting or lying, I found Melvin's grandfather interesting.

Yet I was glad that he was Melvin's grandfather and not mine. Even though he kept dragging his grandfather into conversation, Melvin was ashamed of him. He was always reminding us of his grandfather, not because he wanted to talk about him but just as though he were tossing the old man at our feet for a dare. I can't remember any of us taking him up on it.

Perhaps now that he is an alienist out on the West Coast, he has decided what compelled him to remind us continually of the grandfather he was ashamed of.

The summer that I have in mind was the year that Peanuts moved to Khartoum from Estevan, where his father was an engineer for a coal strip-mining company. Some sort of cousin of the Sweeneys, Peanuts had migrated to Canada from England just a year before. He'd only had three months in Khartoum to pick up the nickname, Peanuts. He was not a Peanuts sort of boy, quite blocky, very full red cheeks, hemp fair hair and flax blue eyes. At ten years of age, I suppose John Bull must have looked a great deal like Peanuts. His given name was actually Geoffrey.

He was quite practical, fertile for all kinds of reasons that a project could not work; this unwillingness to suspend disbelief tore illusion and spoiled pretend games. He had no sense of humor at all, for he seldom laughed at anything Fat said; English into the bargain, he should have been the most unpopular boy in Khartoum. However, he had piano-wire nerves which made up for his shortcomings. When we held our circus that July, he slipped snake after snake down the throat of his blouse, squirmed them past his belt and extricated them one by one from the legs of his stovepipe British woolen pants. They were only garter snakes, but a week later to settle a horticultural argument in Ashford's Grove, he ate a toadstool raw. Just because he didn't die was not proof that he was right and that we were wrong, for immediately after he pulled up and ate two bouquets of wild horse-radish with instantaneous emetic effect.

Now that I think back to a late August day that year, I can see that Peanuts has to share with Melvin's grandfather the credit or the responsibility for Melvin's being today a leading West Coast psychiatrist. It was a day that promised no excitement. The Khartoum Fair was past; Johnny J. Jones' circus had come and gone a month before, posters already nostalgic and wind-tattered on shed and fence and barn walls. We couldn't duck or bottom it in the little Souris River, for it was filled with rusty bloodsuckers and violet-colored algae that caused prairie itch. The bounty was off gopher tails for the rest of the year so there was no point in hunting them.

There was simply nothing to do but sprawl in the adequate shade of McGoogan's hedge, eat clover heads and caragana flowers. With bored languor we looked out over Sixth Street lifting and drifting in the shimmering heat. Without interest we saw the town wagon roll by, darkening the talcum-fine dust with spray; moments later the street was thirsty again, smoking under the desultory August wind.

Fin pulled out the thick glass from a flashlight, focused it to a glowing bead on his pant leg. A thin streamer of smoke was born and we idly watched a fusing spark eat through the cloth until its ant sting bit Fin's knee. He put the glass back into his pocket and said let's go down to the new creamery and chew tar. Someone said let's go look for beer bottles and lead instead; someone else said how about fooling around in the loft of Fat's uncle's livery stable; someone else said the hell with it.

About that time we all got to our feet, for an ice dray came down the street, piled high with frozen geometry. When the leather-chapped driver had chipped and hoisted a cake of ice over his shoulder and left for delivery, we went to the back of the dray. We knew we were welcome to the chips on the floor, and as we always did we popped into our mouths chunks too big for them. The trick was to suck in warm air around the ice until you could stand it no longer, then lower your head, eject and catch.

Someone said let's go over and see Melvin stuck with his grandfather; inhibited by ice and the cool drool of it, no one agreed or disagreed. We wandered up Sixth Street, past the McKinnon girls and Noreen Robins darting in and out of a skipping rope, chanting: "Charlie Chaplin—went to—France —teach the—ladies—how to—dance ..." At the corner of Bison and Sixth we turned east and in two blocks reached the prairie. I think it was the tar-papered and deserted shack between the town's edge and Arbuckles' house that gave us the idea of building a hut. By the time we had reached Melvin's, we had decided it might be more fun to dig a cave which would be lovely and cool.

Melvin was quite agreeable to our building the cave in his back yard; there were plenty of boards for covering it over; if we all pitched in and started right away, we might even have it finished before his grandfather had wakened from his nap.

Shovel and spade and fork plunged easily through the eighteen inches of top soil; but the clay subsoil in this dry year was heart and back breaking. Rock-hard, it loosened under pick and bar in reluctant sugar lumps. Stinging with sweat, our shoulder sockets aching, we rested often, reclining at the lip of our shallow excavation. We idly wished: "If a fellow only had a fresno and team, he could really scoop her out . . ."

"If a fellow could soak her good . . . run her full of water— soften her up—easy digging then."

"If a fellow could only blow her out . . ."

"How?"

"Search me."

"Stumping powder—dynamite . . ."

"Oh," Peanuts said, "yes—dynamite."

"Whumph and she'd blow our cave for us," Fin said.

"She sure would," Fat said.

Melvin said, "Only place I know where they got dynamite— CPR sheds."

"I have dynamite," Peanuts said. "I can get dynamite."

We looked at each other; we looked at Peanuts. Knowing Peanuts, I felt a little sick; Fat and Fin and Melvin didn't look so happy either. We had never even seen a stick of dynamite; it simply did not belong in our world. It had been quite *imaginary* dynamite that we had been tossing about in conversation.

Fat said, "We can't go swiping dynamite."

Fin said, "We don't know a thing about handling dynamite."

"I do," Peanuts said.

"Isn't our yard," Fat said. "We can't set off dynamite in Mel's yard." Peanuts got up purposefully. "Can we, Mel?"

"The cave's a hundred yards from the house," Peanuts said. "Nothing dangerously near it at all." He turned to Melvin. "Are you frightened?"

"Well—no," Melvin said.

"My father has a whole case of sixty percent," Peanuts said. "From the mine. While I get it you have them do the hole."

"What hole?" Melvin said.

"For the dynamite—with the bar—straight down about four feet, I should say."

"The whole goddam case!" Fin said.

"Dead centre, the hole," Peanuts said and started for his house.

"He bringing back the whole case?" Fin said.

Fat got up. "I guess I better be getting on my way ..." His voice fainted as he looked down at us and we looked up at him. "I guess I better—we better—start punching—down that hole," he finished up. "Like Peanuts said." It was not what Fat had started out to say at all.

Peanuts brought back only three sticks of dynamite, and until his return the hole went down rather slowly. He tossed the sticks on the ground by the woodpile and took over authority. He did twice his share of digging the dynamite hole; from time to time he estimated how much further we had to go down. When it seemed to suit him he dropped two of the sticks down, one on top of the other. There was no tenderness in the way he handled that dynamite, inserted the fuse end into the copper tube detonator, crimped it with his teeth, used a spike to work a hole into the third stick to receive the cap and fuse. He certainly knew how to handle dynamite. We watched him shove loose clay soil in around the sticks, tamp it firm with the bar. With his jackknife he split the free end of the fuse protruding from the ground. He took a match from his pocket.

"Hold on a minute," Melvin said. "Where do we—what do we—how long do we ..."

"Once it's going there'll be three minutes," Peanuts said. "Plenty of time to take cover."

"What cover?" Fat said.

"Round the corner of the house," Peanuts said. "You may go there now if you wish. I'll come when the fuse is started. They're hard to start—it will take several matches."

We stayed. The fuse took life at the third match. Fat and Fin and Melvin and I ran the hundred yards to the house. We looked around the corner to Peanuts coming towards us. He did it by strolling. I had begun to count to myself so that I could have a rough notion of when the fuse was near the end of its three minutes. I had reached fifty-nine when I heard the Arbuckle screen slap the stillness.

Fin said, "Judas Priest!"

Melvin said, "He's headed for the back house!"

Fat said, "He's got his knapsack and his hat and his cane on —maybe he's just going out to get lost."

Melvin started round the corner of the house but Fin grabbed him. "Let him keep goin', Mel! Let him keep goin' so's he'll get in the clear!"

"I'll get him," Peanuts said.

"He's my grandfather!" Melvin said.

Fin said, "There ain't even a minute left!" I had no way of telling for I'd stopped counting.

The site of our proposed cave and, therefore, of the dynamite with its burning fuse, was halfway between the back of the Arbuckle house and the privy. Melvin's grandfather stopped by the woodpile. He shook his head and he spat. Peanuts launched himself around the corner of the house, belly to the ground towards the old man. Melvin's grandfather must have thought the running footsteps behind him were those of either Louis Riel or Gabriel Dumont, for without looking back he covered the open ground to the privy in ten seconds, jumped inside and slammed the door. Right in stride, Peanuts pounded past and out to the prairie beyond. There he was still running with his head back, chin out, arms pumping, knees high, when the dynamite let go.

The very first effect was not of sound at all. Initially the Arbuckle yard was taken by one giant and subterranean hiccough, an earth fountain spouted; four cords of wood took flight; the privy leaped straight up almost six feet; two clothes line posts javelined into the air, their wires still stretched between them in an incredible aerial cat's cradle. Not until *then* did the lambasting explosion seem to come. For several elastic seconds all the air-borne things hung indecisively between the thrust of dynamite and the pull of gravity. Gravity won.

At the back of the house we looked at each other wildly; we swallowed to unbung our ears, heard the Japanese chiming of glass shards dropping from Arbuckle windows, the thud of wood chunks returning to earth. I saw Melvin lick with the tip of his tongue at twin blood yarns coming down from his nostrils. No one said anything; we simply moved as a confused body in the direction of the privy. We skirted the great shallow saucer the dynamite had blown, and I remember thinking they would never fill it in; the dirt was gone forever. At the very centre it was perhaps ten feet deep; it would have taken all the lumber from a grain elevator to roof it over for a cave.

"Grampa—Grampa—" Melvin was calling—"Please, Grampa. Please, Grampa."

"We'll have to tip it up," Fin said, "so's we can open the door."

"You're not supposed to move injured people," Fat said.

Melvin squatted down and put his face to the hole and his frightened voice sounded cistern hollow. "Grampa!" Then he really yelled as the varnished willow cane caught him across the bridge of the nose. He straightened up and he said, "He's still alive. Give me a hand."

It took all of us to upright the privy and Melvin's grandfather. He swung at us a couple of times when we opened the door, then he let us help him to the house and into his own room off the kitchen. Seated there on a Winnipeg couch, he stared straight ahead of himself as Melvin removed the boy scout hat, slipped off the packsack. With an arm around the old man's shoulders, Melvin eased him down on the pillow, then motioned us out of the room. Before we got to the door the old man spoke.

"Melvin."

"Yes, Grampa?"

"Sure they're all cleared out now?"

"Yes, Grampa."

He released a long sigh. "Get word to General Middleton."

"For help, Grampa?"

"Not help." The old man shook his head. "Sharply engaged enemy. Routed the barstards!"

We were all whipped that evening, and the balance of our merciful catharsis was earned over a month's quarantine, each in his own yard. When his month's isolation was up, Melvin gained a freedom he'd never known before; he didn't have to knock on another door for his grandfather never wandered again. He sat at the Arbuckle living room window for the next three years, then died.

"One of Khartoum's most famous native sons", Roddy Montgomery had called him at the Chamber of Commerce birthday party in the Elks' Bar; "Dr. Melvin Arbuckle, Portland psychiatrist and mental health trail blazer". In shock therapy—of course.

The Story of the Widow's Son

Mary Lavin

THIS is the story of a widow's son, but it is a story that has two endings.

There was once a widow, living in a small neglected village at the foot of a steep hill. She had only one son, but he was the meaning of her life. She lived for his sake. She wore herself out working for him. Every day she made a hundred sacrifices in order to keep him at a good school in the town, four miles away, because there was a better teacher there than the village dullard that had taught herself.

She made great plans for Packy, but she did not tell him about her plans. Instead she threatened him, day and night, that if he didn't turn out well, she would put him to work on the roads, or in the quarry under the hill.

But as the years went by, everyone in the village, and even Packy himself, could tell by the way she watched him out of sight in the morning, and watched to see him come into sight in the evening, that he was the beat of her heart, and that her gruff words were only a cover for her pride and her joy in him.

It was for Packy's sake that she walked for hours along the road, letting her cow graze the long acre of the wayside grass, in order to spare the few poor blades that pushed up through the stones in her own field. It was for his sake she walked back and forth to the town to sell a few cabbages as soon as ever they were fit. It was for his sake that she got up in the cold dawning hours to gather mushrooms that would take the place of foods that had to be bought with money. She bent her back daily to make every penny she could, and as often happens, she made more by industry, out of her few bald acres, than many of the farmers around her made out of their great bearded meadows. Out of the money she made by selling eggs alone, she paid for Packy's clothes and for the greater number of his books.

When Packy was fourteen, he was in the last class in the school, and the master had great hopes of his winning a scholarship to a big college in the city. He was getting to be a tall lad, and his features were beginning to take a strong cast. His character was strengthening too, under his mother's sharp tongue. The people of the village were beginning to give him the same respect they gave to the sons of the farmers who came from their fine colleges in the summer, with blue suits and bright ties. And whenever they spoke to the widow they praised him up to the skies.

One day in June, when the air was so heavy the scent that rose up from the grass was imprisoned under the low clouds and hung in the air, the widow was waiting at the gate for Packy. There had been no rain for some days and the hens and chickens were pecking irritably at the dry ground and wandering up and down the road in bewilderment.

A neighbour passed.

"Waiting for Packy?" said the neighbour, pleasantly, and he stood for a minute to take off his hat and wipe the sweat of the day from his face. He was an old man.

"It's a hot day!" he said. "It will be a hard push for Packy on that battered old bike of his. I wouldn't like to have to face into four miles on a day like this!"

"Packy would travel three times that distance if there was a book at the other end of the road!" said the widow, with the pride of those who cannot read more than a line or two without wearying.

The minutes went by slowly. The widow kept looking up at the sun.

"I suppose the heat is better than the rain!" she said, at last.

"The heat can do a lot of harm, too, though," said the neighbour, absent-mindedly, as he pulled a long blade of grass from between the stones of the wall and began to chew the end of it. "You could get sunstroke on a day like this!" He looked up at the sun. "The sun is a terror," he said. "It could cause you to drop down dead like a stone!"

The widow strained out further over the gate. She looked up the hill in the direction of the town.

"He will have a good cool breeze on his face coming down the hill, at any rate," she said.

The man looked up the hill. "That's true. On the hottest day of the year you would get a cool breeze coming down that hill on a bicycle. You would feel the air streaming past your cheeks like silk. And in the winter it's like two knives flashing to either side of you, and peeling off your skin like you'd peel the bark off a sally-rod." He chewed the grass meditatively. "That must be one of the steepest hills in Ireland," he said. "That hill is a hill worthy of the name of a hill." He took the grass out of his mouth. "It's my belief," he said, earnestly looking at the widow—"it's my belief that that hill is to be found marked with a name in the Ordnance Survey map!"

"If that's the case," said the widow, "Packy will be able to tell you all about it. When it isn't a book he has in his hand it's a map."

"Is that so?" said the man. "That's interesting. A map is a great thing. A map is not an ordinary thing. It isn't everyone can make out a map."

The widow wasn't listening.

"I think I see Packy!" she said, and she opened the wooden gate and stepped out into the roadway.

At the top of the hill there was a glitter of spokes as a bicycle came into sight. Then there was a flash of blue jersey as Packy came flying downward, gripping the handlebars of the bike, with his bright hair blown back from his forehead. The hill was so steep, and he came down so fast, that it seemed to the man and woman at the bottom of the hill that he was not moving at all, but that it was the bright trees and bushes, the bright ditches and wayside grasses that were streaming away to either side of him.

The hens and chickens clucked and squawked and ran along the road looking for a safe place in the ditches. They ran to either side with feminine fuss and chatter. Packy waved to his mother. He came nearer and nearer. They could see the freckles on his face.

"Shoo!" cried Packy, at the squawking hens that had not yet left the roadway. They ran with their long necks straining forward.

"Shoo!" said Packy's mother, lifting her apron and flapping it in the air to frighten them out of his way.

It was only afterwards, when the harm was done, that the widow began to think that it might, perhaps, have been the flapping of her own apron that frightened the old clocking hen, and sent her flying out over the garden wall into the middle of the road.

The old hen appeared suddenly on top of the grassy ditch and looked with a distraught eye at the hens and chickens as they ran to right and left. Her own feathers began to stand out from her. She craned her neck forward and gave a distracted squawk, and fluttered down into the middle of the hot dusty road.

Packy jammed on the brakes. The widow screamed. There was a flurry of white feathers and a spurt of blood. The bicycle swerved and fell. Packy was thrown over the handlebars.

It was such a simple accident that, although the widow screamed, and although the old man looked around to see if there was help near, neither of them thought that Packy was very badly hurt, but when they ran over and lifted his head, and saw that he could not speak, they wiped the blood from his face and looked around, desperately, to measure the distance they would have to carry him.

It was only a few yards to the door of the cottage, but Packy was dead before they got him across the threshold.

"He's only in a weakness!" screamed the widow, and she urged the crowd that had gathered outside the door to do something for him. "Get a doctor!" she cried, pushing a young labourer towards the door. "Hurry! Hurry! The doctor will bring him around."

But the neighbours that kept coming in the door, quickly, from all sides, were crossing themselves, one after another, and falling on their knees, as soon as they laid eyes on the boy, stretched out flat on the bed, with the dust and dirt and the sweat marks of life on his dead face.

When at last the widow was convinced that her son was dead, the other women had to hold her down. She waved her arms and cried out aloud, and wrestled to get free. She wanted to wring the neck of every hen in the yard.

"I'll kill every one of them. What good are they to me, now? All the hens in the world aren't worth one drop of human blood. That old clocking hen wasn't worth more than six shillings, at the very most. What is six shillings? Is is worth poor Packy's life?"

But after a time she stopped raving, and looked from one face to another.

"Why didn't he ride over the old hen?" she asked. "Why did he try to save an old hen that wasn't worth more than six shillings? Didn't he know he was worth more to his mother than an old hen that would be going into the pot one of these days? Why did he do it? Why did he put on the brakes going down one of the worst hills in the country? Why? Why?"

The neighbours patted her arm.

"There now!" they said. "There now!" and that was all they could think of saying, and they said it over and over again. "There now! There now!"

And years afterwards, whenever the widow spoke of her son Packy to the neighbours who dropped in to keep her company for an hour or two, she always had the same question to ask; the same tireless question.

"Why did he put the price of an old clocking hen above the price of his own life?"

And the people always gave the same answer.

"There now!" they said, "There now!" And they sat as silently as the widow herself, looking into the fire.

But surely some of those neighbours must have been stirred to wonder what would have happened had Packy not yielded to his impulse of fear, and had, instead, ridden boldly over the old clucking hen? And surely some of them must have stared into the flames and pictured the scene of the accident again, altering a detail here and there as they did so, and giving the story a different end. For these people knew the widow, and they knew Packy, and when you know people well it is as easy to guess what they would say and do in certain circumstances as it is to remember what they actually did say and do in other circumstances. In fact it is sometimes easier to invent than to remember accurately, and were this not so two great branches of creative art would wither in an hour: the art of the story-teller and the art of the gossip. So, perhaps, if I try to tell you what I myself think might have happened had Packy killed that cackling old hen, you will not accuse me of abusing my privileges as a writer. After all, what I am about to tell you is no more of a fiction than what I have already told, and I lean no heavier now upon your credulity than, with your full consent, I did in the first instance.

And moreover, in many respects the new story is the same as the old.

It begins in the same way too. There is the widow grazing her cow by the wayside, and walking the long roads to the town, weighted down with sacks of cabbages that will pay for Packy's schooling. There she is, fussing over Packy in the mornings in case he would be late for school. There she is in the evening watching the battered clock on the dresser for the hour when he will appear on the top of the hill at his return. And there too, on a hot day in June, is the old labouring man coming up the road, and pausing to talk to her, as she stood at the door. There he is dragging a blade of grass from between the stones of the wall, and putting it between his teeth to chew, before he opens his mouth.

And when he opens his mouth at last it is to utter the same remark.

"Waiting for Packy?" said the old man, and then he took off his hat and wiped the sweat from his forehead. It will be remembered that he was an old man. "It's a hot day," he said.

"It's very hot," said the widow, looking anxiously up the hill. "It's a hot day to push a bicycle four miles along a bad road with the dust rising to choke you, and sun striking spikes off the handlebars!"

"The heat is better than the rain, all the same," said the old man.

"I suppose it is," said the widow. "All the same, there were days when Packy came home with the rain dried into his clothes so bad they stood up stiff like boards when he took them off. They stood up stiff like boards against the wall, for all the world as if he was still standing in them!" "Is that so?" said the old man. "You may be sure he got a good petting on those days. There is no son like a widow's son. A ewe lamb!"

"Is it Packy?" said the widow, in disgust. "Packy never got a day's petting since the day he was born. I made up my mind from the first that I'd never make a soft one out of him."

The widow looked up the hill again, and set herself to raking the gravel outside the gate as if she were in the road for no other purpose. Then she gave another look up the hill.

"Here he is now!" she said, and she rose such a cloud of dust with the rake that they could hardly see the glitter of the bicycle spokes, and the flash of blue jersey as Packy came down the hill at a breakneck speed.

Nearer and nearer he came, faster and faster, waving his hand to the widow, shouting at the hens to leave the way!

The hens ran for the ditches, stretching their necks in gawky terror. And then, as the last hen squawked into the ditch, the way was clear for a moment before the whirling silver spokes.

Then, unexpectedly, up from nowhere it seemed, came an old clocking hen and, clucking despairingly, it stood for a moment on the top of the wall and then rose into the air with the clumsy flight of a ground fowl.

Packy stopped whistling. The widow screamed. Packy yelled and the widow flapped her apron. Then Packy swerved the bicycle, and a cloud of dust rose from the braked wheel.

For a minute it could not be seen what exactly had happened, but Packy put his foot down and dragged it along the ground in the dust till he brought the bicycle to a sharp stop. He threw the bicycle down with a clatter on the hard road and ran back. The widow could not bear to look. She threw her apron over her head.

"He's killed the clocking hen!" she said. "He's killed her! He's killed her!" and then she let the apron fall back into place, and began to run up the hill herself. The old man spat out the blade of grass that he had been chewing and ran after the woman.

"Did you kill it?" screamed the widow, and as she got near enough to see the blood and feathers she raised her arm over her head, and her fist was clenched till the knuckles shone white. Packy cowered down over the carcass of the fowl and hunched up his shoulders as if to shield himself from a blow. His legs were spattered with blood, and the brown and white feathers of the dead hen were stuck to his hands, and stuck to his clothes, and they were strewn all over the road. Some of the short white inner feathers were still swirling with the dust in the air.

"I couldn't help it, Mother. I couldn't help it. I didn't see her till it was too late!"

The widow caught up the hen and examined it all over, holding it by the bone of the breast, and letting the long neck dangle. Then, catching it by the leg, she raised it suddenly above her head, and brought down the bleeding body on the boy's back, in blow after blow, spattering the blood all over his face and his hands, over his clothes and over the white dust of the road around him.

"How dare you lie to me!" she screamed, gaspingly, between the blows. "You saw the hen. I know you saw it. You stopped whistling! You called out! We were watching you. We saw." She turned upon the old man. "Isn't that right?" she demanded. "He saw the hen, didn't he? He saw it?"

"It looked that way," said the old man, uncertainly, his eye on the dangling fowl in the widow's hand.

"There you are!" said the widow. She threw the hen down on the road. "You saw the hen in front of you on the road, as plain as you see it now," she accused, "but you wouldn't stop to save it because you were in too big a hurry home to fill your belly! Isn't that so?"

"No, Mother. No! I saw her all right but it was too late to do anything."

"He admits now that he saw it," said the widow, turning and nodding triumphantly at the onlookers who had gathered at the sound of the shouting.

"I never denied seeing it!" said the boy, appealing to the on-lookers as to his judges.

"He doesn't deny it!" screamed the widow. "He stands there as brazen as you like, and admits for all the world to hear that he saw the hen as plain as the nose on his face, and he rode over it without a thought!"

"But what else could I do?" said the boy, throwing out his

hand; appealing to the crowd now, and now appealing to the widow. "If I'd put on the brakes going down the hill at such a speed I would have been put over the handlebars!"

"And what harm would that have done you?" screamed the widow. "I often saw you taking a toss when you were wrestling with Jimmy Mack and I heard no complaints afterwards, although your elbows and knees would be running blood, and your face scraped like a gridiron!" She turned to the crowd. "That's as true as God. I often saw him come in with his nose spouting blood like a pump, and one eye closed as tight as the eye of a corpse. My hand was often stiff for a week from sopping out wet cloths to put poultices on him and try to bring his face back to rights again." She swung back to Packy again. "You're not afraid of a fall when you go climbing trees, are you? You're not afraid to go up on the roof after a cat, are you? Oh, there's more in this than you want me to know. I can see that. You killed that hen on purpose—that's what I believe! You're tired of going to school. You want to get out of going away to college. That's it! You think if you kill the few poor hens we have there will be no money in the box when the time comes to pay for books and classes. That's it!" Packy began to redden.

"It's late in the day for me to be thinking of things like that," he said. "It's long ago I should have started those tricks if that was the way I felt. But it's not true. I want to go to college. The reason I was coming down the hill so fast was to tell you that I got the scholarship. The teacher told me as I was leaving the schoolhouse. That's why I was pedalling so hard. That's why I was whistling. That's why I was waving my hand. Didn't you see me waving my hand from once I came in sight at the top of the hill?"

The widow's hands fell to her sides. The wind of words died down within her and left her flat and limp. She didn't know what to say. She could feel the neighbours staring at her. She wished that they were gone away about their business. She wanted to throw out her arms to the boy, to drag him against her heart and hug him like a small child. But she thought of how the crowd would look at each other and nod and snigger. A ewe lamb! She didn't want to satisfy them. If she gave in to her feelings now they would know how much she had been counting on his getting the scholarship. She wouldn't please them! She wouldn't satisfy them!

She looked at Packy, and when she saw him standing there before her, spattered with the furious feathers and crude blood of the dead hen, she felt a fierce disappointment for the boy's own disappointment, and a fierce resentment against him for killing the hen on this day of all days, and spoiling the great news of his success.

Her mind was in confusion. She started at the blood on his face, and all at once it seemed as if the blood was a bad omen of the future that was for him. Disappointment, fear, resentment, and above all defiance, raised themselves within her like screeching animals. She looked from Packy to the onlookers.

"Scholarship! Scholarship!" she sneered, putting as much derision as she could into her voice and expression.

"I suppose you think you are a great fellow now? I suppose you think you are independent now? I suppose you think you can go off with yourself now, and look down on your poor slave of a mother who scraped and sweated for you with her cabbages and her hens! I suppose you think to yourself that it doesn't matter now whether the hens are alive or dead? Is that the way? Well, let me tell you this! You're not as independent as you think. The scholarship may pay for your books and your teacher's fees but who will pay for your clothes? Ah-ha, you forgot that, didn't you?" She put her hands on her hips. Packy hung his head. He no longer appealed to the gawking neighbours. They might have been able to save him from blows but he knew enough about life to know that no one could save him from shame.

The widow's heart burned at sight of his shamed face, as her heart burned with grief, but her temper too burned fiercer and fiercer, and she came to a point at which nothing could quell the blaze till it had burned itself out. "Who'll buy your suits?" she yelled. "Who'll buy your boots?" She paused to think of more humiliating accusations. "Who'll buy your breeches?" She paused again and her teeth bit against each other. What would wound deepest? What shame could she drag upon him? "Who'll buy your nightshirts or will you sleep in your skin?"

The neighbours laughed at that, and the tension was broken. The widow herself laughed. She held her sides and laughed, and as she laughed everything seemed to take on a newer and simpler significance. Things were not as bad as they seemed a moment before. She wanted Packy to laugh too. She looked at him. But as she looked at Packy her heart turned cold with a strange new fear.

"Get into the house!" she said, giving him a push ahead of her. She wanted him safe under her own roof. She wanted to get him away from the gaping neighbours. She hated them, man, woman and child. She felt that if they had not been there things would have been different. And she wanted to get away from the sight of the blood on the road. She wanted to mash a few potatoes and make a bit of potato cake for Packy. That would comfort him. He loved that.

Packy hardly touched the food. And even after he had washed and scrubbed himself there were stains of blood turning up in the most unexpected places: behind his ears, under his finger-nails, inside the cuff of his sleeve.

"Put on your good clothes," said the widow, making a great effort to be gentle, but her manner had become as twisted and as hard as the branches of the trees across the road from her, and even the kindly offers she made sounded harsh. The boy sat on the chair in a slumped position that kept her nerves on edge, and set up a further conflict of irritation and love in her heart. She hated to see him slumping there in the chair, not asking to go outside the door, but still she was uneasy whenever he as much as looked in the direction of the door. She felt safe while he was under the roof; inside the lintel; under her eyes.

Next day she went in to wake him for school, but his room was empty; his bed had not been slept in, and when she ran out into the yard and called him everywhere there was no answer. She ran up and down. She called at the houses of the neighbours but he was not in any house. And she thought she could hear sniggering behind her in each house that she left, as she ran to another one. He wasn't in the village. He wasn't in the town. The master of the school said that she should let the police have a description of him. He said he never met a boy as sensitive as Packy. A boy like that took strange notions into his head from time to time.

The police did their best but there was no news of Packy that night. A few days later there was a letter saying that he was well. He asked his mother to notify the master that he would not be coming back, so that some other boy could claim the scholarship. He said that he would send the price of the hen as soon as he made some money.

Another letter in a few weeks said that he had got a job on a trawler, and that he would not be able to write very often but that he would put aside some of his pay every week and send it to his mother whenever he got into port. He said that he wanted to pay her back for all she had done for him. He gave no address. He kept his promise about the money but he never gave any address when he wrote.

. . . . And so the people may have let their thoughts run on, as they sat by the fire with the widow, many a night, listening to her complaining voice saying the same thing over and over. "Why did he put the price of an old hen above the price of his own life?" And it is possible that their version of the story has a certain element of truth about it too. Perhaps all our actions have this double quality about them; this possibility of alternative, and that it is only by careful watching and absolute sincerity, that we follow the path that is destined for us, and, no matter how tragic that may be, it is better than the tragedy we bring upon ourselves.

First Practice

Gary Gildner

After the doctor checked to see
we weren't ruptured,
the man with the short cigar took us
under the grade school,
where we went in case of attack
or storms, and said
he was Clifford Hill, he was
a man who believed dogs
ate dogs, he had once killed
for his country, and if
there were any girls present
for them to leave now.
                            No one
left. OK, he said, he said I take
that to mean you are hungry
men who hate to lose as much
as I do. OK. Then
he made two lines of us
facing each other,
and across the way, he said,
is the man you hate most
in the world,
and if we are to win
that title I want to see how.
But I don't want to see
any marks when you're dressed,
he said. He said, *Now.*

The Jump Shooter

Dennis Trudell

The way the ball
hung there
against the blue or purple

one night last week
across town
at the playground where

I had gone to spare
my wife
from the mood I'd swallowed

and saw in the dusk
a stranger
shooting baskets a few

years older maybe
thirty-five
and overweight a little

beer belly saw him
shooting there
and joined him didn't

ask or anything simply
went over
picked off a rebound

and hooked it back up
while he
smiled I nodded and for

ten minutes or so we
took turns
taking shots and the thing

is neither of us said
a word
and this fellow who's

too heavy now and slow
to play
for any team still had

the old touch seldom
ever missed
kept moving further out

and finally his t-shirt
a gray
and fuzzy blur I stood

under the rim could
almost hear
a high school cheer

begin and fill a gym
while wooden
bleachers rocked he made

three in a row from
twenty feet
moved back two steps

faked out a patch
of darkness
arched another one and

the way the ball
hung there
against the blue or purple

then suddenly filled
the net
made me wave goodbye

breathe deeply and begin
to whistle
as I walked back home.

The Man He Killed

Thomas Hardy

'Had he and I but met
By some old ancient inn,
We should have sat us down to wet
Right many a nipperkin!

'But ranged as infantry,
And staring face to face,
I shot at him as he at me,
And killed him in his place.

'I shot him dead because—
Because he was my foe,
Just so: my foe of course he was;
That's clear enough; although

'He thought he'd 'list, perhaps,
Off-hand like—just as I—
Was out of work—had sold his traps—
No other reason why.

'Yes; quaint and curious war is!
You shoot a fellow down
You'd treat if met where any bar is,
Or help to half-a-crown.'

Walk Well, My Brother

Farley Mowat

W HEN Charlie Lavery first went north just after
the war, he was twenty-six years old and case hardened by nearly a hundred bombing missions over
Europe. He was very much of the new elite who believed that
any challenge, whether by man or nature, could be dealt with
by good machines in the hands of skilled men. During the following five years, flying charter jobs in almost every part of
the arctic from Hudson Bay to the Alaska border, he had
found no reason to alter this belief. But though his familiarity
with arctic skies and his ability to drive trackless lines across
them had become considerable, he remained a stranger to the
land below. The monochromatic wilderness of rock and tundra, snow and ice, existed outside his experience and compre-
hension, as did the native people whose world this was.

One mid-August day in 1951 he was piloting a war surplus
Anson above the drowned tundra plains south of Queen Maud
Gulf, homeward bound to his base at Yellowknife after a flight
almost to the limit of the aircraft's range. The twin engines
thundered steadily and his alert ears caught no hint of warning
from them. When the machine betrayed his trust, it did so
with shattering abruptness. Before he could touch the
throttles, the starboard engine was dead and the port one
coughing in staccato bursts. Then came silence—replaced almost instantly by a rising scream of wind as the plane nosed
steeply down toward the shining circlet of a pond.

It was too small a pond and the plane had too little altitude. As Lavery frantically pumped the flap hydraulics, the floats smashed into the rippled water. The Anson careened wickedly for a few yards and came to a crunching stop against the frost-shattered rocks along the shore.

Lavery barely glanced at his woman passenger, who had been thrown into a corner of the cabin by the impact. He scrambled past her, flung open the door and jumped down to find himself standing knee deep in frigid water. Both floats had been so badly holed that they had filled and now rested on the rocky bottom.

The woman crawled to the door and Lavery looked up into an oval, warmly tinted face framed in long black hair. He groped for a few Eskimo words he knew:

"*Tingmeak . . . tokoiyo . . .* smashed to hell! No fly! Understand?"

As she stared back uncomprehending, a spasm of anger shook him. What a fool he'd been to take her aboard at all . . . now she was a bloody albatross around his neck.

Four hours earlier he had landed in a bay on the Gulf coast to set out a cache of aviation gas for a prospecting company. No white men lived in that part of the world and Lavery had considered it a lucky accident to find an Eskimo tent pitched there. The two men who had run out to watch him land had been a godsend, helping to unload the drums, float them to tideline and roll them up the beach well above the storm line.

He had given each of them a handful of chocolate bars in payment for their work and had been about to head back for Yellowknife when the younger Eskimo touched his arm and pointed to the tent. Lavery had no desire to visit that squat skin cone hugging the rocks a hundred yards away and it was not the Eskimo's gentle persistence that prevailed on him—it was the thought that these Huskies might have a few white fox pelts to trade.

There were no fox pelts in the tent. Instead there was a woman lying on some caribou hides. *Nuliak*—wife—was the only word Lavery could understand of the Eskimo's urgent attempt at explanation.

The tent stank of seal oil and it was with revulsion that Lavery looked more closely at the woman. She was young and not bad looking—for a Husky—but her cheeks were flushed a sullen red by fever and a trickle of blood had dried at the corner of her mouth. Her dark eyes were fixed upon him with grave intensity. He shook his head and turned away.

T.B. . . . . sooner or later all the Huskies got it . . . bound to the filthy way they lived. It would be no kindness to fly her out to the little hospital at Yellowknife already stuffed with dying Indians. She'd be better off to die at home . . .

Lavery was halfway back to the Anson before the younger Eskimo caught up with him. In his hands he held two walrus tusks, and the pilot saw they were of exceptional quality.

Ah, what the hell . . . no skin off my ass. I'm deadheading anyhow . . .

"*Eeema*. Okay, I'll take your *nuliak*. But make it snappy. *Dwoee, dwoee!*"

While Lavery fired up the engines, the men carried the woman, wrapped in caribou-skin robes, and placed her in the cabin. The younger Eskimo pointed at her, shouting her name: Konala. Lavery nodded and waved them away. As he pulled clear of the beach he caught a glimpse of them standing in the slipstream, as immobile as rocks. Then the plane was airborne, swinging around on course for the long haul home.

Barely two hours later he again looked into the eyes of the woman called Konala . . . wishing he had never seen or heard of her.

She smiled tentatively but Lavery ignored her and pushed past into the cabin to begin sorting through the oddments which had accumulated during his years of arctic flying. He found a rusty .22 rifle and half a box of shells, a torn sleeping bag, an axe and four cans of pork and beans. This, together with a small box of matches and a pocket knife in his stylish cotton flying jacket, comprised a survival outfit whose poverty testified to his contempt for the world that normally lay far below his aircraft.

Shoving the gear into a packsack he waded ashore. Slowly Konala followed, carrying her caribou robes and a large seal-skin pouch. With mounting irritation Lavery saw that she was able to move without much difficulty. Swinging the lead to get a free plane ride, he thought. He turned on her.

"The party's over, lady! Your smart-assed boy friend's got you into a proper mess—him and his goddamn walrus tusks!"

The words meant nothing to Konala but the tone was clear enough. She walked a few yards off, opened her pouch, took out a fishing line and began carefully unwinding it. Lavery turned his back on her and made his way to a ledge of rock where he sat down to consider the situation.

A thin tongue of fear was flickering in the back of his mind. Just what the hell *was* he going to do? The proper drill would be to stick with the Anson and wait until a search plane found him ... except he hadn't kept to his flight plan. He had said he intended to fly west down the coast to Bathurst before angling southwest to Yellowknife ... instead he'd flown a direct course from the cache, to save an hour's fuel. Not so bright maybe, considering his radio was out of kilter. There wasn't a chance in a million they'd look for him this far off-course. Come to that, he didn't even know exactly where he was ... fifty miles or so north of the Back River lakes would be a good guess. There were so damn few landmarks in this godforsaken country ... Well, so he wasn't going to be picked up ... that left Shanks' mare, as the Limeys would say ... but which way to go?

He spread out a tattered aeronautical chart on the knees of his neat cotton pants. Yellowknife, four hundred miles to the southwest, was out of the question ... The arctic coast couldn't be more than a hundred and fifty miles away but there was nobody there except a scattering of Huskies ... How about Baker Lake? He scaled off the airline distance with thumb and forefinger, ignoring the innumerable lakes and rivers across the route. About two hundred miles. He was pretty fit ... should be able to manage twenty miles a day ... ten days, and presto.

Movement caught his eye and he looked up. Konala, a childlike figure in her bulky deerskin clothes, had waded out to stand on the submerged tail of a float. Bent almost double, she was swinging a length of line around her head. She let the weighted hook fly so that it sailed through the air to strike the surface a hundred feet from shore.

Well, there was no way she could walk to Baker. She'd have to stay put until he could bring help. His anger surged up again ... Fishing, for God's sake! What in Jesus' sweet name did she think she was going to catch in that lousy little pond?

He began to check his gear. Lord, no *compass* . . . and the sun was no use this time of year. He'd never bothered to buy one of the pocket kind . . . no need for it . . . but there was a magnetic compass in the instrument panel of the old crate . . .

Lavery hurried back to the Anson, found some tools and went to work. He was too preoccupied to notice Konala haul in her line and deftly slip a fine char off the hook. He did not see her take her curved woman's knife and slice two thick fillets from the fish. The first he knew of her success was when she appeared at the open cabin door. She was so small that her head barely reached the opening. With one hand she held a fillet up to him while with the other she pushed raw pink flesh into her mouth, pantomiming to show him how good it was.

"Jesus, no!" He was revolted and waved her away. "Eat it yourself . . . you animal!"

Obediently Konala disappeared from the doorway. Making her way ashore she scraped together a pile of dry lichens then struck a light with flint and steel. The moss smoked and began to glow. She covered it with dwarf willow twigs, then spread pieces of the fish on two flat rocks angled toward the rising flames. When Lavery descended from the plane with the compass in his hand his appetite woke with a rush at the sight and smell of roasting fish. But he did not go near the fire. Instead he retreated to the rocks where he had left his gear and dug out a can of beans. He gashed his thumb trying to open the can with his pocket knife.

Picking up the axe, he pounded the can until it split. Raging against this wasteland that had trapped him, and the fate that had stripped him of his wings, he furiously shovelled the cold mess into his mouth and choked it down.

Konala sat watching him intently. When he had finished she rose to her feet, pointed northward and asked, "*Peechuktuk?* We walk?"

Lavery's resentment exploded. Thrusting his arms through the straps of the packsack, he heaved it and the sleeping bag into position then picked up the rifle and pointed with it to the southwest.

"You're goddamn right!" he shouted. "Me—*owunga peechuktuk* that way! *Eeetpeet*—you bloody well stay here!"

Without waiting to see if she had understood, he began to climb the slope of a sandy esker that rose to the south of the pond. Near the crest he paused and looked back. Konala was squatting by the tiny fire seemingly unaware that he was deserting her. He felt a momentary twinge of guilt, but shrugged it off . . . no way she could make it with him to Baker, and she had her deerskins to keep her warm. As for food, well, Huskies could eat anything . . . she'd make out. He turned and his long, ungainly figure passed over the skyline.

With a chill of dismay he looked out across the tundra rolling to a measureless horizon ahead of him—a curving emptiness more intimidating than anything he had seen in the high skies. The tongue of fear began to flicker again but he resolutely shut his mind to it and stumbled forward into that sweep of space, his heavy flight boots slipping on rocks and sucking in the muskeg, the straps of the packsack already cutting into his shoulders through the thin cotton jacket.

There is no way of knowing what Konala was thinking as she saw him go. She might have believed he was going hunting, since that would have been the natural thing for a man to do under the circumstances. But in all likelihood she guessed what he intended—otherwise, how to explain the fact that ten days later and nearly sixty miles to the south of the downed plane, the sick woman trudged wearily across a waste of sodden muskeg to climb a gravel ridge and halt beside the unconscious body of Charlie Lavery?

Squatting beside him she used her curved knife to cut away the useless remnants of his leather boots, then wrapped his torn and bloody feet in compresses of wet sphagnum moss. Slipping off her parka, she spread it over his tattered jacket to protect him from the flies. Her fingers on his emaciated and insect-bitten flesh were tender and sure. Later she built a fire, and when Lavery opened his eyes it was to find himself under a rude skin shelter with a can of fish broth being pressed lightly against his lips.

There was a hiatus in his mind. Anxiously he raised himself to see if the aircraft was still on the pond, but there was no pond and no old Anson . . . only that same stunning expanse of empty plains. With a sickening lurch, memory began to function. The seemingly endless days of his journey flooded back upon him: filled with roaring clouds of mosquitoes and flies; with a mounting, driving hunger; the agony of lacerated feet and the misery of rain-swept hours lying shelterless in a frigid void. He remembered his matches getting soaked when he tried to ford the first of a succession of rivers that forever deflected his course toward the west. He remembered losing the .22 cartridges when the box turned to mush after a rain. Above all, he remembered the unbearable sense of loneliness that grew until he began to panic, throwing away first the useless gun, and then the sodden sleeping bag, the axe . . . and finally sent him, in a heart-bursting spasm of desperation, toward a stony ridge that seemed to undulate serpent-like on the otherwise shapeless face of a world that had lost all form and substance.

Konala's face came into focus as she nudged the tin against his lips. She was smiling and Lavery found himself smiling weakly back at this woman who not so long before had roused his contempt and anger.

They camped on the nameless ridge for a week while Lavery recovered some of his strength. At first he could hardly bear to leave the shelter because of the pain in his feet. But Konala seemed always on the move: gathering willow twigs for fires, collecting and cooking food, cutting and sewing a new pair of boots for Lavery from the hides she had brought with her. She appeared tireless, but that was an illusion. Her body was driven to its many tasks only at great cost.

Time had telescoped itself so that Lavery would wake from sleep with shaking hands, hearing the engines of the Anson fail. It would seem to him that the plane had crashed only a few minutes earlier. It would seem that the terrible ordeal of his march south was about to begin again and he would feel a sick return of panic. When this happened, he would desperately fix his thoughts on Konala for she was the one comforting reality in all this alien world.

He thought about her a great deal, but she was an enigma to him. Sick as she was, how had she managed to follow him across those sodden plains and broken rock ridges . . . how had she managed to keep alive in such a country?

After Konala gave him the completed skin boots carefully lined with cotton grass, he began to find answers to some of these questions. He was able to hobble far enough from camp to watch her set sinew snares for gaudy ground squirrels she called *hikik*, scoop suckers from a nearby stream with her bare hands, outrun snow geese that were still flightless after the late-summer moult, and dig succulent lemmings from their peat bog burrows. Watching her, Lavery slowly came to understand that what had seemed to him a lifeless desert was in fact a land generous in its support of those who knew its nature.

Still, the most puzzling question remained unanswered. Why had Konala not stayed in the relative safety of the aircraft or else travelled north to seek her own people? What had impelled her to follow him ... to rescue a man of another race who had abandoned her?

Toward the end of their stay on the ridge, the sun was beginning to dip well below the horizon at night—a warning that summer was coming to an end. One day Konala again pointed north and, with a grin, she waddled duck-like a few paces in that direction. The joke at the expense of Lavery's splayed and painful feet did not annoy him. He laughed and limped after her to show his willingness to follow wherever she might lead.

When they broke camp, Konala insisted on carrying what was left of Lavery's gear along with her own pouch and the roll of caribou hides which was both shelter and bedding for them. As they trekked northward she broke into song—a high and plaintive chant without much melody which seemed as much part of the land as the fluting of curlews. When Lavery tried to find out what the song was all about, she seemed oddly reticent and all he could gather was that she was expressing kinship for someone or for some thing beyond his ken. He did not understand that she was joining her voice to the voice of the land and to the spirits of the land.

Retracing their path under Konala's tutelage became a journey of discovery. Lavery was forever being surprised at how different the tundra had now become from the dreadful void he had trudged across not long since.

He discovered it was full of birds ranging from tiny longspurs whose muted colouring made them almost invisible, to great saffron-breasted hawks circling high above the bogs and lakes. Konala also drew his attention to the endless diversity of tundra plants, from livid orange lichens to azure flowers whose blooms were so tiny he had to kneel to see them clearly.

Once Konala motioned him to crawl beside her to the crest of an esker. In the valley beyond, a family of white wolves was lazily hunting lemmings in a patch of sedge a hundred feet away. The nearness of the big beasts made Lavery uneasy until Konala boldly stood up and called to the wolves in their own language. They drew together then, facing her in a half circle, and answered with a long, lilting chorus before trotting away in single file.

Late one afternoon they at last caught sight of a splash of brilliant colour in the distance. Lavery's heartbeat quickened and he pushed forward without regard for his injured feet. The yellow-painted Anson *might* have been spotted by a search plane during their absence . . . rescue by his own kind might still be possible. But when the man and woman descended the esker to the shore of the pond, they found the Anson exactly as they had left it. There had been no human visitors.

Bitterly disappointed, Lavery climbed into the cockpit, seated himself behind the controls and slumped into black depression. Konala's intention of travelling northward to rejoin her own people on the coast now loomed as an ordeal whose outcome would probably be death during the first winter storm . . . if they could last that long. Their worn clothing and almost hairless robes were already barely adequate to keep the cold at bay. Food was getting harder to find as the birds left, the small animals began to dig in and the fish ran back to the sea. And what about fuel when the weather really began to turn against them?

Lavery was sullen and silent that evening as they ate their boiled fish, but Konala remained cheerful. She kept repeating the word *tuktu*—caribou—as she vainly tried to make him understand that soon they would have the wherewithal to continue the journey north.

As the night wind began to rise he ignored the skin shelter which Konala had erected and, taking one of the robes, climbed back into the plane and rolled himself up on the icy metal floor. During the next few days he spent most of his time in the Anson, sometimes fiddling with the knobs of the useless radio, but for the most part morosely staring through the Plexiglas windscreen at a landscape which seemed to grow increasingly bleak as the first frosts greyed the tundra flowers and browned the windswept sedges.

Early one morning an unfamiliar sound brought him out of a chilled, nightmarish sleep. It was a muffled, subdued noise as of waves rolling in on a distant shore. For one heart-stopping instant he thought it was the beat of an aircraft engine, then he heard Konala's exultant cry.

"*Tuktoraikayai*—the deer have come!"

From the window of the dead machine Lavery looked out upon a miracle of life. An undulating mass of antlered animals was pouring out of the north. It rolled steadily toward the pond, split, and began enveloping it. The rumble resolved itself into a rattling cadence of hooves on rock and gravel. As the animals swept past, the stench of barnyard grew strong even inside the plane. Although in the days when he had flown high above them Lavery had often seen skeins of migrating caribou laced across the arctic plains like a pattern of beaded threads, he could hardly credit what he now beheld . . . the land inundated under a veritable flood of life. His depression began to dissipate as he felt himself being drawn into and becoming almost a part of that living river.

While he stared, awe-struck and incredulous, Konala went to work. Some days earlier she had armed herself with a spear, its shaft made from a paddle she had found in the Anson and its double-edged blade filed out of a piece of steel broken from the tip of the plane's anchor. With this in hand she was now scurrying about on the edge of the herd. The press was so great that individual deer could not avoid her. A snorting buck leapt high as the spear drove into him just behind the ribs. His dying leap carried him onto the backs of some of his neighbours, and as he slid off and disappeared into the ruck, Konala's blade thrust into another victim. She chose the fattest beasts and those with the best hides.

When the tide of caribou finally thinned, there was much work for Konala's knife. She skinned, scraped and staked out several prime hides destined for the making of clothes and sleeping robes, then turned her attention to a small mountain of meat and began slicing it into paper-thin sheets which she draped over dwarf willow bushes. When dry this would make light, imperishable food fit to sustain a man and a woman— one injured and the other sick—who must undertake a long, demanding journey.

Revitalized by the living ambience of the great herd, Lavery came to help her. She glanced up at him and her face was radiant. She cut off a piece of brisket and held it out to him, grinning delightedly when he took it and tore off a piece with his teeth. It was his idea to make a stove out of two empty oil cans upon which the fat which Konala had gathered could be rendered into white cakes that would provide food *and* fuel in the times ahead.

Several days of brisk, clear weather followed. While the meat dried on the bushes, Konala laboured on, cutting and stitching clothing for them both. She worked herself so hard that her cheeks again showed the flame of fever and her rasping cough grew worse. When Lavery tried to make her take things a little easier she became impatient with him. Konala knew what she knew.

Finally on a day in mid-September she decided they were ready. With Lavery limping at her side, she turned her back on the white men's fine machine and set out to find her people.

The skies darkened and cold gales began sweeping gusts of snow across the bogs whose surfaces were already crusting with ice crystals. One day a sleet storm forced them into early camp. Konala had left the little travel tent to gather willows for the fire and Lavery was dozing when he heard her cry of warning through the shrilling of the wind.

There was no mistaking the urgency in her voice. Snatching up the spear he limped from the tent to see Konala running across a narrow valley. Behind her, looming immense and forbidding in the leaden light, was one of the great brown bears of the barrenlands.

Seeing Lavery poised on the slope above her, Konala swerved away, even though this brought her closer to the bear. It took a moment for Lavery to realize that she was attempting to distract the beast, then he raised the spear and flung himself down the slope, shouting and cursing at the top of his lungs.

The bear's interest in the woman shifted to the surprising spectacle Lavery presented. It sat up on its massive haunches and peered doubtfully at him through the veil of sleet.

When he was a scant few yards from the bear, Lavery tripped and fell, rolling helplessly among the rocks to fetch up on his back staring upward into that huge, square face. The bear looked back impassively then snorted, dropped on all fours and shambled off.

The meeting with the bear crystallized the changes which had been taking place in Lavery. Clad in caribou-skin clothing, a dark beard ringing his cheeks, and his hair hanging free to his shoulders, he had acquired a look of litheness and vigour— and of watchfulness. No longer was he an alien in an inimical land. He was a man now in his own right, able to make his way in an elder world.

In Konala's company he knew a unity that he had previously felt only with members of his bombing crew. The weeks they had spent together had eroded the barrier of language and he was beginning to understand much about her that had earlier baffled him. Yet the core of the enigma remained for he had not found the answer to the question that had haunted him since she brought life back to his body on that distant southern ridge.

For some time they had been descending an already frozen and snow-covered river which Konala had given him to understand would lead them to the coast. But with each passing day, Konala had been growing weaker even as Lavery regained his strength. At night, when she supposed him to be asleep, she sometimes moaned softly, and during the day she could walk only for short distances between paroxysms of coughing and left blood stains in the new snow at her feet.

When the first real blizzard struck them, it was Lavery who set up the travel tent and lit the fire of lichens and caribou fat upon which to simmer some dried deer meet. Konala lay under their sleeping robes while he prepared the meal, and when he turned to her he saw how the lines of pain around her mouth had deepened into crevices. He came close and held a tin of warm soup to her dry lips. She drank a mouthful then lay back, her dark eyes glittering too brightly in the meagre firelight. He looked deep into them and read the confirmation of his fear.

Keeping her eyes on his, she took a new pair of skin boots from under the robes and slowly stroked them, feeling the infinitely fine stitching which would keep them waterproof. After a time she reached out and placed them in his lap. Then she spoke, slowly and carefully so he would be sure to understand.

"They are not very good boots but they might carry you to the camps of my people. They might help you return to your own land . . . Walk well in them . . . my brother."

Later that night the gale rose to a crescendo. The cold drove into the tent and, ignoring the faint flicker of the fire, pierced through the thick caribou robes wrapped about Konala and entered into her.

When the storm had blown itself out, Lavery buried her under a cairn of rocks on the high banks of the nameless river. As he made his way northward in the days that followed, his feet finding their own sure way, he no longer pondered the question which had lain in his mind through so many weeks . . . for he could still hear the answer she had made and would forever hear it: Walk well . . . my brother . . .

At Gull Lake: August, 1810

Duncan Campbell Scott

Gull Lake set in the rolling prairie—
Still there are reeds on the shore,
As of old the poplars shimmer
As summer passes;
Winter freezes the shallow lake to the core;
Storm passes,
Heat parches the sedges and grasses,
Night comes with moon-glimmer,
Dawn with the morning-star;
All proceeds in the flow of Time
As a hundred years ago.

Then two camps were pitched on the shore,
The clustered teepees
Of Tabashaw Chief of the Saulteaux.
And on a knoll tufted with poplars
Two gray tents of a trader—
Nairne of the Orkneys.
Before his tents under the shade of the poplars
Sat Keejigo, third of the wives
Of Tabashaw Chief of the Saulteaux;
Clad in the skins of antelopes
Broidered with porcupine quills
Coloured with vivid dyes,
Vermilion here and there
In the roots of her hair,

A half-moon of powder-blue
On her brow, her cheeks
Scored with light ochre streaks.
Keejigo daughter of Launay
The Normandy hunter
And Oshawan of the Saulteaux,
Troubled by fugitive visions
In the smoke of the camp-fires,
In the close dark of the teepee,
Flutterings of colour
Along the flow of the prairies,
Spangles of flower tints
Caught in the wonder of dawn,
Dreams of sounds unheard—
The echoes of echo,
Star she was named for
Keejigo, star of the morning,
Voices of storm—
Wind-rush and lightning,—
The beauty of terror;
The twilight moon
Coloured like a prairie lily,
The round moon of pure snow,
The beauty of peace;
Premonitions of love and of beauty
Vague as shadows cast by a shadow.
Now she had found her hero,
And offered her body and spirit
With abject, unreasoning passion,
As Earth abandons herself
To the sun and the thrust of the lightning.
Quiet were all the leaves of the poplars,
Breathless the air under their shadow,
As Keejigo spoke of these things to her heart
In the beautiful speech of the Saulteaux.

　　　　The flower lives on the prairie,
　　　　The wind in the sky,

I am here my beloved;
The wind and the flower.

The crane hides in the sand-hills,
Where does the wolverine hide?
I am here my beloved,
Heart's-blood on the feathers
The foot caught in the trap.

Take the flower in your hand,
The wind in your nostrils;
I am here my beloved;
Release the captive
Heal the wound under the feathers.

A storm-cloud was marching
Vast on the prairie,
Scored with livid ropes of hail,
Quick with nervous vines of lightning—
Twice had Nairne turned her away
Afraid of the venom of Tabashaw,
Twice had the Chief fired at his tents
And now when two bullets
Whistled above the encampment
He yelled "Drive this bitch to her master."

Keejigo went down a path by the lake;
Thick at the tangled edges,
The reeds and the sedges
Were gray as ashes
Against the death-black water;
The lightning scored with double flashes
The dark lake-mirror and loud
Came the instant thunder.
Her lips still moved to the words of her music,
"Release the captive,
Heal the wound under the feathers."

At the top of the bank
The old wives caught her and cast her down
Where Tabashaw crouched by his camp-fire.
He snatched a live brand from the embers,
Seared her cheeks,
Blinded her eyes,
Destroyed her beauty with fire,
Screaming, "Take that face to your lover."
Keejigo held her face to the fury
And made no sound.
The old wives dragged her away
And threw her over the bank
Like a dead dog.

Then burst the storm—
The Indians' screams and the howls of the dogs
Lost in the crash of hail
That smashed the sedges and reeds,
Stripped the poplars of leaves,
Tore and blazed onwards,
Wasting itself with riot and tumult—
Supreme in the beauty of terror.

The setting sun struck the retreating cloud
With a rainbow, not an arc but a column
Built with the glory of seven metals;
Beyond in the purple deeps of the vortex
Fell the quivering vines of the lightning.
The wind withdrew the veil from the shrine of the moon,
She rose changing her dusky shade for the glow
Of the prairie lily, till free of all blemish of colour
She came to her zenith without a cloud or a star,
A lovely perfection, snow-pure in the heaven of midnight.
And after the beauty of terror the beauty of peace.

But Keejigo came no more to the camps of her people;
Only the midnight moon knew where she felt her way,
Only the leaves of autumn, the snows of winter
Knew where she lay.

Some Objects of Wood and Stone

Margaret Atwood

i) Totems

We went to the park
where they kept the wooden people:
static, multiple
uprooted and trans-
planted.

Their faces were restored,
freshly-painted.
In front of them
the other wooden people
posed for each others' cameras
and nearby a new booth
sold replicas and souvenirs.

One of the people was real.
It lay on its back, smashed
by a toppling fall or just
the enduring of minor winters.
Only one of the heads had
survived intact, and it was
also beginning to decay
but there was a
life in the progressing

of old wood back to
the earth, obliteration

that the clear-hewn
standing figures lacked.

As for us, perennial watchers,
tourists of another kind
there is nothing for us to worship;
no pictures of ourselves, no blue-
sky summer fetishes, no postcards
we can either buy, or
smiling
be.

There are few totems that remain
living for us.
Though in passing,
through glass we notice

dead trees in the seared meadows
dead roots bleaching in the swamps.

  ii) Pebbles

Talking was difficult. Instead
we gathered coloured pebbles
from the places on the beach
where they occurred.

They were sea-smoothed, sea-completed.
They enclosed what they intended
to mean in shapes
as random and necessary
as the shapes of words

and when finally
we spoke
the sounds of our voices fell

into the air   single and
solid and rounded and really
there
and then dulled, and then like sounds
gone,   a fistful of gathered
pebbles there was no point
in taking home, dropped on a beachful
of other coloured pebbles

and when we turned to go
a flock of small
birds flew scattered by the
fright of our sudden moving
and disappeared: hard

sea pebbles
thrown solid for an instant
against she sky

flight of words

iii) Carved Animals

The small carved
animal is passed from
hand to hand
around the circle
until the stone grows warm

touching, the hands do not know
the form of animal
which was made or
the true form of stone
uncovered

and the hands, the fingers the
hidden small bones
of the hands bend to hold the shape,
shape themselves, grow

cold with the stone's cold, grow
also animal, exchange
until the skin wonders
if stone is human

In the darkness later
and even when the animal
has gone, they keep
the image of that
inner shape

hands holding warm
hands holding
the half-formed air

Travelling Through the Dark

William Stafford

Travelling through the dark I found a deer
dead on the edge of the Wilson River road.
It is usually best to roll them into the canyon:
that road is narrow; to swerve might make more dead.

By glow of the tail-light I stumbled back of the car
and stood by the heap, a doe, a recent killing;
she had stiffened already, almost cold.
I dragged her off; she was large in the belly.

My fingers touching her side brought me the reason—
her side was warm; her fawn lay there waiting,
alive, still, never to be born
Beside that mountain road I hesitated.

The car aimed ahead its lowered parking lights;
under the hood purred the steady engine.
I stood in the glare of the warm exhaust turning red;
around our group I could hear the wilderness listen.

I thought hard for us all—my only swerving—
then pushed her over the edge into the river.

The Fish

Elizabeth Bishop

I caught a tremendous fish
and held him beside the boat
half out of water, with my hook
fast in a corner of his mouth.
He didn't fight.
He hadn't fought at all.
He hung a grunting weight,
battered and venerable
and homely. Here and there
his brown skin hung in strips
like ancient wall-paper,
and its pattern of darker brown
was like wall-paper:
shapes like full-blown roses
stained and lost through age.
He was speckled with barnacles,
fine rosettes of lime,
and infested
with tiny white sea-lice,
and underneath two or three
rags of green weed hung down.
While his gills were breathing in
the terrible oxygen
—the frightening gills,
fresh and crisp with blood,

that can cut so badly—
I thought of the coarse white flesh
packed in like feathers,
the big bones and the little bones,
the dramatic reds and blacks
of his shiny entrails,
and the pink swim-bladder
like a big peony.
I looked into his eyes
which were far larger than mine
but shallower, and yellowed,
the irises backed and packed
with tarnished tinfoil
seen through the lenses
of old scratched isinglass.
They shifted a little, but not
to return my stare.
—It was more like the tipping
of an object toward the light.
I admired his sullen face,
the mechanism of his jaw,
and then I saw
that from his lower lip
—if you could call it a lip—
grim, wet, and weapon-like,
hung five old pieces of fish-line,
or four and a wire leader
with the swivel still attached,
with all their five big hooks
grown firmly in his mouth.
A green line, frayed at the end
where he broke it, two heavier lines,
and a fine black thread
still crimped from the strain and snap

when it broke and he got away.
Like medals with their ribbons
frayed and wavering,
a five-haired beard of wisdom
trailing from his aching jaw.
I stared and stared
and victory filled up
the little rented boat,
from the pool of bilge
where oil had spread a rainbow
around the rusted engine
to the bailer rusted orange,
the sun-cracked thwarts,
the oarlocks on their strings,
the gunnels—until everything
was rainbow, rainbow, rainbow!
And I let the fish go.

The Bear on the Delhi Road

Earle Birney

Unreal   tall as a myth
by the road the Himalayan bear
is beating the brilliant air
with his crooked arms
About him two men   bare
spindly as locusts   leap

One pulls on a ring
in the great soft nose   His mate
flicks   flicks with a stick
up at the rolling eyes

They have not led him here
down from the fabulous hills
to this bald alien plain
and the clamorous world   to kill
but simply to teach him to dance

They are peaceful both   these spare
men of Kashmir   and the bear
alive is their living   too
If   far on the Delhi way
around him galvanic they dance
it is merely to wear   wear
from his shaggy body the tranced
wish forever to stay

only an ambling bear
four-footed in berries

It is no more joyous for them
in this hot dust to prance
out of reach of the praying claws
sharpened to paw for ants
in the shadows of deodars
It is not easy to free
myth from reality
or rear this fellow up
to lurch   lurch with them
in the tranced dancing of men

An Astrologer's Day

R. K. Narayan

P UNCTUALLY at midday he opened his bag and
spread out his professional equipment, which consisted of a dozen cowrie shells, a square piece of cloth
with obscure mystic charts on it, a notebook, and a bundle of
palmyra writing. His forehead was resplendent with sacred
ash and vermilion, and his eyes sparkled with a sharp abnor-
mal gleam which was really an outcome of a continual searching look for customers, but which his simple clients took to be
a prophetic light and felt comforted. The power of his eyes
was considerably enhanced by their position—placed as they
were between the painted forehead and the dark whiskers
which streamed down his cheeks: even a half-wit's eyes would
sparkle in such a setting. To crown the effect he wound a saf-
fron-coloured turban around his head. This colour scheme
never failed. People were attracted to him as bees are attracted
to cosmos or dahlia stalks. He sat under the boughs of a
spreading tamarind tree which flanked a path running
through the Town Hall Park. It was a remarkable place in
many ways: a surging crowd was always moving up and down
this narrow road morning till night. A variety of trades and
occupations was represented all along its way: medicine sellers, sellers of stolen hardware and junk, magicians, and, above
all, an auctioneer of cheap cloth, who created enough din all
day to attract the whole town. Next to him in vociferousness
came a vendor of fried groundnut, who gave his ware a fancy
name each day, calling it 'Bombay Ice-Cream' one day, and on

the next 'Delhi Almond,' and on the third 'Raja's Delicacy,' and so on and so forth, and people flocked to him. A considerable portion of this crowd dallied before the astrologer too. The astrologer transacted his business by the light of a flare which crackled and smoked up above the groundnut heap nearby. Half the enchantment of the place was due to the fact that it did not have the benefit of municipal lighting. The place was lit up by shop lights. One or two had hissing gaslights, some had naked flares stuck on poles, some were lit up by old cycle lamps, and one or two, like the astrologer's, managed without lights of their own. It was a bewildering criss-cross of light rays and moving shadows. This suited the astrologer very well, for the simple reason that he had not in the least intended to be an astrologer when he began life; and he knew no more of what was going to happen to others than he knew what was going to happen to himself next minute. He was as much a stranger to the stars as were his innocent customers. Yet he said things which pleased and astonished everyone: that was more a matter of study, practice, and shrewd guesswork. All the same, it was as much an honest man's labour as any other, and he deserved the wages he carried home at the end of a day.

He had left his village without any previous thought or plan. If he had continued there he would have carried on the work of his forefathers—namely, tilling the land, living, marrying, and ripening in his cornfield and ancestral home. But that was not to be. He had to leave home without telling anyone, and he could not rest till he left it behind a couple of hundred miles. To a villager it is a great deal, as if an ocean flowed between.

He had a working analysis of mankind's troubles: marriage, money, and the tangles of human ties. Long practice had sharpened his perception. Within five minutes he understood what was wrong. He charged three pies per question, never opened his mouth till the other had spoken for at least ten minutes, which provided him enough stuff for a dozen answers and advices. When he told the person before him, gazing at his palm, 'In many ways you are not getting the fullest results for your efforts,' nine out of ten were disposed to agree with him. Or he questioned: 'Is there any woman in your family, maybe even a distant relative, who is not well disposed towards you?' Or he gave an analysis of character: 'Most of your troubles are due to your nature. How can you be otherwise with Saturn where he is? You have an impetuous nature and a rough exterior.' This endeared him to their hearts immediately, for even the mildest of us loves to think that he has a forbidding exterior.

The nuts vendor blew out his flare and rose to go home. This was a signal for the astrologer to bundle up too, since it left him in darkness except for a little shaft of green light which strayed in from somewhere and touched the ground before him. He picked up his cowrie shells and paraphernalia and was putting them back into his bag when the green shaft of light was blotted out; he looked up and saw a man standing before him. He sensed a possible client and said: 'You look so careworn. It will do you good to sit down for a while and chat with me.' The other grumbled some reply vaguely. The astrologer pressed his invitation; whereupon the other thrust his palm under his nose, saying: 'You call yourself an astrologer?' The astrologer felt challenged and said, tilting the other's palm towards the green shaft of light: 'Yours is a nature . . .' 'Oh, stop that,' the other said. 'Tell me something worth while. . . .'

Our friend felt piqued. 'I charge only three pies per question, and what you get ought to be good enough for your money. . . .' At this the other withdrew his arm, took out an anna, and flung it out to him, saying: 'I have some questions to ask. If I prove you are bluffing, you must return that anna to me with interest.'

'If you find my answers satisfactory, will you give me five rupees?'

'No.'

'Or will you give me eight annas?'

'All right, provided you give me twice as much if you are wrong,' said the stranger. This pact was accepted after a little further argument. The astrologer sent up a prayer to heaven as the other lit a cheroot. The astrologer caught a glimpse of his face by the matchlight. There was a pause as cars hooted on the road, *jutka* drivers swore at their horses, and the babble of the crowd agitated the semi-darkness of the park. The other sat down, sucking his cheroot, puffing out, sat there ruthlessly. The astrologer felt very uncomfortable. 'Here, take your anna back. I am not used to such challenges. It is late for me today. . . .' He made preparations to bundle up. The other held his wrist and said: 'You can't get out of it now. You dragged me in while I was passing.' The astrologer shivered in his grip; and his voice shook and became faint. 'Leave me today. I will speak to you tomorrow.' The other thrust his palm in his face and said: 'Challenge is challenge. Go on.' The astrologer proceeded with his throat drying up: 'There is a woman . . .'

'Stop,' said the other. 'I don't want all that. Shall I succeed in my present search or not? Answer this and go. Otherwise I will not let you go till you disgorge all your coins.' The astrologer muttered a few incantations and replied: 'All right. I will speak. But you will give me a rupee if what I say is convincing? Otherwise I will not open my mouth, and you may do what you like.' After a good deal of haggling the other agreed. The astrologer said: 'You were left for dead. Am I right?'

'Ah, tell me more.'

'A knife has passed through you once?' said the astrologer.

'Good fellow!' He bared his chest to show the scar. 'What else?'

'And then you were pushed into a well nearby in the field. You were left for dead.'

'I should have been dead if some passer-by had not chanced to peep into the well,' exclaimed the other, overwhelmed by enthusiasm. 'When shall I get at him?' he asked, clenching his fist.

'In the next world,' answered the astrologer. 'He died four months ago in a far-off town. You will never see any more of him.' The other groaned on hearing it. The astrologer proceeded:

'Guru Nayak—'

'You know my name!' the other said, taken aback.

'As I know all other things. Guru Nayak, listen carefully to what I have to say. Your village is two days' journey due north of this town. Take the next train and be gone. I see once again great danger to your life if you go from home.' He took out a pinch of sacred ash and held it to him. 'Rub it on your forehead and go home. Never travel southward again, and you will live to be a hundred.'

'Why should I leave home again?' the other said reflectively. 'I was only going away now and then to look for him and to choke out his life if I met him.' He shook his head regretfully. 'He has escaped my hands. I hope at least he died as he deserved.' 'Yes,' said the astrologer. 'He was crushed under a lorry.' The other looked gratified to hear it.

The place was deserted by the time the astrologer picked up his articles and put them into his bag. The green shaft was also gone, leaving the place in darkness and silence. The stranger had gone off into the night, after giving the astrologer a handful of coins.

It was nearly midnight when the astrologer reached home. His wife was waiting for him at the door and demanded an explanation. He flung the coins at her and said: 'Count them. One man gave all that.'

'Twelve and a half annas,' she said, counting. She was overjoyed. 'I can buy some jaggery and coconut tomorrow. The child has been asking for sweets for so many days now. I will prepare some nice stuff for her.'

'The swine has cheated me! He promised me a rupee,' said the astrologer. She looked up at him. 'You look worried. What is wrong?'

'Nothing.'

After dinner, sitting on the *pyol*, he told her: 'Do you know a great load is gone from me today? I thought I had the blood of a man on my hands all these years. That was the reason why I ran away from home, settled here, and married you. He is alive.'

She gasped. 'You tried to kill!'

'Yes, in our village, when I was a silly youngster. We drank, gambled, and quarrelled badly one day—why think of it now? Time to sleep,' he said, yawning, and stretched himself on the *pyol*.

Porphyria's Lover

Robert Browning

The rain set early in to-night,
  The sullen wind was soon awake,
It tore the elm-tops down for spite,
  And did its worst to vex the lake:
I listened with heart fit to break.
When glided in Porphyria; straight
  She shut the cold out and the storm,
And kneeled and made the cheerless grate
  Blaze up, and all the cottage warm;
Which done, she rose, and from her form
Withdrew the dripping cloak and shawl,
  And laid her soiled gloves by, untied
Her hat and let the damp hair fall,
  And, last, she sat down by my side
And called me. When no voice replied,
She put my arm about her waist,
  And made her smooth white shoulder bare
And all her yellow hair displaced,
  And, stooping, made my cheek lie there,
And spread, o'er all, her yellow hair,
Murmuring how she loved me—she
  Too weak, for all her heart's endeavor,
To set its struggling passion free
  From pride, and vainer ties dissever,
And give herself to me forever.
But passion sometimes would prevail,

Nor could tonight's gay feast restrain
A sudden thought of one so pale
   For love of her, and all in vain:
So, she was come through wind and rain
Be sure I looked up at her eyes
   Happy and proud; at last I knew
Porphyria worshipped me; surprise
   Made my heart swell, and still it grew
While I debated what to do.
That moment she was mine, mine, fair,
   Perfectly pure and good: I found
A thing to do, and all her hair
   In one long yellow string I wound
Three times her little throat around,
And strangled her. No pain felt she;
   I am quite sure she felt no pain.
As a shut bud that holds a bee,
   I warily opened her lids: again
Laughed the blue eyes without a stain.
And I untightened next the tress
   About her neck; her cheek once more
Blushed bright beneath my burning kiss:
   I propped her head up as before,
Only, this time my shoulder bore
Her head, which droops upon it still:
   The smiling rosy little head,
So glad it has its utmost will,
   That all it scorned at once is fled,
And I, its love, am gained instead!
Porphyria's love: she guessed not how
   Her darling one wish would be heard.
And thus we sit together now,
   And all night long we have not stirred,
And yet God has not said a word!

The Late Man

Andreas Schroeder

O N the morning after the storm, the fishermen got up earlier than usual to survey the damage and repair what could be saved. Unusually strong winds and rain had scattered the nets and flattened gardens, bushes, even trees. Fishing boats lay strewn about the beach like broken teeth. Everywhere an exhausted silence hung limply; even the occasional seagull screech seemed blunted and uncertain. Across the mud-flats the faint rush of breakers seemed to fade, though the tide was coming in, slowly and without apparent conviction.

At this time in the morning the fishermen rarely spoke. They arranged their lines, oiled pulleys, checked over their engines and wordlessly pushed out to sea. To break the fragile silence of the first few hours would have been like bursting a delicate membrane without preparation; it was tacitly understood that a man needed more time to clear away in his mind the rubble and destruction of the preceding night, than was available to him between his getting up and the launching of his boat. Even after they had cleared the beach and set their course for the large fishing-grounds farther north, the fishermen rarely raised their voices—as if in instinctive respect for the precariousness of the human mind launched before sunrise on an uncertain sea.

But someone broke the silence that morning; as the last remaining boats poled into deeper water to lower their engines, a young bearded fisherman pointed to a single unattended boat lying on its side on the beach and asked in a low voice: "Where's he?"

The man being addressed looked startled, puzzled, then shrugged his shoulders.

The bearded fisherman risked a further offence. "Could he be sick, d'you think?"

There was no response. The other man slid his oar into the water and pushed them off.

A man opens his cabin door and steps into view. He is the late man, the man whose boat lies untouched on the beach below his cabin. There is nothing particularly unusual about this man except perhaps a certain slight hesitance in his manner; the hesitance of a man for whom the world became at some point intensely suspect, for whom, at that point, a glass on a table became less and less a glass on a table and more and more a thing too strange and amazing to grasp by name. As he stands in his doorway, his hand rests gingerly on the frame, as if constantly ready in case of attack.

About fifteen minutes have passed since the last boat was launched and the late man stepped from his cabin. Now, his boat ready and his outboard spluttering half-submerged, he pushes off and follows the fleet toward the fishing-grounds.

A few hours later the fishing village begins to yawn, stretch and get up; children and fishwives clutter the streets and tangle the air with punctuation marks.

When they return in the early evening and pull their boats out of the water above the high-tide markers, the late man is not with them. During the interval of time between the last fisherman's ascent from his stranded boat to his waiting dinner and the late man's arrival at the launching site fifteen minutes later, silence holds the breach like an indrawn breath. The sound of his prow on the pebbles, therefore, grates in an unusually harsh way on the nerves of the woman waiting for him above the high-tide markers. He has caught fewer fish than the other fishermen.

The next morning the late man appears at his cabin door half an hour after the fisherman have left the beach. Their boats are already vague in the distance when he finally manages to haul his boat to the water-line, which has by this time fallen far below his landing place with the receding tide. He seems somehow weakened, older, leaning wearily against the wheel of his boat. When the fishermen return that night he is an uncertain speck on the horizon, half an hour behind the last of the fishing fleet, and when the catch is scored, he has caught fewer fish than the day before.

Around noon the following day the boats were anchored in clusters to share both lunch and small-talk on the fishing-grounds, and the conversation turned to the late man. "Can't figure 'im out," one fisherman mused, pulling thoughtfully at his beard. "Won't tell nobody what's wrong." "Ain't sayin' a thing," another agreed. "Asked him yesterday what the problem was, but I'll be damned if he didn't seem like he wasn't even listening." There was a pause as if to let the spoken words disperse. Then: "Sea can do that to a man. Catches up with him, it does." The speaker slowly shook his head, threw an orange peel overboard, then absently ignored a deck-hand who had asked him what he meant. The deck-hand finally turned away, assuming his question was naive; he was new in the fleet and often found himself going unanswered. As it was, he was already on the other side of the boat when the old man muttered his answer to no one in particular: "I don't know what happens; I just know it does. Ain't no man can whirl the world by hand."

The next morning the late man launched his boat some forty-five minutes after the fleet had left the beach.

Little is known of the late man's history, though this is not realized until he first begins to attract attention by his mystifying dislocation of schedule; suddenly everyone rummages about in their memory for initial impressions, former opinions, latent suspicions, old predictions. Little in the way of substantial information is collected. It is generally agreed that he is a relatively young man, hard-working and "well-disciplined". Some felt him to be a little too much given to reflection, but one suspects this is said chiefly in reaction to his if not exactly anti-social, at least fairly reticent manner. He cares little for other people, though he has been known to go to the aid of a complete stranger for no reason. A slightly more observant villager notes his peculiar tendency to touch (with a curiously disbelieving air) whatever happens to be around him; the remark is received in uncertain silence. Many frankly admit they have no idea what to make of the whole business, and that the man is probably simply under the attack of some unsettling virus. This fails to explain, however (as someone quickly points out), his consistent, almost plan-like deceleration of pace in relation to the normal fishing schedule of the village—by this time he is reported leaving the beach a full three hours after the last of the other boats has been launched.

By the time the late man pulls his boat from the water, the sun is little more than an almost-submerged leer on a mindless horizon and the waves have jelled to heavy, slowly swirling jibes. Night winds begin to cover the eastern part of the sky with a thick, cumulous ceiling of ridicule. Sardonic chuckles ripple along the water line where the undertow pursues an endless foreplay with beach gravel. The late man stands motionless, looking strangely as if he belongs neither to the water nor the land; his face is a ploughed field but his eyes dart about the beach like frightened piranhas. His boat is a crazily tilted sneer lying on its side in the pebbles, with rope dangling from the prow like corded spittle. Wave upon wave of curling laughter lampoons the beach. Everywhere, everything grins. The late man no longer defends himself. He has committed the blunder of allowing himself and the universe to discover his detective activities, his secret investigations into the nature and composition of himself and whatever he finds it possible to apprehend. But he has allowed this discovery prematurely, before he has had time to properly anaesthetize his specimens, and now, suddenly aware of a spy in their midst, they have disintegrated into countless labyrinthine possibilities and traps and the late man is cut off without the possibility of retreat.

He has long since given up trying to sledge-hammer his brain to sleep.

But a violated universe will not be satisfied with the simple deflection of an inquisitive mind, and as if to make certain that such a trespassing will never again be possible, it has turned glaring spotlights against the late man's brain, blinding and overwhelming it with confusion and derision. Stiffly aligned principles and corollaries suddenly go limp and begin to collapse; endless qualifications overrun simple premises and leave behind a shambles of tattered and useless shreds of belief. Above all, the horror is set creeping up the back stairs of the late man's mind that all this is beyond his control, and that like a retaining pin pulled from a spring-loaded wheel, this destruction will continue relentlessly until it has unrolled the tension from the spring.

There appears to be little he can do but to hold on until all is done, and to hope that he does not become so weakened in the process as to fall prey to a useless madness.

In a matter of months the departures and arrivals of the late man and the fishing fleet have diverged to such an extent that the returning fishermen see the late man's boat heading toward them at dusk, on its way north toward open water. He stands huddled over his wheel, eyes staring unseeing at the darkening horizon as if in purposeful blindness. The fishing fleet parts to let him pass; though no one appears to understand, everyone sees the desperate undertow in his eyes and says nothing. When all the boats are secured and the gear locked away, the late man is a dissolving blotch against black evening. A few moments later he is gone.

The late man had returned the previous morning with no fish at all.

As he sat down to dinner, the young fisherman who had asked about the late man early one morning suddenly spoke of him to his wife. "Nobody knows anything, or they won't say anything. Everybody pretends to ignore him. I've got to find out."

His wife said nothing. He looked at her curiously, then threw down his knife. "Well damn it, here's a man digging his own grave in plain view of a whole fishing village, and nobody has the guts to look into the matter." His wife remained silent but a worried look began to unsettle her face. The young fisherman stood up abruptly. "I'm going to find out," he said, reaching for his squall-jacket and opening the door. "Even if for no other reason than a simple matter of self-defence!" he added as the door slammed shut. Footsteps receded from the cabin. Within minutes the sound of his outboard began to move across the bay toward the fishing grounds and the open sea.

For a time the young fisherman directs his boat through thick total darkness; a bulging cloud cover muffles the moon and the night sways and sidesteps in ponderous movements that are blind but everywhere. The occasional clear splash falls short among the sluggish gurgle and sagging cough of deep-water waves beneath the keel. The young fisherman peers at the bleakness but steers his boat by instinct.

As he moves farther and farther into deeper water the night begins to thin out; his eyes detect edges, outlines, occasional glimpses of phosphoric glitter—eventually the moon disentangles from the clouds and trudges high into the sky, spraying a fine shower of thin light over the fishing grounds. By this time the young fisherman can make out the dark shape of the late man's boat, lying at anchor on his starboard side. The booms on the boat before him are out, trailing thin glistening lines into the water. The late man is fishing.

The young fisherman sits unmoving at his wheel, uncertain as to what should follow. Possibilities dart in and out of his mind, unwilling to bite. He waits, his brain idling slowly, his thoughts loose.

A creak from a rusty tackle interrupts the silence. A glass float dips and scrambles; the late man comes alive and begins to reel it in. A strike.

The young fisherman straightens up and strains to see. The glass float tugs and splashes at the end of a stiff line; the late man's figure curves against the mast, his arms taut like two rigid claws shaking with exertion. The young fisherman feels an instinctive excitement thrill through his body as if the strike were his own. *Something huge is on the end of that line.*

The glass float is almost at boat's edge, momentarily calmer. The late man reaches for his fishnet and plunges it over the side, scooping carefully. His back is turned to the young fisherman, obscuring the float as he brings it to the boat's side. The fishnet rises from the water, then stops.

Surprised, the young fisherman leans forward but sees only the hunched back of the late man leaning over his net. A fierce rippling movement shakes the arm holding the handle as something twists and writhes in the meshes, but the late man makes no move to pull it into the boat. Ten minutes pass; the late man still stands bent over his net, gazing at his catch. The young fisherman is unable to see his face.

Finally, in a slow but deliberate movement, the late man empties his net into the sea and straightens up.

The young fisherman watches, still dumfounded, as the late man repeats the same procedure moments later when another line snaps alive. This time his demeanor seems to indicate recognition or less interest; a short look suffices to make him empty the net again. After a short pause a third float begins to bob and the late man reels it in. Half an hour later he is still engrossed in the net's contents, ignoring all the other lines which are jerking at the boom. Bent over the gunwhale, his hair blowing about his head like spray in the wind, the man stares at his catch in silence, then throws it back into the sea.

As a faint paleness begins to tinge the outermost edges of the dark, the young fisherman stands up stiffly, a nervous flutter in his stomach, strangely excited yet uncertain why. He detects traces of the intoxication of discovery in his feelings, though he has no idea what he has discovered or realized.

Carefully pulling out his oars, he mounts them in the oarlocks and prepares to slip away. By the time the sun appears he will be back in the bay and his cabin. Then there will be time to think.

A small sound from the other boat stops his raised oars short. The late man has emptied his net and stepped back toward the mast. As he half-turns to re-apply bait to one of the lines the young fisherman catches a glimpse of the late man's face. He almost drops his oars.

The late man's face is totally disfigured. Crumbled skin, twitching lips and bleached white hair, he is suddenly old—an uncertain fool barely able to hold his balance in the rocking boat. The young fisherman is stunned. The late man was of the same generation as the others in the fishing fleet—chronologically about thirty years old. Now he looks three times that age.

But there is no time to lose; the horizon is becoming a thin pencil-line of light across the dark and he will be discovered. Stealthily moving his oars, the young fisherman pulls away toward the south and the fishing village.

As his boat moves into the bay, he sees the first cabin doors opening and fishermen walking down the beach toward their boats. Several of them look up, surprised to see his incoming boat at such an odd time. Obviously his wife has said nothing. He steers toward an unused part of the beach and runs his boat aground.

There, his boat bouncing slightly to the rhythm of his fading wash, he sat on the bow and twisted a piece of rope between his fingers; uncertain, almost nervous, uncertain again. The spreading sun warmed his back as he sat, but his stomach remained cold and unsettled; he felt the desperate urge to run, to commit a violence, tear something to shreds, but somehow he was numbed or simply unable to move. For no apparent reason something seemed to have snapped; his senses coiled and bunched in twisting knots, thoughts whirled in ever-tightening circles about his head and a steadily mounting pressure threatened to explode inside him like a surfacing deepwater fish.

Then the faint growl from a distant engine punctured the silence and the tension drained away with an almost audible hiss. The young fisherman looked over his shoulder and watched the late man's boat increase toward the bay. Several of the other fisherman paused and shaded their eyes. For a short while everything hung in suspension . . .

Suddenly the late man's boat is in the bay, its engine silent, drifting toward the beach. As its prow gouges into the sand the late man struggles feebly to climb off the deck onto the gravel, half-falling several times in the process. Then hoisting the bow rope over his shoulder, he attempts to pull his boat higher up onto the beach.

Later, after the late man had been buried and the fishermen had returned to their boats, the young fisherman was heard to say that in a totally paralyzed landscape, the only moving thing had been the late man trying to beach his boat. They had watched him for an incredibly long time, trying to raise the bow above the gravel, and when he finally collapsed, still no one had moved. When they eventually began to climb down toward the fallen figure, the landscape seemed to stretch and expand in every direction and they walked for hours before reaching him. They found him lying on his back, his face contorted with a mixture of agony and amazement; it was the oldest face they had ever seen. So they had buried him, quietly and without looking at each other, and the young fisherman had beached the boat. The next morning, due possibly to the tiring events of the preceding night and day, the young fisherman slept a little longer, and eventually launched his boat some fifteen minutes after the last of the fishing boats had cleared the bay.

A Trip for Mrs. Taylor

Hugh Garner

Characters

MRS. TAYLOR 75; an old-age pensioner
MRS. CONNELL 50; a landlady
A SOLDIER 21;
A YOUNG WOMAN 25; a young mother of two
GARY; a small boy
NEWSY; a railroad news butcher
CONDUCTOR 60; typical railroad conductor
BUS DRIVER; a city bus driver

Scene 1:

A cheap rooming-house room with a door leading to an up-stairs hallway. The furniture consists of a nondescript metal bed on which is an open suitcase, a scruffy kitchen table and two kitchen chairs, a dresser with a mirror, and a low com-mode upon which is a single-burner electric hotplate holding a small kettle. A tall cardboard wardrobe stands beside the door, its top shelf holding a few pieces of chinaware and two or three cans of food. Hanging beneath the shelf are a couple of dresses and a winter coat. On the dresser is a cheap alarm clock, a large black Bible, a milk bottle holding some drooping flowers, brush and comb, and two framed photographs, one of a moustached workman wearing 1929 Sunday clothes, the other of two young men in World War Two army uniforms.

Mrs. Taylor sits at the table eating a slice of bread and marmalade. On the table are a teapot, cup and saucer, a half loaf of bread, jar of marmalade, and a can of evaporated milk. Mrs. Taylor is fully dressed, wearing a high-collared black dress, black stockings, and well polished but run-down black shoes. Her white hair is combed back into a bun.

There is a soft but authoritative knock at the door.

MRS. TAYLOR: (*With a startled glance at the door, then around the room*) Yes! Who is it?

MRS. CONNELL: It's me. Mrs. Connell.

MRS. TAYLOR: Just a minute! (*Scoops the bread and marmalade from the table and hurriedly shoves them onto a shelf in the commode, then opens the door*)

MRS. CONNELL: (*Enters, yawning*) Why, you're all dressed up! What's the matter? (*She is wearing a dressing gown.*)

MRS. TAYLOR: Nothing. I've been up since five o'clock. I hope I didn't disturb anybody?

MRS. CONNELL: (*Looking around the room*) I didn't hear any complaints, and you didn't disturb me, dear. I was awake anyway. It's my bladder again.

MRS. TAYLOR: Oh, I'm so sorry.

MRS. CONNELL: (*Transfers her inspection to Mrs. Taylor*) Where you goin', to a funeral?

MRS. TAYLOR: (*Looking down at herself*) No.

MRS. CONNELL: (*Stares at suitcase on the bed*) Are you goin' away?

MRS. TAYLOR: (*Hurriedly, with a smile*) Not for long.

MRS. CONNELL: Well, it beats all!

MRS. TAYLOR: I'm just going on a little trip.

MRS. CONNELL: (*Petulant*) I thought at least you'd tell me. You were goin' without even lettin' me know.

MRS. TAYLOR: No! No, it isn't—it isn't like that at all, Mrs. Connell.

MRS. CONNELL: Well—(*Walks to the bed and sits down upon it, peering into the empty suitcase*) Are you leavin' town? Takin' a bus?

MRS. TAYLOR: No, I'm catching a train.

MRS. CONNELL: (*Smiles*) That'll be nice. I always like trains. Most of my travellin' has been on trains. They got busses beat all hollow. Joe and me went clear out to the Coast and back on a train once. That was when he was a company representative, of course. Back in the Depression.

MRS. TAYLOR: Yes, it must have been nice. (*Pulls a small washbowl from beneath the electric plate and places it on the table. Puts her cup and saucer, knife, spoon, etc. in it.*)

MRS. CONNELL: Did you hear the Graham's baby coughin' all night?

MRS. TAYLOR:	No.
MRS. CONNELL:	All night I heard it. Sounded like croup to me.
MRS. TAYLOR:	Poor little thing. *(Pours some water into washbowl from the kettle. Gets a dishcloth from the commode and begins washing her dishes. Mrs. Connell makes a useless gesture of fixing her hair.)*
MRS. CONNELL:	I musta nodded off comin' on mornin'. I didn't hear you gettin' up, nor washin' up neither.
MRS. TAYLOR:	*(Takes a dishtowel from a short piece of clothesline across the corner of the room and wipes her dishes. Then she begins putting them away on the top shelf of the wardrobe.)* I kept as quiet as I could. I only gave myself a lick 'n' a spit as they say.
MRS. CONNELL:	*(Pontifically)* In this weather it's no use tryin' to keep clean, Mrs. Taylor. If this heat wave doesn't let up soon I don't know what'll become of us. Joe said it was a hundred-'n'-twenty down at the shop yesterday.
MRS. TAYLOR:	My goodness! *(She folds the towel carefully and places it back in its place.)*
MRS. CONNELL:	I read in last night's paper where six people died of the heat right here in the city. They say it's hard on them that's over fifty.
MRS. TAYLOR:	It doesn't bother me too much. I'm so thin now....
MRS. CONNELL:	Lucky you! You'll be gettin' away from it for a while.
MRS. TAYLOR:	*(Wiping the top of the table with the dishcloth)* I'm so excited I don't know what I'm doing! *(Smiles happily)* It's been years since I went away like this.
MRS. CONNELL:	It seems funny you didn't mention goin' away to me before.
MRS. TAYLOR:	*(Easing herself onto a chair)* I didn't think about it till yesterday. I was downtown for a walk and I went into the station to sit down for a minute— the streets were like an oven—and when I saw everybody going away I made up my mind to go too. I walked right over and bought a ticket.
MRS. CONNELL:	Did you win a sweepstakes or somep'n?
MRS. TAYLOR:	*(Laughs)* No. *(Looks into the past, wearing a*

beatific smile) It came over me all at once. It reminded me of the times in the summer when me and Bert and the boys used to go up to my cousin Flora's in Jamesville. I got the same feeling I used to get then—a warm, picnicky feeling.

MRS. CONNELL: Is that where you're goin' now?

MRS. TAYLOR: To Flora's! No, she's been dead since the 'flu epidemic in 'nineteen.

MRS. CONNELL: *(Petulant)* I'm not one to pry, Mrs. Taylor, you know that, but it seems kind of funny you won't tell me where you're goin'.

MRS. TAYLOR: *(Stands up)* It—well, it's kind of a secret. I'll tell you all about it when I come back.

MRS. CONNELL: *(Reluctantly)* Well, all right then.

Mrs. Taylor picks up the dishpan and exits through the door to empty it. In the moment or two before she comes back, Mrs. Connell gets up from the bed and peers into the wardrobe. She shakes her head sadly. When she hears Mrs. Taylor returning she rushes back to the bed and sits down on the edge of it.

MRS. TAYLOR: *(Enters and glances at the clock on the dresser)* I didn't need to get up so early, I guess. *(Places the dishpan in the bottom of the commode)*

MRS. CONNELL: I'm always the same way.

Mrs. Taylor goes to the wardrobe, takes down a heavy dress, and carries it to the side of the bed.

MRS. CONNELL: You're not takin' that heavy thing with you surely?

MRS. TAYLOR: *(Folds the dress carefully and places it in the suitcase)* Why yes.

MRS. CONNELL: But, my dear, it's too heavy for this time of year. What is it, velvet?

MRS. TAYLOR: Yes. It's the dress Mrs. Eisen gave me last winter for helping her with her cleaning.

MRS. CONNELL: *(Suspiciously)* You're sure you're not leavin' for good?

MRS. TAYLOR: *(Stops on her way to the closet, turns)* My goodness no!

MRS. CONNELL: *(Hurt)* Any time you want to find accommodations somewhere else, you're always free to go, you know.

MRS. TAYLOR: I'm not leaving, Mrs. Connell. *(Goes to wardrobe*

	and takes down a blouse and skirt) It's just that I think packing up and everything is part of the fun of a trip. *(Carries blouse and skirt to the bed)*
MRS. CONNELL:	I hate packin', myself.
	Mrs. Taylor puts the blouse and skirt in the suitcase. Goes to the dresser and from a drawer takes some clean folded underwear, handkerchiefs, and black lisle stockings. From another drawer a clean towel and bar of soap in its wrapper. Carries these things to the bed and places them in the suitcase.
MRS. CONNELL:	*(Watching her)* That bag is too big for what you've got. Let me lend you the small one that Edna gave me last Christmas. It's a light one. *(Brags)* It's air-weight.
MRS. TAYLOR:	Thanks, but this'll do fine. I've got some more things to put in yet. *(Takes the two framed photographs from the top of the dresser, smiles at them for a moment, then cleans their glass with her sleeve.)*
MRS. CONNELL:	You takin' them too!
MRS. TAYLOR:	*(Places the photos in the suitcase)* I couldn't leave them behind.
MRS. CONNELL:	*(Laughs and slaps her hands on her thighs)* I've got it now! Johnny sent you the money to go see your grandchildren! Isn't that ni—
MRS. TAYLOR:	I'm paying my own fare for this trip.
MRS. CONNELL:	*(Inquisitive)* But isn't that expensive? Now I know you won a sweepstake. *(Mrs. Taylor smiles and shakes her head.)* It must be nice to be rich. *(An exaggerated primping of her hair)* When I get the old-age pension myself, I'm gonna take trips too.
MRS. TAYLOR:	*(Sits down on a chair and becomes serious)* Don't wish it on yourself, Mrs. Connell. It might turn out different for you, with your husband living and everything, but it's a struggle, let me tell you, when you're alone. It's nothing but scrimp and scrape all the time to make ends meet. *(Watches her hands as she twists them in her lap)*
MRS. CONNELL:	Hey listen, Mrs. Taylor, I wasn't makin' fun of you! Listen, I know what a struggle you have gettin' along on a few lousy dollars a month.

	(Angrily) If I had my way I'd make the crooks up in . . .
MRS. TAYLOR:	It's not only the money. There's the terrible loneliness too. You don't know what it's like to be cooped up month after month in a dreary little room, without even a radio to keep you company. Without even a cat or a dog or a—or a canary. Nothing but the four walls. *(Indicates them with a wave of her hand)* And a bed, a dresser, and a—an electric plate.
MRS. CONNELL:	But my dear, I don't mind you havin' a radio or—or a canary.
MRS. TAYLOR:	*(Wry smile)* You know I couldn't afford them.
MRS. CONNELL:	Well, it seems to me that your son Johnny could help you out once in a while. There he is with a good job and everythin'—
MRS. TAYLOR:	*(Emphatically)* Johnny's a good boy. He's just—forgetful, that's all.
MRS. CONNELL:	*(Takes the photograph of the two young soldiers from the suitcase)* I always forget which one of these is Johnny.
MRS. TAYLOR:	*(Gets up from the chair and sits beside Mrs. Connell on the edge of the bed)* The one on the right.
MRS. CONNELL:	*(Points at the picture)* I'll bet this one wouldn't have let you live like this if he hadn't—if he was here. That's Bert, isn't it?
MRS. TAYLOR:	He was young Bert. *(Smiles fondly at the photo)* We named him after his father.
MRS. CONNELL:	*(Puts the photograph in the suitcase)* He was a fine-lookin' boy.
MRS. TAYLOR:	Both my boys were fine. Johnny's a fine boy too.
MRS. CONNELL:	*(Puts her arm around Mrs. Taylor's shoulder)* I know he is, dear.
MRS. TAYLOR:	Bert was no better than Johnny.
MRS. CONNELL:	I didn't mean anythin' by what I said. I do think though that after you sendin' him the pipe last Christmas and spendin' all the time you did crochetin' them runners for his wife, that he'd have sent you the fare to go and see your grandchildren. *(Mrs. Taylor walks to the dresser and takes a small tissue-wrapped package from a drawer.)* I'm sure you'd be happier livin' with your

own kith and kin than alone like this. If it was me I'd write to him and—

MRS. TAYLOR: Johnny asked me to go and live with him and Ruth right after the war, but I wouldn't. I've seen women who go and live with their sons and daughters-in-law. There's always squabbling, and they end up either as nuisances or a built-in babysitter. I was always independent, and I ran my own house when I was young. I'll run it now *(Gestures)* even as it is, now I'm old.

MRS. CONNELL: Well, he could ask you down for a visit, and pay your way. *(Catches sight of package in Mrs. Taylor's hand)* What's that you've got?

MRS. TAYLOR: Just some old jewelry.

MRS. CONNELL: *(Holds out her hand)* I've never seen it before. Let's see it, dear. *(Mrs. Taylor unwraps a gold locket and gold chain bangle bearing a small lock, shaped like a heart, and hands them to Mrs. Connell.)* They're lovely!

MRS. TAYLOR: I've had them for years and years.

MRS. CONNELL: I always say old jewelry's better than the junk they're peddlin' nowadays. *(Opens the locket and peers inside)* My, who's the handsome gallant here!

MRS. TAYLOR: *(Please)* That's Bert, my husband. The picture was taken just after we were married.

MRS. CONNELL: He looks like a banker.

MRS. TAYLOR: *(Laughs)* When that was taken he was a teamster for a lumber company.

MRS. CONNELL: It was honest work.

MRS. TAYLOR: *(Takes the locket and stares at the photograph)* He was always a good provider, till he took sick. It took all our savings. And with the boys being overseas at the time and all . . .

MRS. CONNELL: You don't need to tell me how it is. *(Admires the other pieces of jewelry)* This bangle is beautiful. My mother had one exactly like it, but she gave it to my sister Amy just before she passed away. Have you got the key for it?

MRS. TAYLOR: *(Slips the bangle over her wrist)* I lost the key a long time ago, but my hand is so thin now I can put it on without undoing it.

MRS. CONNELL: Put the locket on too, Mrs. Taylor.

	Mrs. Taylor fastens the chain of the locket around her neck, and admires herself in the dresser mirror. Mrs. Connell gets up from the bed and joins her in front of the dresser.
MRS. CONNELL:	Why, you look just like a lady! Like Lady—like Lady Godiva! You look real elegant! *(Mrs. Taylor takes a box of rouge from the dresser drawer and with a guilty wink at her companion rubs a bit of it on her cheeks.)* Whee! *(Both laugh conspiratorially.)* Don't be pickin' up no movie stars on the train! *(Mrs. Taylor takes a straw flower-bordered hat from the bottom drawer of the dresser. Mrs. Connell reaches for it, and then holds it in her hand, admiring it.)* My goodness! A new hat too!
MRS. TAYLOR:	*(Beaming)* I've had it for ages, silly. The flowers are new though. I bought them at the five-and-ten.
MRS. CONNELL:	*(Puts the hat on top of her uncombed hair and with her hands on her hips gazes at herself in the mirror. Pulling a face)* Did you ever see anything so repulsive in your life?
MAN'S VOICE:	*(Coming from downstairs)* Clara!
MRS. CONNELL:	*(Removing the hat and handing it to Mrs. Taylor)* There's the bull-of-the-woods. *(Shouts)* I'm coming! Keep your shirt on! *(To Mrs. Taylor)* Drop in on your way out. *(Looks at the clock)* I hope I haven't made you late. What time does your train leave?
MRS. TAYLOR:	*(Places the hat on the dresser)* Eight o'clock— that's eight Standard Time.
MRS. CONNELL:	What's that, seven our time?
MRS. TAYLOR:	No, nine.
MRS. CONNELL:	Why, you've got hours yet! Look, dear, you lie down for a while. As soon as I get his lordship off to work I'll come back and see you.
MAN'S VOICE:	*(From downstairs)* Clara!
MRS. CONNELL:	Oh shut up! *(She exits.)*
	As soon as the landlady has gone, Mrs. Taylor checks the contents of her suitcase, smiling happily to herself. She begins to fasten the case, then halts as she remembers something she has left out. She walks to the dresser and takes a large

*heavy Bible from the bottom drawer. She weighs
it in her hands in indecision, then brushes it
lovingly with her sleeve before carrying it to the
bed. She opens the suitcase and makes a place for
the Bible beneath the clothing. Then she fastens
the case again with an air of finality and lifts it
heavily to the floor. She lies down on the bed and
stares at the ceiling, a pleasurable smile of
anticipation lighting her face.*

CURTAIN

Scene 2:

*The interior of a large city railroad station on a summer
morning. There is an archway above which is a sign "Track
12". To the side of this archway a sign reads "Lakeshore
Express" and beneath it, from top to bottom, are signs fitted
in slots: Oshawa, Port Hope, Belleville, Kingston, Brockville,
Cornwall, Montreal. The archway is flanked by a pair of waist-
high iron railings, and a railroad gateman sits on a tall wooden
stool. There is a queue of waiting passengers lined up before
the gate.*

    *Mrs. Taylor comes on stage accompanied by a young soldier
carrying her suitcase. They come to a halt away from the line
of people. Mrs. Taylor wears her flowered hat and is carrying a
worn leather purse. The soldier lowers her suitcase to the
floor.*

MRS. TAYLOR: *(Excited and out of breath)* I'm glad I made it in
time.

SOLDIER: *(Glances at the queue and then at his watch)* The
train doesn't leave for a half hour yet.

MRS. TAYLOR: I know, but I was afraid to miss it. You see, I've
been looking forward to this trip for so long.

SOLDIER: Have you bought your ticket yet?

MRS. TAYLOR: Yes, thank you. I bought it yesterday.

SOLDIER: That was a good idea. *(Points behind him at the
gateman)* You'll have to show it to him.

MRS. TAYLOR: Yes. *(Glances at the gateman and back again)* It
was good of you to carry my bag from the street. I
don't think I'd have been able to carry it all that
way by myself.

SOLDIER: It was no trouble at all. It sure is heavy though. *(Smiles)* What are you carrying in it, gold bricks?

MRS. TAYLOR: *(Serious)* Oh no! It's just my things. *(Notices he is joking and smiles)* I've got my Bible in it. It belonged to my husband's family for years. I knew it would weigh me down, but I just couldn't go anywhere without it. *(The Soldier nods.)*

ANNOUNCER'S VOICE: Mr. C.A. Staples, come to the Green Light please! Mr. C.A. Staples, come to the Green Light please!

MRS. TAYLOR: You're pretty young to be in the army.

SOLDIER: I'm twenty-one. Starting my second hitch.

MRS. TAYLOR: Are you taking the Montreal train?

SOLDIER: No, I'm going north to the camp I'm stationed at. *(Looks across the station)* Everybody in the city seems to be taking my train. I hope I get a seat.

MRS. TAYLOR: Oh, I hope you do too! Here I am gabbing with you, and—

SOLDIER: It's okay. I'll get a seat all right.

MRS. TAYLOR: Have you been visiting your mother?

SOLDIER: My mother! *(Begins to laugh but changes his mind)* No. That is—well, my people live in Red Deer, Alberta.

MRS. TAYLOR: My goodness! Away out there?

ANNOUNCER'S VOICE: Last call for the northbound train! Passengers for Barrie, Camp Borden, Bala, Muskoka, MacTier, North Bay, and Sudbury. Train now leaving on Track Seven! A-a-a-all a-b-o-o-oard!

MRS. TAYLOR: That's your train! Don't miss it.

SOLDIER: I don't suppose it'll matter much whether I do or not.

MRS. TAYLOR: Is there another one later?

SOLDIER: No, but I've overstayed my leave anyhow.

MRS. TAYLOR: Well, they might let you off if you go back now. It'll be much worse for you the longer you stay away.

SOLDIER: *(Smiles down at her)* Don't worry about me. I'll carry your bag over to the end of the line-up for your train. *(Picks up the bag and with Mrs. Taylor following him, puts it down at the end of the queue.)* Will you be able to manage with it now?

MRS. TAYLOR: I'll manage fine now, thank you.

SOLDIER: Goodbye. *(Starts to walk away)*

MRS. TAYLOR: Son! *(The Soldier stops and turns.)* I didn't mean to butt into your business. For a minute ... Well, you see, both my own boys were soldiers in the war. The youngest one, Bert—named after his father—well, he didn't come back. Just for a minute you reminded me—

SOLDIER: *(Walks over quickly and kisses her on the cheek)* It's okay, ma'am. *(Smiles)* Goodbye—goodbye, Ma. *(Swings around and hurries away)*

MRS. TAYLOR: Goodbye, son—and thank you! *(The Soldier exits.)* Good luck! Good luck to you, son. *(Stares after him)*

The queue begins moving towards the archway. A man picks up Mrs. Taylor's bag and carrying it as well as his own walks past the gatekeeper. Mrs. Taylor pulls a small pasteboard ticket from her purse and shows it to the gatekeeper as she passes.

CURTAIN

Scene 3:

A section of a railway day-coach. We see one line of seats, as if from the cut-away opposite wall of the car. On one of the seats sits a young woman holding a blanket-wrapped baby. Between her and the window, on the seat, are a pair of paper shopping bags presumably filled with food, baby bottles, diapers, etc. Next to her, near the aisle, sits a five-year-old boy. On the seat between the boy and his mother lies a large celluloid rattle. The boy is wearing light summer clothes, and is bored and restless. His mother is neatly but cheaply dressed in summer clothing, probably Levis and a blouse or sweater. She has the harried, tired look of a woman travelling with young children. People pass down the aisle of the coach searching for seats. A fat man carrying a suitcase makes as if to take the empty seat opposite the young woman with the children, then changes his mind and moves on. The young woman places the baby on the empty, opposite-seat, and places the shopping bags on it too. The young boy picks up the rattle and shakes it loudly while his mother is busy with the baby and the shopping bags.

YOUNG WOMAN: Gary, stop that right now! *(Takes the rattle from him)*

Mrs. Taylor enters the car, lugging her heavy bag, and pauses at the end of the seat holding the baby and the Young Woman's paper bags. She droops, leans against the seat and lowers the bag to the floor. She smiles down at the sleeping baby, then at the Young Woman.

YOUNG WOMAN: *(Lifts little boy to floor)* Gary, you sit over there at the window and watch the choo-choos. Mind the baby now! *(The small boy moves to the seat opposite his mother, and presses his face against the window, staring outside. The Young Woman indicating the seat vacated by the boy, smiles up at Mrs. Taylor.)* You can sit here if you like.

MRS. TAYLOR: Thank you. *(She shoves her suitcase along the floor between the seats and sits down gratefully.)*

YOUNG WOMAN: Would you like me to put your bag up on the rack?

MRS. TAYLOR: It'll be all right there. That is if it won't be in your way?

YOUNG WOMAN: No. It's all right there.

MRS. TAYLOR: *(Shaking the neck of her dress)* It's awfully warm, isn't it?

YOUNG WOMAN: I'll say! *(She bends forward in the seat.)* Gary, be still before you kick the baby.

MRS. TAYLOR: *(Looking at the little boy)* It's the heat that makes them restless.

YOUNG WOMAN: *(Sits up straight again)* He's been a little devil all morning. He thinks he can get away with it on a train.

MRS. TAYLOR: *(Smiling at the other)* I know. I had two boys myself. Is the baby a boy too?

YOUNG WOMAN: Yes. Four months.

MRS. TAYLOR: *(Bends to look at him)* He's a big boy for four months, isn't he?

YOUNG WOMAN: *(Smiling fondly at the baby)* Yes. *(Both women smile down at the sleeping baby, then at each other.)*

MRS. TAYLOR: *(Turning to Young Woman)* Are you going far?

YOUNG WOMAN: To Bathurst, New Brunswick.

MRS. TAYLOR: My goodness! That's an awful long way.

YOUNG WOMAN: You get used to it. My husband's got a job there with a mining company. I wanted my mother to

	see the baby, that's why I made this trip.
MRS. TAYLOR:	*(Wistfully)* I'll bet she was pleased.
YOUNG WOMAN:	Oh yes. We wanted her to come back with us for a month or two, but her arthritis is bad.
MRS. TAYLOR:	*(Nods)* It would have been nice for your mother. *(Changing the subject)* My landlady has trouble with her back. Lumbago I guess it is.
YOUNG WOMAN:	*(Nods politely)*
MRS. TAYLOR:	I love travelling, don't you? People seem more friendly somehow than they do at other times. I don't often get a chance to meet people like this. *(Looks around the car)* The people are just like I hoped they would be.
YOUNG WOMAN:	They're always the same.
MRS. TAYLOR:	I was so excited this morning! I got up at five. *(Lowers her voice)* Do you know, this is going to be my first train trip since my husband died.
YOUNG WOMAN:	It'll be a change for you. How long has it been?
MRS. TAYLOR:	Let's see—*(Stares at the ceiling as she thinks)* Nearly fourteen years.
YOUNG WOMAN:	Fourteen years, my goodness! I suppose you live with one of your children?
MRS. TAYLOR:	No. I get my old-age pension. I have a room of my own, in a rooming house.
YOUNG WOMAN:	*(Sympathetically)* But—
MRS. TAYLOR:	*(Hurriedly)* My oldest boy lives in Montreal, you see. He's married with two small daughters. My youngest one, Bert, was killed in the war. In Italy.
YOUNG WOMAN:	It's none of my business, but can't you stay with your married son?
MRS. TAYLOR:	*(Her face dropping)* Oh, I couldn't do that. My landlady, Mrs. Connell, is always saying the same thing, but I tell her I'm too independent. *The train gives a slight lurch, indicated by both women being jarred back against the seat. The Young Woman bends forward to guard the baby against being toppled to the floor.*
YOUNG WOMAN:	*(Sitting up straight again)* Well, we're on our way at last.
MRS. TAYLOR:	*(Beaming)* I can hardly believe it.
YOUNG WOMAN:	*(To Gary)* You sit up straight, Gary, and watch the choo-choo trains.

MRS. TAYLOR: *(Staring past the Young Woman and through the train window)* I can hardly believe we're moving. It looks as though the station was sliding past.

YOUNG WOMAN: *(Leaning over to listen to her son, who is whispering something to her)* Oh no! Not already!

MRS. TAYLOR: They're all the same. *(Smiles at the little boy)*

YOUNG WOMAN: *(With exasperation)* I've never known it to fail. Before we left home I—

MRS. TAYLOR: You take him. I'll look after the baby.

YOUNG WOMAN: Gee, that'll be swell!

The Young Woman stands up and carefully lifts the small boy from the seat and exits with him, holding him by the hand. Mrs. Taylor moves along the seat to the window, and gazes through it in rapt wonderment. Now and again she glances down at the sleeping baby.

NEWS BUTCHER: *(Off-stage)* Magazines, candy bars, peanuts, popcorn, soft drinks, Toronto and Montreal morning papers!

(Baby's cry)

MRS. TAYLOR: *(Bends over and plays with the baby)* There, there! Did the naughty man wake him up!

The baby continues to cry

MRS. TAYLOR: Oh, he's hot, poor little tyke! Wait till I loosen his clothes.

The baby continues crying as Mrs. Taylor fusses with him. After a moment or two she glances around indecisively, then lifts him into her arms and settles back in her seat. She smiles down at him in his blanket, rocking him back and fro. The baby's crying sinks to a contented gurgle or two, then stops. Mrs. Taylor looks triumphant at first, but as she stares down at him her smile fades and her eyes fill with tears. She stares through the window, trying to wipe her eyes unobtrusively with the knuckles of her hand. Curtain falls momentarily to indicate passage of time.

Curtain rises again on same scene as before, but now Mrs. Taylor is sitting against the window with the little boy seated on her lap. The train is now moving at a moderate speed, as indicated by the swaying of the passengers, the sound of the diesel's whistle, and probably a passenger lurching along the aisle to his seat. In the aisle seat sits the Young Woman. She and Mrs. Taylor have obviously been engaged in conversation for some time.

YOUNG WOMAN: ... A friend of my mother's goes there. Mrs. Bellamy. Do you know her?

MRS. TAYLOR: *(Shaking her head as she tries to remember)* No, I don't think I do. *(Brightens)* Wait a minute! Is she a stout woman with bluish hair, that wears a Persian lamb coat in the winter?

YOUNG WOMAN: Yes, that's her.

MRS. TAYLOR: It's a small world, isn't it?

Mrs. Taylor squeezes the small boy's knee with her hand, and points through the window.

MRS. TAYLOR: *(Turning to the Young Woman)* The city has certainly changed, hasn't it? I was brought up right around here. *(Motions towards the window with her head)* It was nice around here then. There used to be a nice little park where Bert and I used to walk in the evenings. That's where we did our courting. *(Turns to the window again, smiling to herself at the memory)*

MRS. TAYLOR: *(After a pause, and turning from the window to face the Young Woman)* The city looks different from a train, somehow. You pass all the people's backyards, and wonder who lives in the houses. All the backyards with clothes on lines hanging in them, and the kiddies playing, and you think of the women in the house washing up after breakfast, and—You must think I'm crazy!

YOUNG WOMAN: No I don't, Mrs. Taylor.

MRS. TAYLOR: I guess that's what I miss most of all—the feeling that I belong with all this. *(Hugging the small boy to her)* I envy you, Norah, with your kiddies still young and everything. I guess I'd give up every one of the rest of my days just to be young again just for an hour or two, with my boys crawling round on the floor.

YOUNG WOMAN: *(Laying her hand on Mrs. Taylor's forearm)* I know what you mean.

Mrs. Taylor turns away quickly to hide her embarrassment, and whispers to the boy as she points through the window.

YOUNG WOMAN: I'll be glad to see this day go. We'll be in Montreal before supper time. It must make you glad too. *Mrs. Taylor stares at her, suddenly realizing that the other doesn't understand.*

YOUNG WOMAN: You must be looking forward to seeing your grandchildren?

MRS. TAYLOR: *(Trying to make light of it)* I'm not going to Montreal today. I can't afford to go that far.

YOUNG WOMAN: *(Surprised)* Well—well, where are you going then?

MRS. TAYLOR: Just up the line apiece. It's just a short trip. *Mrs. Taylor turns and stares through the window again. The Young Woman begins to say something, but then changes her mind.*

CONDUCTOR: *(Off-stage)* Tickets please! All tickets. Please have your tickets ready.

YOUNG WOMAN: *(Picking up her purse from the seat beside her)* Here's the conductor coming for the tickets, Mrs. Taylor. *Mrs. Taylor takes a small piece of pasteboard from her handbag. It is in contrast to the long ribbon of paper that the Young Woman takes from hers.*

MRS. TAYLOR: *(Turns to the window, then back to her companion)* They're certainly building the city out in every direction. I can remember when all this *(Nods to the window)* was all farmland. And now it's well within the city limits.

YOUNG WOMAN: We won't be out in the real country for miles yet. *The Conductor appears, and begins punching and collecting tickets along the car. Mrs. Taylor stares through the window. The Young Woman looks down at the sleeping baby, moving the blanket from its face.*

When the Conductor reaches their seat the Young Woman hands him her ticket. He punches it, tears off a section, and hands it back to her. Then he reaches across the women and places a small slip of cardboard in the window blind. He then takes Mrs. Taylor's ticket, and places it in his pocket.

CONDUCTOR: *(To Mrs. Taylor)* We'll be at your station in a minute, ma'am. In fact we're slowing down now.

Will you get off at the front end of the car please.
*Mrs. Taylor stands up with the little boy in her
arms. She kisses him and sits him down in the
seat where she has been sitting. She picks up her
suitcase from the floor. The Young Woman is
staring at her openmouthed.*

CONDUCTOR: *(Surprised)* You have luggage, Ma'am!

MRS. TAYLOR: *(Apologetically)* Just this bag.

CONDUCTOR: *(Takes the bag from her)* Here. I'll carry it for
you.
The Conductor exits, carrying the bag.

MRS. TAYLOR: I'll have to say goodbye to you now. You don't
know how much I've enjoyed being with you and
the kiddies.

YOUNG WOMAN: *(Still surprised)* We've enjoyed it too.
*Mrs. Taylor rubs her hand over the little boy's
head, then bends down and kisses the baby.*

MRS. TAYLOR: You be a good boy now, Gary, won't you. *(To the
Young Woman)* You must think I'm crazy just
coming this far. You see I've wanted to take a trip
for so long, and this was sort of—pretending.

YOUNG WOMAN: *(Holding back her tears)* No I don't, Mrs. Taylor. I
just wish you were coming all the way. Thanks so
much for helping me with the children.

MRS. TAYLOR: *(Suddenly shy)* Goodbye, dear, and God bless you.
Have a nice journey. *(She walks along the aisle of
the car.)*

YOUNG WOMAN: *(Shouting after her)* Thanks! Thanks a lot! *(To
the little boy)* Say goodbye to Grandma Taylor,
Gary.
*The small boy mumbles a goodbye and waves his
hand. Mrs. Taylor turns and waves in return
before she exits. As the train begins to move
again the Young Woman and the little boy crowd
against the window waving at someone on the
platform.*

CURTAIN

Scene 4:

The interior of a city bus. We are facing the Driver from his rear, and he is in profile to the audience. He is collecting fares from two or three passengers, but the bus is almost empty. The Driver is wearing a uniform cap, but his uniform jacket is hanging on a hook beside his seat.

Mrs. Taylor climbs the steps, out of breath and obviously weighted down with the heavy suitcase. She places the suitcase down on the floor, and searches in her purse for the fare.

BUS DRIVER: *(Smiling at her)* You look happy, Ma. You must have had a swell vacation.

MRS. TAYLOR: *(Abandons her search in her purse and looks up)* Oh yes. I had a wonderful trip. I'm a little tired though.

BUS DRIVER: I'd never come back to this heat. *(He removes his cap and wipes his forehead on his sleeve.)* Did you just get off a train?

MRS. TAYLOR: Yes, the Montreal train.

BUS DRIVER: *(Enviously)* Montreal, eh? *(Sighs)* It's nice to travel, but it's pretty expensive I guess.

MRS. TAYLOR: *(Smiling at a secret thought)* Yes, but it's almost as expensive staying put these days. *(She finds the fare and deposits it in the fare-box.)*

BUS DRIVER: It must be nice to get away from this heat once during the summer anyway.

MRS. TAYLOR: *(Picking up her suitcase)* Yes it is. *(On a sudden, boastful impulse)* I'm taking another trip next month. But that one'll be on the Winnipeg train! *Mrs. Taylor comes downstage towards the audience, limping a little and lopsided from the weight of the heavy bag. She has to steady herself with her hand on the rear of the seats. Her face lights up and her smile widens as she comes down the aisle of the bus. It is a smile of achievement and triumph beyond happiness.*

FINAL CURTAIN

Do Not Go Gentle Into That Good Night

Dylan Thomas

Do not go gentle into that good night,
Old age should burn and rave at close of day;
Rage, rage against the dying of the light.

Though wise men at their end know dark is right,
Because their words had forked no lightning they
Do not go gentle into that good night.

Good men, the last wave by, crying how bright
Their frail deeds might have danced in a green bay,
Rage, rage against the dying of the light.

Wild men who caught and sang the sun in flight,
And learn, too late, they grieved it on its way,
Do not go gentle into that good night.

Grave men, near death, who see with blinding sight
Blind eyes could blaze like meteors and be gay,
Rage, rage against the dying of the light.

And you, my father, there on the sad height,
Curse, bless, me now with your fierce tears, I pray.
Do not go gentle into that good night.
Rage, rage against the dying of the light.

UNIT 3

NO MAN IS AN ISLAND

More than three centuries ago John Donne observed, "No man is an island." This statement is still often quoted to indicate that human beings cannot live in isolation, unaffected by the people around them. Our lives intertwine with the lives of others, in complex webs of interaction.

Human relationships shape character, provide conflict, motivate behaviour and influence events in our lives. It is not surprising that many writers are interested in various strands of this broad theme. The fascination writers have with human relationships will be apparent to you as you read stories, poems, and essays that reveal the extent to which we are all influenced by our families, friends, and neighbours, by the people with whom we fall in love, and the people with whom we must learn to live. We are related not only to our own generation, but also to the generations that came before us and to the generations that will follow us. No person is an island; our lives are touched by the lives of those around us.

To a Sad Daughter

Michael Ondaatje
For Quintin

All night long the hockey pictures
gaze down at you
sleeping in your tracksuit.
Belligerent goalies are your ideal.
Threats of being traded
cuts and wounds
—all this pleases you.
O my god! you say at breakfast
reading the sports page over the Alpen
as another player breaks his ankle
or assaults the coach.

When I thought of daughters
I wasn't expecting this
but I like this more.
I like all your faults
even your purple moods
when you retreat from everyone
to sit in bed under a quilt.
And when I say 'like'
I mean of course 'love'
but that embarrasses you.
You who feel superior to black and white movies

(coaxed for hours to see *Casablanca*)
though you were moved
by *Creature from the Black Lagoon.*

One day I'll come swimming
beside your ship or someone will
and if you hear the siren
listen to it. For if you close your ears
only nothing happens. You will never change.

I don't care if you risk
your life to angry goalies
creatures with webbed feet.
You can enter their caves and castles
their glass laboratories. Just
don't be fooled by anyone but yourself.

This is the first lecture I've given you.
You're 'sweet sixteen' you said.
I'd rather be your closest friend
than your father. I'm not good at advice
you know that, but ride
the ceremonies
until they grow dark.

Sometimes you are so busy
discovering your friends
I ache with a loss
—but that is greed.
And sometimes I've gone
into *my* purple world
and lost you.

One afternoon I stepped
into your room. You were sitting

at the desk where I now write this.
Forsythia outside the window
and sun spilled over you
like a thick yellow miracle
as if another planet
was coaxing you out of the house
—all those possible worlds!—
and you, meanwhile, busy with mathematics.

I cannot look at forsythia now
without loss, or joy for you.
You step delicately
into the wild world
and your real prize will be
the frantic search.
Want everything. If you break
break going out not in.
How you live your life I don't care
but I'll sell my arms for you,
hold your secrets forever.

If I speak of death
which you fear now, greatly,
it is without answers,
except that each
one we know is
in our blood.
Don't recall graves.
Memory is permanent.
Remember the afternoon's
yellow suburban annunciation.
Your goalie
in his frightening mask
dreams perhaps
of gentleness.

Girl's-Eye View of Relatives

Phyllis McGinley

First Lesson

The thing to remember about fathers is, they're men.
A girl has to keep it in mind.
They are dragon-seekers, bent on improbable rescues.
Scratch any father, you find
Someone chock-full of qualms and romantic terrors,
Believing change is a threat—
Like your first shoes with heels on, like your first bicycle
It took such months to get.

Walk in strange woods, they warn you about the snakes there.
Climb, and they fear you'll fall.
Books, angular boys, or swimming in deep water—
Fathers mistrust them all.
Men are the worriers. It is difficult for them
To learn what they must learn:
How you have a journey to take and very likely,
For a while, will not return.

The Adversary

A mother's hardest to forgive.
Life is the fruit she longs to hand you,
Ripe on a plate. And while you live,
Relentlessly she understands you.

Before Two Portraits of My Mother

Émile Nelligan
(translated by George Johnston)

I love the beautiful young girl of this
portrait, my mother, painted years ago
when her forehead was white, and there was no
shadow in the dazzling Venetian glass

of her gaze. But this other likeness shows
the deep trenches across her forehead's white
marble. The rose poem of her youth that
her marriage sang is far behind. Here is

my sadness: I compare these portraits, one
of a joy-radiant brow, the other care-
heavy: sunrise—and the thick coming on

of night. And yet how strange my ways seem,
for when I look at these faded lips my heart
smiles, but at the smiling girl my tears start.

Cornet at Night

Sinclair Ross

THE wheat was ripe and it was Sunday. "Can't help it—I've got to cut," my father said at breakfast. "No use talking. There's a wind again and it's shelling fast."

"Not on the Lord's Day," my mother protested. "The horses stay in the stables where they belong. There's church this afternoon and I intend to ask Louise and her husband home for supper."

Ordinarily my father was a pleasant, accommodating little man, but this morning his wheat and the wind had lent him sudden steel. "No, today we cut," he met her evenly. "You and Tom go to church if you want to. Don't bother me."

"If you take the horses out today I'm through—I'll never speak to you again. And this time I mean it."

He nodded. "Good—if I'd known I'd have started cutting wheat on Sunday years ago."

"And that's no way to talk in front of your son. In the years to come he'll remember."

There was silence for a moment and then, as if in its clash with hers his will had suddenly found itself, my father turned to me.

"Tom, I need a man to stook for a few days and I want you to go to town tomorrow and get me one. The way the wheat's coming along so fast and the oats nearly ready too I can't afford the time. Take old Rock. You'll be safe with him."

But ahead of me my mother cried, "That's one thing I'll not stand for. You can cut your wheat or do anything else you like yourself, but you're not interfering with him. He's going to school tomorrow as usual."

My father bunched himself and glared at her. "No, for a change he's going to do what I say. The crop's more important than a day at school."

"But Monday's his music lesson day—and when will we have another teacher like Miss Wiggins who can teach him music too?"

"A dollar for lessons and the wheat shelling! When I was his age I didn't even get to school."

"Exactly," my mother scored, "and look at you today. Is it any wonder I want him to be different?"

He slammed out at that to harness his horses and cut his wheat, and away sailed my mother and me in her wake to spend an austere half-hour in the dark, hot, plushy little parlour. It was a kind of vicarious atonement, I suppose, for we both took straight-backed leather chairs, and for all of the half-hour stared across the room at the big pansy-bordered motto on the opposite wall: *As for Me and My House We Will Serve the Lord.*

At last she rose and said, "Better run along and do your chores now, but hurry back. You've got to take your bath and change your clothes, and maybe help a little getting dinner for your father."

There was a wind this sunny August morning, tanged with freedom and departure, and from his stall my pony Clipper whinnied for a race with it. Sunday or not, I would ordinarily have had my gallop anyway, but today a sudden welling-up of social and religious conscience made me ask myself whether one in the family like my father wasn't bad enough. Returning to the house, I merely said that on such a fine day it seemed a pity to stay inside. My mother heard but didn't answer. Perhaps her conscience too was working. Perhaps after being worsted in the skirmish with my father, she was in no mood for granting dispensations. In any case I had to take my bath as usual, put on a clean white shirt, and change my overalls for knicker corduroys.

They squeaked, those corduroys. For three months now they

had been spoiling all my Sundays. A sad, muted, swishing little squeak, but distinctly audible. Every step and there it was, as if I needed to be oiled. I had to wear them to church and Sunday-school; and after service, of course, while the grown-ups stood about gossiping, the other boys discovered my affliction. I sulked and fumed, but there was nothing to be done. Corduroys that had cost four-fifty simply couldn't be thrown away till they were well worn-out. My mother warned me that if I started sliding down the stable roof, she'd patch the seat and make me keep on wearing them.

With my customary little bow-legged sidle I slipped into the kitchen again to ask what there was to do. "Nothing but try to behave like a Christian and a gentleman," my mother answered stiffly. "Put on a tie, and shoes and stockings. Today your father is just about as much as I can bear."

"And then what?" I asked hopefully. I was thinking that I might take a drink to my father, but dared not as yet suggest it.

"Then you can stay quiet and read—and afterwards practise your music lesson. If your Aunt Louise should come she'll find that at least I bring my son up decently."

It was a long day. My mother prepared the midday meal as usual, but, to impress upon my father the enormity of his conduct, withdrew as soon as the food was served. When he was gone, she and I emerged to take our places at the table in an atmosphere of unappetizing righteousness. We didn't eat much. The food was cold, and my mother had no heart to warm it up. For relief at last she said, "Run along and feed the chickens while I change my dress. Since we aren't going to service today we'll read Scripture for a while instead."

And Scripture we did read, Isaiah, verse about, my mother in her black silk dress and rhinestone brooch, I in my corduroys and Sunday shoes that pinched. It was a very august afternoon, exactly like the tone that had persisted in my mother's voice since breakfast time. I think I might have openly rebelled, only for the hope that by compliance I yet might win permission for the trip to town with Rock. I was inordinately proud that my father had suggested it, and for his faith in me forgave him even Isaiah and the plushy afternoon. Whereas with my mother, I decided, it was a case of downright bigotry.

We went on reading Isaiah, and then for a while I played hymns on the piano. A great many hymns—even the ones with awkward sharps and accidentals that I'd never tried before—for, fearing visitors, my mother was resolved to let them see that she and I were uncontaminated by my father's sacrilege. But among these likely visitors was my Aunt Louise, a portly, condescending lady married to a well-off farmer with a handsome motor-car, and always when she came it was my mother's vanity to have me play for her a waltz or reverie, or *Holy Night* sometimes with variations. A man-child and prodigy might eclipse the motor-car. Presently she roused herself, and pretending mild reproof began, "Now, Tommy, you're going wooden on those hymns. For a change you'd better practise *Sons of Liberty*. Your Aunt Louise will want to hear it, anyway."

There was a fine swing and vigour in this piece, but it was hard. Hard because it was so alive, so full of youth and head-high rhythm. It was a march, and it did march. I couldn't take time to practise at the hard spots slowly till I got them right, for I had to march too. I had to let my fingers sometimes miss a note or strike one wrong. Again and again this afternoon I started carefully, resolving to count right through, the way Miss Wiggins did, and as often I sprang ahead to lead my march a moment or two all dash and fire, and then fall stumbling in the bitter dust of dissonance. My mother didn't know. She thought that speed and perseverance would eventually get me there. She tapped her foot and smiled encouragement, and gradually as the afternoon wore on began to look a little disappointed that there were to be no visitors, after all. "Run along for the cows," she said at last, "while I get supper ready for your father. There'll be nobody here, so you can slip into your overalls again."

I looked at her a moment, and then asked: "What am I going to wear to town tomorrow? I might get grease or something on the corduroys."

For while it was always my way to exploit the future, I liked to do it rationally, within the limits of the sane and probable. On my way for the cows I wanted to live the trip to town tomorrow many times, with variations, but only on the explicit understanding that tomorrow there was to be a trip to town. I have always been tethered to reality, always compelled by an unfortunate kind of probity in my nature to prefer a barefaced disappointment to the luxury of a future I have no just claims upon.

I went to town the next day, though not till there had been a full hour's argument that paradoxically enough gave all three of us the victory. For my father had his way: I went; I had my way: I went; and in return for her consent my mother wrung a promise from him of a pair of new plush curtains for the parlour when the crop was threshed, and for me the metronome that Miss Wiggins declared was the only way I'd ever learn to keep in time on marching pieces like the *Sons of Liberty*.

It was my first trip to town alone. That was why they gave me Rock, who was old and reliable and philosophic enough to meet motor-cars and the chance locomotive on an equal and even somewhat supercilious footing.

"Mind you pick somebody big and husky," said my father as he started for the field. "Go to Jenkins' store, and he'll tell you who's in town. Whoever it is, make sure he's stooked before."

"And mind it's somebody who looks like he washes himself," my mother warned. "I'm going to put clean sheets and pillow-cases on the bunkhouse bed, but not for any dirty tramp or hobo."

By the time they had both finished with me there were a great many things to mind. Besides repairs for my father's binder, I was to take two crates of eggs each containing twelve dozen eggs to Mr. Jenkins' store and in exchange have a list of groceries filled. And to make it complicated, both quantity and quality of some of the groceries were to be determined by the price of eggs. Thirty cents a dozen, for instance, and I was to ask for coffee at sixty-five cents a pound. Twenty-nine cents a dozen and coffee at fifty cents a pound. Twenty-eight and no oranges. Thirty-one and bigger oranges. It was like decimals with Miss Wiggins, or two notes in the treble against three in the bass. For my father a tin of special blend tobacco, and my mother not to know. For my mother a box of face powder at the drugstore, and my father not to know. Twenty-five cents from my father on the side for ice-cream and licorice. Thirty-five from my mother for my dinner at the Chinese restaurant.

And warnings, of course, to take good care of Rock, speak politely to Mr. Jenkins, and see that I didn't get machine oil on my corduroys.

It was three hours to town with Rock, but I don't remember them. I remember nothing but a smug satisfaction with myself, an exhilarating conviction of importance and maturity—and that only by contrast with the sudden sag to embarrassed insignificance when finally old Rock and I drove up to Jenkins' store.

For a farm boy is like that. Alone with himself and his horse he cuts a fine figure. He is the measure of the universe. He foresees a great many encounters with life, and in them all acquits himself a little more than creditably. He is fearless, resourceful, a bit of a brag. His horse never contradicts.

But in town it is different. There are eyes here, critical, that pierce with a single glance the little bubble of his self-importance, and leave him dwindled smaller even than his normal size. It always happens that way. They are so superbly poised and sophisticated, these strangers, so completely masters of their situation as they loll in doorways and go sauntering up and down Main Street. Instantly he yields to them his place as measure of the universe, especially if he is a small boy wearing squeaky corduroys, especially if he has a worldly-wise old horse like Rock, one that knows his Main Streets, and will take them in nothing but his own slow philosophic stride.

We arrived all right. Mr. Jenkins was a little man with a freckled bald head, and when I carried in my two crates of eggs, one in each hand, and my legs bowed a bit, he said curtly, "Well, can't you set them down? My boy's delivering, and I can't take time to count them now myself."

"They don't need counting," I said politely. "Each layer holds two dozen, and each crate holds six layers. I was there. I saw my mother put them in."

At this a tall, slick-haired young man in yellow shoes who had been standing by the window turned around and said, "That's telling you, Jenkins—he was there." Nettled and glowering, Jenkins himself came round the counter and repeated, "So you were there, were you? Smart youngster! What did you say was your name?"

Nettled in turn to preciseness I answered, "I haven't yet. It's

Thomas Dickson and my father's David Dickson, eight miles north of here. He wants a man to stook and was too busy to come himself."

He nodded, unimpressed, and then putting out his hand said, "Where's your list? Your mother gave you one, I hope?"

I said she had and he glowered again. "Then let's have it and come back in half an hour. Whether you were there or not, I'm going to count your eggs. How do I know that half of them aren't smashed."

"That's right," agreed the young man, sauntering to the door and looking at Rock. "They've likely been bouncing along at a merry clip. You're quite sure, Buddy, that you didn't have a runaway?"

Ignoring the impertinence I staved off Jenkins. "The list, you see, has to be explained. I'd rather wait and tell you about it later on."

He teetered a moment on his heels and toes, then tried again. "I can read too. I make up orders every day. Just go away for a while—look for your man—anything."

"It wouldn't do," I persisted. "The way this one's written isn't what it really means. You'd need me to explain—"

He teetered rapidly. "Show me just one thing I don't know what it means."

"Oranges," I said, "but that's only oranges if eggs are twenty-nine cents or more—and bigger oranges if they're thirty-one. You see, you'd never understand—"

So I had my way and explained it all right then and there. What with eggs at twenty-nine and a half cents a dozen and my mother out a little in her calculations, it was somewhat confusing for a while; but after arguing a lot and pulling away the paper from each other that they were figuring on, the young man and Mr. Jenkins finally had it all worked out, with mustard and soap omitted altogether, and an extra half-dozen oranges thrown in. "Vitamins," the young man overruled me, "they make you grow"—and then with a nod towards an open biscuit box invited me to help myself.

I took a small one, and started up Rock again. It was nearly one o'clock now, so in anticipation of his noonday quart of oats he trotted off, a little more briskly, for the farmers' hitching-rail beside the lumber-yard. This was the quiet end of town. The air drowsed redolent of pine and tamarack, and resin simmering slowly in the sun. I poured out the oats and waited till he had finished. After the way the town had treated me it was comforting and peaceful to stand with my fingers in his mane, hearing him munch. It brought me a sense of place again in life. It made me feel almost as important as before. But when he finished and there was my own dinner to be thought about I found myself more of an alien in the town than ever, and felt the way to the little Chinese restaurant doubly hard. For Rock was older than I. Older and wiser, with a better understanding of important things. His philosophy included the relishing of oats even within a stone's throw of sophisticated Main Street. Mine was less mature.

I went, however, but I didn't have dinner. Perhaps it was my stomach, all puckered and tense with nervousness. Perhaps it was the restaurant itself, the pyramids of oranges in the window and the dark green rubber plant with the tropical-looking leaves, the indolent little Chinaman behind the counter and the dusky smell of last night's cigarettes that to my prairie nostrils was the orient itself, the exotic atmosphere about it all with which a meal of meat and vegetables and pie would have somehow simply jarred. I climbed onto a stool and ordered an ice-cream soda.

A few stools away there was a young man sitting. I kept watching him and wondering.

He was well-dressed, a nonchalance about his clothes that distinguished him from anyone I had ever seen, and yet at the same time it was a shabby suit, with shiny elbows and threadbare cuffs. His hands were slender, almost a girl's hands, yet vaguely with their shapely quietness they troubled me, because, however slender and smooth, they were yet hands to be reckoned with, strong with a strength that was different from the rugged labour-strength I knew.

He smoked a cigarette, and blew rings towards the window.

Different from the farmer boys I knew, yet different also from the young man with the yellow shoes in Jenkins' store. Staring out at it through the restaurant window he was as far away from Main Street as was I with plodding old Rock and my squeaky corduroys. I presumed for a minute or two an imaginary companionship. I finished my soda, and to be with

him a little longer ordered lemonade. It was strangely important to be with him, to prolong a while this companionship. I
hadn't the slightest hope of his noticing me, nor the slightest
intention of obtruding myself. I just wanted to be there, to be
assured by something I had never encountered before, to store
it up for the three hours home with old Rock.

Then a big, unshaven man came in, and slouching onto the
stool beside me said, "They tell me across the street you're
looking for a couple of hands. What's your old man pay this
year?"

"My father," I corrected him, "doesn't want a couple of men.
He just wants one."

"I've got a pal," he insisted, "and we always go together."

I didn't like him. I couldn't help making contrasts with the
cool, trim quietness of the young man sitting farther along.
"What do you say?" he said as I sat silent, thrusting his stubby
chin out almost over my lemonade. "We're ready any time."

"It's just one man my father wants," I said aloofly, drinking
off my lemonade with a flourish to let him see I meant it.
"And if you'll excuse me now—I've got to look for somebody
else."

"What about this?" he intercepted me, and doubling up his
arm displayed a hump of muscle that made me, if not more in-
clined to him, at least a little more deferential. "My pal's got
plenty, too. We'll set up two stooks any day for anybody else's
one."

"Not both," I edged away from him. "I'm sorry—you just
wouldn't do."

He shook his head contemptuously. "Some farmer—just one
man to stook."

"My father's a good farmer," I answered stoutly, rallying to
the family honour less for its own sake than for what the
young man on the other stool might think of us. "And he
doesn't need just one man to stook. He's got three already.
That's plenty other years, but this year the crop's so big he
needs another. So there!"

"I can just see the place," he said, slouching to his feet and
starting towards the door. "An acre or two of potatoes and a
couple of dozen hens."

I glared after him a minute, then climbed back onto the

stool and ordered another soda. The young man was watching me now in the big mirror behind the counter, and when I glanced up and met his eyes he gave me a slow, half-smiling little nod of approval. And out of all proportion to anything it could mean, his nod encouraged me. I didn't flinch or fidget as I would have done had it been the young man with the yellow shoes watching me, and I didn't stammer over the confession that his amusement and appraisal somehow forced from me. "We haven't three men—just my father—but I'm to take one home today. The wheat's ripening fast this year and shelling, so he can't do it all himself."

He nodded again and then after a minute asked quietly, "What about me? Would I do?"

I turned on the stool and stared at him.

"I need a job, and if it's any recommendation, there's only one of me."

"You don't understand," I started to explain, afraid to believe that perhaps he really did. "It's to stook. You have to be in the field by seven o'clock and there's only a bunkhouse to sleep in—a granary with a bed in it—"

"I know—that's about what I expect." He drummed his fingers a minute, then twisted his lips into a kind of half-hearted smile and went on, "They tell me a little toughening up is what I need. Outdoors, and plenty of good hard work— so I'll be like the fellow that just went out."

The wrong hands: white slender fingers, I knew they'd never do—but catching the twisted smile again I pushed away my soda and said quickly, "Then we'd better start right away. It's three hours home, and I've still some places to go. But you can get in the buggy now, and we'll drive around together."

We did. I wanted it that way, the two of us, to settle scores with Main Street. I wanted to capture some of old Rock's disdain and unconcern; I wanted to know what it felt like to take young men with yellow shoes in my stride, to be preoccupied, to forget them the moment that we separated. And I did. "My name's Philip," the stranger said as we drove from Jenkins' to the drugstore. "Philip Coleman—usually just Phil," and companionably I responded, "Mine's Tommy Dickson. For the last year, though, my father says I'm getting big and should be called just Tom."

That was what mattered now, the two of us there, and not the town at all. "Do you drive yourself all the time?" he asked, and nonchalant and off-handed I answered, "You don't really have to drive old Rock. He just goes, anyway. Wait till you see my chestnut three-year-old. Clipper I call him. Tonight after supper if you like you can take him for a ride."

But since he'd never learned to ride at all he thought Rock would do better for a start, and then we drove back to the restaurant for his cornet and valise.

"Is it something to play?" I asked as we cleared the town. "Something like a bugle?"

He picked up the black leather case from the floor of the buggy and held it on his knee. "Something like that. Once I played a bugle too. A cornet's better, though."

"And you mean you can play the cornet?"

He nodded. "I play in a band. At least I did play in a band. Perhaps if I get along all right with the stooking I will again some time."

It was later that I pondered this, how stooking for my father could have anything to do with going back to play in a band. At the moment I confided, "I've never heard a cornet—never even seen one. I suppose you still play it sometimes—I mean at night, when you've finished stooking."

Instead of answering directly he said, "That means you've never heard a band either." There was surprise in his voice, almost incredulity, but it was kindly. Somehow I didn't feel ashamed because I had lived all my eleven years on a prairie farm, and knew nothing more than Miss Wiggins and my Aunt Louise's gramophone. He went on, "I was younger than you are now when I started playing in a band. Then I was with an orchestra a while—then with the band again. It's all I've done ever since."

It made me feel lonely for a while, isolated from the things in life that mattered, but, brightening presently, I asked, "Do you know a piece called *Sons of Liberty*? Four flats in four-four time?"

He thought hard a minute, and then shook his head. "I'm afraid I don't—not by name anyway. Could you whistle a bit of it?"

I whistled two pages, but still he shook his head. "A nice

tune, though," he conceded. "Where did you learn it?"

"I haven't yet," I explained. "Not properly, I mean. It's been my lesson for the last two weeks, but I can't keep up to it."

He seemed interested, so I went on and told him about my lessons and Miss Wiggins, and how later on they were going to buy me a metronome so that when I played a piece I wouldn't always be running away with it. "Especially a march. It keeps pulling you along the way it really ought to go until you're all mixed up and have to start at the beginning again. I know I'd do better if I didn't feel that way, and could keep slow and steady like Miss Wiggins."

But he said quickly, "No, that's the right way to feel—you've just got to learn to harness it. It's like old Rock here and Clipper. The way you are, you're Clipper. But if you weren't that way, if you didn't get excited and wanted to run some-times, you'd just be Rock. You see? Rock's easier to handle than Clipper, but at his best he's a sleepy old plow-horse. Clipper's harder to handle—he may even cost you some tum-bles. But finally get him broken in and you've got a horse that amounts to something. You wouldn't trade him for a dozen like Rock."

It was a good enough illustration, but it slandered Rock. And he was listening. I know—because even though like me he had never heard a cornet before, he had experience enough to accept it at least with tact and manners.

For we hadn't gone much farther when Philip, noticing the way I kept watching the case that was still on his knee, undid the clasps and took the cornet out. It was a very lovely cornet, shapely and eloquent, gleaming in the August sun like pure and mellow gold. I couldn't restrain myself. I said, "Play it—play it now—just a little bit to let me hear." And in response, smiling at my earnestness, he raised it to his lips.

But there was only one note—only one fragment of a note —and then away went Rock. I'd never have believed he had it in him. With a snort and plunge he was off the road and into the ditch—then out of the ditch again and off at a breakneck gallop across the prairie. There were stones and badger holes, and he spared us none of them. The egg-crates full of grocer-ies bounced out, then the tobacco, then my mother's face pow-der. "Whoa, Rock!" I cried, "Whoa, Rock!" but in the rattle and whir of wheels I don't suppose he even heard. Philip couldn't help much because he had his cornet to hang on to. I tried to tug on the reins, but at such a rate across the prairie it took me all my time to keep from following the groceries. He was a big horse, Rock, and once under way had to run himself out. Or he may have thought that if he gave us a thorough shaking-up we would be too subdued when it was over to feel like taking him seriously to task. Anyway, that was how it worked out. All I dared to do was run round to pat his sweaty neck and say, "Good Rock, good Rock—nobody's going to hurt you."

Besides there were the groceries to think about, and my mother's box of face powder. And his pride and reputation at stake, Rock had made it a runaway worthy of the horse he really was. We found the powder smashed open and one of the egg-crates cracked. Several of the oranges had rolled down a badger hole, and couldn't be recovered. We spent nearly ten minutes sifting raisins through our fingers, and still they felt a little gritty. "There were extra oranges," I tried to encourage Philip, "and I've seen my mother wash her raisins." He looked at me dubiously, and for a few minutes longer worked away trying to mend the egg-crate.

We were silent for the rest of the way home. We thought a great deal about each other, but asked no questions. Even though it was safely away in its case again I could still feel the cornet's presence as if it were a living thing. Somehow its gold and shapeliness persisted, transfiguring the day, quickening the dusty harvest fields to a gleam and lustre like its own. And I felt assured, involved. Suddenly there was a force in life, a current, an inevitability, carrying me along too. The questions they would ask when I reached home—the difficulties in making them understand that faithful old Rock had really run away—none of it now seemed to matter. This stranger with the white, thin hands, this gleaming cornet that as yet I hadn't even heard, intimately and enduringly now they were my possessions.

When we reached home my mother was civil and no more. "Put your things in the bunkhouse," she said, "and then wash here. Supper'll be ready in about an hour."

It was an uncomfortable meal. My father and my mother

kept looking at Philip and exchanging glances. I told them about the cornet and the runaway, and they listened stonily. "We've never had a harvest-hand before that was a musician too," my mother said in a somewhat thin voice. "I suppose, though, you do know how to stook?"

I was watching Philip desperately and for my sake he lied, "Yes, stooked last year. I may have a blister or two by this time tomorrow, but my hands will toughen up."

"You don't as a rule do farm work?" my father asked.

And Philip said, "No, not as a rule."

There was an awkward silence, so I tried to champion him. "He plays his cornet in a band. Ever since he was my age— that's what he does."

Glances were exchanged again. The silence continued.

I had been half-intending to suggest that Philip bring his cornet into the house to play it for us, I perhaps playing with him on the piano, but the parlour with its genteel plushiness was a room from which all were excluded but the equally genteel—visitors like Miss Wiggins and the minister—and gradually as the meal progressed I came to understand that Philip and his cornet, so far as my mother was concerned, had failed to qualify.

So I said nothing when he finished his supper, and let him go back to the bunkhouse alone. "Didn't I say to have Jenkins pick him out?" my father stormed as soon as he had gone. "Didn't I say somebody big and strong?"

"He's tall," I countered, "and there wasn't anybody else except two men, and it was the only way they'd come."

"You mean you didn't want anybody else. A cornet player! Fine stooks he'll set up." And then, turning to my mother, "It's your fault—you and your nonsense about music lessons. If you'd listen to me sometimes, and try to make a man of him."

"I do listen to you," she answered quickly. "It's because I've had to listen to you now for thirteen years that I'm trying to make a different man of him. If you'd go to town yourself instead of keeping him out of school—and do your work in six days a week like decent people. I told you yesterday that in the long run it would cost you dear."

I slipped away and left them. The chores at the stable took me nearly an hour; and then, instead of returning to the house, I went over to see Philip. It was dark now, and there was a smoky lantern lit. He sat on the only chair, and in a hospitable silence motioned me to the bed. At once he ignored and accepted me. It was as if we had always known each other and long outgrown the need of conversation. He smoked, and blew rings towards the open door where the warm fall night encroached. I waited, eager, afraid lest they call me to the house, yet knowing that I must wait. Gradually the flame in the lantern smoked the glass till scarcely his face was left visible. I sat tense, expectant, wondering who he was, where he came from, why he should be here to do my father's stooking.

There were no answers, but presently he reached for his cornet. In the dim, soft darkness I could see it glow and quicken. And I remember still what a long and fearful moment it was crouched and steeling myself, waiting for him to begin.

And I was right: when they came the notes were piercing, golden as the cornet itself, and they gave life expanse that it had never known before. They floated up against the night, and each for a moment hung there clear and visible. Sometimes they mounted poignant and sheer. Sometimes they soared and then, like a bird alighting, fell and brushed each again.

It was *To the Evening Star*. He finished it and told me. He told me the names of all the other pieces that he played: an *Ave Maria, Song of India*, a serenade—all bright through the dark like slow, suspended lightning, chilled sometimes with a glimpse of the unknown. Only for Philip there I could not have endured it. With my senses I clung hard to him—the acrid smell of his cigarettes, the tilted profile daubed with smoky light.

Then abruptly he stood up, as if understanding, and said, "Now we'd better have a march, Tom—to bring us back where we belong. A cornet can be good fun, too, you know. Listen to this one and tell me."

He stood erect, head thrown back exactly like a picture on my reader of a bugler boy, and the notes came flashing gallant through the night until the two of us went swinging along in step with them a hundred thousand strong. For this was another march that did march. It marched us miles. It made the feet eager and the heart brave. It said that life was worth the living and bright as morning shone ahead to show the way.

When he had finished and put the cornet away I said, "There's a field right behind the house that my father started cutting this afternoon. If you like we'll go over now for a few minutes and I'll show you how to stook. . . . You see, if you set your sheaves on top of the stubble they'll be over again in half an hour. That's how everybody does at first but it's wrong. You've got to push the butts down hard, right to the ground— like this, so they bind with the stubble. At a good slant, see, but not too much. So they'll stand the wind and still shed water if it rains."

It was too dark for him to see much, but he listened hard and finally succeeded in putting up a stook or two that to my touch seemed firm enough. Then my mother called, and I had to slip away fast so that she would think I was coming from the bunkhouse. "I hope he stooks as well as he plays," she said when I went in. "Just the same, you should have done as your father told you, and picked a likelier man to see us through the fall."

My father came in from the stable then, and he, too, had been listening. With a wondering, half-incredulous little movement of his head he made acknowledgement.

"Didn't I tell you he could?" I burst out, encouraged to indulge my pride in Philip. "Didn't I tell you he could play?" But with sudden anger in his voice he answered, "And what if he can! It's a man to stook I want. Just look at the hands on him. I don't think he's ever seen a farm before."

It was helplessness, though, not anger. Helplessness to escape his wheat when wheat was not enough, when something more than wheat had just revealed itself. Long after they were both asleep I remembered, and with a sharp foreboding that we might have to find another man, tried desperately to sleep myself. "Because if I'm up in good time," I rallied all my faith in life, "I'll be able to go to the field with him and at least make sure he's started right. And he'll maybe do. I'll ride down after school and help till supper time. My father's reasonable."

Only in such circumstances, of course, and after such a day, I couldn't sleep till nearly morning, with the result that when at last my mother wakened me there was barely time to dress and ride to school. But of the day I spent there I remember nothing. Nothing except the midriff clutch of dread that made it a long day—nothing, till straddling Clipper at four again, I galloped him straight to the far end of the farm where Philip that morning had started to work.

Only Philip, of course, wasn't there. I think I knew—I think it was what all day I had been expecting. I pulled Clipper up short and sat staring at the stooks. Three or four acres of them —crooked and dejected as if he had never heard about pushing the butts down hard into the stubble. I sat and stared till Clipper himself swung round and started for home. He wanted to run, but because there was nothing left now but the half-mile ahead of us, I held him to a walk. Just to prolong a little the possibility that I had misunderstood things. To wonder within the limits of the sane and probable if tonight he would play his cornet again.

When I reached the house my father was already there, eating an early supper. "I'm taking him back to town," he said quietly. "He tried hard enough—he's just not used to it. The sun was hot today; he lasted till about noon. We're starting in a few minutes, so you'd better go out and see him."

He looked older now, stretched out limp on the bed, his face haggard. I tiptoed close to him anxiously, afraid to speak. He pulled his mouth sidewise in a smile at my concern, then motioned me to sit down. "Sorry I didn't do better," he said. "I'll have to come back another year and have another lesson."

I clenched my hands and clung hard to this promise that I knew he couldn't keep. I wanted to rebel against what was happening, against the clumsiness and crudity of life, but instead I stood quiet a moment, almost passive, then wheeled away and carried out his cornet to the buggy. My mother was already there, with a box of lunch and some ointment for his sunburn. She said she was sorry things had turned out this way, and thanking her politely he said that he was sorry too. My father looked uncomfortable, feeling, no doubt, that we were all unjustly blaming everything on him. It's like that on a farm. You always have to put the harvest first.

And that's all there is to tell. He waved going through the gate. I never saw him again. We watched the buggy down the road to the first turn, then with a quick resentment in her voice my mother said, "Didn't I say that the little he gained would in the long run cost him dear? Next time he'll maybe listen to me—and remember the Sabbath Day."

What exactly she was thinking I never knew. Perhaps of the crop and the whole day's stooking lost. Perhaps of the stranger who had come with his cornet for a day, and then as meaninglessly gone again. For she had been listening, too, and she may have understood. A harvest, however lean, is certain every year; but a cornet at night is golden only once.

Father

Dale Zieroth

Twice he took me in his hands and shook
me like a sheaf of wheat, the way a dog shakes
a snake, as if he meant to knock out my tongue
and grind it under his heel right there
on the kitchen floor. I never remembered
what he said or the warnings he gave; she
always told me afterwards, when he
had left and I had stopped my crying. I
was eleven that year and for seven more years
I watched his friends laughing and him
with his great hands rising and falling
with every laugh, smashing down on his knees
and making the noise of a tree when it cracks
in winter. Together they drank chokecherry
wine and talked of the dead friends and the
old times when they were young, and because
I never thought of getting old, their
youth was the first I knew of dying.

Sunday before church he would trim
his fingernails with the hunting knife
his East German cousins had sent, the same
knife he used for castrating pigs and
skinning deer: things that had nothing
to do with Sunday. Communion once

a month, a shave every third day, a
good chew of snuff, these were the things
that helped a man to stand in the sun for
eight hours a day, to sweat through each
cold hail storm without a word, to freeze
fingers and feet to cut wood in winter, to do
the work that bent his back a little more
each day down toward the ground.

Last Christmas, for the first time, he
gave presents, unwrapped and bought
with pension money. He drinks mostly coffee
now, sleeping late and shaving everyday.
Even the hands have changed: white, soft,
unused hands. Still he seems content
to be this old, to be sleeping in the middle
of the afternoon with his mouth open as if there
is no further need for secrets, as if he is
no longer afraid to call his children fools
for finding different answers, different lives.

Those Winter Sundays

Robert Hayden

Sundays too my father got up early
and put his clothes on in the blueblack cold,
then with cracked hands that ached
from labor in the weekday weather made
banked fires blaze. No one ever thanked him.

I'd wake and hear the cold splintering, breaking.
When the rooms were warm, he'd call,
and slowly I would rise and dress,
fearing the chronic angers of that house,

Speaking indifferently to him,
who had driven out the cold
and polished my good shoes as well.
What did I know, what did I know
of love's austere and lonely offices?

Mother and Son

Alden Nowlan

She goes on with her story,
this woman whose twelve-year-old son
has drifted into the party;
her mind is still with her guests.
But her flesh has claimed possession of his.

She pushes his hair back from his eyes,
curls a lock of it around her finger,
while continuing to entertain us
with her wit. The touch of her hand
embarrasses him, but only a little;
he shrugs slightly, that is all.
Now she smiles at him
as if conscious of his presence
for the first time.
It's a loving smile, of course,
but not altogether a friendly one:
there's pride in that smile
and a sense of power,
even a hint of cruelty. She's a normal parent.

She pinches his earlobe now, plays with the buttons
on his shirt, talking with us all the while.
He wriggles for an instant, and then
surrenders, half-gratefully,
half-resentfully, to her caresses.

They both know she's the stronger,
that she'll be the stronger for a while yet,
that he couldn't break away from her
even if he could make up his mind
that it's what he wants.

Warren Pryor

Alden Nowlan

When every pencil meant a sacrifice
his parents boarded him at school in town,
slaving to free him from the stony fields,
the meagre acreage that bore them down.

They blushed with pride when, at his graduation,
they watched him picking up the slender scroll,
his passport from the years of brutal toil
and lonely patience in a barren hole.

When he went in the Bank their cups ran over.
They marvelled how he wore a milk-white shirt
work days and jeans on Sundays. He was saved
from their thistle-strewn farm and its red dirt.

And he said nothing. Hard and serious
like a young bear inside his teller's cage,
his axe-hewn hands upon the paper bills
aching with empty strength and throttled rage.

The Average

W. H. Auden

His peasant parents killed themselves with toil
To let their darling leave a stingy soil
For any of those smart professions which
Encourage shallow breathing, and grow rich.

The pressure of their fond ambition made
Their shy and country-loving child afraid
No sensible career was good enough,
Only a hero could deserve such love.

So here he was without maps or supplies,
A hundred miles from any decent town;
The desert glared into his blood-shot eyes;

The silence roared displeasure: looking down,
He saw the shadow of an Average Man
Attempting the exceptional, and ran.

The Broken Globe

Henry Kreisel

S INCE it was Nick Solchuk who first told me about the opening in my field at the University of Alberta, I went up to see him as soon as I received word that I had been appointed. He lived in one of those old mansions in Pimlico that had once served as town houses for wealthy merchants and aristocrats, but now housed a less moneyed group of people—stenographers, students, and intellectuals of various kinds. He had studied at Cambridge and got his doctorate there and was now doing research at the Imperial College and rapidly establishing a reputation among the younger men for his work on problems which had to do with the curvature of the earth.

His room was on the third floor, and it was very cramped, but he refused to move because he could look out from his window and see the Thames and the steady flow of boats, and that gave him a sense of distance and of space also. Space, he said, was what he missed most in the crowded city. He referred to himself, nostalgically, as a prairie boy, and when he wanted to demonstrate what he meant by space he used to say that when a man stood and looked out across the open prairie, it was possible for him to believe that the earth was flat.

'So,' he said, after I had told him my news, 'you are going to teach French to prairie boys and girls. I congratulate you.' Then he cocked his head to one side, and looked me over and said: 'How are your ears?'

'My ears?' I said. 'They're all right. Why?'

'Prepare yourself,' he said. 'Prairie voices trying to speak French—that will be a great experience for you. I speak from experience. I learned my French pronunciation in a little one-room school in a prairie village. From an extraordinary girl, mind you, but her mind ran to science. Joan McKenzie—that was her name. A wiry little thing, sharp-nosed, and she always wore brown dresses. She was particularly fascinated by earth-quakes. "In 1755 the city of Lisbon, Portugal, was devastated. 60,000 persons died; the shock was felt in Southern France and North Africa; and inland waters of Great Britain and Scandinavia were agitated." You see, I still remember that, and I can hear her voice too. Listen: "In common with the entire solar system, the earth is moving through space at the rate of approximately 45,000 miles per hour, toward the constellation of Hercules. Think of that, boys and girls." Well, I thought about it. It was a lot to think about. Maybe that's why I became a geophysicist. Her enthusiasm was infectious. I knew her at her peak. After a while she got tired and married a solid farmer and had eight children.'

'But her French, I take it, was not so good,' I said.

'No,' he said. 'Language gave no scope to her imagination. Mind you, I took French seriously enough. I was a very serious student. For a while I even practised French pronunciation at home. But I stopped it because it bothered my father. My mother begged me to stop. For the sake of peace.'

'Your father's ears were offended.' I said.

'Oh, no,' Nick said, 'not his ears. His soul. He was sure that I was learning French so I could run off and marry a French girl. . . . Don't laugh. It's true. When once my father believed something, it was very hard to shake him.'

'But why should he have objected to your marrying a French girl anyway?'

'Because,' said Nick, and pointed a stern finger at me, 'be-cause when he came to Canada he sailed from some French port, and he was robbed of all his money while he slept. He held all Frenchmen responsible. He never forgot and he never forgave. And, by God, he wasn't going to have that cursed language spoken in his house. He wasn't going to have any nonsense about science talked in his house either.' Nick was silent for a moment, and then he said, speaking very quietly. 'Curious man, my father. He had strange ideas, but a strange kind of imagination, too. I couldn't understand him when I was going to school or to the university. But then a year or two ago, I suddenly realized that the shape of the world he lived in had been forever fixed for him by some medieval priest in the small Ukrainian village where he was born and where he received an education of sorts when he was a boy. And I suddenly realized that he wasn't mad, but that he lived in the universe of the medieval church. The earth for him was the centre of the universe, and the centre was still. It didn't move. The sun rose in the East and it set in the West, and it moved perpetually around a still earth. God had made this earth especially for man, and man's function was to perpetuate himself and to worship God. My father never said all that in so many words, mind you, but that is what he believed. Everything else was heresy.'

He fell silent.

'How extraordinary,' I said.

He did not answer at once, and after a while he said, in a tone of voice which seemed to indicate that he did not want to pursue the matter further, 'Well, when you are in the middle of the Canadian West, I'll be in Rome. I've been asked to give a paper to the International Congress of Geophysicists which meets there in October.'

'So I heard,' I said. 'Wilcocks told me the other day. He said it was going to be a paper of some importance. In fact, he said it would create a stir.'

'Did Wilcocks really say that?' he asked eagerly, his face reddening, and he seemed very pleased. We talked for a while longer, and then I rose to go.

He saw me to the door and was about to open it for me, but stopped suddenly, as if he were turning something over in his mind, and then said quickly, 'Tell me—would you do something for me?'

'Of course,' I said. 'If I can.'

He motioned me back to my chair and I sat down again. 'When you are in Alberta,' he said, 'and if it is convenient for you, would you—would you go to see my father?'

'Why, yes,' I stammered, 'why, of course. I—I didn't realize he was still . . .'

'Oh, yes,' he said, 'he's still alive, still working. He lives on his farm, in a place called Three Bear Hills, about sixty or seventy miles out of Edmonton. He lives alone. My mother is dead. I have a sister who is married and lives in Calgary. There were only the two of us. My mother could have no more children. It was a source of great agony for them. My sister goes to see him sometimes, and then she sometimes writes to me. He never writes to me. We—we had—what shall I call it—differences. If you went to see him and told him that I had not gone to the devil, perhaps . . .' He broke off abruptly, clearly agitated, and walked over to his window and stood staring out, then said, 'Perhaps you'd better not. I—I don't want to impose on you.'

I protested that he was not imposing at all, and promised that I would write to him as soon as I had paid my visit.

I met him several times after that, but he never mentioned the matter again.

I sailed from England about the middle of August and arrived in Montreal a week later. The long journey West was one of the most memorable experiences I have ever had. There were moments of weariness and dullness. But the very monotony was impressive. There was a grandeur about it. It was monotony of a really monumental kind. There were moments when, exhausted by the sheer impact of the landscape, I thought back with longing to the tidy, highly cultivated countryside of England and of France, to the sight of men and women working in the fields, to the steady succession of villages and towns, and everywhere the consciousness of nature humanized. But I also began to understand why Nick Solchuk was always longing for more space and more air, especially when we moved into the prairies, and the land became flatter until there seemed nothing, neither hill nor tree nor bush, to disturb the vast unbroken flow of land until in the far distance a thin, blue line marked the point where the prairie merged into the sky. Yet over all there was a strange tranquillity, all motion seemed suspended, and only the sun moved steadily, imperturbably West, dropping finally over the rim of the horizon, a blazing red ball, but leaving a superb evening light lying over the land still.

I was reminded of the promise I had made, but when I arrived in Edmonton, the task of settling down absorbed my time and energy so completely that I did nothing about it. Then, about the middle of October, I saw a brief report in the newspaper about the geophysical congress which had opened in Rome on the previous day, and I was mindful of my promise again. Before I could safely bury it in the back of my mind again, I sat down and wrote a brief letter to Nick's father, asking him when I could come out to visit him. Two weeks passed without an answer, and I decided to go and see him on the next Saturday without further formalities.

The day broke clear and fine. A few white clouds were in the metallic autumn sky and the sun shone coldly down upon the earth, as if from a great distance. I drove south as far as Wetaskiwin and then turned east. The paved highway gave way to gravel and got steadily worse. I was beginning to wonder whether I was going right, when I rounded a bend and a grain elevator hove like a signpost into view. It was now about three o'clock and I had arrived in Three Bear Hills, but, as Nick had told me, there were neither bears nor hills here, but only prairie, and suddenly the beginning of an embryonic street with a few buildings on either side like a small island in a vast sea, and then all was prairie again.

I stopped in front of the small general store and went in to ask for directions. Three farmers were talking to the storekeeper, a bald, bespectacled little man who wore a long, dirty apron and stood leaning against his counter. They stopped talking and turned to look at me. I asked where the Solchuk farm was.

Slowly scrutinizing me, the storekeeper asked, 'You just new here?'

'Yes,' I said.

'From the old country, eh?'

'Yes.'

'You selling something?'

'No, no,' I said. 'I—I teach at the University.'

'That so?' He turned to the other men and said, 'Only boy ever went to University from around here was Solchuk's boy, Nick. Real brainy young kid, Nick. Two of 'em never got on together. Too different. You know.'

They nodded slowly.

'But that boy of his—he's a real big-shot scientist now. You know them addem bombs and them hydrergen bombs. He helps make 'em.'

'No, no,' I broke in quickly. 'That's not what he does. He's a geophysicist.'

'What's that?' asked one of the men.

But before I could answer, the little storekeeper asked excitedly, 'You know Nick?'

'Yes,' I said, 'we're friends. I've come to see his father.'

'And where's he now? Nick, I mean.'

'Right now he is in Rome,' I said. 'But he lives in London, and does research there.'

'Big-shot, eh,' said one of the men laconically, but with a trace of admiration in his voice, too.

'He's a big scientist, though, like I said. Isn't that so?' the storekeeper broke in.

'He's going to be a very important scientist indeed,' I said, a trifle solemnly.

'Like I said,' he called out triumphantly. 'That's showing 'em. A kid from Three Bear Hills, Alberta. More power to him!' His pride was unmistakable. 'Tell me, mister,' he went on, his voice dropping, 'does he remember this place sometimes? Or don't he want to know us no more?'

'Oh, no,' I said quickly. 'He often talks of this place, and of Alberta, and of Canada. Some day he plans to return.'

'That's right,' he said with satisfaction. He drew himself up to full height, banged his fist on the table and said, 'I'm proud of that boy. Maybe old Solchuk don't think so much of him, but you tell him old Mister Marshall is proud of him.' He came from behind the counter and almost ceremoniously escorted me out to my car and showed me the way to Solchuk's farm.

I had about another five miles to drive, and the road, hardly more now than two black furrows cut into the prairie, was uneven and bumpy. The land was fenced on both sides of the road, and at last I came to a rough wooden gate hanging loosely on one hinge, and beyond it there was a cluster of small wooden buildings. The largest of these, the house itself, seemed at one time to have been ochre-coloured, but the paint had worn off and it now looked curiously mottled. A few chickens were wandering about, pecking at the ground, and from the back I could hear the grunting and squealing of pigs.

I walked up to the house and, just as I was about to knock, the door was suddenly opened, and a tall, massively built old man stood before me.

'My name is . . .' I began.

But he interrupted me. 'You the man wrote to me?' His voice, though unpolished, had the same deep timbre as Nick's.

'That's right,' I said.

'You a friend of Nick?'

'Yes.'

He beckoned me in with a nod of his head. The door was low and I had to stoop a bit to get into the room. It was a large, low-ceilinged room. A smallish window let in a patch of light which lit up the middle of the room but did not spread into the corners, so that it seemed as if it were perpetually dusk. A table occupied the centre, and on the far side there was a large wood stove on which stood a softly hissing black kettle. In the corner facing the entrance there was an iron bedstead, and the bed was roughly made, with a patchwork quilt thrown carelessly on top.

The old man gestured me to one of the chairs which stood around the table.

'Sit.'

I did as he told me, and he sat down opposite me and placed his large calloused hands before him on the table. He seemed to study me intently for a while, and I scrutinized him. His face was covered by a three-days' stubble, but in spite of that, and in spite of the fact that it was a face beaten by sun and wind, it was clear that he was Nick's father. For Nick had the same determined mouth, and the same high cheek bones and the same dark, penetrating eyes.

At last he spoke. 'You friend of Nick.'

I nodded my head.

'What he do now?' he asked sharply. 'He still tampering with the earth?'

His voice rose as if he were delivering a challenge, and I drew back involuntarily. 'Why—he's doing scientific research, yes.' I told him. 'He's . . .'

'What God has made,' he said sternly, 'no man should touch.'

Before I could regain my composure, he went on, 'He sent

you. What for? What he want?'

'Nothing,' I said, 'Nothing at all. He sent me to bring you greetings and to tell you he is well.'

'And you come all the way from Edmonton to tell me?'

'Yes, of course.'

A faint smile played about his mouth, and the features of his face softened. Then suddenly he rose from his chair and stood towering over me. 'You are welcome in this house,' he said.

The formality with which he spoke was quite extraordinary and seemed to call for an appropriate reply, but I could do little more than stammer a thank you, and he, assuming again a normal tone of voice, asked me if I cared to have coffee. When I assented he walked to the far end of the room and busied himself about the stove.

It was then that I noticed, just under the window, a rough little wooden table and on top of it a faded old globe made of cardboard, such as little children use in school. I was intrigued to see it there and went over to look at it more closely. The cheap metal mount was brown with rust, and when I lifted it and tried to turn the globe on its axis, I found that it would not rotate because part of it had been squashed and broken. I ran my hand over the deep dent, and suddenly the old man startled me.

'What you doing there?' Curiosity seemed mingled with suspicion in his voice and made me feel like a small child surprised by its mother in an unauthorized raid on the pantry. I set down the globe and turned. He was standing by the table with two big mugs of coffee in his hands.

'Coffee is hot,' he said.

I went back to my chair and sat down, slightly embarrassed.

'Drink,' he said, pushing one of the mugs over to me.

We both began to sip the coffee, and for some time neither of us said anything.

'That thing over there,' he said at last, putting down his mug, 'that thing you was looking at—he brought it home one day—he was a boy then—maybe thirteen-year-old Nick. The other day I found it up in the attic. I was going to throw it in the garbage. But I forgot. There it belongs. In the garbage. It is a false thing.' His voice had now become venomous.

'False?' I said. 'How is it false?'

He disregarded my question. 'I remember,' he went on, 'he came home from school one day and we was all here in this room—all sitting around this table eating supper, his mother, his sister and me and Alex, too—the hired man like. And then sudden like Nick pipes up, and he says, we learned in school today, he says, how the earth is round like a ball, he says, and how it moves around and around the sun and never stops, he says. They learning you rubbish in school, I say. But he says, no, Miss McKenzie never told him no lies. Then I say she does, I say, and a son of mine shouldn't believe it. Stop your ears! Let not Satan come in!' He raised an outspread hand and his voice thundered as if he were a prophet armed. 'But he was always a stubborn boy—Nick. Like a mule. He never listened to reason. I believe it, he says. To me he says that—his father, just like that. I believe it, he says, because science has proved it and it is the truth. It is false, I cry, and you will not believe it. I believe it, he says. So then I hit him because he will not listen and will not obey. But he keeps shouting and shouting and shouting. "She moves," he shouts, "she moves, she moves!"'

He stopped. His hands had balled themselves into fists, and the remembered fury sent the blood streaming into his face. He seemed now to have forgotten my presence and he went on speaking in a low murmuring voice, almost as if he were telling the story to himself.

'So the next day, or the day after, I go down to that school, and there is this little Miss McKenzie, so small and so thin that I could have crush her with my bare hands. What you teaching my boy Nick? I ask her. What false lies you stuffing in his head? What you telling him that the earth is round and that she moves for? Did Joshua tell the earth to stand still, or did he command the sun? So she says to me, I don't care what Joshua done, she says, I will tell him what science has discovered. With that woman I could get nowhere. So then I try to keep him away from school, and I lock him up in the house, but it was no good. He got out, and he run to the school like, and Miss McKenzie she sends me a letter to say she will sent up the inspectors if I try to keep him away from the school. And I could do nothing.'

His sense of impotence was palpable. He sat sunk into himself as if he were still contemplating ways of halting the scientific education of his son.

'Two, three weeks after,' he went on, 'he comes walking in this door with a large paper parcel in his hand. Now, he calls out to me, now I will prove it to you, I will prove that she moves. And he tears off the paper from the box and takes out this—this thing, and he puts it on the table here. Here, he cries, here is the earth, and look, she moves. And he gives that thing a little push and it twirls around like. I have to laugh. A toy, I say to him, you bring me a toy here, not bigger than my hand, and it is supposed to be the world, this little toy here, with the printed words on coloured paper, this little cardboard ball. This Miss McKenzie, I say to him, she's turning you crazy in that school. But look, he says, she moves. Now I have to stop my laughing. I'll soon show you she moves, I say, for he is beginning to get me mad again. And I go up to the table and I take the toy thing in my hands and I smash it down like this.'

He raised his fists and let them crash down on the table as if he meant to splinter it.

'That'll learn you, I cry. I don't think he could believe I had done it, because he picks up the thing and he tries to turn it, but it don't turn no more. He stands there and the tears roll down his cheeks, and then, sudden like, he takes the thing in both his hands and he throws it at me. And it would have hit me right in the face, for sure, if I did not put up my hand. Against your father, I cry, you will raise up your hand against your father. Asmodeus! I grab him by the arm, and I shake him and I beat him like he was the devil. And he makes me madder and madder because he don't cry or shout or anything. And I would have kill him there, for sure, if his mother didn't come in then and pull me away. His nose was bleeding, but he didn't notice. Only he looks at me and says, you can beat me and break my globe, but you can't stop her moving. That night my wife she make me swear by all that's holy that I wouldn't touch him no more. And from then on I never hit him again nor talk to him about this thing. He goes his way and I go mine.'

He fell silent. Then after a moment he snapped suddenly, 'You hold with that?'

'Hold with what?' I asked, taken aback.

'With that thing?' He pointed behind him at the little table and at the broken globe. His gnarled hands now tightly inter-locked, he leaned forward in his chair and his dark, brooding eyes sought an answer from mine in the twilight of the room.

Alone with him there, I was almost afraid to answer firmly. Was it because I feared that I would hurt him too deeply if I did, or was I perhaps afraid that he would use violence on me as he had on Nick?

I cleared my throat. 'Yes,' I said then. 'Yes, I believe that the earth is round and that she moves. That fact has been accepted now for a long time.'

I expected him to round on me but he seemed suddenly to have grown very tired, and in a low resigned voice he said, 'Satan has taken over all the world.' Then suddenly he roused himself and hit the table hard with his fist, and cried passion-ately, 'But not me! Not me!'

It was unbearable. I felt that I must break the tension, and I said the first thing that came into my mind. 'You can be proud of your son in spite of all that happened between you. He is a fine man, and the world honours him for his work.'

He gave me a long look. 'He should have stayed here,' he said quietly. 'When I die, there will be nobody to look after the land. Instead he has gone off to tamper with God's earth.'

His fury was now all spent. We sat for a while in silence, and then I rose. Together we walked out of the house. When I was about to get into my car, he touched me lightly on the arm. I turned. His eyes surveyed the vast expanse of sky and land, stretching far into the distance, reddish clouds in the sky and blue shadows on the land. With a gesture of great dignity and power he lifted his arm and stood pointing into the dis-tance, at the flat land and the low-hanging sky.

'Look,' he said, very slowly and very quietly, 'she is flat, and she stands still.'

It was impossible not to feel a kind of admiration for the old man. There was something heroic about him. I held out my hand and he took it. He looked at me steadily, then averted his eyes and said, 'Send greetings to my son.'

I drove off quickly, but had to stop again in order to open the wooden gate. I looked back at the house, and saw him still standing there, still looking at his beloved land, a lonely, towering figure framed against the darkening evening sky.

A Secret Lost in the Water

Roch Carrier

AFTER I started going to school my father scarcely talked any more. I was very intoxicated by the new game of spelling; my father had little skill for it (it was my mother who wrote our letters) and was convinced I was no longer interested in hearing him tell of his adventures during the long weeks when he was far away from the house.

One day, however, he said to me:

'The time's come to show you something.'

He asked me to follow him. I walked behind him, not talking, as we had got in the habit of doing. He stopped in the field before a clump of leafy bushes.

'Those are called alders,' he said.

'I know.'

'You have to learn how to choose,' my father pointed out.

I didn't understand. He touched each branch of the bush, one at a time, with religious care.

'You have to choose one that's very fine, a perfect one, like this.'

I looked; it seemed exactly like the others.

My father opened his pocket knife and cut the branch he'd selected with pious care. He stripped off the leaves and showed me the branch, which formed a perfect Y.

'You see,' he said, 'the branch has two arms. Now take one in each hand. And squeeze them.'

I did as he asked and took in each hand one fork of the Y, which was thinner than a pencil.

'Close your eyes,' my father ordered, 'and squeeze a little harder . . . Don't open your eyes! Do you feel anything?'

'The branch is moving!' I exclaimed, astonished.

Beneath my clenched fingers the alder was wriggling like a small, frightened snake. My father saw that I was about to drop it.

'Hang on to it!'

'The branch is squirming,' I repeated. 'And I hear something that sounds like a river!'

'Open your eyes,' my father ordered.

I was stunned, as though he'd awakened me while I was dreaming.

'What does it mean?' I asked my father.

'It means that underneath us, right here, there's a little fresh-water spring. If we dig, we could drink from it. I've just taught you how to find a spring. It's something my own father taught me. It isn't something you learn in school. And it isn't useless: a man can get along without writing and arithmetic, but he can never get along without water.'

Much later, I discovered that my father was famous in the region because of what the people called his 'gift': before digging a well they always consulted him; they would watch him prospecting the fields or the hills, eyes closed, hands clenched on the fork of an alder bough. Wherever my father stopped, they marked the ground; there they would dig; and from there water would gush forth.

Years passed; I went to other schools, saw other countries, I had children, I wrote some books and my poor father is lying in the earth where so many times he had found fresh water.

One day someone began to make a film about my village and its inhabitants, from whom I've stolen so many of the stories that I tell. With the film crew we went to see a farmer to capture the image of a sad man: his children didn't want to receive the inheritance he'd spent his whole life preparing for them—the finest farm in the area. While the technicians were getting cameras and microphones ready the farmer put his arm around my shoulders, saying:

'I knew your father well.'

'Ah! I know. Everybody in the village knows each other . . . No one feels like an outsider.'

'You know what's under your feet?'

'Hell?' I asked, laughing.

'Under your feet there's a well. Before I dug I called in specialists from the Department of Agriculture; they did research, they analyzed shovelfuls of dirt; and they made a report where they said there wasn't any water on my land. With the family, the animals, the crops, I need water. When I saw that those specialists hadn't found any I thought of your father and I asked him to come over. He didn't want to; I think he was pretty fed up with me because I'd asked those specialists instead of him. But finally he came; he went and cut off a little branch, then he walked around for a while with his eyes shut; he stopped, he listened to something we couldn't hear and then he said to me: "Dig right here, there's enough water to get your whole flock drunk and drown your specialists besides." We dug and found water. Fine water that's never heard of pollution.'

The film people were ready; they called to me to take my place.

'I'm gonna show you something,' said the farmer, keeping me back. 'You wait right here.'

He disappeared into a shack which he must have used to store things, then came back with a branch which he held out to me.

'I never throw nothing away; I kept the alder branch your father cut to find my water. I don't understand, it hasn't dried out.'

Moved as I touched the branch, kept out of I don't know what sense of piety—and which really wasn't dry—I had the feeling that my father was watching me over my shoulder; I closed my eyes and, standing above the spring my father had discovered, I waited for the branch to writhe, I hoped the sound of gushing water would rise to my ears.

The alder stayed motionless in my hands and the water beneath the earth refused to sing.

Somewhere along the roads I'd taken since the village of my childhood I had forgotten my father's knowledge.

'Don't feel sorry,' said the man, thinking no doubt of his farm and his childhood; 'nowadays fathers can't pass on anything to the next generation.'

And he took the alder branch from my hands.

My Father, Playing Father

Deborah Eibel

My father, playing father, held my hand—
A visitor, about to leave again
To teach in distant households of our land.
He left, and took a shortcut through the lane.

My father, playing father, made me cry—
He never let a secret leave his throat;
For strangers only did he prophesy;
He came home only when the overcoat

In which he pilgrimed had to be repaired,
The emblem of desertion. And my mother,
Despite the laughter of the neighbors, spared
No pains for him; she would not love another.

My father, playing father, played the clown—
He prophesied for children not his own.

Between Here and Illinois

Ralph Pomeroy

When my father died
I didn't get my brother's telegram.

Tuesday, the day my sister called,
I wasn't home.
It was sunny at the beach.

On Wednesday I got up at eight,
drank a glass of cold Tropicana,
had raisin toast, instant coffee,
went to work.

The day my brother flew my father's body
from San Fernando to Illinois.

The rest of the week went by.
I was home all the following Sunday
because it was too cold to go swimming.

Monday, my sister reached me.
In the atmosphere of my office
I heard her voice, all the way from Michigan.

She said that the funeral was over.
She described the black vestements and white flowers.
She said that they had all missed me
and were wondering where I was.

If they had reached me
I could have flown from New York to Illinois—
all the way from here to Illinois—
over all the graves that lie between here and Illinois.

The Jukes Family

Frank Sullivan

T HE air is so cluttered with homely little radio programs recounting the daily heartaches and joys of a multitude of families—"The Green Family," "The Brown Family," "This Man's Family," "That Man's Family," and so on—that I have decided to climb on the band wagon with my own program, "The Jukes Family." It will recount, from day to day, the joys and sorrows of an average, homey, not-quite-bright family of the lower lower class.

The matriarch is Ma Jukes, a friendly old party of forty-five who has brought fifteen or twenty children into the world and has learned to take things as they come. She does the best she can to manage her unruly brood, each of whom has some characteristic that sets him or her apart from the herd. For instance, it has long been a subject of frank discussion in the family whether the ears on Laddie, the seventh boy, extend above the top of his head or whether the plateau of his head simply fails to rise to the top of his ears.

The fourth child, Slim, age twenty-two, has a penchant for bigamy which frequently brings upon him the good-natured raillery of the rest of the family. Another of the boys, Timmy, is doing a stretch in Sing Sing, and Mayzetta, the third girl, is in her sophomore year at the Dobbville Home for Delinquent Females. But the glamour girl of the Jukes Family is Babs— tall, striking, with dark, flashing eyes and a head of hair five and a half feet long. And every single strand of it a natural emerald green! Ma Jukes' family (she was a Cabot) all had hair of vivid yellow. Pa's folks' hair had been Alice blue. Nature's alchemy had combined the two colors happily in Babs.

Now then, as our first program opens, we find Ma Jukes setting a kettle of water to boil. A dozen or so of the youngsters, among them her first-born, Jeddie, a fine-looking chap of thirty with white hair and pink eyes, romp boisterously under her feet as she putters about the stove. There is a scuffle among the bairns. Ma intervenes.

"Monongahela!" she admonishes a strapping girl of about ten. "You give Jeddie back his doll. Ain't you ashamed to be playin' with dolls, a big gal like you. . . . Tarnation take it, git out from under my feet afore ye git scalded. Oh, it's you, Chub."

Chub is an attractive child of nineteen, always hanging around the stove because he *likes* to be scalded. Ma goodnaturedly ladles a teaspoonful of hot water on him.

"Now, thar, that's enough. Git along an' quit pesterin' yer pore old ma."

Chub scampers off with a happy scream of agony.

"I declar'," says Ma, philosophizing in the manner of all the Mas on the family radio programs, "I don't know what the younger generation's a-comin' to. When I was a young un we hung around our ma to git the scrapin's from the cake bowl, not to git hot water thrun on us. Now, whatever's a-keepin' yer pa?"

"I'm hongry," cries Eglantine Jukes, a comely sprite of fifteen without a chin.

Here the voice of Chuckles Gladsome, the announcer, is heard. Ma winces. In the cheery voice of the typical family-program announcer, Chuckles says that if little Eglantine is "hongry," she had just better get herself a good, big, heapin' old dish of rich, creamy, juicy, delicious, nourishing Dwerps, the Sweetheart of Breakfast Foods. "So go to your corner grocery store tonight, or at the very latest tomorrow morning, etc., etc.," concludes Chuckles.

"I'm still hongry," says Eglantine.

"Well, yer pa oughta be here any minnit now with the chicken," says Ma. "Wonder what's a-keepin' him? Oh, here he is!"

Pa Jukes enters. He is a jovial soul who takes the responsibilities of a large family in his stride. His face, if you can call it a face, is unlined by the years, and its frank, open expression is enhanced rather than marred by an almost complete absence of chin.

"Howdy, Pa," says Ma. "Where's the chicken? You said you was a-goin' to snag us a chicken fer supper."

"Shucks, Ma, there ain't none," apologizes Pa. "Dad rat it, I was lucky I got out of Ole Man Eddy's hencoop 'thout gettin' a hideful o' buckshot."

Ma's face falls at this news, but only for an instant. She quickly hides her disappointment and presents a brave front to the children. All mothers on family programs are constantly presenting brave fronts in the face of domestic problems. "Tarnation take the ornery ole cuss!" she says. "Can't even leave a neighbor have a measly ole chicken. An' after the way we all pitched in an' helped, the night his barn took fire."

"Now, Ma," says Pa, "you know we wa'n't doin' no mor'n our plain duty in helpin' put that fire out. You know's well's I do, 'twas our Buster set that barn afire."

Buster is the firebug of the Jukes Family, a gay, irrepressible Puck of thirteen with the typical Jukes no-chin, and regarded by the neighbors as quite a tease because of his habit of setting buildings afire every so often.

"Well," says Ma, "I kind o' had my face fixed fer chicken, but I guess we c'n manage. Here, Lump, you run down to Perkins' grocery and fetch up a few cans salmon an' any other vittles ye think might tech the spot."

"Not me," Lump says. "Jedge tole me ef I got caught swipin' any more stuff out'n stores, he'd send me to state's prison sure 'nough."

"That so, young Mister High-an'-Mighty!" snaps Pa Jukes. "Well, lemme tell you one thing, you young whippersnapper, ef state's prison's good enough fer yer brother Timmy, it's plenty good enough fer you."

"Now, Pa," says Ma, soothingly.

"Well, dad rat it, Ma, jest don't let him git so uppity, that's all. I don't know what's got into the younger generation lately. Why, there ain't a nicer crowd o' boys you'd want to meet than the boys at Sing Sing. Leastwise, 'twas so in my day thar."

"Pa, mebbe one o' the children that ain't never been pinched better go," advises Ma. "It'll look better."

There are shouts from the kiddies of "Me, Ma! Let me go! I wanna go, Ma!"

At this point the door bursts open and in comes Wash Jukes, an attractive, coffee-colored lad of fourteen.

"Guess what, Ma!" Wash exults. "The jedge jes' pernounced me a ju-vile delinquent!"

Wash's brothers and sisters are agog with admiration and Ma glows with maternal pride, but Brother Lump is in the clutch of the greeneyed monster.

"Shucks!" says Lump. "I was a ju-vile delinquent when I was ten year old, wa'n't I, Ma?"

"Go on, po' white trash," sneers Wash.

"Wash Jukes!" Ma rebukes. "You lemme hear you call yer brother po' white trash again an' I'll slap ye down. Now git along to the store and fetch back some vittles." She sighs.

"What's wrong, Ma?" asks Pa.

"Pa, I'm a-worrit about about Babs. I wa'n't fixin' to tell ye, because I didn't aim to fret ye none, but she ain't been hum now fer two days and two nights."

"Shucks, Ma, she prob'ly stopped off at some gal friend's house on her way hum from school."

"She hadn't oughta gone an' done it 'thout lettin' me know. I declar', I don't know what the younger generation's a-comin' to. When I was a gal Babs' age, ef I stayed away from hum fer more'n one night a-runnin', I got Hail Columbia from the matron."

"Don't ye fret none about Babs, Ma. She's jest young an' full o' fun. Leave her have her fling. She'll be old soon enough."

"Mebbe yer right, Pa, but it seems to me the young uns don't pay no heed to their elders nowadays nohow. Mebbe I'm a-gettin' old-fashioned, but I kind o' like to know whar my children is o' nights. Say, that reminds me, I got a letter from Timmy today."

'Ye did? Then he's out o' solitary. They don't let ye write no letters when yer in solitary. Leastwise, they didn't in my day at Sing Sing. What's he say?"

"Tarnation take it, how do I know? That's why I'm a-waitin' for Babs to come hum, so's she can read it to me. Buster!"

"Yes, Ma!"

"Quit settin' fire to Chub!"

"But he ast me to set him afire, Ma," Buster says.

"Sure I did, Ma," says Chub.

"Makes no difference," says Ma, sternly. "'Tain't good fer ye. Ye want to grow up all charred?"

"Yes," says Chub, eagerly.

"Well, I swan to glory, I don't know what the younger generation's a-comin' to. Pa, put out Chub, will ye?"

With a good-natured chuckle, Pa throws a pail of water over Chub just as Wash returns from his trip to Perkins' store. The hungry brood crowds around him eagerly.

"Any luck, Wash?" says Ma.

"Naw," says Wash. "Ole Perkins was a-watchin' me all the time. All I could git was this." He takes a ham from beneath his blouse.

"Well," says Ma, "'tain't much, but it's somethin'."

"And this." Wash produces another package.

"A flitch o' bacon," says Ma. "Now, that's real nice." Ma's tone is cheery. She is presenting a brave front.

"And these," says Wash, and he unloads from various crannies of his person a quantity of canned goods, fresh vegetables, assorted table delicacies, a watermelon, and a case of soft drinks.

"That all ye got?" asks Ma, striving to keep the disappointment from her voice. "Well, ye done the best ye could. We'll manage somehow."

Now the door opens and who bursts in but Babs, her handsome eyes flashing and her green hair flying in the wind.

"Ma," cries Babs, "guess what!"

"Babs Jukes, whar you been?" says Ma, severely. "Go tidy up yer hair. Look at ye!"

"Ma!" cries Babs. "I got a job!"

Pa winces at the sound of the ugly three-letter word.

"Whar's the job?" Ma inquires, coldly, after a pause.

"In the circus! Lady Godiva!"

An artistic career! Well, that's different. Not quite to be classed as work. The alarm subsides, and the family is agog to hear about Babs' job.

"My sakes!" says Ma. "To think we got a real, gen-wine actress in the family!"

"Babs, c'n I have yer autograph?" asks little Monongahela.

Ma is thinking happily how she will come it over the neighbor up the alley, Mrs. Kallikak, who has been insufferable ever since her son got the hot squat for the axe murder of seven.

"Reason I ain't been hum," says Babs, "is I had to go to New York right away an' sign up. Guess they was afraid some other circus might grab me."

"I allus knew Babs'd go places," says Pa, with pride.

"Gee Whittaker, I'm tired," says Babs. "I set up on that train from New York the hull night."

"Set down, child," urges Ma. "I'll git ye a cup o' tea."

Babs sinks into a chair and the youngsters crowd around their distinguished sister, beseeching her for details of her new career and entreating her to get them jobs as freaks in the sideshow.

Suddenly, above the childish babble, there is heard a shriek, then a sinister crackling noise, and cries of alarm as the children scurry to safety.

"Buster! You quit that!" Ma shouts, as is her wont whenever she hears crackling, but it is too late. This time Buster's prank has succeeded all too well. By the time rescue measures have been taken Bab's once-glorious mane is a smoldering ruin, naught of it remaining save a charred stubble.

Babs is inconsolable.

"Don't you fret none, dearie," Ma attempts to comfort her. "It'l' grow in again in no time at all. Once, when I had the type-ford fever—"

But here the voice of Chuckles Gladsome interrupts Ma.

"Well, folks," says he, "all I can say is, if Babs Jukes wants that hair to grow again in time for her to join the circus, she had just better go tonight, or tomorrow morning at the very latest, to the nearest drugstore and get a bottle of Stickney's Famous Hair Restorer. Ladies, if your hair bothers you, if it is dull, dry, and hard to manage—"

A shot rings out.

When the smoke clears, Ma Jukes is standing over poor Chuckles with Pa's shotgun in her right hand.

"Got him, by cracky!" she announces, with grim pleasure.

"Ma," Pa says. "Ye hadn't ought to o' gone an' done that.

The law says 'tain't legal to shoot a buck announcer out o' season. Now ye've let ye'se'f in fer a good fine, and whar ye're a-goin' to raise the dough, I don't know."

Well, what will happen to Ma? Will any jury convict? Will any Fish and Game Commission slap a fine on her for shooting an announcer, in season or out? Is Ma on her way to the clink? And how about Bab's hair? Will it grow back in time for her to join the circus? Follow the adventures of that happy-go-lucky, madcap, lovable, charming, irresponsible bunch, the Jukes Family! Tune in on this station tomorrow afternoon at this same hour and find out what happened to Ma Jukes. Your announcer is Paul Parks, substituting for Chuckles Gladsome. Bi-ing, ba-ang, bo-ong!

Great-Aunt Rebecca

Elizabeth Brewster

I remember my mother's Aunt Rebecca
Who remembered very well Confederation
And what a time of mourning it was.
She remembered the days before the railway.
And how when the first train came through
Everybody got on and visited it,
Scraping off their shoes first
So as not to dirty the carriage.
She remembered the remoteness, the long walks between
neighbours.
Her own mother had died young, in childbirth,
But she had lived till her eighties,
Had borne eleven children,
Managed to raise nine of them,
In spite of scarlet fever.
She had clothed them with the work of her own fingers,
Wool from her own sheep, spun at home,
Woven at home, sewed at home
Without benefit of machine.
She had fed them with pancakes and salt pork
And cakes sweetened with maple sugar.
She had taught them one by one to memorize
'The chief end of man is to know God,'
And she had also taught them to make porridge
And the right way of lighting a wood fire,

Had told the boys to be kind and courageous
And the girls never to raise their voices
Or argue with their husbands.

I remember her as an old woman,
Rheumatic, with folded hands,
In a rocking chair in a corner of the living room,
Bullied (for her own good) by one of her daughters.
She marveled a little, gently and politely,
At radios, cars, telephones;
But really they were not as present to her
As the world of her prime, the farmhouse
In the midst of woods, the hayfields
Where her husband and the boys swung their scythes
Through the burning afternoon, until she called for supper.

For me also, the visiting child, she made that world more real
Than the present could be. I too
Wished to be a pioneer,
To walk on snowshoes through remote pastures,
To live away from settlements an independent life
With a few loved people only; to be like Aunt Rebecca,
Soft as silk and tough as that thin wire
They use for snaring rabbits.

Four Generations

Joyce Maynard

MY mother called last week to tell me that my grandmother is dying. She has refused an operation that would postpone, but not prevent, her death from pancreatic cancer. She can't eat, she has been hemorrhaging, and she has severe jaundice. "I always prided myself on being different," she told my mother. "Now I am different. I'm yellow."

My mother, telling me this news, began to cry. So I became the mother for a moment, reminding her, reasonably, that my grandmother is eighty-seven, she's had a full life, she has all her faculties, and no one who knows her could wish that she live long enough to lose them. Lately my mother has been finding notes in my grandmother's drawers at the nursing home, reminding her, "Joyce's husband's name is Steve. Their daughter is Audrey." In the last few years she hadn't had the strength to cook or garden, and she's begun to say she's had enough of living.

My grandmother was born in Russia, in 1892—the eldest daughter in a large and prosperous Jewish family. But the prosperity didn't last. She tells stories of the pogroms and the cossacks who raped her when she was twelve. Soon after that, her family emigrated to Canada, where she met my grandfather.

Their children were the center of their life. The story I

loved best, as a child, was of my grandfather opening every box of Cracker Jack in the general store he ran, in search of the particular tin toy my mother coveted. Though they never had much money, my grandmother saw to it that her daughter had elocution lessons and piano lessons, and assured her that she would go to college.

But while she was at college, my mother met my father, who was blue-eyed and blond-haired and not Jewish. When my father sent love letters to my mother, my grandmother would open and hide them, and when my mother told her parents she was going to marry this man, my grandmother said if that happened, it would kill her.

Not likely, of course. My grandmother is a woman who used to crack Brazil nuts open with her teeth, a woman who once lifted a car off the ground, when there was an accident and it had to be moved. She has been representing her death as imminent ever since I've known her—twenty-five years—and has discussed, at length, the distribution of her possessions and her lamb coat. Every time we said goodbye, after our annual visit to Winnipeg, she'd weep and say she'd never see us again. But in the meantime, while every other relative of her generation, and a good many of the younger ones, has died (nursed usually by her), she has kept making knishes, shopping for bargains, tending the healthiest plants I've ever seen.

After my grandfather died, my grandmother lived, more than ever, through her children. When she came to visit, I would hide my diary. She couldn't understand any desire for privacy. She couldn't bear it if my mother left the house without her.

This possessiveness is what made my mother furious (and then guilt-ridden that she felt that way, when of course she owed so much to her mother). So I harbored the resentment that my mother—and dutiful daughter—would not allow herself. I—who had always performed specially well for my grandmother, danced and sung for her, presented her with kisses and good report cards—stopped writing to her, ceased to visit.

But when I heard that she was dying, I realized I wanted to go to Winnipeg to see her one more time. Mostly to make my mother happy, I told myself (certain patterns being hard to break). But also, I was offering up one more particularly fine accomplishment: my own dark-eyed, dark-skinned, dark-haired daughter, whom my grandmother had never met.

I put on my daughter's best dress for our visit to Winnipeg, the way the best dresses were always put on me, and I filled my pockets with animal crackers, in case Audrey started to cry. I scrubbed her face mercilessly. On the elevator going up to her room, I realized how much I was sweating.

Grandma was lying flat with an IV tube in her arm and her eyes shut, but she opened them when I leaned over to kiss her. "It's Fredelle's daughter, Joyce," I yelled, because she doesn't hear well anymore, but I could see that no explanation was necessary. "You came," she said. "You brought the baby."

Audrey is just one, but she has seen enough of the world to know that people in beds are not meant to be so still and yellow, and she looked frightened. I had never wanted, more, for her to smile.

Then Grandma waved at her—the same kind of slow, finger-flexing wave a baby makes—and Audrey waved back. I spread her toys out on my grandmother's bed and sat her down. There she stayed, most of the afternoon, playing and humming and sipping on her bottle, taking a nap at one point, leaning against my grandmother's leg. When I cranked her Snoopy guitar, Audrey stood up on the bed and danced. Grandma wouldn't talk much anymore, though every once in a while she would say how sorry she was that she wasn't having a better day. "I'm not always like this," she said.

Mostly she just watched Audrey. Sometimes Audrey would get off the bed, inspect the get-well cards, totter down the hall. "Where is she?" Grandma kept asking. "Who's looking after her?" I had the feeling, even then, that if I'd said, "Audrey's lighting matches," Grandma would have shot up to rescue her.

We were flying home that night, and I had dreaded telling her, remembering all those other tearful partings. But in the end, I was the one who cried. She had said she was ready to die. But as I leaned over to stroke her forehead, what she said was, "I wish I had your hair" and "I wish I was well."

On the plane flying home, with Audrey in my arms, I thought about mothers and daughters, and the four generations of the family that I know most intimately. Every one of those mothers loves and needs her daughter more than her daughter will love or need her some day, and we are, each of us, the only person on earth who is quite so consumingly interested in our child.

Sometimes I kiss and hug Audrey so much she starts crying —which is, in effect, what my grandmother was doing to my mother, all her life. And what makes my mother grieve right now, I think, is not simply that her mother will die in a day or two, but that, once her mother dies, there will never again be someone to love her in quite such an unreserved, unquestioning way. No one else who believes that, fifty years ago, she could have put Shirley Temple out of a job, no one else who remembers the moment of her birth. She will only be a mother, then, not a daughter anymore.

Audrey and I have stopped over for a night in Toronto, where my mother lives. Tomorrow she will go to a safe-deposit box at the bank and take out the receipt for my grandmother's burial plot. Then she will fly back to Winnipeg, where, for the first time in anybody's memory, there was waist-high snow on April Fool's Day. But tonight she is feeding me, as she always does when I come, and I am eating more than I do anywhere else. I admire the wedding china (once my grandmother's) that my mother has set on the table. She says (the way Grandma used to say to her, of the lamb coat), "Some day it will be yours."

To a Woman

A.M. Stephen

Who are you?
To one, you were a daughter
in whom he saw his own sunshine refracted—
an image in a drop of dew.

To one, you were a sister,
a weaker self.
Thinking of you,
he was a little contemptuous,
and a little proud.

To one, you were a sweetheart—
beauty incarnate to him—
a star that, following,
he became a hero and a poet.

To one, you were a wife.
Careful of his health,
prudent, useful,
you meant home to him.

To one, you were a mother.
He leaned upon you,
neglected you,

resented your vigilance,
and knew
that your love would not fail.

Yet,
these were but facets of you,
fragmentary gleams through windows
of the house which held your soul.

Teacher, artist, warrior,
ruler, merchant prince, and laborer,
a superb animal,
a strong and beautiful god—
these, too, you were—
a human being—
Man—the microcosm!

But we,
who saw only your sex,
passed you by,
blinded by the illusion
of separateness.

In One Era and Out the Other

Sam Levenson

I T was hard to tell whether the papas and mamas of that era were happily married. The subject was not open for discussion, certainly not with their children:

"Are you happy, Ma?"

"You got nothing else to think about?"

Nobody ever told Mama that marriage was supposed to make her happy; certainly Papa didn't. Nobody had promised him *happy* either.

Mature people prayed for good health, good fortune and an honorable old age. A husband was supposed to make a living and a wife was supposed to make a life of it. Only children talked of happiness; they still believed in fairy tales.

Human beings, the old folks said, don't live happily forever after—most of the time not even during. So it was wise, in marriage and in everything else, to expect the worst. Then if it turned out to be only worse, it still wasn't too bad.

Marriage was one of those things you were supposed to save for your old age, happy or not.

"Love, shmove!" Papa used to say. "I love blintzes; did I marry one?"

The word love embarrassed them. It was an unmentionable, like brassiere, hernia and miscarriage. Not that they didn't believe in love. They felt it but avoided the precise definition that young people demand.

To Mama love was not passion or infatuation or compatibility. She had given birth to ten kids without any of those. "Love," said Mama after many years of marriage, "is what you have been through with someone."

Love was made up of satisfaction ("Ten kids, thank God, is plenty"), sharing ("If he can take it, I can take it"), optimism ("Worse it couldn't get!") and friendship—not in the style of Romeo and Juliet but more like Damon and Pythias.

I knew my parents valued each other because Papa told me always to listen to Mama and Mama told me always to listen to Papa. Because Mama always watched at the window when Papa left for work and whispered to herself about his being "a good man, a learned man, to work so hard in a shop, it's a pity." Because at lunchtime she had me deliver a pot of hot soup two miles in the snow to Papa's shop so "he should know." Because Papa wouldn't spend a penny on himself unless Mama spent on herself. Share and share alike. So the day Mama had all her teeth pulled, Papa bought a suit.

If the papas were at all romantic before marriage, they quickly shed "the foolishness" as soon after as possible. My father never took my mother out before they were married— and afterwards only if they were headed for the maternity hospital, which in Mama's case was often enough to give her rosy cheeks: "If it's nice out we'll walk; if it's raining we'll take an umbrella."

They never had a honeymoon. "We didn't have enough money, so Papa went by himself." There were anniversaries but they went uncelebrated.

"How long are you married, Pa?"

"Please! Not while I'm eating."

No candy, no flowers, no inscribed charms to wear on bracelets; nothing but a big, fat, immovable, indestructible wedding ring. The mamas believed the best way to keep it bright and shiny was to soak it in hot soapy water several times a day. In a large family this was no problem.

At the end of the day Mama could count on Papa to come home with those three little words on his lips that made it all worth while: "What's for supper?"

Every night, after we kids were in bed and supposedly asleep, I could hear Mama and Papa in the kitchen, not making love but reading about it. Papa would read aloud the daily installment of a romantic novel that ran on forever in the Yiddish newspaper.

He read in a dull, monotonous voice, perhaps to avoid betraying any emotional involvement in the subject matter, while Mama pressed his shirts, her tempo getting faster and faster as the story got hotter. "And he drew her toward him, looking into the quivering pupils of her wide blue eyes and kissed her on the trembling lips—"

"Again?" said Mama, her iron coming to a dead stop. "He kissed her only yesterday!" Papa took a closer look at the paper and hurled it against the wall. "You're right! It's yesterday's paper!"

The day my brother and I caught Papa kissing Mama we got hysterical. "What happened?" "I don't know. I think maybe the landlord died!"

It had to be an event of supreme emotional significance. Papa had not kissed Mama even at their wedding. Theirs was a marriage of convenience between two poor families. The first time he met her was at the wedding—and he would never kiss a girl the first time he met her!

Generally, kissing was considered unmanly. The presence of so many children proved his manliness but kissing, especially in the presence of his children, was not the manly thing to do.

If any one of us tried to kiss Mama, we would get brushed off with "Go away, crazy! You got nothing better to do?" Besides it was dangerous to kiss Mama. She always wore a needle near the neckline of her dress and a wild embrace could be fatal to the embracer.

It was not the fashion of those times to smother children with kisses but to smother them with care. I knew I wasn't being kissed but I also knew I was being loved, even more than I deserved. It made one rise to the deserving.

We were living witness to love and marriage at its best—and its worst. Devotion, sacrifice, adoration, sympathy, loyalty, tenderness, along with anger, alienation and bitterness. A loving couple and a quarreling couple could be one and the same couple.

The secret of an enduring marriage was no secret. They quarreled. Married people exercised their marriage the way babies exercised their lungs, by yelling. They strengthened their matrimonial muscles by giving them a daily workout.

Psychiatrists do not look down upon the quarrel. Confrontation is also communication. The wide-open dialogue, the airing of the disparity between "is" and "ought," the itemized bill of particular offenses brought to the surface to be contested, denied and sometimes admitted to, may have been my parents' version of today's encounter sessions.

They would rather fight than switch. Perhaps it wasn't even a fight. Perhaps they instinctively recognized that incompatibility is inherent in people and ideas, that dichotomy is really unity, that positives cannot live without negatives and that opposites need each other.

All of which, if true, led to the conclusion that if a man didn't have a wife he'd have to quarrel with total strangers, and for that they can take you away.

Like the sounds of slamming doors, banging pots, beating rugs and chopping meat, the bickering of bedfellows was an accepted household noise. ("Must you quarrel with me on the street? What do we have a home for?")

Some quarrels started in the morning, were suspended when the man of the house left for work, were resumed in the evening without missing a beat. Marital scraps, like food scraps, could be reheated. "He's home!" Evening events were the best. There was time enough for a 15-rounder.

We didn't need alarm clocks. The Kowalciks' gong rang at 6:00 a.m., the Browns' at 6:30; the Michniks' at 6:45. If a morning fight ran on for a half hour or more, it meant the husband was sick and not going to work that day. If there was no quarrel at all, Mama would worry. "It's been like that all day. Sammy, go see if they are all right."

These were our soap operas. We could tune in any time and pick up snatches of dramatic dialogue. We knew the cast; we knew the lines. But we never tired of them. Monogamy, yes; monotony, no.

Sometimes she talked first: "I don't understand you. Monday you liked fried herring, Tuesday you like fried herring. Now all of a sudden you don't like fried herring!"

"Herring! Herring! It's not the herring! It's the last 20 years."

Sometimes he talked first: "You can always leave me."

"I'm gonna leave you and make you happy?"

A dying quarrel sometimes had to be revived. You can't quarrel alone. "I don't like the way you're sitting there not saying anything."

It would seem that our constant exposure to the quarreling of the mamas and papas around us might have turned us prematurely cynical. On the contrary, our early combat training taught us to bring our "as you like it" in focus with "like it is"—not only on the subject of marriage but on people partnerships in general.

We came to realize every man and woman has something to say in his own defense, that there are not only two sides to an argument but dozens, that in human relations there is no perfect and final answer—that some ideas may never be happily wedded to others, that the dialogue, whispered or shouted, is eternal and that the seeking of the answer is the answer.

We had absorbed a mature point of view. There's nothing wrong with marriage; it's just the living together afterward that's murder.

Handling Teen Calls

Gary Lautens

T HE other evening the telephone rang and a lovely
female voice asked, "Is Stephen there?"
As it happened, our eldest wasn't, so I said, "I'm
sorry, he's out."

I should have left it at that.

However, I broke the cardinal rule of being the father of a
teenager while answering a telephone.

"Is that Debbie?" I asked.

Boom, crash and thud.

As soon as the words were out I knew I had made a terrible
mistake.

"No," was the rather chilly reply. "It's . . ."

Of course it was a totally different name, the name of somebody who obviously didn't know Debbie even exists or, if she
did, wasn't happy about it.

What a fool I am.

With three teenagers in the house, I should know you never
mention a name over the phone and give away a son's (or
daughter's) secrets.

You say, "Hello, there" or, "Hi, I'm sorry but you missed
Stephen. Is there any message?" You can even say, "He's out
but he won't be long."

But you don't cough up a free name and put your teenager
in possible hot water with someone he's probably told is the
only one in his life.

When will I learn?

I am pretty good now in that I never say, when a teenager at our house gets a call, "He (or she) is in the bathroom. I'll take a message."

Bathroom references are "gross."

Also, I never say, "He's over at Bill's. Maybe you can reach him there."

Giving away a teenager's social calendar is just as taboo as giving away a free name. You've got to be noncommittal. "Stephen will be sorry he missed you" is okay. Ditto, "Jane was talking about a movie, but she may have changed her mind," a statement that gives her lots of leeway and will not stand up in a court of law.

On the other hand, a teenager expects his or her father to pump as much information out of a caller as possible.

The absolute minimum is (a) who is calling, (b) the time of the call, (c) where the caller can be reached and (d) the sex of the caller.

You can forget about (a), (b) and (c), but heaven help if you flub (d).

Establishing the sex of the caller is absolutely vital and any father who misses out on that one is definitely in trouble. Unfortunately, when your teenagers have friends whose voices haven't changed yet, it isn't easy.

Other things a teenager expects a father to learn are:

Was the call (in your opinion) to invite said teenaged son or daughter to a party, school dance, etc., or did the caller sound like someone who only wanted the title of the book required for the French course.

As a guess (in the case of a call for a teenaged daughter) would you say the caller was probably six feet tall with a clear complexion?

Why do you think the caller didn't leave a number and, in your estimation, do you think he (or she) will call back if said teenager sits by the telephone for an hour or so?

The pressure of being the father of a teenager is enormous when the telephone rings and sometimes you just want to let it ring rather than risk making a mistake.

Fortunately, with teenagers in the house you know one thing: the call is never for you.

Behind Times

Gary Lautens

O UR Stephen (who is eighteen) came home from a
disco the other evening with distressing news: while
minding his own business on the dance floor, some
girl he had never seen before reached over and pinched him
on the bum.

According to the account we received, the assaulter was
about twenty, had a dynamite figure and gave Stephen a
cheeky grin when he turned in total surprise.

Fortunately, Stephen was with a date, so the whole sordid
business went no further, but Stephen's mother and I were
seething, of course.

Can a young lad no longer boogie in safety on the hardwood
surfaces of this city? Must he keep his wits about him and his
vitals protected even during the intricacies of The Bump to
make certain no lusting female, half-crazed by the sight of his
plunging Pierre Cardin loungewear, takes unwanted liberties
with his person?

For someone of my generation, it's totally unthinkable.
Why, when I was Stephen's age, a male person could fox trot,
waltz and dip to his heart's content in the school gymnasium
without fear of being womanhandled every time he box-
stepped past a dark corner.

In all my years of swinging and swaying with Sammy Kaye,
not once did I have to ward off the impudent grope or the
lecherous pat. Women respected men for their minds then,

and understood when we told them we were "saving" ourselves for marriage.

No more apparently.

"Perhaps this young creature mistook you for somebody else," I suggested hopefully to my eldest. "Or else it was an accident."

"I don't think so," Stephen replied. "I think I can tell a deliberate pinch when I feel one, and she definitely smiled at me."

"You don't suppose she was in the middle of snapping her fingers to the music when your bottom happened to get in the way, do you?"

"No."

"Perhaps she works in a clothing store and was feeling the texture of your trousers. That's how they do it you know, between the fingers."

"She pinched more than cloth," Stephen insisted.

"This is even worse than I suspected," I said. "If you eliminate the music and the cloth, it means she was interested in only—my God! Thank heaven you were with somebody. If you had been alone, it's anyone's guess what might have happened to you."

Stephen shot back an answering nod to indicate he had, indeed, thought about the possibilities.

Unlike other males his age who might have wept and made their complexions blotchy after such a harrowing experience at the hands of a female stranger, Stephen remained composed, and I was proud of him.

"I don't want this one unfortunate incident to change your attitude toward women," I cautioned. "There are lots of them out there who can control their hands at a dance and not get out of line. However, as a precaution, I think you should take some preventative steps to avoid similar pawings in the future."

"Like what?" he asked.

"First, I'd buy trousers that are a size or two too big. You're just asking for trouble if you wear form-fitting ones in front of some sexually liberated, twenty-year-old female who is only interested in a one-night stand.

"Next, for extra protection, put a thick hankie in the back

pocket of the baggy trousers. Not only will it give you a lumpy appearance that should be as good as a cold shower to any female out for a good time, it will provide protection in the event she still tries to get fresh during a Barry Manilow number.

"Finally, try not to turn your back on a female if she is pawing the floor with one foot, has steam coming out of both nostrils and spits in her hands as she walks in your direction. She's obviously up to no good."

Stephen said he would weigh my words carefully because, "I don't think any one in the country knows more about turning off women than you do."

It was difficult holding back the tears. It's not often an eighteen-year-old son pays his father such a glowing tribute.

Adolescence

P. K. Page

In love they wore themselves in a green embrace.
A silken rain fell through the spring upon them.
In the park she fed the swans and he
whittled nervously with his strange hands
And white was mixed with all their colours
as if they drew it from the flowering trees.

At night his two-finger whistle brought her down
the waterfall stairs to his shy smile
which, like an eddy, turned her round and round
lazily and slowly so her will
was nowhere—as in dreams things are and aren't.

Walking along the avenues in the dark
street lamps sang like sopranos in their heads
with a violence they never understood
and all their movements when they were together
had no conclusion.

Only leaning into the question had they motion:
after they parted were savage and swift as gulls.
Asking and asking the hostile emptiness
they were as sharp as partly sculptured stone
and all who watched, forgetting, were amazed
to see them form and fade before their eyes.

Where Have You Gone?

Mari Evans

Where have you gone

with your confident
walk with
your crooked smile

why did you leave
me
when you took your
laughter
and departed

are you aware that
with you
went the sun
all light
and what few stars
there were?

where have you gone
with your confident
walk your
crooked smile the
rent money
in one pocket and
my heart
in another . . .

For Anne

Leonard Cohen

With Annie gone,
whose eyes to compare
With the morning sun?

Not that I did compare,
But I do compare
Now that she's gone.

How Do I Love Thee

Elizabeth Barrett Browning

How do I love thee? Let me count the ways.
I love thee to the depth and breadth and height
My soul can reach, when feeling out of sight
For the ends of Being and ideal Grace.
I love thee to the level of every day's
Most quiet need, by sun and candlelight.
I love thee freely, as men strive for Right;
I love thee purely, as they turn from Praise;
I love thee with the passion put to use
In my old griefs, and with my childhood's faith;
I love thee with a love I seemed to lose
With my lost saints,—I love thee with the breath,
Smiles, tears, all of my life!—and, if God choose,
I shall but love thee better after death.

Love Poem

John Frederick Nims

My clumsiest dear, whose hands shipwreck vases,
At whose quick touch all glasses chip and ring,
Whose palms are bulls in china, burs in linen,
And have no cunning with any soft thing

Except all ill-at-ease fidgeting people:
The refugee uncertain at the door
You make at home; deftly you steady
The drunk clambering on his undulant floor.

Unpredictable dear, the taxi drivers' terror,
Shrinking from far headlights pale as a dime
Yet leaping before red apoplectic streetcars—
Misfit in any space. And never on time.

A wrench in clocks and the solar system. Only
With words and people and love you move at ease.
In traffic of wit expertly manoeuvre
And keep us, all devotion, at your knees.

Forgetting your coffee spreading on our flannel,
Your lipstick grinning on our coat,
So gaily in love's unbreakable heaven
Our souls on glory of spilt bourbon float.

Be with me, darling, early and late. Smash glasses—
I will study wry music for your sake.
For should your hands drop white and empty,
All the toys of the world would break.

Day of the Butterfly

Alice Munro

I do not remember when Myra Sayla came to town, though she must have been in our class at school for two or three years. I start remembering her in the last year, when her little brother Jimmy Sayla was in Grade One. Jimmy Sayla was not used to going to the bathroom by himself and he would have to come to the Grade Six door and ask for Myra and she would take him downstairs. Quite often he would not get to Myra in time and there would be a big dark stain on his little button-on cotton pants. Then Myra had to come and ask the teacher: "Please may I take my brother home, he has wet himself?"

That was what she said the first time and everybody in the front seats heard her—though Myra's voice was the lightest singsong—and there was a muted giggling which alerted the rest of the class. Our teacher, a cold gentle girl who wore glasses with thin gold rims and in the stiff solicitude of certain poses resembled a giraffe, wrote something on a piece of paper and showed it to Myra. And Myra recited uncertainly: "My brother has had an accident, please, teacher."

Everybody knew of Jimmy Sayla's shame and at recess (if he was not being kept in, as he often was, for doing something he shouldn't in school) he did not dare go out on the school grounds, where the other little boys, and some bigger ones, were waiting to chase him and corner him against the back fence and thrash him with tree branches. He had to stay with

Myra. But at our school there were the two sides, the Boys'
Side and the Girls' Side, and it was believed that if you so
much as stepped on the side that was not your own you might
easily get the strap. Jimmy could not go out on the Girls' Side
and Myra could not go out on the Boys' Side, and no one was
allowed to stay in the school unless it was raining or snowing.
So Myra and Jimmy spent every recess standing in the little
back porch between the two sides. Perhaps they watched the
baseball games, the tag and skipping and building of leaf
houses in the fall and snow forts in the winter; perhaps they
did not watch at all. Whenever you happened to look at them
their heads were slightly bent, their narrow bodies hunched in,
quite still. They had long smooth oval faces, melancholy and
discreet—dark, oily, shining hair. The little boy's was long,
clipped at home, and Myra's was worn in heavy braids coiled
on top of her head so that she looked, from a distance, as if
she was wearing a turban too big for her. Over their dark eyes
the lids were never fully raised; they had a weary look. But it
was more than that. They were like children in a medieval
painting, they were like small figures carved of wood, for worship or magic, with faces smooth and aged, and meekly, crypti-
cally uncommunicative.

Most of the teachers at our school had been teaching for a
long time and at recess they would disappear into the teachers'
room and not bother us. But our own teacher, the young
woman of the fragile gold-rimmed glasses, was apt to watch us
from a window and sometimes come out, looking brisk and
uncomfortable, to stop a fight among the little girls or start a
running game among the big ones, who had been huddled together playing Truth or Secrets. One day she came out and
called, "Girls in Grade Six, I want to talk to you!" She smiled
persuasively, earnestly, and with dreadful unease, showing fine
gold rims around her teeth. She said, "There is a girl in Grade
Six called Myra Sayla. She *is* in your grade, isn't she?"

We mumbled. But there was a coo from Gladys Healey.
"Yes, Miss Darling!"

"Well, why is she never playing with the rest of you? Every
day I see her standing in the back porch, never playing. Do
you think she looks very happy standing back there? Do you
think you would be very happy, if *you* were left back there?"

Nobody answered; we faced Miss Darling, all respectful, self-possessed, and bored with the unreality of her question. Then Gladys said, "Myra can't come out with us, Miss Darling. Myra has to look after her little brother!"

"Oh," said Miss Darling dubiously. "Well you ought to try to be nicer to her anyway. Don't you think so? Don't you? You will try to be nicer, won't you? I *know* you will!" Poor Miss Darling! Her campaigns were soon confused, her persuasions turned to bleating and uncertain pleas.

When she had gone Gladys Healey said softly, "You will try to be nicer, won't you? I *know* you will." and then drawing her lip back over her big teeth she yelled exuberantly, "I don't care if it rains or freezes." She went through the whole verse and ended it with a spectacular twirl of her Royal Stuart tartan skirt. Mr. Healey ran a Dry Goods and Ladies' Wear, and his daughter's leadership in our class was partly due to her flashing plaid skirts and organdie blouses and velvet jackets with brass buttons, but also to her early-maturing bust and the fine brutal force of her personality. Now we all began to imitate Miss Darling.

We had not paid much attention to Myra before this. But now a game was developed; it started with saying, "Let's be nice to Myra!" Then we would walk up to her in formal groups of three or four and at a signal, say together, "Hel-lo Myra, Hello *My*-ra!" and follow up with something like, "What do you wash your hair in, Myra, it's so nice and shiny, *My*-ra." "Oh she washes it in cod-liver oil, don't you, Myra, she washes it in cod-liver oil, can't you smell it?"

And to tell the truth there was a smell about Myra, but it was a rotten-sweetish smell as of bad fruit. That was what the Saylas did, kept a little fruit store. Her father sat all day on a stool by the window, with his shirt open over his swelling stomach and tufts of black hair showing around his belly button; he chewed garlic. But if you went into the store it was Mrs. Sayla who came to wait on you, appearing silently between the limp print curtains hung across the back of the store. Her hair was crimped in black waves and she smiled with her full lips held together, stretched as far as they would go; she told you the price in a little rapping voice, daring you to challenge her and, when you did not, handed you the bag of fruit with open mockery in her eyes.

One morning in the winter I was walking up the school hill very early; a neighbour had given me a ride into town. I lived about half a mile out of town, on a farm, and I should not have been going to the town school at all, but to a country school nearby where there were half a dozen pupils and a teacher a little demented since her change of life. But my mother, who was an ambitious woman, had prevailed on the town trustees to accept me and my father to pay the extra tuition, and I went to school in town. I was the only one in the class who carried a lunch pail and ate peanut-butter sandwiches in the high, bare, mustard-coloured cloakroom, the only one who had to wear rubber boots in the spring, when the roads were heavy with mud. I felt a little danger, on account of this; but I could not tell exactly what it was.

I saw Myra and Jimmy ahead of me on the hill; they always went to school very early—sometimes so early that they had to stand outside waiting for the janitor to open the door. They were walking slowly, and now and then Myra half turned around. I had often loitered in that way, wanting to walk with some important girl who was behind me, and not quite daring to stop and wait. Now it occurred to me that Myra might be doing this with me. I did not know what to do. I could not afford to be seen walking with her, and I did not even want to—but, on the other hand, the flattery of those humble, hopeful turnings was not lost on me. A role was shaping for me that I could not resist playing. I felt a great pleasurable rush of self-conscious benevolence; before I thought what I was doing I called, "Myra! Hey, Myra, wait up, I got some Cracker Jack!" and I quickened my pace as she stopped.

Myra waited, but she did not look at me; she waited in the withdrawn and rigid attitude with which she always met us. Perhaps she thought I was playing a trick on her, perhaps she expected me to run past and throw an empty Cracker Jack box in her face. And I opened the box and held it out to her. She took a little. Jimmy ducked behind her coat and would not take any when I offered the box to him.

"He's shy," I said reassuringly. "A lot of little kids are shy like that. He'll probably grow out of it."

"Yes," said Myra.

"I have a brother four," I said. "He's awfully shy." He wasn't. "Have some more Cracker Jack," I said. "I used to eat Cracker Jack all the time but I don't any more. I think it's bad for your complexion."

There was a silence.

"Do you like Art?" said Myra faintly.

"No. I like Social Studies and Spelling and Health."

"I like Art and Arithmetic." Myra could add and multiply in her head faster than anyone else in the class.

"I wish I was as good as you. In Arithmetic," I said, and felt magnanimous.

"But I am no good at Spelling," said Myra. "I make the most mistakes, I'll fail maybe." She did not sound unhappy about this, but pleased to have such a thing to say. She kept her head turned away from me staring at the dirty snowbanks along Victoria Street, and as she talked she made a sound as if she was wetting her lips with her tongue.

"You won't fail," I said. "You are too good in Arithmetic. What are you going to be when you grow up?"

She looked bewildered. "I will help my mother," she said. "And work in the store."

"Well I am going to be an airplane hostess," I said. "But don't mention it to anybody. I haven't told many people."

"No, I won't," said Myra. "Do you read Steve Canyon in the paper?"

"Yes." It was queer to think that Myra, too, read the comics, or that she did anything at all, apart from her role at the school. "Do you read Rip Kirby"

"Do you read Orphan Annie?"

"Do you read Betsy and the Boys?"

"You haven't had hardly any Cracker Jack," I said. "Have some. Take a whole handful."

Myra looked into the box. "There's a prize in there," she said. She pulled it out. It was a brooch, a little tin butterfly, painted gold with bits of coloured glass stuck onto it to look like jewels. She held it in her brown hand, smiling slightly.

I said, "Do you like that?"

Myra said, "I like them blue stones. Blue stones are sapphires."

"I know. My birthstone is sapphire. What is your birthstone?"

"I don't know."

"When is your birthday?"

"July."

"Then yours is ruby."

"I like sapphire better," said Myra. "I like yours." She handed me the brooch.

"You keep it," I said. "Finders keepers."

Myra kept holding it out, as if she did not know what I meant. "Finders keepers," I said.

"It was your Cracker Jack," said Myra, scared and solemn. "You bought it."

"Well you found it."

"No—" said Myra.

"Go on!" I said. "Here, I'll *give* it to you." I took the brooch from her and pushed it back into her hand.

We were both surprised. We looked at each other; I flushed but Myra did not. I realized the pledge as our fingers touched; I was panicky, but *all right*. I thought, I can come early and walk with her other mornings. I can go and talk to her at recess. Why not? *Why not?*

Myra put the brooch in her pocket. She said, "I can wear it on my good dress. My good dress is blue."

I knew it would be. Myra wore out her good dresses at school. Even in midwinter among the plaid wool skirts and serge tunics, she glimmered sadly in sky-blue taffeta, in dusty turquoise crepe, a grown woman's dress made over, weighted by a big bow at the V of the neck and folding empty over Myra's narrow chest.

And I was glad she had not put it on. If someone asked her where she got it, and she told them, what would I say?

It was the day after this, or the week after, that Myra did not come to school. Often she was kept at home to help. But this time she did not come back. For a week, then two weeks, her desk was empty. Then we had a moving day at school and Myra's books were taken out of her desk and put on a shelf in the closet. Miss Darling said, "We'll find a seat when she comes back." And she stopped calling Myra's name when she took attendance.

Jimmy Sayla did not come to school either, having no one to take him to the bathroom.

In the fourth week or the fifth, that Myra had been away, Gladys Healey came to school and said, "Do you know what— Myra Sayla is sick in the hospital."

It was true. Gladys Healey had an aunt who was a nurse. Gladys put up her hand in the middle of Spelling and told Miss Darling. "I thought you might like to know," she said. "Oh yes," said Miss Darling. "I do know."

"What has she got?" we said to Gladys.

And Gladys said, "Akemia, or something. And she has blood transfusions." She said to Miss Darling, "My aunt is a nurse."

So Miss Darling had the whole class write Myra a letter, in which everybody said, "Dear Myra, We are all writing you a letter. We hope you will soon be better and be back to school, Yours truly. . . ." And Miss Darling said, "I've thought of something. Who would like to go up to the hospital and visit Myra on the twentieth of March, for a birthday party?"

I said, "Her birthday's in July."

"I know," said Miss Darling. "It's the twentieth of July. So this year she could have it on the twentieth of March, because she's sick."

"But her *birthday* is in July."

"Because she's sick," said Miss Darling, with a warning shrillness. "The cook at the hospital would make a cake and you could all give a little present, twenty-five cents or so. It would have to be between two and four, because that's visiting hours. And we couldn't all go, it'd be too many. So who wants to go and who wants to stay here and do supplementary reading?"

We all put up our hands. Miss Darling got out the spelling records and picked out the first fifteen, twelve girls and three boys. Then the three boys did not want to go so she picked out the next three girls. And I do not know when it was, but I think it was probably at this moment that the birthday party of Myra Sayla became fashionable.

Perhaps it was because Gladys Healey had an aunt who was a nurse, perhaps it was the excitement of sickness and hospitals, or simply the fact that Myra was so entirely, impressively set free of all the rules and conditions of our lives. We began to talk of her as if she were something we owned, and her party became a cause; with womanly heaviness we discussed it at recess, and decided that twenty-five cents was too low.

We all went up to the hospital on a sunny afternoon when the snow was melting, carrying our presents, and a nurse led us upstairs, single file, and down a hall past half-closed doors and dim conversations. She and Miss Darling kept saying, "Sh-sh," but we were going on tiptoe anyway; our hospital demeanor was perfect.

At this small country hospital there was no children's ward, and Myra was not really a child; they had put her in with two grey old women. A nurse was putting screens around them as we came in.

Myra was sitting up in bed, in a bulky stiff hospital gown. Her hair was down, the long braids falling over her shoulders and down the coverlet. But her face was the same, always the same.

She had been told something about the party, Miss Darling said, so the surprise would not upset her; but it seemed she had not believed, or had not understood what it was. She watched us as she used to watch in the school grounds when we played.

"Well, here we are!" said Miss Darling. "Here we are!"

And we said, "Happy birthday, Myra! Hello, Myra, happy birthday!" Myra said, "My birthday is in July." Her voice was lighter than ever, drifting, expressionless.

"Never mind when it is, really," said Miss Darling. "Pretend it's now! How old are you, Myra?"

"Eleven," Myra said. "In July."

Then we all took off our coats and emerged in our party dresses, and laid our presents, in their pale flowery wrappings on Myra's bed. Some of our mothers had made immense, complicated bows of fine satin ribbon, some of them had even taped on little bouquets of imitation roses and lilies of the valley. "Here Myra," we said, "here Myra, happy birthday." Myra did not look at us, but at the ribbons, pink and blue and speckled with silver, and the miniature bouquets; they pleased her, as the butterfly had done. An innocent look came into her face, a partial, private smile.

"Open them, Myra," said Miss Darling. "They're for you!"

Myra gathered the presents around her, fingering them, with this smile, and a cautious realization, an unexpected pride. She said, "Saturday I'm going to London to St. Joseph's Hospital."

"That's where my mother was at," somebody said. "We went and saw her. They've got all nuns there."

"My father's sister is a nun," said Myra calmly.

She began to unwrap the presents, with an air that not even Gladys could have bettered, folding the tissue paper and the ribbons, and drawing out books and puzzles and cutouts as if they were all prizes she had won. Miss Darling said that maybe she should say thank you, and the person's name with every gift she opened, to make sure she knew whom it was from, and so Myra said, "Thank you, Mary Louise, thank you, Carol," and when she came to mine she said, "Thank you, Helen." Everyone explained their presents to her and there was talking and excitement and a little gaiety, which Myra presided over, though she was not gay. A cake was brought in with *Happy Birthday Myra* written on it, pink on white, and eleven candles. Miss Darling lit the candles and we all sang Happy Birthday to You, and cried, "Make a wish, Myra, make a wish—" and Myra blew them out. Then we all had cake and strawberry ice cream.

At four o'clock a buzzer sounded and the nurse took out what was left of the cake, and the dirty dishes, and we put on our coats to go home. Everybody said, "Goodbye, Myra," and Myra sat in the bed watching us go, her back straight, not supported by any pillow, her hands resting on the gifts. But at the door I heard her call; she called, "Helen!" Only a couple of the others heard; Miss Darling did not hear, she had gone out ahead. I went back to the bed.

Myra said, "I got too many things. You take something."

"What?" I said. "It's for your birthday. You always get a lot at a birthday."

"Well you take something," Myra said. She picked up a leatherette case with a mirror in it, a comb and a nail file and a natural lipstick and a small handkerchief edged with gold thread. I had noticed it before. "You take that," she said.

"Don't you want it?"

"You take it." She put it into my hand. Our fingers touched again.

"When I come back from London," Myra said, "you can

come and play at my place after school."

"Okay," I said. Outside the hospital window there was a clear carrying sound of somebody playing in the street, maybe chasing with the last snowballs of the year. This sound made Myra, her triumph and her bounty, and most of all her future in which she had found this place for me, turn shadowy, turn dark. All the presents on the bed, the folded paper and ribbons, those guilt-tinged offerings, had passed into this shadow, they were no longer innocent objects to be touched, exchanged, accepted without danger. I didn't want to take the case now but I could not think how to get out of it, what lie to tell. I'll give it away, I thought, I won't ever play with it. I would let my little brother pull it apart.

The nurse came back, carrying a glass of chocolate milk.

"What's the matter, didn't you hear the buzzer?"

So I was released, set free by the barriers which now closed about Myra, her unknown, exalted, ether-smelling hospital world, and by the treachery of my own heart. "Well thank you," I said. "Thank you for the thing. Goodbye."

Did Myra ever say goodbye? Not likely. She sat in her high bed, her delicate brown neck, rising out of a hospital gown too big for her, her brown carved face immune to treachery, her offering perhaps already forgotten, prepared to be set apart for legendary uses, as she was even in the back porch at school.

Only Child

P.K. Page

The early conflict made him pale
and when he woke from those long weeping slumbers she
was there
and the air about them—hers and his—
sometimes a comfort to him, like a quilt, but more
often than not a fear.

There were times he went away—he knew not where—
over the fields or scuffing to the shore;
suffered her eagerness on his return
for news of him—where had he been, what done?
He hardly knew, nor did he wish to know
or think about it vocally or share
his private world with her.

Then they would plan another walk, a long
adventure in the country, for her sake—
in search of birds. Perhaps they'd find the blue
heron today, for sure the kittiwake.

Birds were familiar to him now, he knew
them by their feathers and a shyness like his own
soft in the silence.
Of the ducks she said, 'Observe, the
canvas back's a diver,' and her words
stuccoed the slatey water of the lake.

He had no wish to separate them in groups
or learn the Latin,
or, waking early to their song remark, 'the thrush,'
or say at evening when the air is streaked
with certain swerving flying,
'Ah, the swifts.'

Birds were his element like air and not
her words for them—making them statues
setting them apart,
nor were they facts and details like a book.
When she said, 'Look!'
he let his eyeballs harden
and when two came and nested in the garden
he felt their softness, gentle, near his heart.

She gave him pictures which he avoided, showing
strange species flat against a foreign land.
Rather would he lie in the grass, the deep grass of the island
close to the gulls' nests knowing
these things he loved and needed near his hand,
untouched and hardly seen but deeply understood.
Or sail among them through a wet wind feeling
their wings within his blood.

Like every mother's boy he loved and hated
smudging the future photograph she had,
yet struggled within the frames of her eyes and then
froze for her, the noted naturalist—
her very affectionate and famous son.
But when most surely in her grasp, his smile
darting and enfolding her, his words:
'Without my mother's help . . .' the dream occurred.

Dozens of flying things surrounded him
on a green terrace in the sun
and one by one
as if he held caresses in his palm

he caught them all and snapped and wrung their necks
brittle as little sticks.
Then through the bald, unfeathered air
and coldly as a man would walk
against a metal backdrop, he
bore down on her
and placed them in her wide maternal lap
and accurately said their names aloud:
woodpecker, sparrow, meadowlark, nuthatch.

Jamie

Elizabeth Brewster

When Jamie was sixteen,
Suddenly he was deaf. There were no songs,
No voices any more.
He walked about stunned by the terrible silence.
Kicking a stick, rapping his knuckles on doors,
He felt a spell of silence all about him,
So loud it made a whirring in his ears.
People moved mouths without a sound escaping:
He shuddered at the straining of their throats.
And suddenly he watched them with suspicion.
Wondering if they were talking of his faults,
Were pitying him or seeing him with scorn.
He dived into their eyes and dragged up sneers,
And sauntering the streets, imagined laughter behind him.
Working at odd jobs, ploughing, picking potatoes,
Chopping trees in the lumber woods in winter,
He became accustomed to an aimless and lonely labour.
He was solitary and unloquacious as a stone.
And silence grew over him like moss on an old stump.
But sometimes, going to town,
He was sore with the hunger for company among the people
And, getting drunk, would shout at them for friendship,
Laughing aloud in the streets.
He returned to the woods,
And dreaming at night of a shining cowboy heaven
Where guns crashed through his deafness, awoke morose,
And chopped the necks of pine trees in his anger.

Mending Wall

Robert Frost

Something there is that doesn't love a wall,
That sends the frozen-ground-swell under it,
And spills the upper boulders in the sun;
And makes gaps even two can pass abreast.
The work of hunters is another thing:
I have come after them and made repair
Where they have left not one stone on a stone,
But they would have the rabbit out of hiding,
To please the yelping dogs. The gaps I mean,
No one has seen them made or heard them made,
But at spring mending-time we find them there.
I let my neighbor know beyond the hill;
And on a day we meet to walk the line
And set the wall between us once again.
We keep the wall between us as we go.
To each the boulders that have fallen to each.
And some are loaves and some so nearly balls
We have to use a spell to make them balance:
"Stay where you are until our backs are turned!"
We wear our fingers rough with handling them.
Oh, just another kind of outdoor game,
One on a side. It comes to little more:
There where it is we do not need the wall:
He is all pine and I am apple orchard.
My apple trees will never get across
And eat the cones under his pines, I tell him.
He only says, "Good fences make good neighbors."

Spring is the mischief in me, and I wonder
If I could put a notion in his head:
"*Why* do they make good neighbors? Isn't it
Where there are cows? But here there are no cows.
Before I built a wall I'd ask to know
What I was walling in or walling out,
And to whom I was like to give offense.
Something there is that doesn't love a wall,
That wants it down." I could say "Elves" to him,
But it's not elves exactly, and I'd rather
He said it for himself. I see him there
Bringing a stone grasped firmly by the top
In each hand, like an old-stone savage armed.
He moves in darkness as it seems to me,
Not of woods only and the shade of trees.
He will not go behind his father's saying,
And he likes having thought of it so well
He says again, "Good fences make good neighbors."

My Furthest-Back Person— 'The African'

Alex Haley

MY Grandma Cynthia Murray Palmer lived in Henning, Tenn. (pop. 500), about 50 miles north of Memphis. Each summer as I grew up there, we would be visited by several women relatives who were mostly around Grandma's age, such as my Great Aunt Liz Murray who taught in Oklahoma, and Great Aunt Till Merriwether from Jackson, Tenn., or their considerably younger niece, Cousin Georgia Anderson from Kansas City, Kan., and some others. Always after the supper dishes had been washed, they would go out to take seats and talk in the rocking chairs on the front porch, and I would scrunch down, listening, behind Grandma's squeaky chair, with the dusk deepening into night and the lightning bugs flicking on and off above the now shadowy honeysuckles. Most often they talked about our family— the story had been passed down for generations—until the whistling blur of lights of the southbound Panama Limited train *whooshing* through Henning at 9:05 P.M. signaled our bedtime.

So much of their talking of people, places and events I didn't understand: For instance, what was an "Ol' Massa," and "Ol' Missus" or a "plantation"? But early I gathered that white folks had done lots of bad things to our folks, though I couldn't figure out why. I guessed that all that they talked about had happened a long time ago, as now or then Grandma or another, speaking of someone in the past, would excitedly thrust a finger toward me, exclaiming, "Wasn't big as *this* young 'un!" And it would astound me that anyone as old and gray-haired as they could relate to my age. But in time my head began both a recording and picturing of the more graphic scenes they would describe, just as I also visualized David killing Goliath, with his slingshot, Old Pharaoh's army drowning, Noah and his ark, Jesus feeding that big multitude with nothing but five loaves and two fishes, and other wonders that I heard in my Sunday school lessons at our New Hope Methodist Church.

The furthest-back person Grandma and the others talked of —always in tones of awe, I noticed—they would call "The African." They said that some ship brought him to a place that they pronounced " 'Naplis." They said that then some "Mas' John Waller" bought him for his plantation in "Spot-sylvania County, Va." This African kept on escaping, the fourth time trying to kill the "hateful po' cracker" slave-catcher, who gave him the punishment choice of castration or of losing one foot. This African took a foot being chopped off with an ax against a tree stump, they said, and he was about to die. But his life was saved by "Mas' John's" brother—"Mas' William Waller," a doctor, who was so furious about what had happened that he bought the African for himself and gave him the name "Toby."

Crippling about, working in "Mas' William's" house and yard, the African in time met and mated with "the big house cook named Bell," and there was born a girl named Kizzy. As she grew up her African daddy often showed her different kinds of things, telling her what they were in his native tongue. Pointing at a banjo, for example, the African uttered, "*ko*"; or pointing at a river near the plantation, he would say, "*Kamby Bolong*." Many of his strange words started with a "*k*" sound, and the little, growing Kizzy learned gradually that they identified different things.

When addressed by other slaves as "Toby," the master's name for him, the African said angrily that his name was "*Kin-tay*." And as he gradually learned English, he told young Kizzy some things about himself—for instance, that he was not far from his village, chopping wood to make himself a drum, when four men had surprised, overwhelmed, and kidnapped him.

So Kizzy's head held much about her African daddy when at age 16 she was sold away onto a much smaller plantation in North Carolina. Her new "Mas' Tom Lea" fathered her first child, a boy she named George. And Kizzy told her boy all about his African grandfather. George grew up to be such a gamecock fighter that he was called "Chicken George," and people would come from all over and "bet big money" on his cockfights. He mated with Matilda, another of Lea's slaves; they had seven children, and he told them the stories and strange sounds of their African great-grandfather. And one of those children, Tom, became a blacksmith who was bought away by a "Mas' Murray" for his tobacco plantation in Alamance County, N.C.

Tom mated there with Irene, a weaver on the plantation. She also bore seven children, and Tom now told them all about their African great-great-grandfather, the faithfully passed-down knowledge of his sounds and stories having become by now the family's prideful treasure.

The youngest of that second set of seven children was a girl, Cynthia, who became my maternal Grandma (which today I can only see as fated). Anyway, all of this is how I was growing up in Henning at Grandma's, listening from behind her rocking chair as she and the other visiting old women talked of that African (never then comprehended as my great-great-great-great-grandfather) who said his name was "Kin-tay," and said "ko" for banjo, "Kamby Bolong" for river, and a jumble of other "k"-beginning sounds that Grandma privately muttered, most often while making beds or cooking, and who also said that near his village he was kidnapped while chopping wood to make himself a drum.

The story had become nearly as fixed in my head as in Grandma's by the time Dad and Mama moved me and my two younger brothers, George and Julius, away from Henning to be with them at the small black agricultural and mechanical college in Normal, Ala., where Dad taught.

To compress my next 25 years: When I was 17 Dad let me enlist as a mess boy in the U.S. Coast Guard. I became a ship's cook out in the South Pacific during World War II, and at night down by my bunk I began trying to write sea adventure stories; mailing them off to magazines and collecting rejection slips for eight years before some editors began purchasing and publishing occasional stories. By 1949 the Coast Guard had made me its first "journalist"; finally with 20 years' service, I retired at the age of 37, determined to make a full time career of writing. I wrote mostly magazine articles; my first book was "The Autobiography of Malcolm X."

Then one Saturday in 1965 I happened to be walking past the National Archives building in Washington. Across the interim years I had thought of Grandma's old stories—otherwise I can't think what diverted me up the Archives' steps. And when a main reading room desk attendant asked if he could help me, I wouldn't have dreamed of admitting to him some curiosity hanging on from boyhood about my slave forebears. I kind of bumbled that I was interested in census records of Alamance County, North Carolina, just after the Civil War.

The microfilm rolls were delivered, and I turned them through the machine with a building sense of intrigue, viewing in different census takers' penmanship an endless parade of names. After about a dozen microfilmed rolls, I was beginning to tire, when in utter astonishment I looked upon the names of Grandma's parents: Tom Murray, Irene Murray . . . older sisters of Grandma's as well—every one of them a name that I'd heard countless times on her front porch.

It wasn't that I hadn't believed Grandma. You just *didn't* not believe my Grandma. It was simply so uncanny actually seeing those names in print and in official U.S. Government records.

During the next several months I was back in Washington whenever possible, in the Archives, the Library of Congress, the Daughters of the American Revolution Library. (Whenever black attendants understood the idea of my search, documents I requested reached me with miraculous speed.) In one source or another during 1966 I was able to document at least the highlights of the cherished family story. I would have given anything to have told Grandma, but, sadly, in 1949 she had gone. So I went and told the only survivor of those Henning front-porch storytellers: Cousin Georgia Anderson, now in her 80's in Kansas City, Kan. Wrinkled, bent, not well herself, she was so overjoyed, repeating to me the old stories and sounds; they were like Henning echoes: "Yeah, boy, that African say his name was '*Kin-tay*'; he say the banjo was '*ko*,' an' the river '*Kamby Bolong*,' an' he was off choppin' some wood to make his drum when they grabbed 'im!" Cousin Georgia grew so excited we had to stop her, calm her down, "You go'head, boy! Your grandma an' all of 'em—they up there watching what you do!"

That week I flew to London on a magazine assignment. Since by now I was steeped in the old, in the past, scarcely a tour guide missed me—I was awed at so many historical places and treasures I'd heard of and read of. I came upon the Rosetta stone in the British Museum, marveling anew at how Jean Champollion, the French archaeologist, had miraculously deciphered its ancient demotic and hieroglyphic texts . . .

The thrill of that just kept hanging around in my head. I was on a jet returning to New York when a thought hit me. Those strange, unknown-tongue sounds, always part of our family's old story . . . they were obviously bits of our original African "*Kin-tay*'s" native tongue. What specific tongue? Could I somehow find out?

Back in New York, I began making visits to the United Nations Headquarters lobby; it wasn't hard to spot Africans. I'd stop any I could, asking if my bits of phonetic sounds held any meaning for them. A couple of dozen Africans quickly looked at me, listened, and took off—understandably dubious about some Tennesseean's accent alleging "African" sounds.

My research assistant, George Sims (we grew up together in Henning), brought me some names of ranking scholars of African linguistics. One was particularly intriguing: a Belgian- and English-educated Dr. Jan Vansina; he had spent his early career living in West African villages, studying and tape-recording countless oral histories that were narrated by certain very old African men; he had written a standard textbook, "The Oral Tradition."

So I flew to the University of Wisconsin to see Dr. Vansina. In his living room I told him every bit of the family story in the fullest detail that I could remember it. Then, intensely, he queried me about the story's relay across the generations, about the gibberish of "*k*" sounds Grandma had fiercely muttered to herself while doing her housework, with my brothers and me giggling beyond her hearing at what we had dubbed "Grandma's noises."

Dr. Vansina, his manner very serious, finally said, "These sounds your family has kept sound very probably of the tongue called 'Mandinka.'"

I'd never heard of any "Mandinka." Grandma just told of the African saying "*ko*" for banjo, or "*Kamby Bolong*" for a Virginia river.

Among Mandinka stringed instruments, Dr. Vansina said, one of the oldest was the "*kora*."

"*Bolong*," he said, was clearly Mandinka for "river." Preceded by "*Kamby*," it very likely meant "Gambia River."

Dr. Vansina telephoned an eminent Africanist colleague, Dr. Philip Curtin. He said that the phonetic "*Kin-tay*" was correctly spelled "*Kinte*," a very old clan that had originated in Old Mali. The Kinte men traditionally were blacksmiths, and the women were potters and weavers.

I knew I must get to the Gambia River.

The first native Gambian I could locate in the U.S. was named Ebou Manga, then a junior attending Hamilton College in upstate Clinton, N.Y. He and I flew to Dakar, Senegal, then took a smaller plane to Yundum Airport, and rode in a van to Gambia's capital, Bathurst. Ebou and his father assembled eight Gambia government officials. I told them Grandma's stories, every detail I could remember, as they listened intently, then reacted. "'*Kamby Bolong*' of course is Gambia River!" I heard. "But more clue is your forefather's saying his name was '*Kinte*.'" Then they told me something I would never ever have fantasized—that in places in the back country lived very old men, commonly called *griots*, who could tell centuries of the histories of certain very old family clans. As for *Kintes*, they pointed out to me on a map some family villages, Kinte-Kundah, and Kinte-Kundah Janneh-Ya, for instance.

The Gambian officials said they would try to help me. I returned to New York dazed. It is embarrassing to me now, but despite Grandma's stories, I'd never been concerned much with Africa, and I had the routine images of African people living mostly in exotic jungles. But a compulsion now laid hold of me to learn all I could, and I began devouring books about Africa, especially about the slave trade. Then one Thursday's mail contained a letter from one of the Gambian officials, inviting me to return there.

Monday I was back in Bathurst. It galvanized me when the officials said that a *griot* had been located who told the *Kinte* clan history—his name was Kebba Kanga Fofana. To reach him, I discovered, required a modified safari: renting a launch to get upriver, two land vehicles to carry supplies by a roundabout land route, and employing finally 14 people, including three interpreters and four musicians, since a *griot* would not speak the revered clan histories without background music.

The boat Baddibu vibrated upriver, with me acutely tense: Were these Africans maybe viewing me as but another of the pith-helmets? After about two hours, we put in at James Island, for me to see the ruins of the once British-operated James Fort. Here two centuries of slave ships had loaded thousands of cargoes of Gambian tribespeople. The crumbling stones, the deeply oxidized swivel cannon, even some remnant links of chain seemed all but impossible to believe. Then we continued upriver to the left-bank village of Albreda, and there put ashore to continue on foot to Juffure, village of the *griot*. Once more we stopped, for me to see *toubob kolong*, "the white man's well," now almost filled in, in a swampy area with abundant, tall, saw-toothed grass. It was dug two centuries ago to "17 men's height deep" to insure survival drinking water for long-driven, famishing coffles of slaves.

Walking on, I kept wishing that Grandma could hear how her stories had led me to the "*Kamby Bolong*." (Our surviving storyteller Cousin Georgia died in a Kansas City hospital during this same morning, I would learn later.) Finally, Juffure village's playing children, sighting us, flashed an alert. The 70-odd people came rushing from their circular, thatch-roofed, mud-walled huts, with goats bounding up and about, and parrots squawking from up in the palms. I sensed him in advance somehow, the small man amid them, wearing a pillbox cap and an off-white robe—the *griot*. Then the interpreters went to him, as the villagers thronged around me.

And it hit me like a gale wind: every one of them, the whole crowd, was *jet black*. An enormous sense of guilt swept me—a sense of being some kind of hybrid ... a sense of being impure among the pure. It was an awful sensation.

The old *griot* stepped away from my interpreters and the crowd quickly swarmed around him—all of them buzzing. An interpreter named A.B.C. Salla came to me; he whispered: "Why they stare at you so, they have never seen here a black American." And that hit me: I was symbolizing for them twenty-five millions of us they had never seen. What did they think of me—of us?

Then abruptly the old *griot* was briskly walking toward me. His eyes boring into mine, he spoke in Mandinka, as if instinctively I should understand—and A.B.C. Salla translated:

"Yes ... we have been told by the forefathers ... that many of us from this place are in exile ... in that place called America ... and in other places."

I suppose I physically wavered, and they thought it was the heat; rustling whispers went through the crowd, and a man brought me a low stool. Now the whispering hushed—the musicians had softly begun playing *kora* and *balafon*, and a canvas sling lawn seat was taken by the *griot*, Kebba Kanga Fofana, aged 73 "rains" (one rainy season each year). He seemed to gather himself into a physical rigidity, and he began speaking the *Kinte* clan's ancestral oral history; it came rolling from his mouth across the next hours ... 17th- and 18th-century *Kinte* lineage details, predominantly what men took wives; the children they "begot," in the order of their births; those children's mates and children.

Events frequently were dated by some proximate singular physical occurrence. It was as if some ancient scroll were printed indelibly within the *griot*'s brain. Each few sentences or so, he would pause for an interpreter's translation to me. I distill here the essence:

The *Kinte* clan began in Old Mali, the men generally blacksmiths "... who conquered fire," and the women potters and weavers. One large branch of the clan moved to Mauretania from where one son of the clan, Kairaba Kunta Kinte, a Moslem Marabout holy man, entered Gambia. He lived first in the village of Pakali N'Ding; he moved next to Jiffarong village; ". . . and then he came here, into our own village of Juffure."

In Juffure, Kairaba Kunta Kinte took his first wife, ". . . a Mandinka maiden, whose name was Sireng. By her, he begot two sons, whose names were Janneh and Saloum. Then he got a second wife, Yaisa. By her, he begot a son, Omoro."

The three sons became men in Juffure. Janneh and Saloum went off and found a new village, Kinte-Kundah Janneh-Ya. "And then Omoro, the youngest son, when he had 30 rains, took as a wife a maiden, Binta Kebba.

"And by her, he begot four sons—Kunta, Lamin, Suwadu, and Madi . . ."

Sometimes, a "begotten," after his naming, would be accompanied by some later-occurring detail, perhaps as ". . . in time of big water (flood), he slew a water buffalo." Having named those four sons, now the *griot* stated such a detail.

"About the time the king's soldiers came, the eldest of these four sons, Kunta, when he had about 16 rains, went away from his village, to chop wood to make a drum . . . and he was never seen again . . ."

Goose-pimples the size of lemons seemed to pop all over me. In my knapsack were my cumulative notebooks, the first of them including how in my boyhood, my Grandma, Cousin Georgia and the others told of the African *"Kin-tay"* who always said he was kidnapped near his village—while chopping wood to make a drum . . .

I showed the interpreter, he showed and told the *griot*, who excitedly told the people; they grew very agitated. Abruptly then they formed a human ring, encircling me, dancing and chanting. Perhaps a dozen of the women carrying their infant babies rushed in toward me, thrusting the infants into my arms conveying, I would later learn, "the laying on of hands . . . through this flesh which is us, we are you, and you are us." The men hurried me into their mosque, their Arabic praying later being translated outside: "Thanks be to Allah for returning the long lost from among us." Direct descendants of Kunta Kinte's blood brothers were hastened, some of them from nearby villages, for a family portrait to be taken with me, surrounded by actual ancestral sixth cousins. More symbolic acts filled the remaining day.

When they would let me leave, for some reason I wanted to go away over the African land. Dazed, silent in the bumping Land Rover, I heard the cutting staccato of talking drums. Then when we sighted the next village, its people came thronging to meet us. They were all—little naked ones to wizened elders—waving, beaming; amid a cacophony of crying out; and then my ears identified their words: *"Meester Kinte! Meester Kinte!"*

Let me tell you something: I am a man. But I remember the sob surging up from my feet, flinging up my hands before my face and bawling as I had not done since I was a baby . . . the jet-black Africans were jostling, staring . . . I didn't care, with the feelings surging. If you really knew the odyssey of us millions of black Americans, if you really knew how we came in the seeds of our forefathers, captured, driven, beaten, inspected, bought, branded, chained in foul ships, if you really knew, you needed weeping . . .

Back home, I knew that what I must write, really, was our black saga, where any individual's past is the essence of the millions'. Now flat broke, I went to some editors I knew, describing the Gambian miracle, and my desire to pursue the research; Doubleday contracted to publish, and Reader's Digest to condense the projected book; then I had advances to travel further.

What ship brought Kinte to Grandma's " 'Naplis" (Annapolis, Md., obviously)? The old *griot*'s time reference to "king's soldiers" sent me flying to London. Feverish searching at last identified, in British Parliament records, "Colonel O'Hare's Forces," dispatched in mid-1767 to protect the then British-held James Fort whose ruins I'd visited. So Kunta Kinte was down in some ship probably sailing later that summer from the Gambia River to Annapolis.

Now I feel it was fated that I had taught myself to write in the U.S. Coast Guard. For the sea dramas I had concentrated on had given me years of experience searching among yellowing old U.S. maritime records. So now in English 18th Century marine records I finally tracked ships reporting themselves in and out to the Commandant of the Gambia River's James Fort. And then early one afternoon I found that a Lord Ligonier under a Captain Thomas Davies had sailed on the Sabbath of July 5, 1767. Her cargo: 3,265 elephants' teeth, 3,700 pounds of beeswax, 800 pounds of cotton, 32 ounces of Gambian gold, and 140 slaves; her destination: "Annapolis."

That night I recrossed the Atlantic. In the Library of Congress the Lord Ligonier's arrival was one brief line in "Shipping In The Port Of Annapolis—1748-1775." I located the author, Vaughan W. Brown in his Baltimore brokerage office. He drove to Historic Annapolis, the city's historical society, and found me further documentation of her arrival on Sept. 29, 1767. (Exactly two centuries later, Sept. 29, 1967, standing, staring seaward from an Annapolis pier, again I knew tears). More help came in the Maryland Hall of Records. Archivist Phebe Jacobsen found the Lord Ligonier's arriving customs declaration listing, "98 Negroes"—so in her 86-day crossing, 42 Gambians had died, one among the survivors being 16-year-old Kunta Kinte. Then the microfilmed Oct. 1, 1767, Maryland Gazette contained, on page two, an announcement to prospective buyers from the ship's agents, Daniel of St. Thos. Jenifer and John Ridout (the Governor's secretary): "from the River GAMBIA, in AFRICA . . . a cargo of choice, healthy SLAVES . . ."

No Man is an Island (from Meditation 17)

John Donne

NO man is an island, entire of itself; every man is a piece of a continent, a part of the main. If a clod be washed away by the sea, Europe is the less, as well as if a promontory were, as well as if a manor of thy friend's or of thine own were. Any man's death diminishes me because I am involved in mankind, and therefore never send to know for whom the bell tolls; it tolls for thee.

UNIT 4

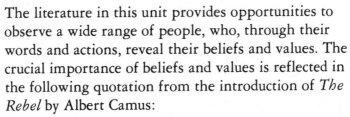

WHAT I BELIEVE

The literature in this unit provides opportunities to observe a wide range of people, who, through their words and actions, reveal their beliefs and values. The crucial importance of beliefs and values is reflected in the following quotation from the introduction of *The Rebel* by Albert Camus:

If we believe in nothing, if nothing has any meaning, and if we can affirm no values whatsoever, then everything is possible and nothing has any importance. There is no pro and con: the murderer neither right nor wrong. We are free to stoke the crematory fires or to devote ourselves to the care of lepers. Evil and virtue are mere chance or caprice.

As this quotation emphasizes, beliefs and values are necessary for the preservation of humanity. They provide the motivation for an individual's behaviour in critical situations, and influence the nature of the society in which we live.

As writers explore the relations between beliefs and actions, they comment on the human condition. As we read literature which emphasizes action based on beliefs and values, we speculate on how we might interact in similar conditions and with similar characters. This unit, which includes literature from a variety of cultures, provides us with opportunities to examine other people's beliefs and values as well as our own.

Dreams

Langston Hughes

Hold fast to dreams
For if dreams die
Life is a broken-winged bird
That cannot fly.

Hold fast to dreams
For when dreams go
Life is a barren field
Frozen with snow.

I Saw a Man Pursuing the Horizon

Stephen Crane

I saw a man pursuing the horizon;
Round and round they sped.
I was disturbed at this;
I accosted the man.
"It is futile," I said,
"You can never—"
"You lie," he cried,
And ran on.

"Truth," Said a Traveller

Stephen Crane

"Truth," said a traveller,
"Is a rock, a mighty fortress;
Often have I been to it,
Even to its highest tower,
From whence the world looks black."

"Truth," said a traveller,
"Is a breath, a wind,
A shadow, a phantom;
Long have I pursued it,
But never have I touched
The hem of its garment."

And I believed the second traveller;
For truth was to me
A breath, a wind,
A shadow, a phantom,
And never had I touched
The hem of its garment.

Nationality

Mary Gilmore

I have grown past hate and bitterness,
I see the world as one;
But though I can no longer hate,
My son is still my son.

All men at God's round table sit
And all men must be fed;
But this loaf in my hand,
This loaf is my son's bread.

You Should Have Seen the Mess

Muriel Spark

I AM now more than glad that I did not pass into the grammar school five years ago, although it was a disappointment at the time. I was always good at English, but not so good at the other subjects!!

I am glad that I went to the secondary modern school, because it was only constructed the year before. Therefore, it was much more hygienic than the grammar school. The secondary modern was light and airy, and the walls were painted with a bright, washable gloss. One day, I was sent over to the grammar school, with a note for one of the teachers, and you should have seen the mess! The corridors were dusty, and I saw dust on the window ledges, which were chipped. I saw into one of the classrooms. It was very untidy in there.

I am also glad that I did not go to the grammar school, because of what it does to one's habits. This may appear to be a strange remark, at first sight. It is a good thing to have an education behind you, and I do not believe in ignorance, but I have had certain experiences, with educated people, since going out into the world.

I am seventeen years of age, and left school two years ago last month. I had my A certificate for typing, so got my first job, as a junior, in a solicitor's office. Mum was pleased at this, and Dad said it was a first-class start, as it was an old-established firm. I must say that when I went for the interview, I was surprised at the windows, and the stairs up to the offices were also far from clean. There was a little waiting-room, where some of the elements were missing from the gas fire, and the carpet on the floor was worn. However, Mr Heygate's office, into which I was shown for the interview, was better. The furniture was old, but it was polished, and there was a good carpet, I will say that. The glass of the bookcase was very clean.

I was to start on the Monday, so along I went. They took me to the general office, where there were two senior shorthand-typists, and a clerk, Mr Gresham, who was far from smart in appearance. You should have seen the mess!! There was no floor covering whatsoever, and so dusty everywhere. There were shelves all round the room, with old box files on them. The box files were falling to pieces, and all the old papers inside them were crumpled. The worst shock of all was the tea-cups. It was my duty to make tea, mornings and afternoons. Miss Bewlay showed me where everything was kept. It was kept in an old orange box, and the cups were all cracked. There were not enough saucers to go round, etc. I will not go into the facilities, but they were also far from hygienic. After three days, I told Mum, and she was upset, most of all about the cracked cups. We never keep a cracked cup, but throw it out, because those cracks can harbour germs. So Mum gave me my own cup to take to the office.

Then at the end of the week, when I got my salary, Mr Heygate said, 'Well, Lorna, what are you going to do with your first pay?' I did not like him saying this, and I nearly passed a comment, but I said, 'I don't know.' He said, 'What do you do in the evenings, Lorna? Do you watch Telly?' I did take this as an insult, because we call it TV, and his remark made me out to be uneducated. I just stood, and did not answer, and he looked surprised. Next day, Saturday, I told Mum and Dad about the facilities, and we decided I should not go back to that job. Also, the desks in the general office were rickety. Dad was indignant, because Mr Heygate's concern was flourishing, and he had letters after his name.

Everyone admires our flat, because Mum keeps it spotless, and Dad keeps doing things to it. He has done it up all over, and got permission from the Council to re-modernize the kitchen. I well recall the Health Visitor, remarking to Mum,

'You could eat off your floor, Mrs Merrifield.' It is true that you could eat your lunch off Mum's floors, and any hour of the day or night you will find every corner spick and span.

Next, I was sent by the agency to a publisher's for an interview, because of being good at English. One look was enough!! My next interview was a success, and I am still at Low's Chemical Co. It is a modern block, with a quarter of an hour rest period, morning and afternoon. Mr Marwood is very smart in appearance. He is well spoken, although he has not got a university education behind him. There is special lighting over the desks, and the typewriters are the latest models.

So I am happy at Low's. But I have met other people, of an educated type, in the past year, and it has opened my eyes. It so happened that I had to go to the doctor's house, to fetch a prescription for my young brother, Trevor, when the epidemic was on. I rang the bell, and Mrs Darby came to the door. She was small, with fair hair, but too long, and a green maternity dress. But she was very nice to me. I had to wait in their living-room, and you should have seen the state it was in! There were broken toys on the carpet, and the ash trays were full up. There were contemporary pictures on the walls, but the furniture was not contemporary, but old-fashioned, with covers which were past standing up to another wash, I should say. To cut a long story short, Dr Darby and Mrs Darby have always been very kind to me, and they meant everything for the best. Dr Darby is also short and fair, and they have three children, a girl and a boy, and now a baby boy.

When I went that day for the prescription, Dr Darby said to me, 'You look pale, Lorna. It's the London atmosphere. Come on a picnic with us, in the car, on Saturday.' After that I went with the Darbys more and more. I liked them, but I did not like the mess, and it was a surprise. But I also kept in with them for the opportunity of meeting people, and Mum and Dad were pleased that I had made nice friends. So I did not say anything about the cracked lino, and the paintwork all chipped. The children's clothes were very shabby for a doctor, and she changed them out of their school clothes when they came home from school, into those worn-out garments. Mum always kept us spotless to go out to play, and I do not like to say it, but those Darby children frequently looked like the Leary family, which the Council evicted from our block, as they were far from houseproud.

One day, when I was there, Mavis (as I called Mrs Darby by then) put her head out the window, and shouted to the boy, 'John, stop peeing over the cabbages at once. Pee on the lawn.' I did not know which way to look. Mum would never say a word like that from the window, and I know for a fact that Trevor would never pass water outside, not even bathing in the sea.

I went there usually at the week-ends, but sometimes on week-days, after supper. They had an idea to make a match for me with a chemist's assistant, whom they had taken up too. He was an orphan, and I do not say there was anything wrong with that. But he was not accustomed to those little extras that I was. He was a good-looking boy, I will say that. So I went once to a dance, and twice to films with him. To look at, he was quite clean in appearance. But there was only hot water at the week-end at his place, and he said that a bath once a week was sufficient. Jim (as I called Dr Darby by then) said it was sufficient also, and surprised me. He did not have much money, and I do not hold that against him. But there was no hurry for me, and I could wait for a man in a better position, so that I would not miss those little extras. So he started going out with a girl from the coffee bar, and did not come to the Darbys very much then.

There were plenty of boys at the office, but I will say this for the Darbys, they had lots of friends coming and going, and they had interesting conversation, although sometimes it gave me a surprise, and I did not know where to look. And sometimes they had people who were very down and out, although there is no need to be. But most of the guests were different, so it made a comparison with the boys at the office, who were not so educated in their conversation.

Now it was near the time for Mavis to have her baby, and I was to come in at the week-end, to keep an eye on the children, while the help had her day off. Mavis did not go away to have her baby, but would have it at home, in their double bed, as they did not have twin beds, although he was a doctor. A girl I knew, in our block, was engaged, but was let down, and even she had her baby in the labour ward. I was sure the bedroom was not hygienic for having a baby, but I did not mention it.

One day, after the baby boy came along, they took me in the car to the country, to see Jim's mother. The baby was put in a carry-cot at the back of the car. He began to cry, and without a word of a lie, Jim said to him over his shoulder, "Oh shut your gob, you little bastard." I did not know what to do, and Mavis was smoking a cigarette. Dad would not dream of saying such a thing to Trevor or I. When we arrived at Jim's mother's place, Jim said, 'It's a fourteenth-century cottage, Lorna.' I could well believe it. It was very cracked and old, and it made one wonder how Jim could let his old mother live in this tumble-down cottage, as he was so good to everyone else. So Mavis knocked at the door, and the old lady came. There was not much anyone could do to the inside. Mavis said, 'Isn't it charming, Lorna?' If that was a joke, it was going too far. I said to the old Mrs Darby, 'Are you going to be re-housed?' but she did not understand this, and I explained how you have to apply to the Council, and keep at them. But it was funny that the Council had not done something already, when they go round condemning. Then old Mrs Darby said, 'My dear, I shall be re-housed in the Grave.' I did not know where to look.

There was a carpet hanging on the wall, which I think was there to hide a damp spot. She had a good TV set, I will say that. But some of the walls were bare brick, and the facilities were outside, through the garden. The furniture was far from new.

One Saturday afternoon, as I happened to go to the Darbys, they were just going off to a film and they took me too. It was the Curzon, and afterwards we went to a flat in Curzon Street. It was a very clean block, I will say that, and there were good carpets at the entrance. The couple there had contemporary furniture, and they also spoke about music. It was a nice place, but there was no Welfare Centre to the flats, where people could go for social intercourse, advice and guidance. But they were well-spoken, and I met Willy Morley, who was an artist. Willy sat beside me, and we had a drink. He was young, dark, with a dark shirt, so one could not see right away if he was clean. Soon after this, Jim said to me, 'Willy wants to paint you, Lorna. But you'd better ask your Mum.' Mum said it was all right if he was a friend of the Darbys.

I can honestly say that Willy's place was the most unhygienic place I have seen in my life. He said I had an unusual type of beauty, which he must capture. This was when we came back to his place from the restaurant. The light was very dim, but I could see the bed had not been made, and the sheets were far from clean. He said he must paint me, but I told Mavis I did not like to go back there. 'Don't you like Willy?' she asked. I could not deny that I liked Willy, in a way. There was something about him, I will say that. Mavis said, 'I hope he hasn't been making a pass at you, Lorna.' I said he had not done so, which was almost true, because he did not attempt to go to the full extent. It was always unhygienic when I went to Willy's place, and I told him so once, but he said, 'Lorna, you are a joy.' He had a nice way, and he took me out in his car, which was a good one, but dirty inside, like his place. Jim said one day, 'He has pots of money, Lorna,' and Mavis said, 'You might make a man of him, as he is keen on you.' They always said Willy came from a good family.

But I saw that one could not do anything with him. He would not change his shirt very often, or get clothes, but he went round like a tramp, lending people money, as I have seen with my own eyes. His place was in a terrible mess, with the empty bottles, and laundry in the corner. He gave me several gifts over the period, which I took as he would have only given them away, but he never tried to go to the full extent. He never painted my portrait, as he was painting fruit on a table all that time, and they said his pictures were marvellous, and thought Willy and I were getting married.

One night, when I went home, I was upset as usual, after Willy's place. Mum and Dad had gone to bed, and I looked round our kitchen which is done in primrose and white. Then I went into the living-room, where Dad has done one wall in a patterned paper, deep rose and white, and the other walls pale rose, with white woodwork. The suite is new, and Mum keeps everything beautiful. So it came to me, all of a sudden, what a fool I was, going with Willy. I agree to equality, but as to me marrying Willy, as I said to Mavis, when I recall his place, and the good carpet gone greasy, not to mention the paint oozing out of the tubes, I think it would break my heart to sink so low.

Quality

John Galsworthy

I knew him from the days of my extreme youth, because he made my father's boots; inhabiting with his elder brother two little shops let into one, in a small by-
street—now no more, but then most fashionably placed in the
West End.

That tenement had a certain quiet distinction; there was no
sign upon its face that he made for any of the Royal Family—
merely his own German name of Gessler Brothers; and in the
window a few pairs of boots. I remember that it always troubled me to account for those unvarying boots in the window,
for he made only what was ordered, reaching nothing down,
and it seemed so inconceivable that what he made could ever
have failed to fit. Had he bought them to put there? That, too,
seemed inconceivable. He would never have tolerated in his
house leather on which he had not worked himself. Besides,
they were too beautiful—a pair of pumps, so inexpressibly
slim, the patent leathers with cloth tops, making water come
into one's mouth, the tall brown riding-boots with marvellous
sooty glow, as if, though new, they had been worn a hundred
years. Those pairs could only have been made by one who saw
before him the Soul of Boot—so truly were they prototypes in-
carnating the very spirit of all footgear. These thoughts, of
course, came to me later, though even when I was promoted to
him, at the age of perhaps fourteen, some inkling haunted me
of the dignity of himself and brother. For to make boots—such

boots as he made—seemed to me then, and still seems to me, mysterious and wonderful.

I remember well my shy remark, one day, while stretching out to him my youthful foot:

"Isn't it awfully hard to do, Mr. Gessler?"

And his answer, given with a sudden smile from out of the sardonic redness of his beard: "Id is an Ardt!"

Himself, he was a little as if made from leather, with his yellow crinkly face, and crinkly reddish hair and beard, and neat folds slanting down his cheeks to the corners of his mouth, and his guttural and one-toned voice; for leather is a sardonic substance, and stiff and slow of purpose. And that was the character of his face, save that his eyes, which were grey-blue, had in them the simple gravity of one secretly possessed by the Ideal. His elder brother was so very like him—though watery, paler in every way, with a great industry—that sometimes in early days I was not quite sure of him until the interview was over. Then I knew that it was he, if the words, "I will ask my brudder," had not been spoken; and, that if they had, it was his elder brother.

When one grew old and wild and ran up bills, one somehow never ran them up with Gessler Brothers. It would not have seemed becoming to go in there and stretch out one's foot to that blue iron-spectacled glance, owing him for more than— say—two pairs, just the comfortable reassurance that one was still his client.

For it was not possible to go to him very often—his boots lasted terribly, having something beyond the temporary— some, as it were, essence of boot stitched into them.

One went in, not as into most shops, in the mood of: "Please serve me, and let me go!" but restfully, as one enters a church; and, sitting on the single wooden chair, waited—for there was never anybody there. Soon, over the top edge of that sort of well—rather dark, smelling soothingly of leather— which formed the shop, there would be seen his face, or that of his elder brother, peering down. A guttural sound, and the tip-tap of bast slippers beating the narrow wooden stairs, and he would stand before one without coat, a little bent, in leather apron, with sleeves turned back, blinking—as if awakened from some dream of boots, or like an owl surprised in daylight and annoyed at this interruption.

And I would say: "How do you do, Mr. Gessler? Could you make me a pair of Russia leather boots?"

Without a word he would leave me, retiring whence he came, or into the other portion of the shop, and I would continue to rest in the wooden chair, inhaling the incense of his trade. Soon he would come back, holding in his thin, veined hand a piece of gold-brown leather. With eyes fixed on it, he would remark: "What a beaudiful biece!" When I, too, had admired it, he would speak again. "When do you wand dem?" And I would answer: "Oh! As soon as you conveniently can." And he would say: "To-morrow fordnighd?" Or if he were his elder brother: "I will ask my brudder!"

Then I would murmur: "Thank you! Good-morning, Mr. Gessler." "Goot-morning!" he would reply, still looking at the leather in his hand. And as I moved to the door, I would hear the tip-tap of his bast slippers restoring him, up the stairs, to his dream of boots. But if it were some new kind of footgear that he had not yet made me, then indeed he would observe ceremony—divesting me of my boot and holding it long in his hand, looking at it with eyes at once critical and loving, as if recalling the glow with which he had created it, and rebuking the way in which one had disorganized this masterpiece. Then, placing my foot on a piece of paper, he would two or three times tickle the outer edges with a pencil and pass his nervous fingers over my toes, feeling himself into the heart of my requirements.

I cannot forget that day on which I had occasion to say to him: "Mr. Gessler, that last pair of town walking-boots creaked, you know."

He looked at me for a time without replying, as if expecting me to withdraw or qualify the statement, then said:

"Id shouldn'd 'ave greaked."

"It did, I'm afraid."

"You goddem wed before dey found demselves?"

"I don't think so."

At that he lowered his eyes, as if hunting for memory of those boots, and I felt sorry I had mentioned this grave thing.

"Zend dem back!" he said; "I will look at dem."

A feeling of compassion for my creaking boots surged up in

me, so well could I imagine the sorrowful long curiosity of regard which he would bend on them.

"Some boods," he said slowly, "are bad from birdt. If I can do noding wid dem, I dake dem off your bill."

Once (once only) I went absent-mindedly into his shop in a pair of boots bought in an emergency at some large firm's. He took my order without showing me any leather, and I could feel his eyes penetrating the inferior integument of my foot. At last he said:

"Dose are nod my boods."

The tone was not one of anger, nor of sorrow, not even of contempt, but there was in it something quiet that froze the blood. He put his hand down and pressed a finger on the place where the left boot, endeavouring to be fashionable, was not quite comfortable.

"Id 'urds you dere," he said. "Dose big virms 'ave no self-respect. Drash!" And then, as if something had given way within him, he spoke long and bitterly. It was the only time I ever heard him discuss the conditions and hardships of his trade.

"Dey get id all," he said, "dey get id by adverdisement, nod by work. Dey dake id away from us, who lofe our boods. Id gomes to this—bresently I haf no work. Every year id gets less —you will see." And looking at his lined face I saw things I had never noticed before, bitter things and bitter struggle— and what a lot of grey hairs there seemed suddenly in his red beard!

As best I could, I explained the circumstances of the purchase of those ill-omened boots. But his face and voice made so deep an impression that during the next few minutes I ordered many pairs. Nemesis fell! They lasted more terribly than ever. And I was not able conscientiously to go to him for nearly two years.

When at last I went I was surprised to find that outside one of the two little windows of his shop another name was painted, also that of a bootmaker—making, of course, for the Royal Family. The old familiar boots, no longer in dignified isolation, were huddled in the single window. Inside, the now contracted well of the one little shop was more scented and darker than ever. And it was longer than usual, too, before a face peered down, and the tip-tap of the bast slippers began. At last he stood before me, and gazing through those rusty iron spectacles, said:

"Mr.—, isn'd it?"

"Ah! Mr. Gessler," I stammered, "But your boots are really *too* good, you know! See, these are quite decent still!" And I stretched out to him my foot. He looked at it.

"Yes," he said; "beople do not wand good boods, id seems."

To get away from his reproachful eyes and voice I hastily remarked: "What have you done to your shop?"

He answered quietly: "Id was too exbensif. Do you wand some boods?"

I ordered three pairs, though I had only wanted two, and quickly left. I had, I do not know quite what feeling of being part, in his mind, of a conspiracy against him; or not perhaps so much against him as against his idea of boot. One does not, I suppose, care to feel like that; for it was again many months, before my next visit to his shop, paid, I remember, with the feeling: "Oh! well, I can't leave the old boy—so here goes! Perhaps it'll be his elder brother!"

For his elder brother, I knew, had not character enough to reproach me, even dumbly.

And, to my relief, in the shop there did appear to be his elder brother, handling a piece of leather.

"Well, Mr. Gessler," I said, "How are you?"

He came close, and peered at me.

"I am breddy well," he said slowly; "but my elder brudder is dead."

And I saw that it was indeed himself—but how aged and wan! And never before had I heard him mention his brother. Much shocked, I murmured: "Oh! I am sorry."

"Yes," he answered, "he was a good man, he made a good bood; but he is dead." And he touched the top of his head, where the hair had suddenly gone as thin as it had been on that of his poor brother, to indicate, I suppose, the cause of death. "He could nod ged over losing de oder shop. Do you wand any boods?" And he held up the leather in his hand. "Id's a beaudiful biece."

I ordered several pairs. It was very long before they came—but they were better than ever. One simply could not wear them out. And soon after that I went abroad.

It was over a year before I was again in London. And the first shop I went to was my old friend's. I had left a man of sixty, I came back to one of seventy-five, pinched and worn and tremulous, who genuinely, this time, did not at first know me.

"Oh! Mr. Gessler," I said, sick at heart; "how splendid your boots are! See, I've been wearing this pair nearly all the time I've been abroad; and they're not half worn out, are they?"

He looked long at my boots—a pair of Russia leather, and his face seemed to regain steadiness. Putting his hand on my instep, he said:

"Do dey vid you here? I 'ad drouble wid dat bair, I remember."

I assured him that they had fitted beautifully.

"Do you wand any boods?" he said. "I can make dem quickly; id is a slack dime."

I answered: "Please, please! I want boots all round—every kind!"

"I will make a vresh model. Your food must be bigger." And with utter slowness, he traced my foot, and felt my toes, only once looking up to say:

"Did I dell you my brudder was dead?"

To watch him was painful, so feeble had he grown; I was glad to get away.

I had given those boots up, when one evening they came. Opening the parcel, I set the four pairs out in a row. Then one by one I tried them on. There was no doubt about it. In shape and fit, in finish and quality of leather, they were the best he had ever made me. And in the mouth of one of the town walking-boots I found his bill. The amount was the same as usual, but it gave me quite a shock. He had never sent it in till quarter day. I flew downstairs, and wrote a cheque, and posted it at once with my own hand. A week later, passing the little street, I thought I would go in and tell him how splendidly the new boots fitted. But when I came to where his shop had been, his name was gone. Still there, in the window, were the slim pumps, the patent leathers with cloth tops, the sooty riding-boots.

I went in, very much disturbed. In the two little shops—
again made into one—was a young man with an English face.

"Mr. Gessler in?" I said.

He gave me a strange, ingratiating look.

"No, sir," he said, "no. But we can attend to anything with
pleasure. We've taken the shop. You've seen our name, no
doubt, next door. We make for some very good people."

"Yes, yes," I said; "but Mr. Gessler?"

"Oh!" he answered; "dead."

"Dead! But I only received these boots from him last
Wednesday week."

"Ah!" he said; "a shockin' go. Poor old man starved 'imself."

"Good God!"

"Slow starvation, the doctor called it! You see he went to
work in such a way! Would keep the shop on; wouldn't have a
soul touch his boots except himself. When he got an order, it
took him such a time. People won't wait. He lost everybody.
And there he'd sit, goin' on and on—I will say that for him—
not a man in London made a better boot! But look at the competition! He never advertised! Would 'ave the best leather, too,
and do it all 'imself. Well, there it is, What could you expect
with his ideas?"

"But starvation—!"

"That may be a bit flowery, as the sayin' is—but I know myself he was sittin' over his boots day and night, to the very
last. You see I used to watch 'im. Never gave 'imself time to
eat; never had a penny in the house. All went in rent and
leather. How he lived so long I don't know. He regular let his
fire go out. He was a character. But he made good boots."

"Yes," I said, "he made good boots."

And I turned and went out quickly, for I did not want that
youth to know that I could hardly see.

My Very Good Dear Friends . . .

Chief Dan George

WAS it only yesterday that men sailed around the moon . . . and can they now stand up on its barren surface? You and I marvel that man should travel so far and so fast. . . . Yet, if they have travelled far then I have travelled farther . . . and if they have travelled fast, then I faster . . . for I was born a thousand years ago . . . born in a culture of bows and arrows. But within the span of half a lifetime I was flung across the ages to the culture of the atom bomb. . . . And from bows and arrows to atom bombs is a distance far beyond a flight to the moon.

I was born in an age that loved the things of nature and gave them beautiful names like Tes-wall-u-wit instead of dried-up names like Stanley Park.

I was born when people loved all nature and spoke to it as though it had a soul. . . . I can remember going up Indian River with my father when I was very young. . . . I can remember him watching the sun light fires on Mount Pay-nay-nay as it rose above its peak. I can remember him singing his thanks to it as he often did . . . singing the Indian word "thanks . . ." so very, very softly.

And then the people came . . . more and more people came . . . like a crushing rushing wave they came . . . hurling the years aside!! . . . and suddenly I found myself a young man in the midst of the twentieth century.

I found myself and my people adrift in this new age . . . but not a part of it.

Engulfed by its rushing tide, but only as a captive eddy . . . going round and round . . . on little reserves, on plots of land we floated in a kind of grey unreality . . . ashamed of our culture which you ridiculed . . . unsure of who we were or where we were going . . . uncertain of our grip on the present . . . weak in our hope of the future. . . . And that is pretty well where we stand today.

I had a glimpse of something better than this. For a few brief years I knew my people when we lived the old life. . . . I knew them when there was still a dignity in our lives and a feeling of worth in our outlook. I knew them when there was unspoken confidence in the home and a certain knowledge of the path we walked upon. But we were living on the dying energy of a dying culture . . . a culture that was slowly losing its forward thrust.

I think it was the suddenness of it all that hurt us so. We did not have time to adjust to the startling upheaval around us. We seemed to have lost what we had without a replacement for it. We did not have time to take our twentieth-century progress and eat it little by little and digest it. It was forced feeding from the start and our stomachs turned sick and we vomited.

Do you know what it is like to be without moorings? Do you know what it is like to live in surroundings that are ugly and everywhere you look you see ugly things . . . strange things . . . strange and ugly things? It depresses man, for man must be surrounded by the beautiful if his soul is to grow.

What did we see in the new surroundings you brought us? Laughing faces, pitying faces, sneering faces, conniving faces. Faces that ridiculed, faces that stole from us. It is no wonder we turned to the only people who did not steal and who did not sneer, who came with love. They were the missionaries and they came with love and I for one will ever return that love.

Do you know what it is like to feel you are of no value to society and those around you? To know that people came to help you but not to work with you for you knew that they knew you had nothing to offer . . . ?

Do you know what it is like to have your race belittled and to come to learn that you are only a burden to the country? Maybe we did not have the skills to make a meaningful contribution, but no one would wait for us to catch up. We were shoved aside because they thought we were dumb and could never learn.

What is it like to be without pride in your race, pride in your family, pride and confidence in yourself? What is it like? You don't know for you never tasted its bitterness.

I shall tell you what it is like. It is like not caring about tomorrow for what does tomorrow matter. It is like having a reserve that looks like a junk yard because the beauty in the soul is dead and why should the soul express an external beauty that does not match it? It is like getting drunk for a few brief moments, an escape from ugly reality, and feeling a sense of importance. It is most of all like awaking next morning to the guilt of betrayal. For the alcohol did not fill the emptiness but only dug it deeper.

And now you hold out your hand and you beckon to me to come across the street . . . come and integrate you say. . . . But how can I come? I am naked and ashamed. How can I come in dignity? I have no presents . . . I have no gifts. What is there in my culture you value? . . . My poor treasure you can only scorn. Am I then to come as a beggar and receive all from your omnipotent hand? Somehow I must wait . . . I must delay. I must find myself. I must find my treasure. I must wait until you want something of me . . . until you need something that is me. Then I can raise my head and say to my wife and family . . . listen . . . they are calling . . . they need me . . . I must go. . . .

Then I can walk across the street and I will hold my head high for I will meet you as an equal. I will not scorn you for your demeaning gifts and you will not receive me in pity. Pity I can do without; my manhood I cannot.

I can only come as Chief Capilano came to Captain Vancouver . . . as one sure of his authority . . . certain of his worth . . . master of his house and leader of his people. I shall not come as a cringing object of your pity. I shall come in dignity or I shall not come at all.

You talk big words of integration in the schools. Does it really exist? Can we talk of integration until there is social integration? Unless there is integration of hearts and minds you have only a physical presence . . . and the walls are as high as the mountain range.

Come with me to the playgrounds of an integrated high school ... see how level and flat and ugly the black top is.... But look ... now it is recess time ... the students pour through the doors ... soon over here is a group of white students ... and see ... over there near a fence ... a group of native students ... and look again ... the black is no longer level ... mountain ranges rising ... valleys falling ... and a great chasm seems to be opening up between the two groups ... yours and mine ... and no one seems capable of crossing over. But wait.... Soon the bell will ring and the students will leave the play yard. Integration has moved indoors. There isn't much room in a classroom to dig chasms so there are only little ones there ... only little ones ... for we won't allow big ones ... at least, not right under our noses ... so we will cover it all over with black top ... cold ... black ... flat ... and full of ugliness in its sameness.

I know you must be saying ... tell us what *do* you want. What do we want? We want first of all to be respected and to feel we are people of worth. We want an equal opportunity to succeed in life ... but we cannot succeed on your terms ... we cannot raise ourselves on your norms. We need specialized help in education ... specialized help in the formative years ... special courses in English. We need guidance counselling ... we need equal job opportunities for graduates, otherwise our students will lose courage and ask what is the use of it all.

Let no one forget it ... we are a people with special rights guaranteed to us by promises and treaties. We do not beg for these rights, nor do we thank you ... we do not thank you for them because we paid for them ... and, God help us, the price we paid was exorbitant. We paid for them with our culture, our dignity, and self-respect. We paid and paid and paid until we became a beaten race, poverty-stricken and conquered.

But you have been kind to listen to me and I know that in your heart you wished you could help. I wonder if there is much you can do and yet I believe there is a lot you can do ... when you meet my children in your classroom, respect each one for what he is ... a child of our Father in heaven, and your brother. Maybe it all boils down to that.

And now it is the end. May I say thanks to you for the warmth of your understanding.

The Tractor

Peter Cowan

SHE watched him coming back from the gate, walking towards the slightly ornate suburban-style house she felt to be so incongruous set down on the bare rise, behind it the sheds and yards and the thin belt of shade trees. Yet he and his family were proud of it, grateful for its convenience and modernity, and had so clearly not understood her first quizzical remarks that she had never repeated them.

He stood on the edge of the veranda, and she saw in his face the anger that seemed to deepen because he knew the feeling to be impotent.

She said, "What is it?"

"Mackay's two big tractors—that they were going to use for the scrub-clearing—they've been interfered with. Sand put into the oil. The one they started up will cost a few hundred to repair."

"But no one would do that," she said, as if already it were settled, her temporizing without point.

"We know who did it."

"Surely he didn't come right up to the sheds—as close as that to the house—."

"No. They left the tractors down in the bottom paddock. Where they were going to start clearing."

"And now—they can't?"

"Now they can't. Not till the tractor's repaired."

She looked towards the distant line of the low scrub that

was deepening in colour as the evening came. She said, "That is what he wanted."

"What he wants is to make as much trouble as he can. We haven't done anything to him."

"You were going to clear the land along the bottom paddock at the back of Mackay's. Where he lives."

"Where he lives?"

"You told me he lived in the bush there."

"He lives anywhere. And he takes the ball floats off the taps in the sheep tank and the water runs to waste, and he breaks the fences when he feels like it, and leaves the gates open—"

"You think he does this deliberately?"

"How else?"

"Oh," she said, "yet it is all so ruthless."

"You mean what he does?"

"No. You only ever think of what he does."

"Well, I'll admit he's given us a few things to think about."

"Clearing with those tractors and the chain," she said. "Everything in their path goes—kangaroos—all the small things that live in the scrub—all the trees—"

He looked at her as if her words held some relevance that must come to him. He said, "We clear the land. Yes."

"You clear it," she said. "It seems to be what is happening everywhere today."

"I don't know what you mean, Ann," he said.

She got up from the chair by the steps. "Perhaps he feels something should be left."

"Look," he said, "maybe you teach too much nature study at school. Or you read all this stuff about how we shouldn't shoot the bloody 'roos—so that when some crazy swine wrecks our property you think he's some sort of a—"

"Some sort of a what?"

"I don't know," he said, aware she mocked him. "Better than us."

"No," she said. "Perhaps just different."

"Different all right."

"What are you going to do?"

"Get the police," he said. "They don't take much notice most of the time, but they will of this." He looked at her as if he would provoke the calm he felt to be assumed. "We'll burn him out if we can't get him any other way."

She looked up quickly and for a moment he was afraid.

"You wouldn't do that."

"He's gone too far this time," he said stubbornly.

The long thin streamers of cloud above the darkening line of scrub were becoming deep and hard in colour, scarlet against the dying light. He watched her face that seemed now calm, remote, as if their words were erased. She was small, slight, somehow always neat, contained. Her dark hair was drawn straight back, her brows clearly marked, lifting slightly so that they seemed to give humour sometimes to her serious expression, her firm mouth.

"I'd better go, Ken."

"The family expect you for tea."

"It's Sunday night. I've to work in the morning. I have some things to prepare."

"Look," he said. "If it's this business—"

"No. I'm just tired. And I've assignments to mark."

"All right," he said.

As they drove she watched the long shadows that spread across the road and over the paddocks from the few shade trees, the light now with a clarity denied through the heat of the day. She would have liked to make some gesture to break the tension between them, to explain to him why she had been unwilling to stay and listen to the inevitable talk of what had happened. But to tell him that at such times she became afraid, as if she could never become one of them, certain that the disagreements now easily enough brought to a truce must in the end defeat them, would not lessen their dissension.

He said suddenly, "You're worried about it, aren't you?"

She knew he referred to themselves, as if he had been aware of her own thoughts.

"Yes," she said. "Sometimes."

"It could be all right, Ann. You'd come to like it here."

"In so many ways I do."

"It's nothing like it used to be. This light land has come good now. We've done well. We've got everything—you wouldn't be without anything you'd have in the city."

"I know that, Ken," she said.

"But you're not sure of it."

She thought he perhaps did this deliberately, seeking to provoke an issue on material grounds, these at least being demonstrable of some conclusion, that he was lost, unwilling, in the face of their real uncertainty. He was more perceptive, she knew, than he cared to reveal, but he had a stubbornness she felt was perhaps impossible to defeat. Before it, she relented a little.

"Not sure of some things. You must give me time. After all, I—hadn't thought to live here. It's different for you."

The few high trees stood out darkly above the low thick scrub, and beyond she could see the roofs of the town.

He said, "This other business will probably be over next week, anyhow."

She supposed he deliberately minimized this which perhaps he did not understand, preferring evasion, the pretence that when it was settled it would not matter. As to him it might not. But he was so clearly afraid that she would escape. She reached out quickly and touched his hand.

He stopped the car before the house near the end of the main street, where she boarded. Farther down, near the club, she could see the cars parked, and people moving without haste along the pavements.

There was no wind, and in the darkness the street was hot, as if the endless heat of summer was never to be dissipated. As he closed the door of the car he said, "I have to go out to the paddock on the way back. It won't take long."

She made no comment and he said, as if to prevent her censure, "I've got to take some stuff from the store out there."

"They haven't found him?"

"No. The police think he's moved out. But we know he hasn't. He makes fools of them in the bush. They've been looking since Sunday, but they've given it up now. Anyhow, you could walk right past him at three feet. And there are no tracks."

"To be able to dodge them like that he must know all this country very well."

"I suppose he does."

"Almost—more than that. He must understand it."

"He doesn't seem to do anything else all day."

She smiled. "Well, do you?"

"I'm not sure what you mean by that. You mean we don't understand it?"

"Perhaps in a different way. You're making it something you can understand."

"Here we go again." He banged his hand against the steering wheel. "We never take a trick. Why don't you go and live with this character?"

She laughed suddenly. "I'm sorry, Ken. But how long has he been here? That's a harmless enough question!"

"He's been around here something like ten years. I remember when I was at school. He's mad."

She said, "All those who oppose us are mad."

"Well," he said, "we're going to get him out this time. We're taking shifts down at the tractors, and we've got a watch on a camp of his we found."

"A camp?"

"Made out of boughs." His voice was grudging. "Pretty well made. You could live in it. We flushed him out, because he left some food, and a radio."

"That's not in keeping—a radio."

"It doesn't work. May never have been any good. But it might be only that the batteries are flat. We'll find out. But he could have camps like that all through the bush. We'll be lucky if he comes back to this one."

They turned off through a fence gate, and down along a track that followed a side fence. He switched off the car lights and drove slowly.

"He'll hear the car," he said. "Still, the lights are a giveaway."

Suddenly they were close to the dark thick scrub, and then she saw the forms of the tractors, gaunt, high, like grotesque patches of shadow. Two men moved up to the car. One of them started to say something, then saw her, and paused.

He said, "He came back, Ken. Got the food. We never saw him."

They carried rifles, and suddenly she began to laugh. They looked at her with a surprise that had not yet become hostility.

"It—it just seems funny," she said weakly.

"It's not funny," Ken said. She was aware of their anger.

"We'll get him," the man she recognized as Don Mackay said. "We'll get him this time."

She was reminded suddenly of the boys at school in the playground at the lunch period, confronted by some argument that physical force could not immediately solve. Even their voices sound alike, she thought. Perhaps it is not so serious. But when they had taken the box Ken handed out to them, they stepped back from the car and she saw again the guns they carried, and the parallel frightened her.

"How long will they be repairing the tractor?" she asked.

"End of the week." His voice was brusque. She knew she had belittled him before his friends. She moved closer to him as he drove, and he looked briefly at her small, serious face shadowed in the half-light of the car.

"We'll go through there next week. I wish he'd get between the tractors when they're dragging the chain, that's all."

"Is he armed?"

"Yes," he said. "He is. He's lived off the land for years. And by taking food. He might be dangerous now."

She said slowly, "I wonder what made him begin to live like that?"

"No one will know that."

"You'll have to take care."

"There'll be a few of us there to watch for him."

"Actually, he hasn't ever threatened anyone, has he?"

"No. But he's never damaged anything big like this. And the police have never bothered about him before, either. You can see why. He's made fools of them."

"And of you."

"All right. And of us."

"Oh, Ken," she said, "I'm sorry. It's—it's just that I wish somehow you could just let him be."

"And have him do what he likes?"

"Well, he's not done anything much."

"Only wrecked a tractor."

"He would hate the tractors," she said, as if she no longer spoke to him, but was trying to work something out to her own satisfaction.

"Well, it's a reason why we can't leave him there."

"I suppose," she said, "you have to clear that land?"

"Of course. We clear some land every year. It's a tax deduction. And we need it the way taxation is."

"So there can't be anybody who wants things to stay the way they are for a while?"

He looked at her strangely. "Stay the way they are?"

If it was not what she meant she could not perhaps find words that were any more adequate. It was not a simple thing of statement, of definition, this that she felt. She saw with a sudden desolating clarity the grey sprawl of suburbs crossed by the black lines of roads, the cluster of city buildings that clawed up like a sudden focus, the endless tawdry, over-decorated little houses like the one he and his family had placed on the long low rise of land from which almost all else had been erased. As though, she thought painfully, he hated this land she had herself, incongruously enough, come to feel for in the brief time she had been close to it. And it was perhaps worse that he did not see what he was doing, himself a part of some force beyond him. Duped by pride. It was as if she had made some discovery she could not communicate to him and that set them apart.

She said desperately, "Do we have to change everything? Wipe out everything so that everlastingly we can grow things, make things, get tax deductions? You don't even leave a few acres of timber, somewhere for animals and birds—"

"Animals and birds," he said. "You can't stop progress."

"The unanswerable answer," she said. Before them the shade trees showed briefly along the road as it turned near the farm. "So we must all conform."

He slowed the car for the house gate, and in the headlights she saw the façade of the house as if they had turned into a suburban street. As he stopped the motor the silence held them. For a moment they did not move, then he drew her against him, his arm lightly about her shoulders, the gesture token of a security they might both have willed, denying the words with which they had held themselves separate.

"Maybe," he said slowly, "it's because you're so crazy I have to have you. You—you're different—"

"I'm sorry, Ken. Because I'm afraid I do love you—I suppose I have to have you, too."

"And you'd rather you didn't."

"Perhaps," she said, "I would rather I didn't."

"It's a mess, isn't it?"

"It might sort out," she said, and she laughed with him. At the house the front door opened briefly, the light shining across the entrance porch as someone looked out at the car.

At the week-end she had arranged to stay at the farm, and she expected him to call for her soon after breakfast. She put her small case on the veranda, but as he did not come she went back inside. Idly, rather irritated at his lateness, she took out her paints and began to work on the flower illustrations she was making. She had begun to paint the native flowers, their grotesque seeds and leaves, to use for her teaching, but the work had begun to absorb her, and she spent whatever time she could searching for new examples. Many, at first, she could not identify. Now, though she told no one, she had begun to hope the paintings might be publishable if she could complete series of different areas.

It was mid-morning when she heard him outside. In the car as they drove he said, "Some of the fences were broken, out by Hadley's boundary. We've been too busy this week to look down there, and the sheep had gone through into the scrub. We got most of them back."

"You lost some?"

"Some."

"I'm sorry," she said, as if somehow it were her fault.

"He knows we're going to clear that land, and he's out to do as much damage as he can first."

She had no wish to draw him, as if she deliberately sought their disagreement, but it seemed she must form the words, place them before him, his evasion too easy.

"You're sure about it, Ken, aren't you? That he's just getting his own back? That it's as simple as that?"

"It's obvious. He's done pretty well so far."

"And that's the only side there is to it?"

"What else could there be? He can't expect to stop us."

"He might know that."

"Well—that proves it."

"No—perhaps we've all got to make a gesture of some sort. For the things we believe in."

He shook his head. "You put it your way if you like. But what I believe in is using that land."

"Yes, Ken."

"We can't all be dreamers." And then, refusing to be further drawn, he laughed. "It's funny the way I've got caught up with one. Perhaps it will sort out, like you said. You do the dreaming. I'll do the work."

She ran her hands lightly over her arms, smiling at him. "You think we might convert one another?"

"It's a risk we'll have to take."

"Yes. I suppose we're young enough."

"I'll be out a bit this week-end, Ann. We've got to stop this somehow. While we've a few sheep left."

He went out late in the afternoon, and she helped his mother in the kitchen. The older woman had a quietness and a kind of insight that she found attractive, and they had always got on well together, though sometimes Ann was irritated by her acceptance of the men's decisions and views, as if this was something she no longer questioned, or perhaps, Ann thought, she had never questioned.

When Ken came back she heard him talking to his father on the veranda, and then the older man's voice raised in disagreement, though she could distinguish only a few of the words. She went out through the kitchen door and the men stopped talking.

As she came towards them Ken said, "We've found one of his camps. Ted and Don found it, but this time they turned off and kept away. They didn't go near enough for him to realize they'd seen it. We made that mistake last time."

"Where is this?" she said.

"It's new. So he may still be there. It's down in the paddock off the side road to Mackay's. Straight in from the dam. About half a mile north in the scrub."

"There."

"Yes. By the new land. Where we were going to build." He looked at her as if she might have contradicted him. "When we were married."

"What will you do?"

His father said, "I told them to get the police."

"He walked away from the police last time." For a moment

his eyes met the girl's. "And us. All right. We were no better. And the reporters came up from town. Photographers all over the place. A seven-day wonder for the suburbanites."

"It's not something that happens every day," she said. "Naturally, it was news."

"They'll make it news again, if we let them. But this time it will be different. We don't do anything until tomorrow night. That way he won't be suspicious if he sees our tracks near the camp. Then Sunday night we'll make a line north of the camp, and if the wind's right we'll burn back towards the firebreak along the paddock. He'll have to break out through the paddock. We'll have a chance that way."

"I think it's too big a risk," his father said. "You'll burn the whole of that country. You can't do it."

"We were going to clear it, anyway."

"You can't start a fire like that."

"If we try to close in on the camp he'll hear us."

"You could still get him. There's enough of you."

"He'd go between us in the bush. No matter how close we were. You know that. No one's been able to get a sight of him in the bush. The police had trackers there last week. They found plenty of tracks. But he kept as far ahead or behind them as he liked. No," he said, "he's made fools of us long enough. I think we've got a chance now."

He turned suddenly towards the girl and she stood beside him, not moving. His words seemed to her to hold a kind of defiance as if he did not himself believe in them, and she thought that it was not simply that he doubted their ability to carry out the plan, but that he did not really believe in the idea of the fire himself. That if she or his father did not further pursue it he might be glad to drop it. But she could not be certain, and before she could speak, as if he intended to prevent her words, he said, "Let's forget this now, Ann. We'll go over to Harris's after tea. They've got a bit of a show on there for May's birthday."

Almost all those she had come to know seemed to have found their way to the party. And all of them discussed the hermit, as they called him; she realized it was general knowledge that he was expected to be caught soon. She listened to the undercurrent of derision that the police with all their resources had been mocked by this man it seemed none of them had seen, as if in this they were on his side. Some of the older people she spoke to claimed to have caught glimpses of him when, some years earlier, he had taken food quite freely for a time from the farmhouses. Some claimed to know his name. But it seemed to her, as she mixed with them and listened to them, that none of them really cared. She felt they simply accepted the idea that he must be denied, driven from cover and killed if necessary, as they might have accepted the killing of a dingo or a fox, a creature for them without motive or reason. When she tried to turn their words, to question them, they looked at her with a kind of surprise, or the beginning of suspicion, perhaps in doubt of her as a teacher of their children. And she saw that quite quickly they exhausted the topic, turning to the enjoyment of the evening, as if already the whole thing was disposed of. In the end she thought it was their lack of involvement, their bland rejection of responsibility, that irritated her to the point of anger, so that she was forced to hold herself from rudeness.

It was late when they returned, and in her room, after she had changed, she stood for a time by the window in the darkness. There was a small moon that seemed scarcely to break the dark ground shadow, and beyond the paddocks she could not see where the scrub began. Her sense of anger had given place to dejection and a kind of fear. She tried to imagine the man who in the darkness slept in what they had described as his camp, something she could picture only as a kind of child's cubby house in the thick scrub. But she could form no picture of him as a physical being, only that it seemed to her he must possess imagination and sensibility beyond that of his pursuers, that he must be someone not difficult to talk to, someone who would understand her own feeling about these things for which he was persecuted. And who might even, she thought, be glad to know, however briefly, that they were shared. She was aware of a sense of disloyalty, but the image persisted, and it was suddenly monstrous that the darkness of the scrub should be swept by the glare of fire, as she would see it from the window where she stood now, the man stumbling from it in some unimaginable indignity. And though she had doubted the men's intention to carry out their plan, it seemed now in the darkness only too probable that in anger they might do what she, and perhaps they, feared. And it was impossible. Her hands felt the cold of the sill, she was aware of the faint wind that blew in through the window, cool upon her skin, and she could hear it in the boughs of the few shade trees behind the house.

On Sunday, in the afternoon, Ken left to make arrangements with the other men. His parents were resting, but she knew they would not question her going out, they were used to her wandering about the farm, looking for the plants she wished to paint. She went down through the yard gate, across the paddock towards the track that led out to the belt of scrub and timber. It seemed, in the heat, farther than she had expected.

She walked along the side fence, where the brush began, feeling that it would hide her if any of the men were watching. If she met them she would say she had come to look for Ken. She could see the dam ahead, the smooth red banks rising steeply, to one side a few thin trees, motionless in the heat.

At the dam she paused. The side track to Mackay's had turned some distance back to the left. In front of her, facing north, the scrub was thick, untouched, she was suddenly reluctant to go beyond the fence on the far side of the dam.

She pushed the wires down and stepped through. She began to pick her way through the scrub, choosing the small, most imperceptible pockets where the bushes were thinner. It was only after a time, when she could no longer see the dam or the trees beside it, that she realized her method of walking had led her away from a straight line. She had no clear idea how far she had come. She went on until she was certain she had covered half a mile, but as she stopped it was suddenly clear she could have deviated in any direction.

The bushes grew upward on their thin sparse stems to a rounded umbrella-like top, the leaves tough, elongated and splindly. They stretched away like endless replicas, rising head-high, become too thick for her to go farther. As she looked about it seemed improbable she had come so far. In the heat the scrub was silent. Along the reddish ground, over the thin stalks, the ants moved, in places she had walked round their mud-coloured mounds. She looked down at the ground, at the hard brittle twigs and fallen leaves, some of them already cemented by the ants. In a kind of fear she began to walk.

A short distance to the right a thin patch of trees lifted above the bushes, and though she thought it was the wrong direction she began to push her way towards it. The trees were like some sharp variation in the endless grey pattern of the brush that rose about her.

Beneath them the bark and leaves were thick upon the ground. She stood in the patch of shade, and she tried to reason that she could not have come far, that she could find her way back if she was careful. And in the silence she thought again, as she had the night before, of the man she had come to warn. It had seemed that if she could explain to him, he must understand, and that perhaps he would go. She had relied on there being understanding between them, that at least in these things they must feel alike. So that it had seemed her words would have effect. Now, in the heat and the silence, it was a dream, holding in this place no reality. She could never have thought to do it. And it was here he had spent ten years. It was like nothing she could encompass. She felt a sharp, childish misery, as if she might have allowed herself tears.

It occurred to her that if she could climb one of the trees she might gain an idea of direction. But the trunks were slippery, without foothold, and at the second attempt she fell, twisting her leg. She leant against the trunk, afraid of the pain, trying to deny it, as if she would will herself to be without injury that might imprison her.

She was not aware of any movement or sound, but she looked up, and turned slightly, still holding to the smooth trunk. He was standing just at the edge of the clump of trees. He might have been there all the time. Or been attracted by the noise she had made.

She said weakly, "I—didn't see you——"

His face held no expression she could read. His hair was grey and short, and she was vaguely surprised, as if she had imagined something different, but cut crudely, and streaked across his head by sweat. He was very thin, all the redundant flesh might long ago have been burnt from him, his arms stick-like, knotted and black. His hands held a rifle, and she knew a sudden fear that he would kill her, that somehow she must place words between them before he took her simply as one of his persecutors.

She said quickly, "I came to warn you—they have found your camp—tonight they mean to drive you out towards the paddock——"

But they were not the words she had planned. His eyes gave her no sign. They were very dark, sharp somehow, and she knew suddenly they were like the eyes of an animal or a bird, watchful, with their own recognition and knowledge which was not hers. The stubble of beard across his face was whitish, his skin dark from the sun.

"I—if only you would go from here," she said. "They only want you to go—they don't understand——"

The words were dead in the heat and the silence. She saw the flies that crawled across his face.

"I wanted to help you," she said, and she despised herself in her terror. Only his hands seemed to move faintly about the rifle. His stillness was insupportable. Abruptly she began to sob, the sound loud, gulping, ridiculous, her hands lifting to her face.

He seemed to step backwards. His movement was somehow liquid, unhuman, and then she thought of the natives she had once seen in the north, not the town natives whose movements had grown like her own. But with a strange inevitability he moved like an animal or the vibration of the thin sparse trees before the wind. She did not see him go. She looked at the boles of the trees where he had stood, and she could hear her own sobbing.

Some time in the afternoon she heard the sudden sound of shots, flat, unreal, soon lost in the silence. But she walked towards where the sound had seemed to be, and after a time, without warning she came on the track that ran towards Mackay's place. She had gone only a short distance when she heard the voices, and called out. The men came through the scrub and she saw them on the track. She began to run towards them, but checked herself. Farther down she saw a Landrover and one of the police. Ken said, "We missed you—

we've been searching—it was only that Ted saw where you'd walked down the fence—"

She said, "The shots—I heard them—"

"We were looking for you. We didn't see him. He tried to get past us, then shot at Don—we had to shoot."

She did not speak and he said, "We had to do it, Ann. We sent for the police. But where were you? How did you get out here?"

There was nothing she could tell him. She said, "I was looking for you, I think."

The Landrover had drawn up beside them, and the driver opened the door for her. They moved back down the dry rutted track where the thin shade had begun to stretch in from the broken scrub.

999 Smiles

Atukwei Okai

(*to Guy Warren*)

nine hundred and ninety-nine smiles
plus
one quarrel ago, our eyes and our
hearts
were in agreement full that still

The sun rises in the East
And sets in the West, that
Still
Rains fall from above
Downward to the earth
That
Still smokes rise from the
Earth, reaching for the sky
That
Still our earth is round and
Not flat like a spread-out
Mat

and yet . . .
        see where
               today

you have
        gone
            to sit . . .
throwing . . .
            stones
                at us . . .
poisonous . . .
            stones
                at us . . .
satanic . . .
            stones . . .
                at us . . .

And if I still had my hands
On my shoulders I should raise
One of my hands above my
Head
And gauge and catch your
Stones, one by one, while they
Were still hot in the cool
Air,

and yet . . .
            see where . . .
                        today
you have
        gone
            to sit . . .
hurling . . .
            stones . . .
                at us . . .
hurling . . .
            stones . . .
                at us . . .

infernal . . .

        stones . . .

                at us . . .

sinister . . .

        stones . . .

                at us . . .

But all the same, I shall not even
Utter your name, lest the fast and
Faithful
Winds repeat it to the hearing of
Our ancestors who are asleep
With
Their eyes, but not asleep with
Their ears, lest our ancestors
Angrily
Rise out of their nest and
Breathe out the winds that can
Shake
Till it breaks, the decayed drooping

Branch
upon which

        of all

            people

you today

        have gone

            to sit . . .

hurling . . .

        stones . . .

                at us . . .

wrathful . . .

        stones . . .

                at us . . .

saddening . . .

        stones . . .

                at us . . .

Charging precisely to our
Head, and if I still had my
Hands about me, I would
Gather
Your stones into a heap, and
Leave them there to lie till
Some morrow when we might
Use

Them to bring down to the warm
Tongues of some fire, fleshy
Birds, that above our heads are
Perched,
Just like you, upon the slippery
Branch of the air; and if still
I had my hands with me, I would
Catch
And keep your stones without thinking
Of throwing them back at you—but
The hands too soon you have stolen away
With

you
    to where
            today
you have
        gone
           to perch
throwing . . .
          stones . . .
               at us . . .
venomous . . .
          stones . . .
               at us . . .
spiteful . . .
          stones . . .
               at us . . .

nine hundred and ninety-nine smiles
plus
one quarrel ago our eyes and our
hearts
were in agreement full that still

When a man lifts his foot, it is
Forward
That he places it, that still, each
Human
Being owns only ten fingers on two
Hands

Flight

Doris Lessing

A BOVE the old man's head was the dovecote, a tall wire-netted shelf on stilts, full of strutting, preening birds. The sunlight broke on their grey breasts into small rainbows. His ears were lulled by their crooning, his hands stretched up towards his favourite, a homing pigeon, a young plump-bodied bird which stood still when it saw him and cocked a shrewd bright eye.

'Pretty, pretty, pretty,' he said, as he grasped the bird and drew it down, feeling the cold coral claws tighten around his finger. Content, he rested the bird lightly on his chest, and leaned against a tree, gazing out beyond the dovecote into the landscape of a late afternoon. In folds and hollows of sunlight and shade, the dark red soil, which was broken into great dusty clods, stretched wide to a tall horizon. Trees marked the course of the valley; a stream of rich green grass the road.

His eyes travelled homewards along this road until he saw his grand-daughter swinging on the gate underneath a frangipani tree. Her hair fell down her back in a wave of sunlight, and her long bare legs repeated the angles of the frangipani stems, bare, shining-brown stems among patterns of pale blossoms.

She was gazing past the pink flowers, past the railway cottage where they lived, along the road to the village.

His mood shifted. He deliberately held out his wrist for the bird to take flight, and caught it again at the moment it spread its wings. He felt the plump shape strive and strain under his fingers; and, in a sudden access of troubled spite, shut the bird into a small box and fastened the bolt. 'Now you stay there,' he muttered; and turned his back on the shelf of birds. He moved warily along the hedge, stalking his grand-daughter, who was now looped over the gate, her head loose on her arms, singing. The light happy sound mingled with the crooning of the birds, and his anger mounted.

'Hey!' he shouted; saw her jump, look back, and abandon the gate. Her eyes veiled themselves, and she said in a pert neutral voice: 'Hullo, Grandad.' Politely she moved towards him, after a lingering backward glance at the road.

'Waiting for Steven, hey?' he said, his fingers curling like claws into his palm.

'Any objection?' she asked lightly, refusing to look at him.

He confronted her, his eyes narrowed, shoulders hunched, tight in a hard knot of pain which included the preening birds, the sunlight, the flowers. He said: 'Think you're old enough to go courting, hey?'

The girl tossed her head at the old-fashioned phrase and sulked. 'Oh, Grandad!'

'Think you want to leave home, hey? Think you can go running around the fields at night?'

Her smile made him see her, as he had every evening of this warm end-of-summer month, swinging hand in hand along the road to the village with that red-handed, red-throated, violent-bodied youth, the son of the postmaster. Misery went to his head and he shouted angrily: 'I'll tell your mother!'

'Tell away!' she said, laughing, and went back to the gate.

He heard her singing, for him to hear:

'I've got you under my skin
I've got you deep in the heart of . . .'

'Rubbish,' he shouted. 'Rubbish. Impudent little bit of rubbish!'

Growling under his breath he turned towards the dovecote, which was his refuge from the house he shared with his daughter and her husband and their children. But now the house would be empty. Gone all the young girls with their laughter and their squabbling and their teasing. He would be left, uncherished and alone, with that square-fronted, calm-eyed woman, his daughter.

He stooped, muttering, before the dovecote, resenting the absorbed cooing birds.

From the gate the girl shouted: 'Go and tell! Go on, what are you waiting for?'

Obstinately he made his way to the house, with quick, pathetic persistent glances of appeal back at her. But she never looked around. Her defiant but anxious young body stung him into love and repentance. He stopped. 'But I never meant . . .' he muttered, waiting for her to turn and run to him. 'I didn't mean . . .'

She did not turn. She had forgotten him. Along the road came the young man Steven, with something in his hand. A present for her? The old man stiffened as he watched the gate swing back, and the couple embrace. In the brittle shadows of the frangipani tree his grand-daughter, his darling, lay in the arms of the postmaster's son, and her hair flowed back over his shoulder.

'I see you!' shouted the old man spitefully. They did not move. He stumped into the little whitewashed house, hearing the wooden veranda creak angrily under his feet. His daughter was sewing in the front room, threading a needle held to the light.

He stopped again, looking back into the garden. The couple were now sauntering among the bushes, laughing. As he watched he saw the girl escape from the youth with a sudden mischievous movement, and run off through the flowers with him in pursuit. He heard shouts, laughter, a scream, silence.

'But it's not like that at all,' he muttered miserably. 'It's not like that. Why can't you see? Running and giggling, and kissing and kissing. You'll come to something quite different.'

He looked at his daughter with sardonic hatred, hating himself. They were caught and finished, both of them, but the girl was still running free.

'Can't you *see*!' he demanded of his invisible grand-daughter, who was at that moment lying in the thick green grass with the postmaster's son.

His daughter looked at him and her eyebrows went up in tired forbearance.

'Put your birds to bed?' she asked, humouring him.

'Lucy,' he said urgently. 'Lucy . . .'

'Well, what is it now?'

'She's in the garden with Steven.'

'Now you just sit down and have your tea.'

He stumped his feet alternatively, thump, thump, on the hollow wooden floor and shouted: 'She'll marry him. I'm telling you, she'll be marrying him next!'

His daughter rose swiftly, brought him a cup, set him a plate.

'I don't want any tea. I don't want it, I tell you.'

'Now, now,' she crooned. 'What's wrong with it? Why not?'

'She's eighteen. Eighteen!'

'I was married at seventeen and I never regretted it.'

'Liar,' he said. 'Liar. Then you should regret it. Why do you make your girls marry? It's you who do it. What do you do it for? Why?'

'The other three have done fine. They've three fine husbands. Why not Alice?'

'She's the last,' he mourned. 'Can't we keep her a bit longer?'

'Come, now, dad. She'll be down the road, that's all. She'll be here every day to see you.'

'But it's not the same.' He thought of the other three girls, transformed inside a few months from charming petulant spoiled children into serious young matrons.

'You never did like it when we married,' she said. 'Why not? Every time, it's the same. When I got married you made me feel like it was something wrong. And my girls the same. You get them all crying and miserable the way you go on. Leave Alice alone. She's happy.' She sighed, letting her eyes linger on the sunlit garden. 'She'll marry next month. There's no reason to wait.'

'You've said they can marry?' he said incredulously.

'Yes, Dad, why not?' she said coldly, and took up her sewing.

His eyes stung, and he went out onto the veranda. Wet spread down over his chin and he took out a handkerchief and mopped his whole face. The garden was empty.

From around the corner came the young couple; but their faces were no longer set against him. On the wrist of the postmaster's son balanced a young pigeon, the light gleaming on its breast.

'For me?' said the old man, letting the drops shake off his chin. 'For me?'

'Do you like it?' The girl grabbed his hand and swung on it. 'It's for you, Grandad. Steven brought it for you.' They hung about him, affectionate, concerned, trying to charm away his wet eyes and his misery. They took his arms and directed him to the shelf of birds, one on each side, enclosing him, petting him, saying worldlessly that nothing would be changed, nothing could change, and that they would be with him always. The bird was proof of it, they said, from their lying happy eyes, as they thrust it on him. 'There, Grandad, it's yours. It's for you.'

They watched him as he held it on his wrist, stroking its soft, sun-warmed back, watching the wings lift and balance.

'You must shut it up for a bit,' said the girl intimately. 'Until it knows this is its home.'

'Teach your grandmother to suck eggs,' growled the old man.

Released by his half-deliberate anger, they fell back, laughing at him. 'We're glad you like it.' They moved off, now serious and full of purpose, to the gate, where they hung, backs to him, talking quietly. More than anything could, their grown-up seriousness shut him out, making him alone; also, it quietened him, took the sting out of their tumbling like puppies on the grass. They had forgotten him again. Well, so they should, the old man reassured himself, feeling his throat clotted with tears, his lips trembling. He held the new bird to his face, for the caress of its silken feathers. Then he shut it in a box and took out his favourite.

'*Now* you can go,' he said aloud. He held it poised, ready for flight, while he looked down the garden towards the boy and the girl. Then, clenched in the pain of loss, he lifted the bird on his wrist, and watched it soar. A whirr and a spatter of wings, and a cloud of birds rose into the evening from the dovecote.

At the gate Alice and Steven forgot their talk and watched the birds.

On the veranda, that woman, his daughter, stood gazing, her eyes shaded with a hand that still held her sewing.

It seemed to the old man that the whole afternoon had stilled to watch his gesture of self-command, that even the leaves of the trees had stopped shaking.

Dry-eyed and calm, he let his hands fall to his sides and stood erect, staring up into the sky.

The cloud of shining silver birds flew up and up, with a shrill cleaving of wings, over the dark ploughed land and the darker belts of trees and the bright folds of grass, until they floated high in the sunlight, like a cloud of motes of dust.

They wheeled in a wide circle, tilting their wings so there was flash after flash of light, and one after another they dropped from the sunshine of the upper sky to shadow, one after another, returning to the shadowed earth over trees and grass and field, returning to the valley and the shelter of night.

The garden was all a fluster and a flurry of returning birds. Then silence, and the sky was empty.

The old man turned, slowly, taking his time; he lifted his eyes to smile proudly down the garden at his granddaughter. She was staring at him. She did not smile. She was wide-eyed, and pale in the cold shadow, and he saw the tears run shivering off her face.

My Neighbor's Son

Pearl Buck

I
T is autumn. The streets of our village and the road
at the end of our lane are quiet. The children are back at
school, the little ones and the big ones, the first-graders
to whom school is a wonder because they know nothing about
it, and the high school seniors who know all about it and are
already impatiently anticipating the year beyond when they
must face the decision of armed services or college or job.

In the houses on the farms and on the streets parents are
thoughtful, too. The summer has brought them new acquaintance with their children, and they feel pride, vague alarm, exasperation, and hope. Never was there an age so difficult for
parents as this age in which we live. We know too well that
the world our children face is not the world we faced at their
age, and we doubt our ability to help them. They think their
parents do not know enough.

It has always been a phase of youth to feel itself misunderstood until maturity brings its own humor and commonsense
to dispel the miasma. Yet our children feel more than the
pains of growing independence. They conclude, quite simply,
that their parents and their teachers do not know enough
about our suddenly changed world to warrant faith, and therefore they must discover for themselves what the facts are.

And, aware of this withdrawal, parents read the newspapers
and learn of other people's children. They read of boys, not
children but young men, who go out to rob and torture and

murder innocent and unknown persons. Nor are these the children of bad parents. They may be the sons of respectable, hard-working people who have tried to build good homes and make a decent environment for their children. Their parents cannot believe that the young men, handcuffed and in the custody of the police, are their sons.

"They have always been such good boys!" the parents cry.

"Why didn't you keep them off the streets?" the police retort. "Why didn't you know where your sons were at midnight?"

The parents cannot answer. Anyone who knows teen-age boys today, and even teen-age girls, knows that it is not easy to insist upon knowing where they are at midnight. Because they do not have faith in their parents they do not respect them. They assert their independence and they think it is part of independence to come and go as they please. What can a middle-aged couple do when a tall, able-bodied son refuses to obey? What are the punishments that can be meted out to a young man by an old one? The young man sneers at threats; he is contemptuous of appeal.

"I don't have to take anything from anybody," I heard a young man shout in the house of the good man who is my neighbor and his father.

The boy, six feet two, strode out of the house and the father looked at me.

"What do I do now?" he asked helplessly.

"I don't know," I answered, equally helplessly.

I came home and reflected upon question and answer. Knowing the father, I felt an unwilling sympathy for the son; and knowing the son, I felt the same sympathy for the father. How is it that the son of my neighbor, whom I first saw when he was a curly-haired baby learning to walk, has grown into this hooligan? He was an amiable baby, smiling and friendly. He is not amiable now and he is not friendly and his smile is usually a sneer. What happened? His parents are plain, good folk. The mother has a high school education, the father went to a technical school and earns a fair salary as a mechanical engineer. There are two children, a girl in junior high school and a younger boy. They were smiling babies, too, but they, too, are not happy children now. Yet their home is pleasant enough and they have the comforts which today we think of as necessities. The family goes to church with reasonable regularity, although the children use the church as a social center rather than as a religious source. The mother has never worked outside her home. She seldom goes anywhere, except for her monthly club meeting, and she is a good cook and housekeeper. The family reads very little but they like popular music, and they have a television set which occasionally causes strife, for the parents do not enjoy seeing murders and the children do.

It is significant that children today crave scenes of violence. It is because they are angry deep in their souls, so deep that they do not know it. They want to strike back, even vicariously, at a world they fear. Dangerous! Youth, when happy, is in love with life and beauty.

What is wrong in my neighbor's house? Anyone entering it would say that it is a good home. All the furniture and equipment for a good home are there, including parents and children. But when I have stayed there awhile, I have a strange feeling that the house is empty. Nobody is really living there except perhaps the mother in the kitchen.

I wonder why the house feels empty, and after thinking about it, it seems to me that it is because the home is not connected with the stream of life in the community or the nation or the world. It is an island apart, striving to maintain itself in a sea of change. But we human beings need each other, near and far. The separation of the individual or nation or race, whether voluntary or compelled, has dangerous results. We must have constant replenishment from the stream of human life or we thirst and die.

The rebellion of my neighbor's son is inevitable and right. He is rebelling unconsciously and therefore with all his strength against the tomb of his home. He has nothing to do in this house. Oh yes, chores, but why should he work to maintain a tomb? What purpose is there for him in keeping a lawn neat, in weeding vegetable or flower gardens, in washing windows or sweeping out the cellar? They are all parts of the tomb. He has an interest in washing the car and even spending a day or two in simonizing it because there is life in a car. It can take him away from home. Here at home everything is as it has always been as long as he can remember. His father has not changed his mind or his opinions in twenty years, which for the boy is a lifetime. His mother has a flow of talk but no ideas, as far as he is concerned, beyond the cost of food and her longing for a new refrigerator that the father cannot afford. The boy is too young to tap the simple wisdom of his father's philosophy and his mother's compliance. They have discovered that a cup can only hold a cupful. A cup in the kitchen and a cup of life are the same. It contains only so much as it can hold. The parents have settled for what they have. It is a sort of wisdom—call it resignation, if you like.

But the young cannot be resigned unless they have been wounded or deformed. They will not believe that life is no more than a cupful. There must be more somewhere, outside this house. Somewhere there must be joy, peace, security, companionship, understanding, communion. Else why were they born? And the young are right. They, too, have their wisdom.

My neighbor that day watched his tall, strong son climb into the family car and whirl away. I saw despair on his face and bleak helplessness in his eyes.

He said, "We ought to put them all into the Army at sixteen."

I cried out against such defeat. "Oh, don't say that—it means we don't know how to make a world for the young as well as the old."

"I've done all I can," he said, and he turned and went into the house and shut the door.

So the house is really empty and I do not blame the son for leaping into the car and riding away. And yet I know that my neighbor is right when he says that he has done all he can. He faces a task greater than one man can perform.

The whole community must help the parents with their sons and daughters. Schoolteachers must not only teach school, preachers may not only save the souls, police may not merely arrest the criminals, the city fathers may not simply attend to city affairs. They must all help the parents with their children.

In ancient countries, where the social unit is the big family, where grandparents and parents, uncles and aunts and cousins all live together within one surrounding wall and function as a community, the children belong to all. The family community is itself the stream of life, leading into nation and world. But two people struggling to make a living in our highly competitive society in a fluctuating era cannot at the same time feed, clothe, educate, train, and inspire a family of restless and lively children.

No two parents have that much strength. And when I say educate, I mean education in the fullest sense, for what teachers have to teach children is very little compared to what parents have to teach children if these parents are conscientious.

In pre-Communist China, for example, the responsibilities of the schoolteacher were much greater than they are here. When parents brought their son to school, they gave him, in a sense, to the teacher. They said, in effect, he is yours not only to teach but to make into a good man. The teachers shared with the parents the responsibility of building character in the pupil. Ancestors, too, helped the parents. Precepts were handed down which all obeyed, young and old, and the son obeyed his dead ancestors as he did his living grandparents and parents.

Had my neighbor lived in old China, scores of people would have helped him with his son, and his son would have felt himself linked to them all and therefore part of the human stream. Instead of this, my neighbor struggles alone with the bewildered help of the boy's mother and the uncertain and intermittent interest of church and school. My sympathies are certainly with my neighbor, for nobody taught him how to be a parent. He spent years learning how to be an engineer. Yet of his two jobs, fatherhood is far more difficult and important than engineering. As for the mother parent, cooking and housekeeping is the least part of being a mother. And nobody helps those parents, not the dead or the living. Yet they are blamed for whatever their son does. In spite of their bewilderment and sense of defeat, they keep on trying.

The boy is wrong, of course, when he is contemptuous of his parents and feels they are useless to him. He has no conception of what heavy hearts they have when they think of him and how much they love him. I do not expect such sensitivity in a boy or girl nowadays. Ours is not a sensitive age. We have been hardened by atrocities. Nevertheless, the son owes it to himself to be courteous and helpful to his parents, regardless of whether he loves them or respects them. When he behaves without courtesy or helpfulness, he is less than fair to himself. But nobody seems to have taught him that. Nor does he know that feeling can follow action or that action must be based on principle and not on feelings.

"Do I have to say I am sorry when I am not?" One of my own sons, when small, made this demand after injustice to his younger sister.

"Indeed you must say you are sorry, and whether you are or not," I replied. "You must *do* right, however you *feel*. You cannot make yourself feel something you do not feel, but you can make yourself do right in spite of your feelings. And you'll be surprised, because when you have learned the habit of saying you are sorry when you should be, you will actually begin to feel sorry."

I learned that precept long ago when I was a child, and my teacher was a wise old man who was not of my race or my religion. I have found it true throughout my life.

And having acted without courtesy or respect toward his father, what satisfaction will my neighbor's son find this afternoon, wherever he is going? He is whirling down the street in a cloud of dust, and my heart goes with him, badly as he has behaved, for I fear he will not find what he really craves, which is to be part of the stream of human life. He will spend the afternoon on the football field and then, with his friends whom he calls "the gang," he will go to the garage, which is today's substitute for the country store or the city saloon, and they will talk about football scores and whether they want to finish high school and what movies they will see and what girls they know and which branch of the service is the easiest and least likely to force them to kill men they have never seen before.

It is a hopeful fact that most of our young people do not want to kill—they still would rather not. I do not believe that those boys I read about in the morning paper, who roamed the city streets, beating and torturing and killing strangers, really wanted to do such things. It is against man's nature to kill his kind. Those boys were pressed beyond endurance by the cruel aspect of the world about them, and in the loneliness of their youth they tried to seize what they thought was life. If someday they must be compelled to violate every natural instinct, then let it be now. They wanted life whatever it had to be. It might as easily have been the saving of lives, if anybody had shown them that in this world, even today, there is the delirious possibility of peace and good will.

There was no such conscious reasoning in these tragic boys who, in their ignorance, mistook death for life, but it is unconscious reasoning that we must fear, the despair of the young soul who thinks he cannot escape what he foresees and fears and hates and therefore rushes to meet it. And, looking back, he knows there is no refuge, either, in the life he has lived in the past.

My neighbor's son flees his empty childhood home, but alas, the football field, the garage, the movie, even the girl he takes out for a few nights and then abandons because she does not satisfy his mind and soul—which do mean more to him, though he does not know it, than his body—these are also empty, for they, too, are not in the mainstream of the world's life.

For I believe that my neighbor's son knows instinctively that there are important and therefore interesting and exciting things to be done in the world, in the nation and even in this home town of his, and he has a vague, blind longing to throw himself into something important and therefore interesting and exciting. His need is the need of the individual to be needed and therefore essential.

How do I know? Once I walked in the evening through the woods at the far end of our farm. I heard the sound of human sobbing, and I stopped to listen. It was a man sobbing, a young man, his voice still breaking. I followed the sound and there, in a small dell, I found my neighbor's son, sitting on a log, his head in his hands. He was crying.

"Are you in trouble?" I asked.

He was startled at the sound of my voice, and he tried to hide his face. "It's nothing," he said. He searched for his handkerchief and, not finding it, he used his shirttail to wipe his eyes.

"Of course it is something," I said, "but I won't ask if you'd rather not talk."

"It's just something personal," he said.

"Troubles are always just personal," I said. "I've had them myself and I know."

I sat down on the far end of the log and waited. It had been a lovely autumn day; the air was warm, the sky clear, the trees flaming.

"I wouldn't know how to pin it down to one trouble," he said at last. "I just feel pushed around."

"Who pushes you?" I asked. His parents were certainly lenient—permissive is the word.

"Oh, everything ... sort of ..."

"You have nothing that you really care about doing," I suggested.

"That's it," he said.

"Or," I suggested, "you haven't found what you really want to do and you don't know where to look."

"I guess so," he said unwillingly.

He looked away from me. "Well, I have to go."

"So do I," I said, getting up from my end of the log. "I just want to say, though, that I hope you won't give up looking for what you really want to do. For I do assure you the world is a wonderful, big place, far beyond your imagination, and there is certainly something in it that you want to do and people who need desperately what you can do. Just keep looking—and be patient with yourself."

"Okay."

He nodded and went off through the woods, and I walked homeward. The very paucity of his speech was a sign of trouble and doubtless added to his frustration. He knew too few words with which to explain himself, and speech is a bottleneck for his surging feelings. "Sort of—." ... "I guess so—." ... "Okay!" Such words are the rubber-stamp vocabulary of most of our young people.

But his real suffering is the universal human yearning to belong to something bigger than himself, to be indispensable to his fellowmen and valued as an individual.

I observe that our American young suffer more deeply than the young of other countries from this conviction of uselessness. Their childhood is prolonged until it becomes a vacuum into which they pour sports, entertainment, jaunting around, "hacking"—all harmless activities but all empty in themselves and none of them substitutes for soul-satisfying work in the mainstream of human life. No one can grow and find content in himself unless he knows that he is contributing his share to the growing, expanding, developing life of the human race.

My neighbor's son has never been taught this deep and simple truth, and so he is lonely and he goes into the woods to weep without knowing why. I hope it is not too late for him to learn. I hope his life will be larger than a cup meagerly filled. Yet he should have begun long ago to learn, when he was still a curly-haired little boy with a smile. We have wasted his youth and strength, as we waste so much of our youth.

Every town and village and city and countryside wastes its young people. Why does so much remain undone? It is because our children have no connection with life. They live in a child world of which they weary and yet which they do not know how to leave. I do not believe in a child world. It is a fantasy world. I believe the child should be taught from the very first that the whole world is his world, that adult and child share one world, that all generations are needed.

If I were the mayor of a town, I would see to it that even first-graders know that they are citizens, and that, as citizens, they have duties. They would be given no privileges but they would have rights. Their very first duties would be essential to the general welfare. They would receive neither pay nor reward for doing their duty, and part of their duty would be to consider how the town could be improved, from their point of view, and their opinions would be given full weight.

If I were the mayor of a town, I would see to it that even a first-grader knows the names of our fine leading citizens, and that he understands what makes men and women good citizens. I would hold the children responsible for part of the care of museums and monuments and public buildings. I would make them realize that it is their duty to cooperate with the police, who are protectors of good people but who in their job as employees of the public must not behave in cruel and tyrannous ways and thus abuse the power which is vested in them by tax-paying citizens.

At each age level the responsibility of the child-citizen should increase. By the time he is twelve, he should understand the government of his town so well that he can assess the character of a man or woman running for public office, because he knows what that person has achieved in character and public service. He should be held responsible for that knowledge by his parents and teachers who, in turn, must furnish him the means of learning. And the child must be given a recognized way of expressing his opinion by a graduated vote.

Had my neighbor's son been part even of the streamlet of life in his own home town, I do not believe he would have gone off to weep in the woods because he was lonely. Responsibility breeds respect, and when our young people assume responsibility, they deserve our respect. I grieve to see how little the young are respected in our society.

We love our children and we shower them with privilege, we pamper them with pretty clothes and dashing cars, we indulge ourselves by being proud of them in a self-centered sort of way whereby the child is the possession of the parent— "He's my kid, ain't he? So he's none of your business—" But we do not respect our children as human beings and individuals. Young Americans, quite contrary to usual judgment at home and abroad, suffer almost universally from deep convictions of inferiority. Their bombastic loudness or their negative withdrawals are signs of self-doubt. And who can blame them for not respecting themselves when they are not respected by society? The respect of one's fellowmen is the source of self-respect, and for a child it is the primary atmosphere of growth.

My sympathies are still with my neighbor's son. He has had very little to help him to grow. His amusements at eighteen are childish and repetitious or destructive, and yet they are the only ones to be had. He reads almost nothing, for he is not really literate, in spite of years of schooling, and so he does not know that the cream of all human thought is between the covers of books. Instead, he looks at comics and those sad funny papers.

I remember once that my mother refused to read a certain magazine, popular in her day, on the grounds that it was only trash. Whether it was trash I do not remember—and it was not important then nor is it now—but what she said was so important that I have never forgotten it.

She said, "I would no more put trash into my mind than I would put garbage into my mouth."

It was her way of expressing an old Biblical wisdom: "As a

man thinketh, so he is."

The mind becomes a sewer if it is fed sewage. If, in the name of freedom, we allow the uncontrolled flow of sewage of murder and crime and violence and absurd fantasy to seep continually into the minds of our children, then in the name of freedom we ought to strive with all effort to counteract the flow of evil with a powerful surge of good.

And I deny the sophist who says that good and evil depend upon the person and the standards of his society. Good and evil can be universally defined in their basic essentials, and are so defined by people everywhere. In the many countries in which I have lived and traveled I have been impressed by the discovery that a good human being in one country is considered a good human being in every other. We know instinctively, wherever we were born, what is good and what is evil, but our instincts can become confused.

I think my neighbor's son is confused, and that is part of his trouble. He has been fed on poor fare, mentally and spiritually, and this while his body has been stuffed with good food and vitamins. Little has been expected of him, and he has been limited in his development by that meager expectation.

I do not approve severity but I believe in the inexorable demand for responsibility at each age level of all citizens, and deprivation, if not punishment, when duty is ignored. We need to restore the full meaning of that old word, duty. It is the other side of rights. Each of us has a duty to every human being, and the proper performance of such duty is duty to one's self. Nor is discipline the means to performance. There is a void to be filled in the lives of our young people, and discipline in itself is negative, a prohibition and not a fulfillment.

No, we have to teach our young that they will never find contentment until they put themselves into the mainstream of human life. And then, in the wonderful, rewarding way that life has, peace and happiness—when not sought for their own sakes—come stealing in through the doors of duty fulfilled. Duty is not hateful or tedious or destructive. Duty fulfilled is gratifying and enjoyable and restoring to the soul, and serenity is its fruit.

I pray there is still time for my neighbor's son to know it.

Black Jackets

Thom Gunn

In the silence that prolongs the span
Rawly of music when the record ends,
    The red-haired boy who drove a van
In weekday overalls but like his friends,

    Wore cycle boots and jacket here
To suit the Sunday hangout he was in,
    Heard, as he stretched back from his beer,
Leather creak softly round his neck and chin.

    Before him, on a coal-black sleeve
Remote exertion had lined, scratched, and burned
    Insignia that could not revive
The heroic fall or climb where they were earned.

    On the other drinkers bent together,
Concocting selves for their impervious kit,
    He saw it as no more than leather
Which, taut across the shoulders grown to it,

    Send through the dimness of a bar
As sudden and anonymous hints of light
    As those that shipping give, that are
Now flickers in the Bay, now lost in night.

He stretched out like a cat, and rolled
The bitterish taste of beer upon his tongue,
   And listened to a joke being told:
The present was the things he stayed among.

   If it was only loss he wore,
He wore it to assert, with fierce devotion,
   Complicity and nothing more.
He recollected his initiation,

   And one especially of the rites.
For on his shoulders they had put tattoos:
   The group's name on the left, The Knights,
And on the right the slogan Born To Lose.

Walking on Water

Janette Turner Hospital

I
N places where the wind had flayed the snow into fantastic waves, they would come upon barrens of black ice, smooth as agate. Earth's vital fluids, seen through a glass darkly. And sometimes fish with startled gills, who had surfaced too close to the edge of winter, would stare at them out of the clear ebony.

Poor things, Gillian would think, cupping her leather mitts and calling to the others. "Another one! Here's another frozen fish!"

Only the suggestion of her shouting would reach them, an intimation of being hailed, her voice flaking and blowing in a thousand directions. Her husband and children would pause and turn, stamping feet laced into heavy mukluks, pounding out on the frozen lake a weird basso counterpoint to the coloratura shrieks of wind. They were anxious to keep moving, to get it over with, but she refused to let them treat the crossing in this grimly dutiful way. She insisted it be memorable, an *occasion*: enjoy yourselves! Savor these extraordinary and freakish sights!

On the line of her will she reeled them in, and reluctantly they turned back, sighing into their scarves but obedient, crouching beside her on the ice and feigning an interest in snap-frozen smelts.

"See!" She had to shout above the wind. "It's mouth is open. It was so sudden."

"His death of cold!" Allison's words came to them in a blather of snow so that the sound stung their cheeks. "You could say"—she gasped as the air scoured her lungs—"he caught his death of cold."

Gillian laughed and hugged her younger child for the act of cooperation, for the conscientious effort to wring pleasure from February. She glanced at her son, but James merely frowned and cradled his mittened hands under his armpits. Gillian averted her eyes quickly in case he saw the begging in them.

Of course it was no laughing matter, this instant glaciation. It happened, they knew only too well, to people too. There were local faces cratered into braille records of unplanned exposures (the car stalled in a blizzard; the cross-country skier stranded with a broken ski); a nose, an ear, even lips lost to frostbite. And the boy in a snowbank just a few weeks ago, found smiling in a sleep from which he would never waken.

It was not a climate that made allowances for human error.

James was staring back at the fish with spooked and sombre eyes. Suddenly, scooping up handfuls of snow from a baroquely curlicued drift, he brushed a shroud over the tiny death suspended like an air bubble between winter and spring. His movements were quick and unconscious, small acts of instinctive decency.

His father intimated, though not by squandering breath and body heat on words, that they should keep moving.

Cats, Gillian knew, forgot their progenitors entirely and mated with them. Birds left the nest to find private slipstreams. Every parent knew that high school was a country of aliens, but James was not quite 15 and how could it be happening already? And if he had to leave, why the rush? Why in the dead of winter, when planes skewed themselves on icy runways and fell out of the sky with a full cargo of deaths, splattering across the front pages of newspapers? Why now? California would keep until summer. Or at least until spring.

All this had been said, of course.

"I'll be *back* by spring," James would point out. "And you can phone me any day of the week."

What objection could possibly be made to his spending half

a term in a California high school, living with her own brother and his family?

She could not say: There is something about the suddenness of this arrangement that makes me uneasy.

She could not say: The driving is bad; you might be killed between here and Toronto. There will be ice on the wings of your plane; you might not survive takeoff. Or landing: there is nearly always fog over Los Angeles, and the flight patterns are too heavy, and what confidence can one place in substitute air-traffic controllers?

She could not say: I am overwhelmed by the fragility of human life, my children's in particular. I fear this first separation as I would fear amputation. What if you never come back? What if you come back a stranger?

"Why do you want to leave home?"

"*Leave home?*" He would echo the words with a lift of the eyebrows. As if he were an exasperated language teacher who found her misuse of idiom shoddily unacceptable. "Six weeks is leaving home?"

Well then. At least they would keep this family rite before he went. She had insisted, although they all thought it slightly foolish of her. One of her eccentricities, the annual lake-hike.

"My wife has a thing about ritual," Bill would tease at parties. "She thinks it will work like a witch doctor's charm. The family that performs secret ceremonies together stays together."

"Very funny," she would say, flushing.

But were not these the events that glued their years together? When, inevitably, they moved on again, when the time came for them to ask, "How many years did we live in that place, that cold place on the lake?" then an answer would come: "For three winter crossings." Or four. Or whatever it turned out to be. Remember how the wind . . . ? they would ask. And the way the fish . . . ? Nostalgia would warm them like an old blanket smelling of past happiness.

It was not even seriously cold, given the month and place: only 5 below, no more than 20 below with the windchill factor. Choosing the right day was an art: far enough into winter for the ice to be safely thick, yet not so bitter a day that exposure was deadly. She thought of the crossing as interestingly arduous.

And so would the others by tomorrow. *Walked across Lake Ontario*, they would say casually at office coffee-break and in the school cafeteria. *As far as Wolfe Island anyway*—sheepishly, self-deprecatingly, as if admitting to reading comic books or watching *Lassie* reruns. *Walked to the U.S.A.* They would bask in the murmur of tribute, yet next winter would demand again: "Do we *really* need . . . ?"

"Please," she would cajole.

And annually they would humor her, enjoying mainly the feat accomplished.

She, drunk perhaps on the profligacy of oxygen that barreled along the Great Lakes from prairies to ocean, had always felt a taut hum of exultation above the pained protest of her body.

Below us, she would think, where the sluggish lower currents buffet the lake silt, there is French gold stamped with the image of Bourbon kings and lost since the days of Cartier and Frontenac. Below us are greedy fathoms that have swallowed ships and men and centuries. Here and there, stirring like sleepers far below our padded boots, lie American and British gunboats that foundered in 1812, and Iroquois canoes slicked with algae, and snowmobiles that skated on the margins of last year's thaw.

The thrill of the anomalous had become an annual addiction.

Walking on water.

Walking on history.

And walking south—toward the sun and the countries of their past.

She turned to look at the town they had left. Domed and spired and provincial, a huddle of pretentious limestone, it leaned back from the lakeshore as prissily as a society matron testing the waters with a well-manicured toe. Smugness rose from its streets in a fug of steam.

It seemed very distant now. It had nothing to do with them.

This defines us, she thought. This no-man's-land, this mere crust of hardened water temporary as a few weeks of winter, this dissolving border between nations—in both of which we have lived, and on three other continents besides. This is where, if anywhere, we belong—trekking over the bones of other wanderers, French explorers and Indian scouts, the flotsam of history. We are of that new tribe, the 20th-century nomads, who live where rarefied specializations and high technologies demand, transitory as the glaze on the lake. We have passports, but where is home?

The symbols of our culture are airports and transit lounges. Our independence is so stunning that we dream of trees doing headstands on water, their roots trailing into the sky like seaweed. And therefore this walk across the lake is our Christmas and our Hanukkah and our Thanksgiving and our Fourth of July.

She would have liked to join hands with her husband and children, to form a magic circle and offer incantations:

Here we four are, solitary between border posts, held by a wafer of ice between the empty sky and the unstable bowels of earth. We have each other and the memories we have told and retold, meting them out to ourselves like a lifeline.

If she could have said that, they would all be safe. Then James would change his mind, postponing experiments and adulthood.

James had invented a private term for the way things were: penalty-shot time. There were only seconds of play left, packed stands, a tied score, and he in the hot spot with the ball in his hands. Everything depended on his getting a basket.

Each morning when he woke he thought: this could be it, and the end of the game. And he would pull the sheet up over his eyes to block out Stuart's face smiling blue and mournful from its snowdrift.

It's so unfair, so crazy, he would rage silently to his ceiling. Why me? I scarcely knew the guy. Why should I have to be one of the last to see him alive? And by such a fluke, by such bizarre chance.

James had discovered randomness and found it totally, obscenely unacceptable.

Benched for five minutes, he had made for the water fountain in the lobby. Just for a sip, to moisten his salty mouth, to recharge himself for the last quarter of a hard night's game against their archrivals.

And that was where he and Stuart—a kid he knew only from his science class—had had their last conversation.

"You can't come in," two senior girls were saying. "School rule, and you know it perfectly well. You're drunk."

"Am not!" Stuart protested angrily. "Am shertainly not! Hey James! Tell th' ladies here I'm poziv-itely not ... ?" He leaned over the desk in front of the girls and laid his head gently on the small metal box full of dollar bills and closed his eyes.

"We'll get the bouncers," one girl said.

"He'll be okay." James knew him only as the quiet kid four desks away in science, an A student, diligent and shy. Not the athletic type at all. "You won't need a bouncer. He's not the type. I know him."

"Oh man," Stuart groaned, sliding onto the floor. "Not my day, James. Definitely not my day. C'mon ladies, lemme into the warm. 'Sbeen a rotten day."

He was groping for something by which to pull himself up and clasped the leg of one of the girls. She gave a shriek of shock and anger and signaled the bouncer, who hailed one of the taxis outside the gym. When the doors opened, the icy air rushed in like a brace of linebackers. Stuart glanced back at them all and laughed and made a defiant sign with his finger. Disturbed, James hesitated, entertained fleetingly the thought of pulling team player's rank, of insisting Stuart be allowed in. Then he went back inside to the game and instantly forgot about the boy in the lobby. Which was like forgetting the ball in your hands during a penalty shot in the last second of play.

Afterward he thought: If I had insisted they let him in ... If I had been there when he told the driver: "This will be okay, I'll walk from here. Cold air will sober me up. Wouldn't want my mom to see me like this." If I had walked with him by the lake ... If I had been there to shake him when he lay down drowsy in the snow. . . .

Hypothermia. It was a word that had fastened itself onto his consciousness like excess baggage. He dragged it through waking and sleeping.

And at night in the dark, after all the other questions, shameful thoughts would surface. If I had gone to the water fountain just five minutes earlier. Or five minutes later. If I had been in a different science section this year. Then it would have nothing to do with me at all. Nothing at all.

And then he would begin to get angry. (But at whom?) Why me? he would demand. Why should I feel so guilty? Where were Stuart's friends, why didn't *they* ... ?

How could he, James, possibly be held responsible?

How could he *not* be responsible?

He knew now that death was not just something that happened to other people in newspapers. It waited like a spider on the wall of his 14 years, velvetly watching, malevolent. Every day, every waking moment bristled with dangers, anything was possible. In another second, perhaps, the lake ice would yawn open beneath their feet and they would sway rigid in their deaths till spring, gaping like the fish. On any day his parents might say: we are getting divorced; we are moving to China; you will have to change schools; you will have to change languages—your father has been transferred to Germany. Tomorrow a policeman might knock on his door: an accident, your parents and sister, you are all alone.

What would he do if he were suddenly all alone? He had lived in five countries. Which was home? Who would take him in? He hardly knew the grandparents who lived beyond an ocean, or the uncle and aunt and cousins in California.

In sleep he stumbled over Stuart, lost his hold on the certainties of each day, careened through unknown places, down, down. Free-falling through Himalayan abysses, past the tundra layers, past the steaming tropical strata of other years of his life, past empty spaces into a dark nothingness. But then. He had pulled a cord at his chest, and a silken parachute had bellied into the wind and snagged itself on a way station, an explorer's cabin.

Yes, he thought waking. I need safety devices, I need way stations. And he had written to his uncle and aunt in California, ports in a storm. He would establish a chain of defences, he would be prepared.

He applied himself with a sort of pleasurable savagery to the walk across the lake. If the ice held them up this time, if the wind did not shroud their still bodies with snow on this crossing, it would be like an immunization. A small and salvific draft of risk that might ward off greater dangers.

In the restaurant on the island, they drank hot chocolate and decided to go back by ferry from the dock two kilometres farther down. Enough was enough. A point had been made, their eyes were bloodshot, their hands and feet white with pain.

Watching the under-ice cables and pressurized air smash open a channel for the ferry, Gillian said with awe: "When you see how easily it breaks. . . ."

"You *know* that the fishermen can make holes with only a handsaw," James accused. "We could have dropped through like winter bait."

Gillian was stung. "It's not nearly as dangerous as flying at this time of year. *Why* can't you wait until. . . ."

"It's not safe to wait."

"Not *safe* to wait?"

"No one can ever tell when. Don't you see? I have to get used to living without you. We don't even know our own relatives. What if you and dad were killed? What if you split up . . . ?"

"James, what on earth are you talking about? If we split up?! We have no intention. . . ."

"Yeah. Everyone's parents said that before the divorce."

She was shocked, dumbfounded.

"Is *this* what you . . . ? Are you actually afraid that we . . . ?"

But now he was red-faced.

"No, no. Sorry, Mom, I'm raving. It's just . . . I have to feel safer. I'm sorry, I'm just . . . lately I'm not . . . It's Stuart's death."

"Stuart?"

"Stuart Anderson."

She squeezed her eyes shut in concentration, and the name surfaced from a newspaper headline.

"That boy who died from exposure! You never said anything. I didn't realize you knew him."

"Only slightly. He was in my science class. I guess it shook me up badly, that's all. I just want to . . . hedge my bets. I want to know my relatives better. I have to feel safer."

"But James. . . ." She was going to protest that his plane might fall out of the sky. That California was so very far away, that the Los Angeles freeways coiled lethal as snakes through her imagination, that he would be beyond her protective reach. Instead she laid her cheek momentarily against his because it came to her that all four of them, tentative as waifs, must walk their own stretches of water.

The Only Lesson I Still Remember

Barry Dickie

E VERYTHING I learned at university I owe to a janitor. Indeed, this Man of the Broom taught me the only
lesson I still remember.

I met him during a mathematics lecture at the University of
Toronto. He was a skinny man with a black mustache and a
gray uniform. He entered our class, checked his watch and
started pushing his broom.

We hardly noticed. Our eyes were glued to the blackboard
where the professor was proving a theorem called Russell's
Paradox. This is no ordinary theorem; it is more like a poem
—a passionate burst of logic which proves that there is no
universe. You can imagine the suspense on that fateful morning in 1970.

After the janitor had finished sweeping, he took a brush
from the blackboard ledge and was beginning to erase the theorem. Using broad, lazy strokes he was demolishing Bertrand
Russell's masterpiece faster than the professor could write it
down. It was a race between brush and chalk, Time and Truth.
The professor once stopped to glare at the janitor, but he
didn't say anything. Maybe he was afraid of Big Labor, or
maybe he had personal reasons. Soon the janitor caught up to
the professor and settled into a yet slower pace, killing the
logic one line at a time. After writing the last line and watch-

ing it vanish, the professor walked to the window and looked out. The janitor checked his watch again and left the room.

The incident changed my life. I sensed that the janitor knew something we didn't. I wondered if all people with simple jobs knew something I didn't know. For 10 years now, I have been trying to find out.

It hasn't been easy. The first problem was finding a simple, menial job. I went to CN and asked to be hired on as a Lantern-Swinger: someone who walks beside the train swinging a lantern and smoking a pipe. CN didn't want me. They gave me an aptitude test and told me I wasn't mentally fit to be a Lantern-Swinger. It hurt. As consolation, they offered to train me as a computer programmer, but the damage had already been done.

So I lowered my sights and got a clerical job with the federal Government. I was a CR-2 working in the Old Age Security Department. It was fun: all I had to do was carry papers back and forth between the filing cabinets and the desks where the CR-3 sat. The fun lasted until they promoted me to a CR-3. As a CR-3, I had to do complex arithmetic; I also had to tell pensioners their Guaranteed Income Supplement had been cut off. I lacked the social finesse for this, so I quit and shovelled snow for the Toronto Transit Commission.

This was my big break. The moment I touched the shovel something clicked inside me. A new vitality surged through my body. I felt alive. It is hard to describe the joy of pushing slush off a bus stop. For once, I knew who I was: I was a laborer.

Since then I have had dozens and dozens of laboring jobs. I have laid sod, picked worms, mixed cement, crushed rock, dug holes, sawed trees, loaded trucks and slung garbage *ad euphoria*. Each job has been special in its own way. Each job has brought me a step closer to the wisdom of that skinny janitor.

Of course, the Path has crossed some rough terrain. I dodged rats while loading sacks of flour into a Russian ship moored in Halifax Harbour. I watched a man lose his arm under a bending machine in a steel factory. I forfeited my dream of being a concert pianist, for my hands are numb with callouses. I have known boredom and I have known pain.

There has been beauty, too. I watched rainbows dance as I

swept the morning dew from a golf-green with a bamboo pole. I heard the earth sigh as I scratched her back with a pickax. I heard hailstones playing drums on my hardhat.

There has been heroism. I remember one September afternoon in 1972 when I was picking tomatoes on a farm near Chatham, Ont. The farmer ran from his house, shouting across the field to us: "We won! We won!" I learned later, after many cruel hours in the field, why the farmer was so excited: it was because Paul Henderson had scored the winning goal for Team Canada. Yes, it was a glorious day: it was the day I picked 120 hampers of back-breaking, homegrown Canadian tomatoes. It was a day of tears, a day of joy.

Most laborers have a specialty. I do not. I am a general, all-round, unskilled laborer. You might call me freelance. Leaving a job is half the fun. The very notion of a permanent job disturbs me: it is a total contradiction of what the janitor was trying to teach me about Time and the passing of all things.

Now I am working for Metro Parks, laying sod and putting up snow fences. It's getting chilly. I am looking forward to winter layoff. There's something romantic about a Separation Certificate: it is like a ticket into the Unknown.

I still think about the janitor. Last week I was at the university, looking everywhere for the janitor. I couldn't find him. I asked a few students if they had seen him but, no, students don't take much notice of janitors. Oh, well, maybe he retired.

Hmmm . . . maybe the university is looking for a good man to fill his shoes.

Overlaid

Robertson Davies

Characters

POP
ETHEL
GEORGE BAILEY

The scene is a farmhouse kitchen in rural Canada. It is a cluttered and inconvenient room containing a wood range, a dresser, a kitchen table, a radio and several chairs. There is a door leading to the farmyard and another to the house. A light cord, fitted with a double socket, hangs nakedly from the ceiling; a basket of unironed clothes sits under the table; an ironing board and an electric iron are in the corner and on the top of the range respectively.

As the curtain rises the radio rings with the applause of a great audience. POP, *a farmer of seventy, sitting in a kitchen armchair and wearing an ancient and battered top hat, is applauding also; on his hands he wears white cotton workman's gloves.*

RADIO VOICE:	Once again our principals are led on by Mr. Panizzi ... and they bow. You can hear the rapturous applause of this Saturday matinee audience. [*Sound of applause rises.*]
POP:	Attaboy! Yippee!
RADIO VOICE:	Our lovely Lucia, in her handsome green and gold first-act costume, steps forward to acknowledge a special tribute.... [*Tremendous applause.*]
POP:	Hot dog!
RADIO VOICE:	And now, ladies and gentlemen, we have arrived at the first intermission in this Saturday afternoon

performance of *Lucia di Lammermoor*, brought to you from the stage of the Metropolitan Opera House in New York City, and in just a few moments I shall ask the president of our Opera Radio Guild, Mrs. August Belmont, to address you.

POP: Yay, Miz' Belmont!

[ETHEL, POP'S *daughter, enters; she is a hard-faced woman of forty; she takes the basket of clothes from under the table.*]

ETHEL: Poppa, turn that thing down; I can't hear myself think.

RADIO VOICE: [*female*] Friends of the Opera Guild everywhere . . .

POP: Quiet, gal; Miz' Belmont's goin' to speak.

ETHEL: I don't care who it is. You always turn it up loudest when they're clapping. My head's splitting.

POP: Leave'er be.

ETHEL: Oh, don't be so contrary! [*She turns the radio down to a murmur.*] I've got one of my sick headaches; that racket just goes through and through me like a knife. I've got ironing to do out here. [*She sets up her board from the table to a chair back, and then plugs in her iron, climbing on a chair to reach the central light socket.*]

POP: Oh no you don't. Bump, bump, bump all through my op'ry. You just wait. Go lie down again. Rest your head.

ETHEL: It's got to be done. Can't wait. Plenty to do without waiting till half-past five for that row to be over.

POP: Row, eh? Say, whose house is this anyways? Mine or your'n?

ETHEL: Yours, of course, but I do the work and keep things decent and Jim works the farm. You can't expect to have everything your own way; you know that.

POP: I'll have this my own way. Now you turn up that radio so's I can hear Miz' Belmont.

ETHEL: Oh, don't be so childish! What do you want to hear some society woman in New York for?

POP: What for? Because she's my kind, that's what for! I'm a member of the Op'ry Radio Guild; paid my three bucks and got a ticket says so. This here Miz' Belmont, she's boss of the Guild. Guess I can hear her if I want!

ETHEL: Your kind! Ptuh! [*She tests her iron by spitting on it.*]

POP: Yes, my kind and no "ptuh" about it neither. Just because you were a schoolmarm before you married a dumb farmer you think you're everybody, don't you? Well, you never had no ear for music, nor no artistic soul. You ain't never been one of the artistic crowd.

ETHEL: And you are, I suppose? [*She is now ironing as though she were punishing the clothes, sprinkling and thumping ill-naturedly.*]

POP: Durn right I am! Look at me! I'm at the op'ry, the only fella in this township that is, I betcha. And where's Jim? Layin' out in the barn asleep, though you think he's workin'. And where are you? Layin' on the bed, hatin' the world and feelin' sick, and he thinks you're workin'. You're emotionally understimulated, the both of you—

ETHEL: What did you say?

POP: You heard me good enough.

ETHEL: Listen, Poppa. I've stood a good deal from you, but I won't have that kind of talk.

POP: What's wrong with it?

ETHEL: You know, well enough. Emotion, and that. Suppose little Jimmy was to hear?

POP: Well, what if he does?

ETHEL: A child like that? Putting ideas in his head!

POP: Do him good. Any ideas he gets in this house he'll have to get from me. You and Jim ain't got none. [*He turns up the radio.*]

RADIO VOICE: [*female*] If our lives lack beauty, we are poor indeed . . .

ETHEL: Emotionally understimulated! You were always loose.

POP: Hey?

ETHEL: I know what Mother went through. [*Turns radio down.*]

POP: Oh, you do, do you? Well, you don't. Your Ma was kinda like you—just as dumb but not as mean.

ETHEL: Don't speak so of Mother!

POP: I knew your Ma better than you did. She worked like a nigger on this farm: we both did. When she wasn't

	workin' she was up to some religious didoes at the church. Then come forty-five or fifty she broke down and had to have a spell in the bughouse. Never properly got over it. More and more religion: more and more hell-raisin' at home. Folks say I drove her crazy. It's a lie. Emotional undernourishment is what done it, and it'll do the same for you. You an' your sick headaches!
ETHEL:	Poppa, that's the meanest thing you ever said! You're a wicked old man!
POP:	Yeh, but I'm happy, an' that's more than most of 'em can say 'round here. I'm the bohemian set of Smith township, all in one man. Now you let Miz' Belmont speak. [*He turns up the radio:* JIMMY'S *voice, the changing voice of a boy of fourteen, is heard outside.*]
JIMMY:	Hey, Maw! Hey, Maw!
RADIO VOICE:	No life today need be starved for the fulfilment which the noblest art can give. It is to be had for the taking: great music, great drama ...
ETHEL:	[*at the door, fondly*] What is it, Lover?
JIMMY:	Car comin' in from the road.
ETHEL:	Do you know whose?
JIMMY:	Naw: from town by the looks of it.
ETHEL:	Well—don't get cold, will you, Lover? [*She closes the door and turns down radio.*]
POP:	Lover! Huh!
ETHEL:	Well, what about it? He's my own son, isn't he?
POP:	Yeh. Bet you never called Jim "Lover."
ETHEL:	Of course not. To a grown person it ain't—isn't decent.
POP:	You said ain't!
ETHEL:	Living with you it's a wonder any of my Normal School sticks to me at all.
POP:	Never could figure why they call them things Normal. Now who's comin' here to bust in on my Saturday afternoon; the one time o' the week when I get a little food for my immortal soul.
ETHEL:	[*from window*] It's that insurance agent from town.
POP:	Aw, him! What's he want? [*A loud knock at the door and* GEORGE BAILEY *enters; he is a fat man with a frequent, phlegmy laugh.*]

G.B.: Well, well, lots o' snow you got out here, eh? Afternoon, Miz' Cochran. Hi, Grandpop! Holy Gol, what are you doin' in that get-up, for Pete sake?

POP: Awright now, G.B.; awright; say your say and don't be all day over it. I'm busy.

ETHEL: Poppa, what a way to talk to a man who's just come in out of the cold. Will you have a cup of tea, Mr. Bailey?

G.B.: Sure, thanks, if you got it handy.

ETHEL: Right on the stove; always keep some going.

G.B.: Now then, Grandpop, what's the big idea? Gettin' ready for an Orange Walk, or something?

POP: If you got to know, I'm listenin' to the op'ry on the radio. I listen every Saturday afternoon. I'm a paid-up member of the Op'ry Radio Guild, same as Miz' August Belmont. This hat is what's called an op'ry hat, but I guess you wouldn't understand about that.

G.B.: [*uproarious*] Holy smoke! And what's the idea of the furnaceman's gloves?

POP: In New York white gloves for the op'ry are *dee rigger*. That's French for you can't get in without 'em.

G.B.: [*choking*] Well by gollies, now I seen everything.

POP: No you ain't: you ain't seen nothin', nor been anywheres. That's what's wrong with you and a lot more like you. Now what do you want?

G.B.: Keep your shirt on, Grandpop. I'm here on business: 32096-B Pay Life is finished, washed up, and complete.

POP: Hey?

G.B.: Yep. Now, what d'you want to do with the money?

POP: What money?

G.B.: Your money. Your insurance policy is paid up. You were seventy a couple of days ago, weren't you?

POP: Yeh.

G.B.: Well, then—You got twelve hundred dollars comin' to you.

POP: Is that right?

G.B.: You bet it's right. Didn't you know?

POP: I'd kinda forgotten.

G.B.: Gol, you farmers! I wonder you're not all on relief, the kind of business men you are.

POP: Aw shut up. I been payin' so long I guess I forgot I

was payin' for anything except to save you from honest work. Twelve hundred bucks, eh?

G.B.: A cool twelve hundred.

POP: When do I get it?

G.B.: Well, now, just a minute, now. You don't have to take the money.

POP: Oh, I don't, eh?

G.B.: No. There's a couple of options. If you want, we'll give you a hundred dollars a year in twelve equal monthly instalments, for twelve years, and if you die before it's all gone (which you will, o'course) the balance will go to your heirs, minus certain deductions for accounting and adjustment. Or if you'd rather we'll give you two hundred cash and a paid-up policy for a thousand, which would give you a smart burial and leave five or six hundred for Miz' Cochran and Jim.

ETHEL: Here's your tea.

G.B.: Yeah, thanks. [*Gulps some of it.*] What do you think he ought to do?

ETHEL: Well—it's hard to say. With twelve hundred we could make a lot of improvements 'round the farm. I know Jim wants a tractor the worst way. But then, the thousand in the hand after Poppa's called home would certainly be welcome. Of course, we hope that won't be for many years yet.

G.B.: Nope. The old codger looks good for a while yet. Still, you know, Grandpop, at your time of life anything can happen.

POP: Yeh? Well, with all that fat on you, and that laugh you got, you might have a stroke any minute. Ever look at it that way?

G.B.: By gollies, you're a card. Ain't he a card, eh? Seventy and smart as a steel trap. A regular card.

POP: You talk like nobody ever lived to seventy before.

G.B.: The average life expectancy for men on farms is sixty-point-two years; you're living on borrowed time, Grandpop.

POP: Borrowed from who?

G.B.: What a card! Borrowed from who, he says. It's just a way of speaking; technical.

POP: Borrowed from you, I hope.

G.B.:   Aw now, don't get sore. What do you want to do?
        Personally I'd advise the two-hundred-down-and-a-
        thousand-at-death plan. Nice, clean-cut proposition,
        and fix up for Jim and Miz' Cochran when you're
        gone.

POP: I ain't gone yet. I'll take the twelve hundred in cash.
        Got it on you?

G.B.:   Eh? No. I can write you a cheque. But are you sure
        you want it that way?

POP: Sure I'm sure.

ETHEL: What are you up to, Poppa?

POP: None of your business.

ETHEL: He'll let you know on Monday, Mr. Bailey.

POP: I just told him. You keep out o' this.

ETHEL: Poppa and Jim and I'll talk it over tonight. We'll
        phone you on Monday.

POP: You and Jim nothin'. I made up my mind.

ETHEL: You haven't considered.

POP: Say, whose money is this? Ain't it my insurance?

ETHEL: Didn't you take it out to provide for your family?

POP: Damned if I remember what I took it out for after
        all these years. Likely I took it out because some
        insurance agent bamboozled me into it. Never knew
        it would bring me in anything.

ETHEL: Now, Poppa, you don't want to do anything foolish
        after all those years of paying the premium. You
        took out the policy to protect your family and
        properly speaking it's family money, and the family
        will decide what to do with it.

POP: What makes you so sure I'd do somethin' foolish?

ETHEL: Well, what would you do?

POP: I'd go to New York and spend it—that's what.

ETHEL: You'd what?

G.B.:   Go on a tear, eh, Grandpop? By gollies you're a card!

POP: No, I ain't a card. That's what I'm goin' to do. You
        can write the cheque right now, and I'll catch the
        9:15 into town. I got enough money to get me quite
        a piece of the ways without cashin' it.

G.B.:   Go on! You ain't serious?

POP: Durn right I'm serious.

G.B.:   You can't do that.

POP: Why not?

G.B.: Because you can't. You don't want to go to New York.

POP: Who says I don't?

G.B.: You don't know nobody there. Where'd you sleep an' eat?

POP: Hotel.

G.B.: Go on!

ETHEL: He's just keeping this up to torment me, Mr. Bailey.

POP: You keep out o' this.

G.B.: Lookit, Grandpop—are you serious?

POP: Say, how often do I have to tell you I'm serious?

G.B.: Aw, but lookit—two hundred'll buy you a nice trip if you got to go somewheres.

POP: Two hundred won't last a week where I'm goin! Gimme the twelve hundred an' make it quick!

G.B.: Say lookit—do you know how much twelve hundred dollars is?

POP: 'Tain't much, but it'll have to do.

G.B.: Ain't much! Say lookit, do you know what's wrong with you? You're crazy, that's what! What'd you do in New York with twelve hundred dollars?

POP: [*very calmly and with a full sense of the effect of what he says on* ETHEL *and* BAILEY] I'll tell you what I'd do, since you're so nosey: I'd get some stylish clothes, and I'd go into one o' these restrunts, and I'd order vittles you never heard of—better 'n the burnt truck Ethel calls food—and I'd get a bottle o' wine—cost a dollar, maybe two—and drink it all, and then I'd mosey along to the Metropolitan Opera House and I'd buy me a seat right down beside the trap-drummer, and there I'd sit an' listen, and holler and hoot and raise hell whenever I liked the music, an' throw bookies to the gals, an' wink at the chorus, and when it was over I'd go to one o' these here night-clubs an' eat some more, an' drink whisky, and watch the gals that take off their clothes—every last dud, kinda slow an' devilish till they're bare-naked— an' maybe I'd give one of 'em fifty bucks for her brazeer—

ETHEL: [*scandalized*] Poppa!

G.B.: Jeepers!

ETHEL: You carnal man!

POP: An' then I'd step along Park Avenoo, an' I'd go right up to the door, an' I'd say, "Is this were Miz' August Belmont lives?" an' the coon would say, "Yessiree!" an' I'd say, "Tell her one o' the Op'ry Guild gang from up in Canada is here, an' how'd she like to talk over things—"

G.B.: Say listen, Grandpop: you're nuts.

ETHEL: He must be. Mother was like that at the last, you know.

POP: She was not: your Ma used to think the Baptist preacher was chasin' her to cut the buttons off her boots, but that was as far as she got. She never had the gumption to pump up a real good dream. Emotional undernourishment: that was what ailed your Ma.

ETHEL: There you go again! He's been talking that indecent stuff all afternoon.

POP: 'Tain't indecent. It's the truth. No food for your immortal souls—that's what ails everybody 'round here—little, shriveled-up, peanut-size souls. [*He turns up the radio with a jerk.*]

RADIO VOICE: [*blaring*] . . . render life gracious with the boon of art. . . .

ETHEL: [*turning radio down*] Is that what your soul feeds on? Restrunts with shameless women in 'em?

POP: Yeah, an' music an' booze an' good food an' high-toned conversation—all the things a man can't get here because everybody's too damn dumb to know they're alive. Why do you think so many people go to the bughouse around here, anyways? Because they've starved an' tormented their souls, that's why! Because they're against God an' don't know it, that's why!

ETHEL: That's blasphemous!

POP: It ain't blasphemous! They try to make God in their own little image an' they can't do it same as you can't catch Niagara Falls in a teacup. God likes music an' naked women an' I'm happy to follow his example.

ETHEL: [*shrieks in outrage*] Eeeeeek!

G.B.: [*on firm moral ground at last*] That'll do now! That'll just do o' that! I ain't goin' to listen to no such smut: I got a kiddy at home not three yet! Do you think I'm goin' to give you twelve hundred dollars for that kind o' thing? It wouldn't be business ethics! Say, you better look out I don't report this to the Ministerial Alliance! They'd tell you where you got off, darn soon!

POP: You mean you won't give me the money?

G.B.: Naw!

POP: You want me to have to write to head office an' ask why?

G.B.: I'll tell 'em. Unsound mind, that's why.

POP: What's your proof?

G.B.: You just say what you said about God to any doctor, that's all.

POP: Yeah, but if I don't?

G.B.: Well—

POP: You'd look kinda silly, wouldn't you?

G.B.: Now lookit—

POP: Would it cost you the agency, do you think?

G.B.: Aw, now lookit here—

POP: A libel suit'd come pretty dear to your company, anyways.

G.B.: Libel?

POP: Libellous to say a man's crazy.

G.B.: Miz' Cochran would back me up.

POP: Serious thing, tryin' to put a man in the bughouse just when he gets some money. Look bad in court.

G.B.: [*deflated*] Aw, have it your own way. I'll write you a cheque. [*He sits at the table and does so.*]

POP: Make it nice an' plain, now. [*He turns up the radio.*]

RADIO VOICE: [*male, again*] You have been listening to Mrs. August Belmont, president of the Metropolitan Opera Guild, in one of the series of intermission talks which is a regular feature of this Saturday afternoon broadcast. And now to give you a brief outline of Act II of Gaetano Donizetti's romantic masterwork, *Lucia di Lammermoor*: the curtain rises to disclose the magnificent hall of Sir Henry Ashton's castle. Norman (played this afternoon by the American baritone Elmer Backhouse) tells Sir Henry (Mr. Dudelsack) that he need have no fear that Lucy will offer opposition to the proposed marriage with Lord Arthur Bucklaw (played this

afternoon by Listino di Prezzi) as her letters to
Edgar (Mr. Posaun in today's performance) have
been intercepted and forgeries substituted for them
which will leave no doubt of his faithlessness. At
this point Lucia (Miss Fognatura) enters (in a gown
of greenish-blue taffeta relieved by cerise gussets
and a fichu) to a delicately orchestrated passage for
wind and strings. Then, supported entirely by wind,
Lucy tells her brother that her hand is promised to
another, whereupon he produces the forged letters.
"The papers," she cries: "La lettera, mio Dio!"
whereupon follows a lively upward rush of brass. . . .

G.B.: [*during the foregoing*] Here. Well, g'day, Miz'
Cochran. [*He listens to the radio ecstasies.*] Cheest!
[*He goes out.*]

ETHEL: [*turning the radio down*] Well?

POP: Yeah?

ETHEL: When you've squandered the money—what then?

POP: I'll be back. This is my farm, remember. I'll have
some stories to tell you, Ethel. Maybe that Home an'
School Club o' yours'll ask me to address 'em on my
experiences. I'll show 'em the programs from the
op'ry—maybe even let 'em see my fifty-buck
brazeer. [*A pause.*]

ETHEL: [*sitting down*] Listen, Poppa; you haven't thought
about this.

POP: Are we goin' to go through all that again?

ETHEL: Yes. You know what people will say when you come
back. They'll say a fool and his money are soon
parted. They'll say there's no fool like an old fool.

POP: What do I care what they say?

ETHEL: This dream of yours is crazy, like Mr. Bailey says. If
you go to New York you'll just be a lost old man,
and everybody will laugh at you and rob you.

POP: How do you know?

ETHEL: I know. You don't belong there. You belong right
here in this township, though you've been
ungrateful and abused it, just because it isn't full of
opera and restrunts and hussies. This township's
been good to you—given you a good living—

POP: You mean I've been able to work like an ox here and
keep the sheriff the other side o' the gate?

ETHEL: That's more than many people have had.

POP: Well 'tain't enough for me. What about my soul? What's this township ever give me for that, eh? There was just one purty thing in sight o' this farm —row of elms along the road; they cut down the elms to widen the road an' then never widened it.

ETHEL: You talk about your soul in a way that makes me blush. Soul to you just means the pleasures of the flesh. We got a fine church, with almost half the debt paid off on it—

POP: Yeah, an' your Ma pretty near bled me white over that debt. Last fifty bucks I gave 'em was for a bell, and what'd they do? Bought a new stove with it.

ETHEL: They needed a stove.

POP: Yeah, an' they needed a bell. But that's always the way around here; necessities first, every time.

ETHEL: And what's wrong with that?

POP: Because there's always a gol-danged necessity to get in the way whenever you want somethin' purty. There's always somebody starvin', or a sewer needs diggin', or some damn necessary nuisance to hog all your time an' energy an' money if you go lookin' for it. Somebody's got to take the bull by the horns an' ignore the necessities if we're ever goin' to have any o' the things that make life worth livin'.

ETHEL: What makes life worth living? You seem to think nothing is worth having but a high old time. Don't you ever think of duty?

POP: I've had a bellyful o' duty. I've got somethin' in me that wants more than duty an' work.

ETHEL: Yes, and you've told me what it is. Rich food and alcohol and lewd women. A fine thing, at your age!

POP: Aw—that's just a way of speakin'. I want what's warm an'—kind of mysterious; somethin' to make you laugh an' talk big, an'—oh, you wouldn't know. You just sit there, lookin' like a meat-axe, an' won't even try to see what I'm drivin' at. Say listen, Ethel: what d'you get out o' life anyways?

ETHEL: Well, that's a fine question!

POP: Now don't get mean about it. You called my New York trip a dream; what's your dream?

ETHEL: I'm not the dreaming kind.

POP: Oh yes you are. You cranky ones, you're the ones

with dreams, all right. What do you think o' yourself, Ethel?

ETHEL: Well—[*Pause.*]—I think I'm a dutiful woman.

POP: A good woman?

ETHEL: [*overcoming her aversion to the luxury of direct self-praise*] Yes.

POP: And is that what you want out o' life?

ETHEL: It's my reward for a lot of work and self-denial.

POP: Go on.

ETHEL: You talk about dreams. Why do you think I live the way I do? Because it's right, first of all. And there are rewards on earth, too. When I walk into church or a meeting I know what people say: they say "There's Ethel Cochran; she stands on her own two feet, and never asks anything from anybody; she has a hard enough row to hoe, too, but you never hear a peep out of her."

POP: An' you like that, eh? Kind o' strong-woman stuff?

ETHEL: I'm glad I'm well-thought-of. "You never see *her* wash out after Monday noon," they say.

POP: And that's what you want in life? To be a woman that nobody can help or give anything to? Come on, Ethel; what else?

ETHEL: Well—you wouldn't understand.

POP: I'm trying. Go on.

ETHEL: I want to be remembered.

POP: Yeah? How?

ETHEL: You're not going to New York, are you?

POP: Who says I ain't?

ETHEL: Then let's not go on talking.

POP: Now Ethel, we ain't goin' to stop. I want to know what goes on inside you. Get yourself a cup o' tea, and give me one too an' let's have this out. [ETHEL *goes to get the tea.*] I think I see what you're up to. You don't want me to go to New York because you want the money for somethin' else. Is that it?

ETHEL: Here's your tea.

POP: Sit down.

ETHEL: Rather stand.

POP: Now what is it you want? Not a tractor, I bet. Come on, now. Is it something for Lover? You want to send him to college, maybe?

ETHEL: Naturally I want to see Jimmy get a good start in life. I—I've done a little saving toward it.

POP: Yeah, I know. Cheatin' on me an' Jim. I know where you got it hid, too. But that ain't it. I can tell.

ETHEL: Of course you'd made it sound ugly. I'm determined that my boy shall be a pharmacist, and I've had to find my own way of financing it.

POP: But that ain't your real ambition. Come on, Ethel.

ETHEL: No.

POP: Unless you tell me, I'm certain to go on my trip and spend all the money, and bang goes your dream. But if you tell me, you've got a chance. It's up to you. [*Pours his tea in his saucer and drinks noisily.*]

ETHEL: That'd look fine in a New York restrunt. What would the brazen women say?

POP: They'd put up with it long's I had a dollar. Don't stall, Ethel. We got nearest to your dream when you said you wanted to be remembered. Come on, now.

ETHEL: I won't tell you.

POP: Don't, then. [*Rises purposefully.*] Got a clean shirt for me? I'll be getting ready to go.

ETHEL: [*wavers for a moment, then breaks into painful, ugly tears*] Poppa!

POP: Yeah?

ETHEL: I want—a headstone.

POP: You want a what?

ETHEL: A headstone. A granite one.

POP: [*sits, flabbergasted*] Well good God Almighty!

ETHEL: [*weeping freely now*] Mother's grave just has a plain marker. But it's in a wonderful position. Soon all the land around it will be sold off and who can tell where we'll be buried? Higgledy-piggledy all over the place, most likely. We ought to have a proper family plot, with a chain fence round it, and a headstone with the family name on it. A headstone! Oh, a big family headstone! We could get that plot surrounding mother, right on the crest of the hill, and it'd be seen from every place in the cemetery. A headstone! Not a broken pillar, or a draped urn, or anything flashy and cheap, but a great big block of granite—the grey, not the red— smooth-finished on the faces, but rough on the sides and top, and the name on the base, cut deep!

	Dignified! Quiet! But the best quality—the finest in the cemetery. I want it! I want it! Then Mother and I, and Lover and Jim and you could all be there together at last—
POP:	Envied by every stiff in the township!
ETHEL:	I want it! I want it!
POP:	I can see that.
ETHEL:	Not even a text. No "Rest in the Lord" or "Till The Day Break" or anything. Just the name.
POP:	And that's what you want more than anything else?
ETHEL:	Yes, You had to know. Now you know. Jim doesn't care about—well, about nice things like that. And of course it isn't his name.
POP:	And when Bailey came in here with twelve hundred bucks for me you seen your gravestone as good as raised?
ETHEL:	Yes.
POP:	Pretty vain idea, ain't it?
ETHEL:	No it ain't—isn't. We've been something in this township. You would never run for council, though you could have been reeve if you'd tried. But Mother was a real figure here, especially the four or five years before—she had to go to That Place. And I've tried to follow where she went. She deserves something, and so do I. Missions, Temperance, the W.A.—we've done our share and more. And when we're gone we deserve something that'll last. That money would cover it all, and leave a little something to provide for Perpetual Care. It's not vain to want your due.
POP:	Don't follow your Ma's trail as far as the bughouse, Ethel. It'd cost a darn sight more than my insurance money to keep you there.
ETHEL:	It was silly of me to tell you. You've got no feeling for anything that really matters. I've just put a stick in your hand to beat me with.
POP:	Drink your tea an' blow your nose an' shut up. Ain't there a pen-an'-ink someplace here? [*He searches in the dresser drawers.*] Yeah, here she is. Y'know, I never could play no instrument nor draw worth a cent, but before my fingers got so stiff I was a real pretty writer. Your Ma once got me to write out a presentation address to a preacher that was leavin',

and when it was done it just looked like a page o' copperplate. There, Ethel; there's your cheque, endorsed and made over to you.

[ETHEL *takes the cheque, amazed.*]

ETHEL: Poppa!

POP: Buy yourself a nice tombstone. [*He sits.*] Y'know, when you was a little thing, you was as pretty as all-get-out, and till you got to be about fourteen you meant more to me than anything else on God's earth. But then you got religion, and began to favour your Ma, and I guess it was as if you'd died to me, and everything I liked. So far as I'm concerned, this here tombstone's mostly for the little one I lost.

ETHEL: Poppa, we've had our disagreements, but that's past. It'll be different now. [*She has put the cheque in her pocket, changed her mind, and tucked it in her bosom.*]

POP: Because I bought you a tombstone? Naw. You've changed, Ethel, and you've been what you are more than twice as long as you were my child.

ETHEL: But I don't understand. You do this wonderful, generous thing, and yet you seem so bitter. I know you haven't much feeling for me.

POP: Oh, yes I have; I pity you twelve hundred bucks' worth an' maybe more.

ETHEL: But why—?

POP: Aw, never mind. Ethel, you've got the power of goodness.

ETHEL: [*modest*] Oh, Poppa!

POP: Don't take it as a compliment. There's a special kind o' power that comes from the belief that you're right. Whether you really are right or not doesn't matter: it's the belief that counts. Your belief in your own goodness makes you awful strong, Ethel, and you've kind of overlaid me with it. I can't stand up to it.

ETHEL: I don't know what you're talking about. I don't know what to say about this, Poppa. There must be depths of good in you I never suspected. It just goes to show that we shouldn't judge.

JIMMY'S
VOICE: [*outside*] Hey, Maw!

POP: There's your future druggist hollerin'.

ETHEL: [*at the door, her voice trilling with happiness*] Yes, Lover?

JIMMY'S
VOICE: How long till supper, Maw?

ETHEL: Oh, you greedy thing! More'n an hour. D'you want me to fix you a piece?

JIMMY'S
VOICE: Naw, I'll wait.

ETHEL: I'm going to open a jar of maple surrp. Pancakes, Lover! [*She closes the door.*]

POP: Lover! Emotional understimulation!
[ETHEL *comes behind him and gives him a dry, shy kiss on the brow. Then she goes to the radio and turns it on, with an indulgent smile toward him. It hums a little as it warms.*]

POP: Naw. Turn it off. Don't want it now. I been overlaid and I got to get myself back in shape. Maybe I been emotionally overstimulated. But I ain't overlaid for good, Ethel, an' that stone'll rest lighter on me than it will on you.

During this speech ETHEL *has been getting flour, bowls and other supplies out of the dresser, with her back to* POP. *He has fished a long pair of black stockings out of the clothesbasket and wrapped them round his arm like a mourner's crêpe; he now tilts back in his chair and surveys* ETHEL'S *back quizzically, whistling an air from* Lucia, *which mingles with the sound of* ETHEL'S *eggbeater as the Curtain falls.*

The Singing Silence

Eva-Lis Wuorio

O LD Vicente of Formentera was perhaps the happiest man I've ever known. And also, perhaps, the poorest.

He was a cadaverous, bent juniper of a man, brown and lined, and he owned not one piece of clothing that was not patched. He lived at Cala Pujol, in a lean-to made of stone and driftwood and brush, with a rusty iron brazier for his kitchen and a couple of cracked iron pots, discarded by the fishermen, from which to eat. But he owned also an excellent snorkel and a pair of rubber flippers and a diver's mask, and, as I say, I don't believe there was a happier man.

I had been coming to Formentera for several years before Vicente stood out in my eyes from the old fishermen who drew their boats up under the brush and the bamboo shelters at the end of the beach where the rocks begin. At last I realized he was not a fisherman. He had no time to fish.

I had some Ibicenco, his dialect, a language quite different from the Castilian Spanish, so I could tell, that day I first saw him, that he was asking with dignity, not pleading, for the loan of a fisherman's small boat. I could not understand, thinking him a fisherman, how he got along without a boat, but I offered to lend him the one I always rent in Formentera. I do not use it often anyhow. He thanked me, and again his dignity impressed me.

I watched him load the boat with the snorkel and the flippers and the face mask, an earthen jug of water, and a small parcel of provisions. There was no fishing gear, no underwater gun to go with his other equipment. I wondered what he intended to catch and how. I watched him row out, facing the horizon, a small man, intent.

I watched until he was but a speck on the horizon, and then I forgot about him. At Cala Pujol it is easy to forget. The turquoise waters are deep and clear to the bottom, the sand is untrodden, there is a long sweep of white-silver shore—the year I speak of, it was still that way—and the sun is a constant benediction. In peace, one forgets.

There came a day when the wind blew from Africa and the sea was sultry and the fishermen did not go out. They sat in the bamboo-roofed little bar on the beach and drank red wine and talked. "Vicente got in?"

"Not yet."

"He is *loco, este hombre*, a little crazy."

"Not at all, not so much. He has the good intention."

"You think so? You, too, are *loco*."

"Me? Not at all. I see the point. I understand very well."

"Vicente?" I asked. "He is the old man with the underwater equipment?"

"Ah," they said, "aha. Ah."

I asked for another bottle of the wine of the island, for only that is drunk there. We do not try to be smart by taking better-known wines.

And, so sitting there, with the wind from Africa blowing and stirring up the sea until it was muddy below and racing, sheep-white, above, I heard the story of Vicente.

He had been an ambitious boy 60 years ago, and he had left Formentera, the little island of the past. But 60 years ago there was not much for a Spaniard to do in his country of Spain. So Vicente went to sea in foreign ships, and after a time he came back. He walked the country, trying all sorts of jobs, but he ended where better men than he had ended, as a porter on the quays of Barcelona—a *mozo*.

He had had a dream, but dreams fail a man sometimes. So he carried the luggage of others: the rich Spaniards, the visitors, the tourists. Until ten years ago he stood there at the quay, a number on his hat, waving his hand at the passengers from the boats, pointing to himself and shouting, "Me? Me! Number Seventy-three!"

One day a rich American from a Palma boat saw his frantic wave and beckoned. Vicente got in line with the other porters and pushed his way up the gangplank to the white boat. There this rich American said to him, "Here are six suitcases, and that thing. Be careful with it; it's an antique".

Vicente recognized the earthen vessel. It was an amphora, a Phœnician one, a fine, rare specimen of the big jugs used for transporting wine or grain. In the old days fishermen some-times caught them in their nets. They had often thrown them back into the sea, but this they did no longer, not since the *señores* from the town came to buy them for their museums.

Vicente hoisted the bags on his back, picked up the big, pinkish, sea-encrusted jug and started down the gangplank. The people were pushing and pulling, getting off the boat, coming on board, and he shouted as they shouted. He came to the quay, and another porter, stumbling on a mooring rope, fell against him and he dropped the amphora.

Two thousand years went down in a dusty sound of earth falling. Well.

Ten years before there were still amphoræ and other relics of the Greeks and Phœnicians and Romans in the shallow coves of the islands of Ibiza, but now there were mostly only almost valueless objects of more recent times; valuable specimens were very rare. The American had paid $500 for this water jug of a Phœnician sailor, having had it verified as authentic by the authorities. Naturally he was angry.

But he was also a sensible man and knew that never in a lifetime could the porter Vicente make $500, so he was re-signed and ready to forget his loss.

Not so Vicente. He knew the value men set now on these useless old jugs and pots; he had seen the disappointment on the face of the American. Vicente was an honorable man and he wanted to make amends.

He followed the American to his hotel, pleaded for his name and address, and promised to pay him back. A ragged piece of paper torn from a diary and scribbled with Abraham Lincoln Smith, 72 Hudson Avenue, Milwaukee, Wisconsin, U.S.A. became his most valuable possession. It was to him the ultimate milepost on the long road of his search.

I believe that somehow, in his dreams, Vicente saw himself

at last arriving in Milwaukee, Wisconsin, U.S.A., with the ancient Phoenician amphora under his arm, receiving with joy the praise that would greet him there.

Vicente knew that he would never have the money to buy an amphora, but what was to prevent his finding one? Others had, dozens of them in the time of his boyhood. Why not he?

He had no family, so it did not take him long to bid farewell to his life in Barcelona, that bustling, busy city by the sea, where he had carried bags for the price of a small glass of wine in a smoky wineshop, and a windowless room to roof his nights.

When he had sold his few possessions he had the deck fare to Ibiza, and a little more. From the stern of the boat he looked back and saw the city sink into the sea, and for the first time he knew that his years there had been a prison of his own making. He had never, there, lifted up his eyes from the narrow streets to the wide sky. *Personification*

And once again, as when he was a boy, the sea sang to him.

Back on the islands he set about the task he had chosen. He learned where the last amphora had been found, and he realized, as had others before him, that since the ancient pieces were valuable, all the inshore places must have been searched and emptied of their treasure.

Young Sandik, of Santa Eulalia del Rio, the carpenter's son, had made himself a reputation as an undersea swimmer. He had found a cannon at the bottom of the sea—but that's another story. To consult him, Vicente travelled by bus to Santa Eulalia del Rio, and Sandik's advice was brief. Get a mask, get flippers, go far out into the sea. There, way out, were still unknown shallows, no deeper than the height of a man, or twice or thrice the height of a man, and caught in the caves of the sea bottom, treasures might still be.

Now Vicente, like many of the island-born, had never learned to swim. But he spent the rest of his money, as Sandik advised, on a good snorkel and flippers and a mask. Then he took the little mail boat *Manolito* back to his island of Formentera. There, camping on the beach, scrounging his meals, intent as are all men with a singleness of purpose to urge them on, he set about teaching himself to swim.

He was over 60 then. An old man, as time makes men like Vicente old. Yet he was young in his urgency to learn and go on toward the far horizon of his purpose.

He learned to swim, and he learned to dive with the snorkel and the flippers and the mask, a froglike, crablike figure in the clear shallows about the beaches of Cala Pujol. He ventured farther and farther, to where the water turned purple, where the deeps began. This was the most talkative time of his life, after his first dives, for he could not contain his wonder at the unexpected beauty of the deep sea. The gardens of starfish, the varicolored, bug-eyed gentle fish that followed him, the slant of translucent sunlight on the mysterious caves and rocks— these he recounted to the fishermen who toiled upon the surface of the sea. And his tales were touched with wonder and awe. Never, he swore, had he known such freedom as at the bottom of the sea.

"But you can't breathe there!"

"One breathes with one's eyes, one's pores."

Never had he heard such music.   *Simile*

"But there is only silence under the sea?"

"It is a singing silence. Like many instruments sending their purest sounds up to the sky."

There is that to the Spanish language. The plowman often speaks the language of poetry. It is the way the words arrange themselves.

Day by day, week by week, month by month, and so into the years, Vicente, searching for the amphora which in honor he felt he must find to replace the one he had broken, grew happier. Each day was a new delight, a new adventure. No longer were his days imprisoned by the needs of the hours. Somehow there was always something for those needs, a fish to grill, a glass of wine, a piece of bread, a box of matches. To the fishermen his search had become a part of their life on the beach and the sea, and their generosity was quick, unthinking.

They told me the story of Vicente, that day the wind blew from Africa and stirred up the depths of the sea and sent the high green waves scurrying, and I, too, searched the horizon for the little boat. Then I turned to Father Pedro, the curé of San Fernando, who had joined us.

"What do you think, Father?" I said. "Will old Vicente find his amphora?"

The fat little priest joined his fingers. His eyes, too, were on the horizon, but he seemed undisturbed. The wind from Africa swayed the bamboo shelter over us.

"Well, now, you see," he said, "Vicente has the search. It is not what one finds, you know, but the search itself that is important. Only the search."

Last year, on another day, when the sea rose suddenly, stirred to tumult by the wind, the little boat Vicente had borrowed was tossed back to the beach.

No one saw the old man again.

The seas had been heavy.

But tied securely, wrapped in seaweed at the bottom of the boat, was an amphora, an ancient Phoenician vessel salvaged from the centuries and the sea.

Father Pedro and the fishermen who had been Vicente's friends asked me, since I knew English, to write to Abraham Lincoln Smith of Milwaukee, Wisconsin, U.S.A. I did. I wrote a number of times to the address we had and finally to the mayor of the city.

No one had heard of him.

Annoyed by the foolish old man who had dropped his souvenir, the American had fabricated a name to get rid of him. Perhaps, however, he did come from Milwaukee. We do not know.

To Set Our House in Order

Margaret Laurence

WHEN the baby was almost ready to be born, something went wrong and my mother had to go to the hospital two weeks before the expected time. I was wakened by her crying in the night, and then I heard my father's footsteps as he went downstairs to phone. I stood in the doorway of my room, shivering and listening, wanting to go to my mother, but afraid to go lest there be some sight there more terrifying than I could bear.

"Hello, Paul?" my father said, and I knew he was talking to Doctor Cates. "It's Beth. I'm only thinking of what happened the last time, and another like that would be—Yes, I think that would be the best thing. Okay, make it as soon as you can."

He came back upstairs, looking bony and dishevelled in his pyjamas, and running his fingers through his sand-coloured hair. At the top of the stairs he came face to face with Grandmother MacLeod, who was standing there in her quilted black-satin dressing gown, her light figure held straight and poised, as though she was unaware that her hair was bound grotesquely like white-feathered wings in the snare of her coarse night-time hairnet.

"What is it, Ewen?"

"It's all right, Mother. Beth's having . . . a little trouble. I'm going to take her to the hospital. You go back to bed."

"I told you," Grandmother MacLeod said in her clear voice, never loud, but distinct and ringing like the tap of a silver spoon on a crystal goblet, "I did tell you, Ewen, did I not, that you should have got a girl in to help her with the housework? She should have rested more."

"I couldn't afford to get anyone in," my father said. "If you thought she should've rested more, why didn't you ever . . . Oh God, I'm out of my mind tonight. Just go back to bed, Mother, please. I must get back to Beth."

When my father went down to open the front door for Doctor Cates, my need overcame my fear and I slipped into my parents' room. My mother's black hair, so neatly pinned up during the day, was startlingly spread across the white pillowcase. I stared at her, not speaking, and then she smiled, and I rushed from the doorway and buried my head upon her.

"It's all right, Vanessa," she said. "Honey, the baby's just going to come a little early, that's all. You'll be all right. Grandmother MacLeod will be here."

"How can she get the meals?" I wailed, fixing on the first thing that came to mind. "She never cooks. She doesn't know how."

"Yes, she does," my mother said. "She can cook as well as anyone when she has to. She's just never had to very much, that's all. Don't worry, she'll keep everything in order, and then some."

My father and Doctor Cates came in, and I had to go, without saying anything I had wanted to say. I went back to my own room and lay with the shadows all around me, listening to the night murmurings that always went on in that house, sounds that never had a source—rafters and beams contracting in the dry air, perhaps, or mice in the walls, or a sparrow that had flown into the attic through the broken skylight there. After a while, although I would not have believed it possible, I slept.

The next morning, though summer vacation was not quite over, I did not feel like going out to play with any of the kids. I was very superstitious and felt that if I left the house, even for a few hours, some disaster would overtake my mother. I did not, of course, mention this to Grandmother MacLeod, for she did not believe in the existence of fear, or if she did, she never let on.

I spent the morning morbidly, seeking hidden places in the

house. There were many of these—odd-shaped nooks under the stairs, and dusty tunnels and forgotten recesses in the heart of the house where the only things actually to be seen were drab oil paintings stacked upon the rafters and trunks full of outmoded clothing and old photograph albums. But the unseen presences in these secret places I knew to be those of every person, young or old, who had ever belonged to the house and had died, including Uncle Roderick who got killed on the Somme and the baby who would have been my sister if only she had come to life. Grandfather MacLeod, who had died a year after I was born, was present in the house in more tangible form. At the top of the main stairs hung a mammoth picture of a darkly uniformed man riding a horse whose prancing stance and dilated nostrils suggested the battle was not yet over, that it might continue until Judgement Day. The stern man was the Duke of Wellington, but at the time I believed him to be my Grandfather MacLeod, still keeping an eye on things.

We had moved in with Grandmother MacLeod when the depression got bad and she could no longer afford a housekeeper; yet the MacLeod house never seemed like home to me. Its dark-red brick was grown over at the front with Virginia creeper that turned crimson in the fall until you could hardly tell brick from leaves. It boasted a small tower in which Grandmother MacLeod kept a weed-like collection of anaemic ferns. The veranda was embellished with a profusion of wrought-iron scrolls, and the circular rose window upstairs contained many-coloured glass that permitted an outlooking eye to see the world as a place of absolute sapphire or emerald or, if one wished to look with a jaundiced eye, a hateful yellow. In Grandmother MacLeod's opinion, these features gave the house style. To me, they seemed fascinating, but rather as the paraphernalia of an alchemist's laboratory might be, things to be peered at curiously but with caution, just in case.

Inside, a multitude of doors led to rooms where my presence, if not actually forbidden, was not encouraged. One was Grandmother MacLeod's bedroom, with its stale and old-smelling reek of medicines and lavender sachets. Here resided her monogrammed dresser silver—brush and mirror, nail buffer and button hook and scissors—none of which must even be fingered by me now, for she meant to leave them to me in her will and intended to hand them over in their original flawless and unused condition. Here, too, were the silver-framed photographs of Uncle Roderick—as a child, as a boy, as a man in his army uniform. The massive walnut spool bed had obviously been designed for queens or giants, and my tiny grandmother used to lie within it all day when she had migraines, contriving somehow to look like a giant queen.

The day my mother went to the hospital, Grandmother MacLeod called me at lunch-time, and when I appeared, smudged with dust from the attic, she looked at me distastefully.

"For mercy's sake, Vanessa, what have you been doing with yourself? Get washed this minute. Not that way. Use the back stairs, young lady. Get along now. Oh, your father phoned."

I swung around. "What did he say? How is she? Is the baby born?"

"Curiosity killed the cat," Grandmother MacLeod said, frowning. "I cannot understand Beth and Ewen telling you all these things at your age. What sort of vulgar person you'll grow up to be, I dare not think. No, it's not born yet. Your mother's just the same. No change."

I looked at my grandmother, not wanting to appeal to her, but unable to stop myself. "Will she—will she be all right?"

Grandmother MacLeod straightened her already straight back. "If I said definitely yes, Vanessa, that would be a lie, and the MacLeods do not tell lies, as I have tried to impress upon you before. What happens is God's will. 'The Lord giveth, and the Lord taketh away.'"

Appalled, I turned away so she would not see my face. Surprisingly, I heard her sigh and felt her papery white and perfectly manicured hand upon my shoulder.

"When your Uncle Roderick got killed," she said, "I thought I would die. But I didn't die, Vanessa."

At lunch she chatted animatedly, and I realized she was trying to cheer me in the only way she knew. "When I married your Grandfather MacLeod, he said to me, 'Eleanor, don't think because we're going to the prairies that I expect you to live roughly. You're used to a proper house, and you shall have one.' He was as good as his word. Before we'd been in Manawaka three years, he'd had this place built. He earned a good deal of money in his time, your grandfather. He soon had more patients than either of the other doctors. We ordered our dinner service and all our silver from Birks in Toronto. We had resident help in those days, of course, and never had less than twelve guests for dinner parties. When I had a tea, it would always be twenty or thirty. Never any less than half a dozen different kinds of cake were ever served in this house. Well, no one seems to bother much these days. Too lazy, I suppose."

"Too broke," I suggested. "That's what Dad says."

"I can't bear slang," Grandmother MacLeod said. "If you mean hard up, why don't you say so? It's mainly a question of management, anyway. My accounts were always in good order, and so was my house. No unexpected expenses that couldn't be met, no fruit cellar running out of preserves before the winter was over. Do you know what my father used to say to me when I was a girl?"

"No," I said. "What?"

" 'God loves order,' " Grandmother MacLeod replied with emphasis. "You remember that, Vanessa, 'God loves order.' He wants each one of us to set our house in order. I've never forgotten those words of my father's. I was a MacInnes before I got married. The MacInnes is a very ancient clan, the lairds of Morven and the constables of the Castle of Kinlochaline. Did you finish that book I gave you?"

"Yes," I said. Then, feeling additional comment was called for, I added, "It was a swell book, Grandmother."

This was somewhat short of the truth. I had been hoping for her cairngorm brooch on my tenth birthday and had received instead the plaid-bound volume entitled *The Clans and Tartans of Scotland*. Most of it was too boring to read, but I had looked up the motto of my own family and those of some of my friends' families. *Be then a wall of brass. Learn to suffer. Consider the end. Go carefully.* I had not found any of these slogans reassuring. What with Mavis Duncan learning to suffer, and Laura Kennedy considering the end, and Patsy Drummond going carefully, and I spending my time in being a wall of brass, it did not seem to me that any of us were going to lead very interesting lives. I did not say this to Grandmother MacLeod.

"The MacInnes motto is *Pleasure arises from work*," I said.

"Yes," she agreed proudly. "And an excellent motto it is, too. One to bear in mind."

She rose from the table, rearranging on her bosom the looped ivory beads that held the pendant on which a full-blown ivory rose was stiffly carved.

"I hope Ewen will be pleased," she said.

"What at?"

"Didn't I tell you?" Grandmother MacLeod said. "I hired a girl this morning for the housework. She's to start tomorrow."

When my father got home that evening, Grandmother MacLeod told him her good news. He ran a hand distractedly across his forehead.

"I'm sorry, Mother, but you'll just have to unhire her. I can't possibly pay anyone."

"It seems odd," Grandmother MacLeod snapped, "that you can afford to eat chicken four times a week."

"Those chickens," my father said in an exasperated voice, "are how people are paying their bills. The same with the eggs and the milk. That scrawny turkey that arrived yesterday was for Logan MacCardney's appendix, if you must know. We probably eat better than any family in Manawaka, except Niall Cameron's. People can't entirely dispense with doctors or undertakers. That doesn't mean to say I've got any cash. Look, Mother, I don't know what's happening with Beth. Paul thinks he may have to do a Caesarean. Can't we leave all this? Just leave the house alone. Don't touch it. What does it matter?"

"I have never lived in a messy house, Ewen," Grandmother MacLeod said, "and I don't intend to begin now."

"Oh, Lord," my father said. "Well, I'll phone Edna, I guess, and see if she can give us a hand, although God knows she's got enough, with the Connor house and her parents to look after."

"I don't fancy having Edna Connor in to help," Grandmother MacLeod said.

"Why not?" my father shouted. "She's Beth's sister, isn't she?"

"She speaks in such a slangy way," Grandmother MacLeod said. "I have never believed she was a good influence on Vanessa. And there is no need for you to raise your voice to me, Ewen, if you please."

I could barely control my rage. I thought my father would surely rise to Aunt Edna's defence. But he did not.

"It'll be all right," he soothed her. "She'd only be here for part of the day, Mother. You could stay in your room."

Aunt Edna strode in the next morning. The sight of her bobbed black hair and her grin made me feel better at once. She hauled out the carpet sweeper and the weighted polisher and got to work. I dusted while she polished and swept, and we got through the living room and front hall in next to no time.

"Where's her royal highness, kiddo?" she inquired.

"In her room," I said. "She's reading the catalogue from Robinson and Cleaver."

"Good glory, not again?" Aunt Edna cried. "The last time she ordered three linen tea cloths and two dozen napkins. It came to fourteen dollars. Your mother was absolutely frantic. I guess I shouldn't be saying this."

"I knew anyway," I assured her. "She was at the lace-handkerchief section when I took up her coffee."

"Let's hope she stays there. Heaven forbid she should get onto the banqueting cloths. Well, at least she believes the Irish are good for two things—manual labour and linen-making. She's never forgotten Father used to be a blacksmith, before he got the hardware store. Can you beat it? I wish it didn't bother Beth."

"Does it?" I asked and immediately realized this was a wrong move, for Aunt Edna was suddenly scrutinizing me.

"We're making you grow up before your time," she said. "Don't pay any attention to me, Nessa. I must've got up on the wrong side of the bed this morning."

But I was unwilling to leave the subject. "All the same," I said thoughtfully, "Grandmother MacLeod's family were the lairds of Morven and the constables of the Castle of Kinlochaline. I bet you didn't know that."

Aunt Edna snorted. "Castle, my foot. She was born in Ontario, just like your Grandfather Connor, and her father was a horse doctor. Come on, kiddo, we'd better shut up and get down to business here."

We worked in silence for a while.

"Aunt Edna," I said at last, "what about Mother? Why won't they let me go and see her?"

"Kids aren't allowed to visit maternity patients. It's tough for you, I know. Look, Nessa, don't worry. If it doesn't start tonight, they're going to do the operation. She's getting the best of care."

I stood there, holding the feather duster like a dead bird in my hands. I was not aware that I was going to speak until the words came out. "I'm scared," I said.

Aunt Edna put her arms around me, and her face looked all at once stricken and empty of defences.

"Oh, honey, I'm scared, too," she said.

It was this way that Grandmother MacLeod found us when she came stepping lightly down into the front hall with her order for two dozen lace-bordered handkerchiefs of pure Irish linen.

I could not sleep that night, and when I went downstairs, I found my father in the den. I sat down on the hassock beside his chair, and he told me about the operation my mother was to have the next morning. He kept saying it was not serious nowadays.

"But you're worried," I put in, as though seeking to explain why I was.

"I should at least have been able to keep from burdening you with it," he said in a distant voice, as though to himself. "If only the baby hadn't got twisted around——"

"Will it be born dead, like the little girl?"

"I don't know," my father said. "I hope not."

"She'd be disappointed, wouldn't she, if it was?" I said, wondering why I was not enough for her.

"Yes, she would," my father replied. "She won't be able to have any more, after this. It's partly on your account that she wants this one, Nessa. She doesn't want you to grow up without a brother or sister."

"As far as I'm concerned, she didn't need to bother."

My father laughed. "Well, let's talk about something else, and then maybe you'll be able to sleep. How did you and Grandmother make out today?"

"Oh, fine, I guess. What was Grandfather MacLeod like, Dad?"

"What did she tell you about him?"

"She said he made a lot of money in his time."

"Well, he wasn't any millionaire," my father said, "but I suppose he did quite well. That's not what I associate with him, though." He reached across to the bookshelf, took out a small leather-bound volume and opened it. On the pages were mysterious marks, like doodling, only much neater and more patterned.

"What is it?" I asked.

"Greek," my father explained. "This is a play called *Antigone*. See, here's the title in English. There's a whole stack of them on the shelves there. *Oedipus Rex. Electra. Medea.* They belonged to your Grandfather MacLeod. He used to read them often."

"Why?" I inquired, unable to understand why anyone would pore over those undecipherable signs.

"He was interested in them," my father said. "He must have been a lonely man, although it never struck me that way at the time. Sometimes a thing only hits you a long time afterward."

"Why would he be lonely?" I wanted to know.

"He was the only person in Manawaka who could read these plays in the original Greek," my father said. "I don't suppose many people, if anyone, had even read them in English translation. Maybe he once wanted to be a classical scholar—I don't know. But his father was a doctor, so that's what he was. Maybe he would have liked to talk to somebody about these plays. They must have meant a lot to him."

It seemed to me that my father was talking oddly. There was a sadness in his voice that I had never heard before, and I longed to say something that would make him feel better, but I could not, because I did not know what was the matter.

"Can you read this kind of writing?" I asked hesitantly.

My father shook his head. "Nope. I was never very intellectual, I guess. Your Uncle Rod was always brighter than I, in school, but even he wasn't interested in learning Greek. Perhaps he would've been later, if he'd lived. As a kid, all I ever wanted to do was go into the merchant marine."

"Why didn't you?"

"Oh, well," my father said, "a kid who'd never seen the sea wouldn't have made much of a sailor. I might have turned out to be the seasick type."

I had lost interest, now that he was once more speaking like himself.

"Grandmother MacLeod was pretty cross today about the girl," I said.

"I know," my father said. "Well, we must be as nice as we can to her, Nessa, and after a while she'll be all right."

Suddenly I did not care what I said.

"Why can't she be nice to *us* for a change?" I burst out. "We're always the ones who have to be nice to her."

My father put his hand down and tilted my head until I was forced to look at him. "Vanessa," he said, "she's had troubles in her life which you really don't know much about. That's why she sometimes gets migraines and has to go to bed. It's not easy for her these days. The house is still the same, so she thinks other things should be, too. It hurts her when she finds they aren't."

"I don't see——" I began.

"Listen," my father said, "you know we were talking just now about what people are interested in, like Grandfather MacLeod being interested in Greek plays? Well, your grandmother was interested in being a lady, Nessa, and for a long time it seemed to her that she was one."

I thought of the Castle of Kinlochaline and of horse doctors in Ontario.

"I didn't know——" I stammered.

"That's usually the trouble with most of us," my father said. "Now you go on up to bed. I'll phone tomorrow from the hospital as soon as the operation's over."

I did sleep at last, and in my dreams I could hear the caught sparrow fluttering in the attic and the sound of my mother crying and the voices of dead children.

My father did not phone until afternoon. Although Grandmother MacLeod said I was being silly, for you could hear the phone ringing all over the house, I refused to move out of the den. I had never before examined my father's books, but now, at a loss for something to do, I took them out one by one and read snatches here and there. After several hours, it dawned on me that most of the books were the same kind. I looked again at the titles.

Seven League Boots. Travels in Arabia Deserta. The Seven Pillars of Wisdom. Travels in Tartary, Thibet and China. Count Luckner, the Sea Devil. And a hundred more. On a shelf by themselves were copies of the *National Geographic Magazine.* I had looked at these often enough, but never with the puzzling compulsion which I felt now, as though I was on the verge of some discovery, something which I had to find out and yet did not want to know. I riffled through the picture-filled pages. Hibiscus and wild orchids grew in soft-petaled profusion. The Himalayas stood lofty as gods, with the morning sun on their peaks of snow. Leopards snarled from the depth of a thousand jungles. Schooners buffeted their white sails like the wings of giant angels against the sea winds.

"What on earth are you doing?" Grandmother MacLeod inquired waspishly, from the doorway. "You've got everything scattered all over the place. Pick it all up this minute, Vanessa, do you hear?" So I picked up the books and magazines and put them neatly away.

When the telephone finally rang, I was afraid to answer it. At last I did. My father sounded far away, and the relief in his voice made it unsteady.

"It's okay, honey. Everything's fine. The boy was born alive and kicking after all. Your mother's pretty weak, but she's going to be all right."

I could hardly believe it. I did not want to talk to anyone. I wanted to be by myself, to assimilate the presence of my brother, toward whom, without even having seen him, I felt such tenderness and such resentment.

That evening, Grandmother MacLeod approached my father, who at first did not take her seriously when she asked what they planned to call the child.

"Oh, I don't know. Hank, maybe, or Joe. Fauntleroy, perhaps."

She ignored his levity. "Ewen, I wish you would call him Roderick."

His face changed. "I'd rather not."

"I think you should," Grandmother MacLeod insisted, in a voice as pointed and precise as her silver nail scissors.

"Don't you think Beth ought to decide?" my father asked.

"Beth will agree if you do."

My father did not bother to deny something that even I knew to be true. He did not say anything. Then Grandmother MacLeod's voice, astonishingly, faltered a little. "It would mean a great deal to me," she said.

I remembered what she had told me—*When your Uncle Roderick got killed, I thought I would die. But I didn't die.* All at once her feeling for that unknown dead man became a reality for me. And yet I held it against her, as well, for I could see that she was going to win now.

"All right," my father said. "We'll call him Roderick."

Then, alarmingly, he threw back his head and laughed, "Roderick Dhu!" he cried. "That's what you'll call him, isn't it? Black Roderick. Like before. Don't you remember? As though he was a character out of Sir Walter Scott, instead of an ordinary kid who——"

He broke off and looked at her with a kind of desolation in his face.

"God, I'm sorry, Mother," he said. "I had no right to say that."

Grandmother MacLeod did not flinch, or tremble, or indicate that she felt anything at all. "I accept your apology, Ewen," she said.

My mother had to stay in bed for several weeks after she arrived home. The baby's crib was kept in my parents' room, and I could go in and look at the small creature who lay there with his tightly closed fists and his feathery black hair. Aunt Edna came in to help each morning, and when she had finished the housework, she would have coffee with my mother. They kept the door closed, but this did not prevent me from eavesdropping, for there was an air register in the floor of the spare room that was linked somehow with the register in my parents' room. If you put your ear to the iron grille, it was almost like a radio.

"Did you mind very much, Beth?" Aunt Edna was saying.

"Oh, it's not the name I mind," my mother replied. "It's just that Ewen felt he had to. You knew that Rod only had the sight of one eye, didn't you?"

"Sure, I knew. So what?"

"There was only a year and a half between Ewen and Rod," my mother said, "so they often went around together when they were youngsters. It was Ewen's air rifle that did it."

"Oh, Lord," Aunt Edna said. "I suppose she always blamed him?"

"No, I don't think it was so much that, really. It was how he felt himself. I think he even used to wonder sometimes if—but people shouldn't let themselves think like that, or they'd go crazy. Accidents do happen, after all. When the war came, Ewen joined up first. Rod should never have been in the army at all, but he couldn't wait to get in. He must have lied about his eyesight. It wasn't so very noticeable unless you looked at him closely, and I don't suppose the medicals were very thorough in those days. He got in as a gunner, and Ewen applied to have him in the same company. He thought he might be able to watch out for him, I guess. Rod being at a disadvantage. They were both only kids. Ewen was nineteen and Rod was eighteen when they went to France. And then the Somme. I don't know, Edna, I think Ewen felt that if Rod had had proper sight, or if he hadn't been in the same outfit and had been sent somewhere else—you know how people always think these things afterward, not that it's ever a bit of use. Ewen wasn't there when Rod got hit. They'd lost each other somehow, and Ewen was looking for him, not bothering about anything else, you know, just frantically looking. Then he stumbled across him quite by chance. Rod was still alive, but——"

"Stop it, Beth," Aunt Edna said. "You're only upsetting yourself."

"Ewen never spoke of it to me," my mother went on, "until his mother showed me the letter he'd written to her at the time. It was a peculiar letter, almost formal, saying how gallantly Rod had died, and all that. I guess I shouldn't have, but I told him she'd shown it to me. He was very angry that she had. And then, as though for some reason he was terribly ashamed, he said, 'I had to write something to her, but men don't really die like that, Beth. It wasn't that way at all.' It was only after the war that he decided to study medicine and go into practice with his father."

"Had Rod meant to?" Aunt Edna asked.

"I don't know," my mother said. "I never felt I should ask Ewen that."

Aunt Edna was gathering up the coffee things, for I could hear the clash of cups and saucers being stacked on the tray. "You know what I heard her say to Vanessa once, Beth? *'The MacLeods never tell lies.'* Those were her exact words. Even then, I didn't know whether to laugh or cry."

"Please, Edna." My mother sounded worn out now. "Don't."

"Oh, glory," Aunt Edna said, "I've got all the delicacy of a two-ton truck. I didn't mean Ewen, for heaven's sake. That wasn't what I meant at all. Here, let me plump up your pillows for you."

Then the baby began to cry, so I could not hear anything more of interest. I took my bike and went out beyond Manawaka, riding aimlessly along the gravel highway. It was late summer, and the wheat had changed colour, but instead of being high and bronzed in the fields, it was stunted and desiccated, for there had been no rain again this year. Yet on the bluff where I stopped and crawled under the barbed-wire fence and lay stretched out on the grass, the plentiful poplar leaves were turning to a luminous yellow and shone like church windows in the sun. I put my head down very close to the earth and looked at what was going on. Grasshoppers with enormous eyes ticked and twitched around me, as though the dry air was perfect for their purposes. A ladybug laboured mightily to climb a blade of grass, fell off and started all over again, seeming to be unaware that she possessed wings and could have flown up.

I thought of the accidents that might easily happen to a person—or, of course, might not happen, might happen to somebody else. I thought of the dead baby, my sister, who might as easily have been I. Would she, then, have been lying here in my place, the sharp grass making its small toothmarks on her brown arms, the sun warming her to the heart? I thought of the leather-bound volumes of Greek, and of the six different kinds of iced cakes that used to be offered always in the MacLeod house, and of the pictures of leopards and green seas. I thought of my brother, who had been born alive after all, and now had been given his life's name.

I could not really comprehend these things, but I sensed their strangeness, their disarray. I felt that whatever God might love in this world, it was certainly not order.

Of Children

Kahlil Gibran

And a woman who held a babe against her bosom
said, Speak to us of Children.
And he said:
Your children are not your children.
They are the sons and daughters of Life's longing
for itself.
They come through you but not from you,
And though they are with you yet they belong
not to you.

You may give them your love but not your
thoughts,
For they have their own thoughts.
You may house their bodies but not their souls,
For their souls dwell in the house of tomorrow,
which you cannot visit not even in your dreams.
You may strive to be like them, but seek not to
make them like you.
For life goes not backward nor tarries with
yesterday.

You are the bows from which your children as
living arrows are sent forth.
The archer sees the mark upon the path of the
infinite, and he bends you with His might that
His arrows may go swift and far.
Let your bending in the archer's hand be for
gladness;
For even as He loves the arrow that flies, so He
loves also the bow that is stable.

In Time of "The Breaking of Nations"

Thomas Hardy

Only a man harrowing clods
   In a slow silent walk,
With an old horse that stumbles and nods
   Half asleep as they stalk.

Only thin smoke without flame
   From the heaps of couch-grass;
Yet this will go onward the same
   Though Dynasties pass.

Yonder a maid and her wight
   Come whispering by:
War's annals will cloud into night
   Ere their story die.

To Every Thing There is a Season

Ecclesiastes 3:1-8

1   To every thing there is a season,
    and a time to every purpose under the heaven:
2   A time to be born, and a time to die;
    a time to plant, and time to pluck up that which is
    planted;
3   A time to kill, and a time to heal;
    a time to break down, and a time to build up;
4   A time to weep, and a time to laugh;
    a time to mourn, and a time to dance;
5   A time to cast away stones,
    and a time to gather stones together;
    a time to embrace, and a time to refrain from embracing;
6   A time to get, and a time to lose;
    a time to keep, and a time to cast away;
7   A time to rend, and a time to sew;
    a time to keep silence, and a time to speak;
8   A time to love, and time to hate;
    a time of war, and a time of peace.

(from the *The King James Bible*)

Everything That Happens in This World . . .

Ecclesiastes 3:1-8

1 Everything that happens in this world happens at the
  time God chooses.
2 He sets the time for birth and
      the time for death,
    the time for planting and the
      time for pulling up,
3 the time for killing and the
      time for healing,
    the time for tearing down and
      the time for building.
4 He sets the time for sorrow
      and the time for joy,
    the time for mourning and the
      time for dancing,
5 the time for making love and
      the time for not making love,
    the time for kissing and the
      time for not kissing.
6 He sets the time for finding
      and the time for losing,
    the time for saving and the
      the time for throwing away,

7   the time for tearing and the
        time for mending,
     the time for silence and the
        time for talk.
8   He sets the time for love and
        the time for hate,
     the time for war and the time
        for peace.

(*The Good News Bible*)

Invictus

William Ernest Henley

Out of the night that covers me,
   Black as the Pit from pole to pole,
I thank whatever gods may be
   For my unconquerable soul.

In the fell clutch of circumstance
   I have not winced nor cried aloud.
Under the bludgeoning of chance
   My head is bloody, but unbowed.

Beyond this place of wrath and tears
   Looms but the Horror of the shade,
And yet the menace of the years
   Finds, and shall find, me unafraid.

It matters not how strait the gate,
   How charged with punishments the scroll,
I am the master of my fate;
   I am the captain of my soul.

What I Believe

E. M. Forster

I do not believe in Belief. But this is an age of faith, and there are so many militant creeds that, in self-defence, one has to formulate a creed of one's own. Tolerance, good temper and sympathy are no longer enough in a world which is rent by religious and racial persecution, in a world where ignorance rules, and science who ought to have ruled, plays the subservient pimp. Tolerance, good temper and sympathy—they are what matter really, and if the human race is not to collapse they must come to the front before long. But for the moment they are not enough, their action is no stronger than a flower, battered beneath a military jack-boot. They want stiffening, even if the process coarsens them. Faith, to my mind, is a stiffening process, a sort of mental starch, which ought to be applied as sparingly as possible. I dislike the stuff. I do not believe in it, for its own sake, at all. Herein I probably differ from most people, who believe in Belief, and are only sorry they cannot swallow even more than they do. My law-givers are Erasmus and Montaigne, not Moses and St. Paul. My temple stands not upon Mount Moriah but in that Elysian Field where even the immoral are admitted. My motto is: "Lord, I disbelieve—help thou my unbelief."

I have, however, to live in an Age of Faith—the sort of epoch I used to hear praised when I was a boy. It is extremely unpleasant really. It is bloody in every sense of the word. And I have to keep my end up in it. Where do I start?

With personal relationships. Here is something comparatively solid in a world full of violence and cruelty. Not absolutely solid, for Psychology has split and shattered the idea of a "Person," and has shown that there is something incalculable in each of us, which may at any moment rise to the surface and destroy our normal balance. We don't know what we are like. We can't know what other people are like. How, then, can we put any trust in personal relationships, or cling to them in the gathering political storm? In theory we cannot. But in practice we can and do. Though A is not unchangeably A or B unchangeably B, there can still be love and loyalty between the two. For the purpose of living one has to assume that the personality is solid, and the "self" is an entity, and to ignore all contrary evidence. And since to ignore evidence is one of the characteristics of faith, I certainly can proclaim that I believe in personal relationships.

Starting from them, I get a little order into the contemporary chaos. One must be fond of people and trust them if one is not to make a mess of life, and it is therefore essential that they should not let one down. They often do. The moral of which is that I must, myself, be as reliable as possible, and this I try to be. But reliability is not a matter of contract—that is the main difference between the world of personal relationships and the world of business relationships. It is a matter for the heart, which signs no documents. In other words, reliability is impossible unless there is a natural warmth. Most men possess this warmth, though they often have bad luck and get chilled. Most of them, even when they are politicians, *want* to keep faith. And one can, at all events, show one's own little light here, one's own poor little trembling flame, with the knowledge that it is not the only light that is shining in the darkness, and not the only one which the darkness does not comprehend. Personal relations are despised to-day. They are regarded as bourgeois luxuries, as products of a time of fair weather which is now past, and we are urged to get rid of them, and to dedicate ourselves to some movement or cause instead. I hate the idea of causes, and if I had to choose between betraying my country and betraying my friend, I hope I should have the guts to betray my country. Such a choice may scandalise the modern reader, and he may stretch out his patriotic hand to the telephone at once and ring up the police. It would not have shocked Dante, though. Dante places Brutus and Cassius in the lowest circle of Hell because they had chosen to betray their friend Julius Caesar rather than their country Rome. Probably one will not be asked to make such an agonising choice. Still, there lies at the back of every creed something terrible and hard for which the worshipper may one day be required to suffer, and there is even a terror and a hardness in this creed of personal relationships, urbane and mild though it sounds. Love and loyalty to an individual can run counter to the claims of the State. When they do—down with the State, say I, which means that the State would down me.

This brings me along to Democracy, "even Love, and Beloved Republic, which feeds upon Freedom and lives." Democracy is not a Beloved Republic really, and never will be. But it is less hateful than other contemporary forms of government, and to that extent it deserves our support. It does start from the assumption that the individual is important, and that all types are needed to make a civilisation. It does not divide its citizens into the bossers and the bossed—as an efficiency-regime tends to do. The people I admire most are those who are sensitive and want to create something or discover something, and do not see life in terms of power, and such people get more of a chance under a democracy than elsewhere. They found religions, great or small, or they produce literature and art, or they do disinterested scientific research, or they may be what is called "ordinary people," who are creative in their private lives, bring up their children decently, for instance, or help their neighbours. All these people need to express themselves; they cannot do so unless society allows them liberty to do so, and the society which allows them most liberty is a democracy.

Democracy has another merit. It allows criticism, and if there is not public criticism there are bound to be hushed-up scandals. That is why I believe in the Press, despite all its lies and vulgarity, and why I believe in Parliament. Parliament is often sneered at because it is a Talking Shop. I believe in it *because* it is a talking shop. I believe in the Private Member who makes himself a nuisance. He gets snubbed and is told that he is cranky or ill-informed, but he does expose abuses which would otherwise never have been mentioned, and very often an abuse gets put right just by being mentioned. Occasionally, too, a well-meaning public official starts losing his head in the cause of efficiency. Well, there will be questions about them in Parliament sooner or later, and then they will have to mind their steps. Whether Parliament is either a representative body or an efficient one is questionable, but I value it because it criticises and talks, and because its chatter gets widely reported.

So two cheers for Democracy: one because it admits variety and two because it permits criticism. Two cheers are quite enough: there is no occasion to give three. Only Love the Beloved Republic deserves that.

What about Force, though? While we are trying to be sensitive and advanced and affectionate and tolerant, an unpleasant question pops up: does not all society rest upon force? If a government cannot count upon the police and the army, how can it hope to rule? And if an individual gets knocked on the head or sent to a labour camp, of what significance are his opinions?

This dilemma does not worry me as much as it does some. I realise that all society rests upon force. But all the great creative actions, all the decent human relations, occur during the intervals when force has not managed to come to the front. These intervals are what matter. I want them to be as frequent and as lengthy as possible, and I call them "civilisation." Some people idealise force and pull it into the foreground and worship it, instead of keeping it in the background as long as possible. I think they make a mistake, and I think that their opposites, the mystics, err even more when they declare that force does not exist. I believe that it exists, and that one of our jobs is to prevent it from getting out of its box. It gets out sooner or later, and then it destroys us and all the lovely things which we have made. But it is not out all the time, for the fortunate reason that the strong are so stupid. Consider their conduct for a moment in the Niebelung's Ring. The giants there have the guns, or in other words the gold; but they do nothing with it and the castle of Walhalla, insecure but glorious, fronts the storms. Fafnir, coiled round his hoard, grumbles and grunts;

we can hear him under Europe to-day; the leaves of the wood already tremble, and the Bird calls its warnings uselessly. Fafnir will destroy us, but by a blessed dispensation he is stupid and slow, and creation goes on just outside the poisonous blast of his breath. The Nietzschean would hurry the monster up, the mystic would say he did not exist, but Wotan, wiser than either, hastens to create warriors before doom declares itself. The Valkyries are symbols not only of courage but of intelligence; they represent the human spirit snatching its opportunity while the going is good, and one of them even finds time to love. Brünnhilde's last song hymns the recurrence of love, and since it is the privilege of art to exaggerate, she goes even further, and proclaims the love which is eternally triumphant and feeds upon freedom, and lives.

So that is what I feel about force and violence. It is, alas! the ultimate reality on this earth, but it does not always get to the front. Some people call its absences "decadence"; I call them "civilisation" and find in such interludes the chief justification for the human experiment. I look the other way until fate strikes me. Whether this is due to courage or to cowardice in my own case I cannot be sure. But I know that if men had not looked the other way in the past, nothing of any value would survive. The people I respect most behave as if they were immortal and as if society was eternal. Both assumptions are false: both of them must be accepted as true if we are to go on eating and working and loving, and are to keep open a few breathing holes for the human spirit. No millennium seems likely to descend upon humanity; no better and stronger League of Nations will be instituted; no form of Christianity and no alternative to Christianity will bring peace to the world or integrity to the individual; no "change of heart" will occur. And yet we need not despair, indeed, we cannot despair; the evidence of history shows us that men have always insisted on behaving creatively under the shadow of the sword; that they have done their artistic and scientific and domestic stuff for the sake of doing it, and that we had better follow their example under the shadow of the aeroplanes. Others, with more vision or courage than myself, see the salvation of humanity ahead, and will dismiss my conception of civilisation as paltry, a sort of tip-and-run game. Certainly it is presumptuous to say that we *cannot* improve, and that Man, who has only been in power for a few thousand years, will never learn to make use of his power. All I mean is that, if people continue to kill one another as they do, the world cannot get better than it is, and that since there are more people than formerly, and their means for destroying one another superior, the world may well get worse. What is good in people—and consequently in the world—is their insistence on creation, their belief in friendship and loyalty for their own sakes; and though Violence remains and is, indeed, the major partner in this muddled establishment, I believe that creativeness remains too, and will always assume direction when violence sleeps. So, though I am not an optimist, I cannot agree with Sophocles that it were better never to have been born. And although, like Horace, I see no evidence that each batch of births is superior to the last, I leave the field open for the more complacent view. This is such a difficult moment to live in, one cannot help getting gloomy and also a bit rattled, and perhaps short-sighted.

In search of a refuge, we may perhaps turn to hero-worship. But here we shall get no help, in my opinion. Hero-worship is a dangerous vice, and one of the minor merits of a democracy is that it does not encourage it, or produce that unmanageable type of citizen known as the Great Man. It produces instead different kinds of small men—a much finer achievement. But people who cannot get interested in the variety of life, and cannot make up their own minds, get discontented over this, and they long for a hero to bow down before and to follow blindly. It is significant that a hero is an integral part of the authoritarian stock-in-trade to-day. An efficiency-regime cannot be run without a few heroes stuck about it to carry off the dullness—much as plums have to be put into a bad pudding to make it palatable. One hero at the top and a smaller one each side of him is a favourite arrangement, and the timid and the bored are comforted by the trinity, and, bowing down, feel exalted and strengthened.

No, I distrust Great Men. They produce a desert of uniformity around them and often a pool of blood too, and I always feel a little man's pleasure when they come a cropper. Every now and then one reads in the newspapers some such statement as: "The coup d'etat appears to have failed, and Admiral Toma's whereabouts is at present unknown." Admiral Toma had probably every qualification for being a Great Man—an iron will, personal magnetism, dash, flair, sexlessness—but fate was against him, so he retires to unknown whereabouts instead of parading history with his peers. He fails with a completeness which no artist and no lover can experience, because with them the process of creation is itself an achievement, whereas with him the only possible achievement is success.

I believe in aristocracy, though—if that is the right word, and if a democrat may use it. Not an aristocracy of power, based upon rank and influence, but an aristocracy of the sensitive, the considerate and the plucky. Its members are to be found in all nations and classes, and all through the ages, and there is a secret understanding between them when they meet. They represent the true human tradition, the one permanent victory of our queer race over cruelty and chaos. Thousands of them perish in obscurity, a few are great names. They are sensitive for others as well as for themselves, they are considerate without being fussy, their pluck is not swankiness but the power to endure, and they can take a joke. I give no examples —it is risky to do that—but the reader may as well consider whether this is the type of person he would like to meet and to be, and whether (going farther with me) he would prefer that this type should *not* be an ascetic one. I am against asceticism myself. I am with the old Scotsman who wanted less chastity and more delicacy. I do not feel that my aristocrats are a real aristocracy if they thwart their bodies, since bodies are the instruments through which we register and enjoy the world. Still, I do not insist. This is not a major point. It is clearly possible to be sensitive, considerate and plucky and yet be an ascetic too, and if anyone possesses the first three qualities, I will let him in! On they go—an invincible army, yet not a victorious one. The aristocrats, the elect, the chosen, the Best People—all the words that describe them are false, and all attempts to organise them fail. Again and again Authority, seeing their value, has tried to net them and to utilise them as the

Egyptian Priesthood or the Christian Church or the Chinese Civil Service or the Group Movement, or some other worthy stunt. But they slip through the net and are gone; when the door is shut, they are no longer in the room; their temple, as one of them remarked, is the Holiness of the Heart's Affection, and their kingdom, though they never possess it, is the wide-open world.

With this type of person knocking about, and constantly crossing one's path if one has eyes to see or hands to feel, the experiment of earthly life cannot be dismissed as a failure. But it may well be hailed as a tragedy, the tragedy being that no device has been found by which these private decencies can be transmitted to public affairs. As soon as people have power they go crooked and sometimes dotty as well, because the possession of power lifts them into a region where normal honesty never pays. For instance, the man who is selling newspapers outside the Houses of Parliament can safely leave his papers to go for a drink and his cap beside them: anyone who takes a paper is sure to drop a copper into the cap. But the men who are inside the Houses of Parliament—they cannot trust one another like that, still less can the Government they compose trust other governments. No caps upon the pavement here, but suspicion, treachery and armaments. The more highly public life is organised the lower does its morality sink; the nations of to-day behave to each other worse than they ever did in the past: they cheat, rob, bully and bluff, make war without notice, and kill as many women and children as possible; whereas primitive tribes were at all events restrained by taboos. It is a humiliating outlook—though the greater the darkness, the brighter shine the little lights, reassuring one another, signalling: "Well, at all events, I'm still here. I don't like it very much, but how are you?" Unquenchable lights of my aristrocracy! Signals of the invincible army! "Come along —anyway, let's have a good time while we can." I think they signal that too.

The Saviour of the future—if ever he comes—will not preach a new Gospel. He will merely utilise my aristocracy, he will make effective the good will and the good temper which are already existing. In other words, he will introduce a new technique. In economics, we are told that if there was a new technique of distribution, there need be no poverty, and people would not starve in one place while crops were being ploughed under in another. A similar change is needed in the sphere of morals and politics. The desire for it is by no means new; it was expressed, for example, in theological terms by Jacopone da Todi over six hundred years ago. "*Ordina questo amore, O tu che m'ami,*" he said; "O thou who lovest me—set this love in order." His prayer was not granted, and I do not myself believe that it ever will be, but here, and not through a change of heart, is our probable route. Not by becoming better, but by ordering and distributing his native goodness, will man shut up Force into its box, and so gain time to explore the universe and to set his mark upon it worthily. At present he only explores it at odd moments, when Force is looking the other way and his divine creativeness appears as a trivial by-product, to be scrapped as soon as the drums beat and the bombers hum.

Such a change, claim the orthodox, can only be made by Christianity, and will be made by it in God's good time: man always has failed and always will fail to organise his own goodness, and it is presumptuous of him to try. This claim—solemn as it is—leaves me cold. I cannot believe that Christianity will ever cope with the present world-wide mess, and I think that such influence as it retains in modern society is due to the money behind it, rather than to its spiritual appeal. It was a spiritual force once, but the indwelling spirit will have to be restated if it is to calm the waters again, and probably restated in a non-Christian form. Naturally a lot of people, and people who are not only good but able and intelligent, will disagree here; they will vehemently deny that Christianity has failed, or they will argue that its failure proceeds from the wickedness of men, and really proves its ultimate success. They have Faith, with a large F. My faith has a very small one, and I only intrude it because these are strenuous and serious days, and one likes to say what one thinks while speech is comparatively free: it may not be free much longer.

The above are the reflections of an individualist and a liberal who has found liberalism crumbling beneath him and at first felt ashamed. Then, looking around, he decided there was no special reason for shame, since other people, whatever they felt, were equally insecure. And as for individualism—there seems no way of getting off this, even if one wanted to. The dictator-hero can grind down his citizens till they are all alike, but he cannot melt them into a single man. That is beyond his power. He can order them to merge, he can incite them to mass-antics, but they are obliged to be born separately, and to die separately, and, owing to these unavoidable termini, will always be running off the totalitarian rails. The memory of birth and the expectation of death always lurk within the human being, making him separate from his fellows and consequently capable of intercourse with them. Naked I came into the world, naked I shall go out of it! And a very good thing too, for it reminds me that I am naked under my shirt, whatever its colour.

The World is Too Much With Us

William Wordsworth

The world is too much with us; late and soon,
Getting and spending, we lay waste our powers:
Little we see in Nature that is ours;
We have given our hearts away, a sordid boon!
This Sea that bares her bosom to the moon;
The winds that will be howling at all hours,
And are up-gathered now like sleeping flowers;
For this, for everything, we are out of tune;
It moves us not.—Great God! I'd rather be
A Pagan suckled in a creed outworn;
So might I, standing on this pleasant lea,
Have glimpses that would make me less forlorn;
Have sight of Proteus rising from the sea;
Or hear old Triton blow his wreathèd horn.

Author Biographies

MARGARET ATWOOD (1939-   )

Margaret Atwood, poet and writer of fiction, was born in Ottawa and grew up in Toronto. She studied at Victoria College, University of Toronto, and received an A. M. degree from Harvard in 1962. She has taught writing and Canadian literature at several universities, and has won numerous prizes for her work, including the Governor General's Award for poetry (*The Circle Game*, 1962) and a Guggenheim Fellowship in 1983. In 1982-83, she was President of The Writers' Union of Canada, and she is also well-known outside of Canada, not only for her writing but for her active pursuit of social issues through such organizations as Amnesty International. Widely published, her writing can be found in most Canadian libraries and in many anthologies.

ROSEMARY AUBERT (1946-   )

Rosemary Aubert was born in Niagara Falls, N.Y., and currently lives in Toronto where she works as a free-lance writer. She has edited for both McGraw-Hill Ryerson, from 1974-79, and Harlequin Books, from 1979-82. She has written several novels, published by Harlequin, under the pseudonym Lucy Snow. Her books of poetry include *Two Kinds of Honey* (1977). She has contributed articles, poems, and reviews to many of Canada's leading literary publications, including *Tamarack Review*, *Fiddlehead*, *Quill & Quire*, *Prism*, and *Canadian Forum*.

W.H. AUDEN (1907-1973)

English by birth, Wystan Hugh Auden travelled extensively during the 1930s and took an active interest in the political developments of his day. In 1937, he served as an ambulance driver for the Loyalists in the Spanish Civil War. In 1939 he settled in the United States and served in the U.S. Army during World War II. He became an American citizen in 1946. Some critics have labelled him the greatest poet of his age, for the astonishing versatility of his writing. He was an all-around man of letters and believed that his duty was to interpret his times and to deal with the moral and intellectual problems of public concern. He was an intelligent and perceptive book reviewer, and a major literary critic, a prolific writer of poetry and critical essays, as well as a university professor. His poetry is extremely varied, entertaining, and intellectually challenging. Auden's work includes almost all literary genres—from serious forms such as odes, elegies, verse essays, quasi-dramas, short stories, critical essays, and sonnet sequences, to lighter forms such as limericks, clerihews, ribald epigrams, ballads, and other songs. In 1948, he was awarded the Pulitzer Prize for poetry for *The Age of Anxiety*, and in 1956 he won the National Book Award for *The Shield of Achilles*. *Forewords and Afterwords*, a collection of his criticism, was published in 1973.

MARIA BANUS (1914-   )

Maria Banus, who was born in Bucharest, Rumania, had her first poem published when she was fourteen. She studied law and philology and demonstrated a considerable talent for languages. She has translated poetry from German, French, Russian, Spanish, and Turkish, including poems by Goethe, Rimbaud, Pushkin, Neruda, and Hikmet. In addition to poetry, she has written plays and articles. Her works include *The Girl's Country* (1937), *Joy* (1947), *I am Speaking to You, America!* (1955), *Metamorphosis* (1963), and *Anyone and Something* (1972). Her work published shortly after the war reflects a Stalinist stance, but her later poems are frequently defiantly individualistic, recapturing much of the freshness of her best early work.

EARLE BIRNEY (1904-   )

Born in Calgary, and educated at the Universities of British Columbia, Toronto, Berkeley, and London, Earle Birney has had an important career as a poet, playwright, novelist, editor, and teacher of creative writing and literature. He has won the Governor General's Award for poetry twice (for *David*, 1943, and for *Now is the Time*, 1946), the Stephen Leacock Medal (for *Turvey*, 1949), and the Lorne Pierce Medal for Literature (1953). He has taught at several Canadian universities, principally the University of British

Columbia, where he taught Chaucer and Old English and was influential in establishing Canada's first department of Creative Writing. His most impressive contribution, however, has been to modern Canadian poetry. Using a wide variety of forms and a sensitive but often playful attitude towards language, Birney has produced an exceedingly rich body of literature. Extensive travels in Europe, Latin America, and the Far East have provided subjects for a number of his poems, including "The Bear on the Delhi Road," which Birney wrote after seeing two Kashmiri men and a bear on a roadside in northern India.

ELIZABETH BISHOP (1911-1979)

Elizabeth Bishop was born in Worchester, Massachusetts and lived in New England, Nova Scotia, Mexico and Brazil. In more than thirty years as a poet, she published five volumes of poetry, including *Poems: North and South* (1946) and *A Cold Spring* (1955), for which she won the Pulitzer Prize for poetry in 1956. Many of her poems were featured in *The New Yorker*. Her poetry is notable for its clarity of perception, sharpness of imagery, and capacity to reveal the extraordinary aspects of everyday experience. She was awarded an honorary Doctor of Laws degree by Dalhousie University in Halifax shortly before her death in 1979.

HERMAN CHARLES BOSMAN (1905-1951)

Herman Bosman was born near Capetown, South Africa, of Afrikaner parents, and went to school in Johannesburg. He became a teacher in an isolated rural district in the western Transvaal, which had been settled by Boers who had trekked there to escape British rule after the Boer War. In this frontier setting he met characters and heard tales that strongly influenced his writing. After a year, back in Johannesburg, he was involved in a shooting incident in which his stepbrother was killed. He was found guilty of murder and sentenced to death, but the sentence was commuted and he was released after four and a half years in prison. He is reputed to have been a gentle, humane man who retained his sense of humour throughout a rather turbulent life as a journalist and fiction writer. After spending nine years in Europe during the 1930s he returned to South Africa and published his best works, *Cold Stone Jug*, a novel based on his prison experience, and

Mafeking Road, a collection of short stories which includes "Unto Dust."

ROBERT BOURDEAU (1931-   )

The cover image and three of the four photographs in this volume are by Robert Bourdeau who was born in Kingston, Ontario and currently lives in Ottawa. (The photograph in Unit 1 is of Robert Bourdeau by Mary Bourdeau.) The Winnipeg Art Gallery has recently launched a retrospective of his work which will travel throughout Canada and the United States for two years (1988-90). He has exhibited widely in Canada and abroad and his work can be found in a number of public, museum and corporate collections. He was a student of Minor White and worked as an architectural technologist until the mid 1980's when he was able to retire and devote himself full-time to his art. His work is exhibited frequently at the Jane Corkin Gallery, Toronto.

RAY BRADBURY (1920-   )

Ray Bradbury, born in Waukegan, Illinois, is one of the most popular science fiction and fantasy writers in the English language. His work, while highly entertaining, also illustrates a serious campaign in literary form against those who attempt to control freedom of thought and expression. Many of his novels and short stories have been adapted to television and cinema. Some of his most popular works are *The Martian Chronicles* (1950), *Fahrenheit 451* (1953), *Switch on the Night* (1955), *A Medicine for Melancholy* (1959), and *Something Wicked This Way Comes* (1962).

ELIZABETH BREWSTER (1922-   )

Elizabeth Brewster, who was born in Chipman, New Brunswick, began writing poetry as a child. Many of her early poems reflect her rural childhood in an intensely personal yet remarkably objective way. She graduated with first-class honours in English and Greek from U.N.B, then continued her education at Radcliffe College, King's College, London, the University of Toronto, and Indiana University. She worked as a librarian for many years before joining the English Department at the University of Saskatchewan in 1972. Although Brewster has published two novels and two short story collections, she is best known for her nine volumes of poetry, including *Passage of Summer* (1969), *Sunrise North* (1972), and *The Way Home* (1982).

ELIZABETH BARRETT BROWNING (1806-1861)

Elizabeth Barrett published her first verse when she was fourteen and continued to write with spirit and curiosity even after she suffered a spinal injury while horseback riding. Her health declined, and she lived as an invalid under her father's stern control. By the year 1845, when Robert Browning introduced himself to her, Elizabeth Barrett was an established poet. During their secret courtship, Elizabeth wrote *Sonnets from the Portuguese*, a sequence of forty-four sonnets in which she proclaimed her love for Browning. She presented the sonnets to her husband three years after they were married. She is chiefly remembered for these sonnets, which are some of the most beautiful love poems in the English language.

ROBERT BROWNING (1812-1889)

Robert Browning, a bank clerk's son, was born in the London suburb of Camberwell and was largely self-educated, having read widely in his father's well-stocked library. Browning's attempts at achieving fame through playwriting failed, but his early practice in dramatic form served him well in his later poetic dramatic monologues, for which he is justly famous. His masterpiece, *The Ring and the Book* (1868-69), is a long poem in which he tells through dramatic monologues the story of a Roman murder as seen through the eyes of the participants. Browning's celebrated romance with Elizabeth Barrett began when he introduced himself to her after receiving a favourable mention in a volume of her poetry. Elizabeth, an invalid living in seclusion under the care of her father, eloped to Italy with Robert Browning after a secret courtship. The couple spent most of their time there until Elizabeth's death in 1861.

PEARL S. BUCK (1892-1973)

The daughter of American missionaries, Pearl S. Buck grew up in China and worked throughout her life to encourage better understanding between the United States and China. After spending time in the United States to complete her university education and teach psychology in Virginia, she returned to China to teach English in Nanjing from 1921-31. Her writings include *The Spirit and the Flesh*, a biography of her parents, as well as *The House of Earth*, her trilogy about peasant life in China. *The Good Earth*, the first book of the trilogy, was awarded the Pulitzer Prize in 1931. In addition to writing novels, stories, and essays, she also wrote children's stories and two autobiographical narratives, *My Several Worlds* (1954) and *A Bridge for Passing* (1962). In 1938, Pearl S. Buck became the first woman from the United States to receive the Nobel Prize for literature.

HORTENSE CALISHER (1911-   )

A highly regarded American writer of novels and short stories, Hortense Calisher has published more than a dozen volumes of fiction. Her work also appears in numerous anthologies, including *50 Best American Short Stories, 1915-1965*, *Great American Short Stories*, and *Mid-Century: An Anthology of Distinguished American Short Stories*. Her fiction is particularly noteworthy for the psychological insight with which she explores the lives and interactions of her characters. Among the various literary awards she has received are four O. Henry prizes for short stories. In addition to her fiction she has also published an autobiographical memoir, *Herself* (1972).

JUNE CALLWOOD (1924-   )

Born in Chatham, Ontario, June Callwood began her career as a reporter for the Brantford *Expositor* and the Toronto *Globe and Mail*. During the 1950s she gained prominence for her articles in various magazines, particularly *Maclean's*. She has worked tirelessly for a number of social causes, such as homeless youth, women's rights, rehabilitation of drug addicts, Amnesty International, and freedom from censorship. She has received many honours for this work, including the Order of Canada in 1978. Among her numerous books are *Love, Hate, Fear, and Anger* (1964), *The Law is Not for Women* (1976), and *Portrait of Canada* (1981).

ROCH CARRIER (1937-   )

Roch Carrier's fiction is rooted in his childhood and adolescent experiences in Sainte-Justine-de-

Dorchester, the small Québec village where he was born. After leaving his village, Carrier was educated at the Université de Montréal and at the Sorbonne in Paris, where he earned a doctoral degree in literature. He became the resident dramatist for the Théâtre du Nouveau Monde in Montréal, for which he has written stage adaptations of his novels. These novels, which take a satirical view of English-French relations, have been translated into English, and Carrier has become one of the most widely read Québecois authors in English Canada as well as in Québec. *La guerre, yes sir!* (1968, trans. 1970) is probably his most popular novel; it depicts the pressures put upon individuals and upon village life at the start of World War II.

He is a successful lecturer in both English and French. Twenty of his short stories, or contes, are collected in his book *Les enfants du bonhomme dans la lune*, which is published in English as *The Hockey Sweater and Other Stories* (1979). These contes are shorter than most short stories in English, and remind an English reader of comic anecdotes or parables. They deal with the coming-of-age experiences of the narrator, who may be a persona for Carrier himself, in rural Québec.

LEONARD COHEN (1934-   )

Leonard Cohen, who became internationally known during the 1960s as a songwriter and performer, has also gained prominence as a poet and novelist. His first book of poetry, *Let Us Compare Mythologies* (1956), contains for the most part poems which were written between the ages of fifteen and twenty. Cohen is often thought of as a romantic poet because of the captivating love lyrics in his most popular book of poetry, *The Spice Box of Earth* (1961). However, he has a darker, more despairing vision as well, which is revealed in the poetry of *Flowers for Hitler* (1964) and the novels *The Favourite Game* (1963) and *Beautiful Losers* (1966). In 1968 he won a Governor General's Award but declined it. Cohen's novels, poems, and songs often weave together elements as diverse as religion, sex, death, beauty, and power through a sensuous use of language. His poetic tones range from sweet and lyrical to black and brooding, and in his fiction he frequently reveals a wild, outrageous sense of humour. His work has been widely translated, making him one of Canada's best-known writers outside of this country.

PETER COWAN (1914-   )

Peter Cowan was born in Perth, Western Australia and educated at the University of Western Australia, where he has taught English since 1964. Prior to his teaching career at the university level, he was a clerk, farm labourer, casual worker, and teacher. His keen interest in nature, wildlife conservation, and environmental issues are reflected in various literary works, including the short story, "The Tractor." Among his publications are three volumes of short stories, *Drift* (1944), *The Unploughed Land* (1958), and *The Empty Street* (1965), and two novels, *Summer* (1964), and *Seed* (1966). He has also edited and contributed to a number of anthologies of Australian literature.

STEPHEN CRANE (1871-1900)

A writer most famous for introducing realism into American fiction, Stephen Crane started writing stories at the age of eight. He wrote *The Red Badge of Courage* (1895), often considered the world's greatest war novel, without ever having experienced war. As a free-lance journalist and fiction writer, however, he sought to follow his romantic craving to experience all life's sensations. Having spent his early life in New Jersey, as the fourteenth child of a Methodist minister, he sought experience in New York, in the American prairies and southwest, and as a war correspondent in combat areas in Mexico, Greece, and Cuba. En route to Cuba in 1896, he was involved in a shipwreck, and with several other passengers spent four days drifting in an open boat before being rescued. This experience provided the material for one of his greatest short stories, "The Open Boat," but permanently impaired his health. He died four years later at the age of 29. While known primarily as a fiction writer, Crane wrote several volumes of poetry, *The Black Rider and Other Lines* (1895) and *War is Kind* (1899). His poems are generally short, epigrammatic and characterized by startling images. They frequently achieve their impact through symbolism or irony.

ROBERTSON DAVIES (1913-   )

Robertson Davies was born in southwestern Ontario and educated at Upper Canada College, Queen's University, and Oxford. He participated in stage productions as a child and developed a lifelong interest in drama. His thesis at Oxford,

Shakespeare's Boy Actors, was published in 1939. He worked for two seasons with the Old Vic Repertory Company in London, and he played a major role in launching the Canadian Stratford Festival during the 1950s. He was literary editor of *Saturday Night* (1940-42), editor and publisher of the Peterborough *Examiner* (1942-65), and a teacher of literature at the University of Toronto (1960-1981). Davies, a very prolific and versatile author, has been acclaimed as an essayist, dramatist, and novelist. He is well-known as the creator of the entertaining and crusty Samuel Marchbanks, whose observations of life fill three volumes of humorous essays. Among the most widely-acclaimed of his numerous novels are *Leaven of Malice* (1954), which won the Stephen Leacock Medal for Humour; *Fifth Business* (1970); and *The Manticore* (1972), which won the Governor General's Award for fiction.

BARRY DICKIE (1949-   )

Barry Dickie was born in Halifax, attended the University of Toronto, and now lives in Toronto. He has travelled in South America, and between "frequent intervals of happy unemployment" has held a variety of occupations, such as a free-lance writer, government worker, and labourer in dozens of different jobs. He draws on this varied employment background as content for the essay included in this anthology, "The Only Lesson I Still Remember," which appeared in the Toronto *Globe and Mail* in 1980.

JOHN DONNE (1572-1631)

One of the greatest English poets and preachers of the seventeenth century, and a descendent of Sir Thomas More, Donne was born a Roman Catholic but converted to Anglicanism in his twenties. After years of struggling to support himself and his family, he became an Anglican priest in 1615. Because of his power as a preacher and the influence of King James I, he rose to the position of Dean of St. Paul's Cathedral in 1621, a position he held until his death. Although Donne published only four poems during his lifetime, he wrote many poems on a wide range of subjects and greatly influenced a number of his contemporary poets. The poems in *Satires and Elegies*, written early in his career, blend classical forms with modern subjects. In *Songs and Sonnets*, perhaps his best-known group of poems, he wrote both tenderly and cynically about love and death. In later life,

he turned to writing religious poetry and produced a superb series of *Holy Sonnets*, which includes "Death Be Not Proud" and "Batter My Heart, Three Personed God."

DEBORAH EIBEL (1940-   )

Deborah Eibel was born in Montréal and educated at McGill University and Radcliffe College in Cambridge, Massachusetts. Her poetry has been published in numerous journals in Canada and the United States. A volume of her poetry entitled *Kayak Sickness* (1972) has been published by Sono Nis Press. She has received several Canada Council Arts Bursaries, and in 1965 she was awarded the Davison Ficke Sonnet Prize of the Poetry Society of America.

MARI EVANS (1923-   )

Mari Evans was born in Toledo, Ohio, attended the University of Toledo, and taught at Indiana University and Purdue University. She was also producer, director, and writer for the television program "The Black Experience," 1968-73. She has written a number of books for juveniles and several volumes of poetry, including *Where Is All the Music?* (1968), *I Am a Black Woman* (1970), and *Night Star* (1981). Her poetry is represented in more than 200 anthologies and textbooks. It has also been choreographed and used on record albums, filmstrips, television specials, and in two off-Broadway productions.

E.M. FORSTER (1879-1970)

British novelist, essayist, and literary critic, Edward Morgan Forster was born in London and educated at Cambridge. On leaving Cambridge, he decided to devote his life to writing. He gained considerable critical acclaim for his novels *A Room with a View* (1908) and *Howards End* (1910), but *A Passage to India* (1924) is generally regarded as his masterpiece. This novel set in India, which Forster had visited in 1912-13 and again in 1921, deals with the difficulties of communication between people brought up in different cultures. After the success of *A Passage to India*, Forster was asked to deliver the Clark Lectures at Cambridge, which formed the basis for his most widely known critical work *Aspects of the Novel* (1927).

ROBERT FROST (1874-1963)

Robert Frost lived most of his life in New England and is considered to be a poet of that region of the United States. He attended both Dartmouth College and Harvard University, but did not graduate from either. After working at various times as a teacher, newspaper editor, shoemaker, and farmer, he moved in 1912 with his wife and four children to England because he was unhappy with his inability to gain recognition as a poet in his native land. In 1915, after publishing two books of his verse in England, he returned to New England as a famous poet. From that time on, Frost continued to publish his poetry and to divide his time between teaching in colleges and universities and farming in Vermont. His close association with the natural world of the farmer is revealed in his poetry. Robert Frost was awarded the Pulitzer Prize for poetry four times, in 1924, 1931, 1937, and 1943.

JOHN GALSWORTHY (1867-1933)

Known primarily as a novelist and playwright, John Galsworthy was born in Devonshire, England, and educated at Harrow and New College, Oxford. His series of novels, collectively titled *The Forsyte Saga*, detail the extreme possessiveness of the Forsyte family over the later Victorian period. Galsworthy depicted this society as having lost its purpose, principles, and faith after World War I. He felt that his purpose as a novelist was to guide people by showing impartially both the good and the evil in life.

HUGH GARNER (1913-1979)

Hugh Garner was born in Yorkshire, England, but his family emigrated to Canada when he was six. Soon after, his father abandoned the family, and Garner grew up in the poor neighbourhoods of Toronto, which later became the setting for much of his work, including his best-known novel *Cabbagetown* (1968). He rode the rails during the Depression and fought in the Spanish Civil War and World War II. He was a prolific writer who produced seventeen books, a hundred short stories, and hundreds of articles and radio and television scripts. He is most well-known for his realistic fiction focusing on the lives of working class people. In 1963 he won the Governor General's Award for *Hugh Garner's Best Short Stories*.

WILLARD GAYLIN (1925-   )

A native of Cleveland, Ohio, Dr. Willard Gaylin is a noted clinical psychiatrist who has taught at Columbia University and served as president of the Institute of Society, Ethics, and the Life Sciences. He has published widely on psychiatry, mental health, ethical issues in biology and medicine, penal reform, amnesty, and bias in the justice system. In the essay contained in this anthology, "What You See is the Real You," Dr. Gaylin comments from a psychiatrist's perspective on the self, ethics, and the limitations of mental science.

CHIEF DAN GEORGE (1899-1981)

Chief Dan George, whose Indian name was Teswahno, gained international recognition as an actor, public speaker and author. At the age many people retire, he began his career as an actor. He had already been a longshoreman, logger, musician, and Chief of the Squamish Band of Burrard Inlet, B.C. before being "discovered" at the age of 60 and subsequently becoming a television and movie actor. As well as playing a number of roles in CBC productions such as "Cariboo Country" and "The Ecstasy of Rita Joe," he appeared in at least eight feature films including *Smith* (1969), *Little Big Man* (1970), *Harry and Tonto* (1974) and *The Outlaw Josey Wales* (1975). Although he never became a political activist, he only accepted roles in which he could portray a positive image of his people. In his writing and public addresses, he strove to develop mutual respect and understanding among peoples. Two of his most widely read works are the prose-poems *My Heart Soars* (1974) and *My Spirit Soars* (1982).

KAHLIL GIBRAN (1883-1931)

The Lebanese poet Kahlil Gibran published thirteen books of poetry and prose-poems from *The Madman* in 1918 to *A Tear and a Smile* in 1950. His reputation as a poet of a spiritual and philosophical nature rests primarily upon his most famous and best-selling work, *The Prophet*, which was published in 1923. Gibran also drew illustrations for his works.

GARY GILDNER (1938-   )

Gary Gildner was born in Michigan and is best-known for his poetry, but he has also written novels and short stories and has edited poetry anthologies. He has held the positions of professor and writer-in-residence at several universities in the United States. His works include *First Practice* (1969), *Digging for*

Indians (1971), *Nails* (1975), *Letters from Vicksburg* (1976), *The Crush* (1983), and *Blue Like the Heavens: New and Selected Poems* (1984), as well as *Out of This World: Poems from the Hawkeye State* (1975), which he edited with his wife Judith.

MARY GILMORE (1864-1962)

In addition to being one of Australia's most acclaimed poets, Mary Gilmore was, at various times in her long, eventful life, a teacher, the wife of a sheep-shearer, editor of the labour-oriented Sydney *Worker*, a social activist, an encourager of other writers, and a collector of Australian pioneer lore and legend. Between 1920 and 1940 she published six volumes of poetry and three volumes of prose. In 1937, in recognition of her achievements as a writer she received the title Dame of the British Empire. Throughout her life she constantly worked to improve the welfare of the young and old, sick and helpless, depressed and underprivileged, and spoke out forcefully against privilege and corruption. Her best poetry enshrines the values of love, courage, and selflessness.

LOIS GOULD (1938-   )

A former police reporter and executive editor of *Ladies' Home Journal*, Lois Gould is now primarily a novelist and a columnist for *The New York Times*. Gould has been associated with the feminist movement from time to time, and her novels have served to popularize various facets of feminism. In her collection of essays, *Not Responsible for Personal Articles* (1978), Gould examines various issues including pornography, liberation of the family, and the loss of traditional courtesies to liberated women. Her novels include *Such Good Friends* (1970), *Necessary Objects* (1972), *Final Analysis* (1974), and *Sea Change* (1977).

GRAHAM GREENE (1904-1991)

A major twentieth-century British writer, Graham Greene was born in Berkhamsted, Hertfordshire, and educated at Oxford. A prolific author, Greene wrote twenty-one novels, seven short story collections, ten plays, a collection of poems, and seventeen other volumes including essays, literary criticism, journals, and juvenile fiction. Among his most famous novels are *Brighton Rock* (1938), *The Heart of the Matter* (1948), and *The Power and the Glory* (1940).

Greene was a superb story-teller who spent a number of years as a film critic and screen-writer. In his novels he used cinematic techniques, such as cutting from image to image, in order to achieve pace, contrast, and immediate impact on the reader. In his later years, Greene more frequently turned to comedy, with works such as *Our Man in Havana* (1958), *May We Borrow Your Husband?* (1967), and *Travels with My Aunt* (1969).

THOM GUNN (1929-   )

Thom Gunn was born in England and earned a B.A. at Cambridge University. He served two years in the British Army and has travelled and lived in Paris, Rome, Berlin, and Texas. He studied at Stanford University in California during the 1950s and taught at the University of California at Berkeley from 1958-1966. Since 1966, he has been a free-lance writer. He once commented, "I live by various jobs, sometimes teaching for a term, sometimes doing other things, none regular." He currently resides near San Francisco. In his poetry, through dramatic flourishes with powerful images and rhythms Gunn stresses his existential themes concerning the power of the will and experiments with harsh and rigorous rhetoric. Some critics have claimed that he worships action (often violent) as opposed to sensibility, but in his poetry Gunn is also capable of expressing intellectual subtlety, complexity, and tenderness without sentimentality.

PETER GZOWSKI (1934-   )

Peter Gzowski is best known to Canadians as host of a number of radio and television shows including *This Country in the Morning*, *90 Minutes Live*, and *Morningside*. As an interviewer, he is personable, good-natured and remarkably effective at drawing out his subjects and making them feel at ease. He has received two ACTRA Awards for radio broadcasting and three National Magazine Awards for print journalism. Gzowski's extensive experience as a journalist includes serving as an editor of *Maclean's* and the *Star Weekly*. His published works, covering a wide range of subjects, include *Peter Gzowski's Book About This Country in the Morning* (1974), *Spring Tonic* (1979), *The Sacrament* (1980), and *The Game of Our Lives* (1981). As part of his research for *The Game of Our Lives*, a story about hockey and what it means in the lives of Canadians, Gzowski spent the 1980-81 season travelling around the NHL with the Edmonton Oilers.

ALEX HALEY (1921-   )

The writer Alex Haley was born in Ithaca, New York, and raised primarily in Henning, Tennessee. In 1939 he joined the U.S. Coast Guard, and while in the service, he taught himself to write. After retiring from the Coast Guard in 1959, Haley turned to writing full time. His first major work was a collaboration on *The Autobiography of Malcolm X* (1965), about the life of the Black Muslim leader. In the mid-1960s, he initiated a study of his family background, beginning with stories his grandmother had told him, a family folklore of traditions passed from each generation to the next. After ten years of research, he published *Roots* (1976), detailing seven generations of his family from their African roots to their enslavement in the United States, and finally to their freedom in that country. In 1977, Haley was awarded a special Pulitzer Prize for his work.

THOMAS HARDY (1840-1928)

Born in Dorset, England, Thomas Hardy was educated by his mother and the local schoolteacher, and, with much home study, he mastered both Latin and Greek. When he settled in London as the apprentice to an ecclesiastical architect, he became caught up in the intellectual excitement of the age and turned to writing poetry. His poems did not sell, so Hardy began to write fiction and was quickly successful. It was thirty years before he returned to verse; still, his *Collected Poems* (1930) contains more than eight hundred pieces. Although his writing continued into the twentieth century, his poems retain the regularity of form of nineteenth-century poetry.

ROBERT E. HAYDEN (1913-1980)

Robert E. Hayden was born in Detroit, Michigan and educated at Wayne State University and the University of Michigan. While a professor of English at Fisk University, in Nashville, Tennessee, and at the University of Michigan, Hayden was very active as a poet and editor. Through editing books such as *Kaleidoscope: Poems by American Negro Poets* and *Afro-American Literature: An Introduction* he was influential in bringing to public awareness the

work of other black American writers. Among his volumes of poetry are *Heart Shape in the Dust* (1940), *Figure of Time* (1955), *A Ballad of Remembrance* (1962), *Selected Poems* (1966), and *Words in the Mourning Time* (1973).

WILLIAM ERNEST HENLEY (1849-1903)

Henley, a British poet, is as well-known for his courageous spirit as he is for his poetry. He spent most of his life fighting a crippling disease, tubercular arthritis. He had one leg amputated in 1867, but refused his doctor's advice to have his other leg amputated in 1873. Instead he put himself under the care of Joseph Lister, who was gaining recognition for the development of antiseptic surgery. Lister saved Henley's leg, but the poet spent twenty pain-filled months in hospital undergoing treatment. "Invictus," which was written towards the end of Henley's stay in hospital, expresses both the invalid's triumph over his physical handicap and his exultation in his spiritual independence as he jubilantly prepares to leave the hospital and enter the wonderful world outside.

JANETTE TURNER HOSPITAL (1942-   )

Janette Turner Hospital was born in Melbourne, Australia, and has lived for extended periods of time in Australia, the United States, Canada, England, and India. She was a high-school teacher of English in Brisbane, Australia from 1963-66 and a librarian at Harvard University in Cambridge, Massachusetts from 1967-71. She did graduate work at Queen's University in Kingston and taught English in several Canadian institutions from 1973-82, including Queen's. She once commented, "I am very conscious of being at ease in many countries but belonging nowhere. All my writing reflects this. My characters are always caught between worlds or between cultures or between subcultures." She won the First Novel Award from Seal Books in 1982 for *The Ivory Swing* and the following year published *The Tiger in the Tiger Pit*.

LANGSTON HUGHES (1902-1967)

A black American, (James) Langston Hughes often used black folk or jazz rhythms in his poetry, which frequently depicts the life of the urban American black in an objective and sardonic manner. In addition to writing poetry, plays, novels, short stories, song lyrics, and juvenile books, he also wrote translations of various works and *Fight for Freedom* (1962), an account of the National Association for the Advancement of Colored People. He was also a successful lecturer and editor. As a young man, Hughes served as a seaman on voyages to Africa and Europe and lived in Mexico, France, Italy, Spain, and the Soviet Union. He was first recognized as an important literary figure in the 1920s, a period called the "Harlem Renaissance" because of the many fine black writers who were living and writing in New York's Harlem ghetto. Though his early work gained critical praise, Hughes was criticized by many black intellectuals for portraying an unattractive view of black life. They felt that black writers should only depict their "better" selves when writing for an audience that included white readers. Hughes wrote about that controversy, ". . . I felt that the masses of our people had as much in their lives to put into books as did those more fortunate ones who had been born with some means and the ability to work up to a master's degree at a Northern college. Anyway, I didn't know the upper-class Negroes well enough to write much about them. I knew only the people I had grown up with, and they weren't people whose shoes were always shined, who had been to Harvard, or who had heard of Bach. But they seemed to me good people, too."

BASIL JOHNSTON (1929-   )

Basil Johnston is a teacher of Ojibwa (Anishinanbae) language, history, and mythology, who currently works in the Department of Ethnology at the Royal Ontario Museum in Toronto. Educated in reserve schools in Ontario (an experience recalled in *Indian School Days*, 1988) and at Loyola College in Montréal, he has published a collection of humorous stories about reserve life entitled *Moose Meat and Wild Rice* (1978, reprinted 1988). Among his other works are *Ojibway Heritage* and *Ojibway Ceremonies* (both reprinted in 1988), and an Ojibway language lexicon and course outline published by the Department of Indian and Northern Affairs. The short story "Cowboys and Indians," included in this anthology, is based on a story told to him by Benjamin Pease.

GARRISON KEILLOR (1942-   )

Garrison Keillor, who calls himself "America's

tallest radio humourist," has gained fame as the host of Minnesota Public Radio's weekly show "A Prairie Home Companion." In his monologues he frequently spins humorous and poignant stories from life's most ordinary events, as he brings his listeners up-to-date on the happenings of the residents of his fictional hometown, Lake Wobegone, Minnesota. Many of the selections in his two popular volumes of stories *Lake Wobegon Days* (1985) and *Happy to be Here* (1983) had their origins in his radio show and were first published in *The New Yorker* and *The Atlantic Monthly*.

NAGASE KIYOKO (1906-   )

Nagase Kiyoko was born in Okayama Prefecture. She began to write and publish poetry when she was eighteen, and published her first collection of poetry when she was twenty-four. Many of her poems deal with the complexities of family relationships. In 1927 she married and went to live in Osaka, then moved to Tokyo in 1931. In 1945 she fled devastated Tokyo to return to her home province of Okayama, where she worked in agriculture and continued to produce many volumes of poetry. She has also published a collection of essays describing the difficulties of being a woman poet in pre-war Japan, entitled (in translation) *A Woman Poet's Notebook*, (1952).

JOY KOGAWA (1935-   )

Joy Kogawa and her family were among the thousands of Japanese Canadians forcibly moved from the West Coast to the interior of British Columbia or the prairies during World War II. She grew up in Coaldale, Alberta, and attended the University of Calgary. She also spent a year studying music at the Toronto Conservatory of Music, and has worked as a correspondent in Prime Minister Trudeau's office. The experience of the evacuation is the subject of her novel *Obasan* (1981) and several of her most frequently anthologized poems. Her poetry collections, *The Splintered Moon* (1968), *A Choice of Dreams* (1974), and *Jericho Road* (1978), contain a number of poems which reflect her Japanese heritage. Her poetry is characterized by sensitivity, controlled emotion, and careful craftsmanship.

HENRY KREISEL (1922-1991)

Kreisel was born in Vienna, Austria, emigrated

to England with his family in 1938 when the Nazi movement threatened his homeland, and was among the thirty thousand refugees interned as "enemy aliens" in 1940. He was one of the two thousand refugees sent to Canada. After arriving in Canada he completed his education at the University of Toronto and became a Canadian citizen. From 1947 he taught at the University of Alberta, including terms as head of the English department, associate and acting dean of graduate studies, and academic vice-president. Both of Kreisel's novels, *The Rich Man* (1948) and *The Betrayal* (1964), explore the experience of immigrants to Canada who have left, but have difficulty extricating themselves from, the turbulence of Europe. "The Broken Globe," one of Kreisel's best-known short stories, was published in his short story collection, *The Almost Meeting* (1981).

PATRICK LANE (1939-   )

Born in Nelson, British Columbia, Patrick Lane has worked at a variety of jobs, including construction, logging, mining, and farm labour, and has travelled extensively through North and South America. Both his work experience and his travels figure prominently in his poems, which are frequently about incidents in the lives of poor or working class people in western Canada or Latin America. His poems frequently combine a narrative or anecdotal element with a violently beautiful lyricism. Among his numerous volumes of poetry are *Beware the Months of Fire* (1974); *Albino Pheasants* (1977); *Poems: New and Selected* (1978), for which he received a Governor General's Award; *The Measure* (1980); and *Old Mother* (1982). He has taught creative writing or been writer-in-residence at the Universities of Notre Dame at Nelson, Manitoba, Ottawa, and Alberta. He now lives in Regina.

MARGARET LAURENCE (1926-1987)

Margaret Laurence was born in Neepawa, Manitoba, a town she made famous as the fictional setting "Manawaka." Having decided to become a writer as a child, she contributed to school and college magazines, but began writing in earnest while living in Africa from 1950 to 1957. As a result of her African experiences she wrote *The Tomorrow-Tamer* (1963, short stories), *This Side Jordan* (1960, her first novel), and *The Prophet's Camel Bell* (1963, a memoir of her life in Somaliland). Returning to Canada,

she began work on her "Manawaka" novels, which include *The Stone Angel* (1961); *A Jest of God* (1966), which won a Governor General's Award and was made into the feature film *Rachel, Rachel*; *The Fire-Dwellers* (1969); and *The Diviners* (1974), which also won a Governor General's Award. *A Bird in the House* (1970), a collection of linked short stories, is also set in Manawaka. In addition to her adult fiction, Margaret Laurence has written a number of children's books, the most well-known of which, *The Olden Days Coat* (1979, revised in 1982), was made into an award-winning television drama. Some of her best essays have been collected and published as *Heart of a Stranger* (1976). An inspiration to many of her fellow writers, Laurence was made a Companion of the Order of Canada in 1971 for her outstanding contributions to Canadian literature.

GARY LAUTENS (1928-   )

Gary Lautens is a humourist and journalist whose columns have appeared for many years in the *Star Weekly* and the *Toronto Star*. At the time his first child was born, in 1959, Lautens was a sports columnist, but like Lynn Johnson, the cartoonist whose illustrations appear in his books, he soon found that his growing family was a rich source of material for humorous articles. A recipient of the Stephen Leacock Award for Humour, Lautens has published two books based on his newspaper columns, *Take My Family . . . Please!* (1980) and *No Sex Please—We're Married* (1963).

MARY LAVIN (1912-   )

Born in Massachusetts, Mary Lavin has lived in Ireland since she was a child. She studied at the National University in Dublin and wrote her first short story while working on a doctoral thesis about Virginia Woolf. After being left a widow, she took care of three children and a farm. Discussing short fiction in the Preface to her *Selected Stories* (1981), Lavin wrote, ". . . the short story, shape as well as matter, is determined by the writer's own character. Both are one. Short-story writing—for me—is only looking closer than normal into the human heart. . . ."

DORIS LESSING (1919-   )

The daughter of a British Army captain, Doris Lessing was born in Iran while her father was stationed there; in 1924, the family moved to a farm in Rhodesia (now Zimbabwe), where she remained until she settled in England in 1949. She is well-known for her novels and short stories, which are primarily concerned with people involved in the political and social upheavals of the twentieth century. Her first published book, *The Grass Is Singing* (1950), is about a white farmer, his wife, and their African servant in Rhodesia. *Children of Violence* (1964-65) is a two-volume novel about Martha Quest, who, like Lessing, grows up in southern Africa and settles in England. Lessing has also written science fiction.

SAM LEVENSON (1911-1980)

A humourist, Sam Levenson is better known as a television and nightclub entertainer than as a writer, although he wrote several books, including *In One Era and Out the Other* (1973). He frequently used his experiences of growing up in a large Jewish immigrant family and teaching high school in Brooklyn, New York, as content for the homespun humour of his writing and monologues. During the 1950s he hosted "The Sam Levenson Show" on television.

SANDFORD LYNE (1945-)

Born in Kendalville, Indiana, Lyne moved with his family soon after to Ocala, Florida, and then to Paducah, Kentucky. He received a B.A. in English literature from Oberlin College and a Master's in Fine Arts in Creative Writing from the University of Iowa. His work experience includes being a rehabilitation counselor in an alcoholism clinic in Charlottesville, Virginia.

SID MARTY (1944-)

Sid Marty was born in England, raised in Medicine Hat, Alberta, and educated at Mount Royal College in Calgary and Sir George. Williams University in Montréal. He worked as a ranger in Yoho and Jasper National Parks from 1966 to 1973, and since then he has worked as a park warden in Banff National Park. His poetry collections, *Headwaters* (1973) and *Nobody Danced with Miss Rodeo* (1981), draw upon his experience in the mountains. In his poetry he explores the themes of loneliness, love, and death as part of the life cycle, contemplates the effects of civilization encroaching on nature, and reflects on the joys and challenges of raising a family in the wilderness. *Men for the Mountains* (1978) is an eloquent prose documentary about the work of the wardens in Canada's national parks.

FREDELLE BRUSER MAYNARD (1922-1989)

Fredelle Maynard was born in Saskatchewan and grew up in a number of prairie towns. *Raisins and Almonds* (1972), an account of her childhood experiences as part of the only Jewish family in a small prairie town, is set in Birch Hills, Saskatchewan, where her family moved when she was three and left when she was nine. Maynard attended the University of Manitoba and the University of Toronto, and received her doctorate from Radcliffe. She taught at Wellesley College in Massachusetts and the University of New Hampshire before returning to Canada to become a free-lance writer, addressing areas such as education, child care, current medical research, family and personal relationships, and cultural trends.

JOYCE MAYNARD (1953-)

Joyce Maynard's article "An Eighteen-Year-Old Looks Back at Life" appeared in the Sunday magazine of *The New York Times* when she was a freshman at Yale University. She was immediately acclaimed as a spokesperson for her age group, which she had described as a "generation of unfulfilled expectations." The article was later expanded and published in book form as *Looking Back: A Chronicle of Growing Old in the Sixties* (1973). She is also the author of a novel, *Baby Love* (1981), which deals with the impact of parenthood on teenage mothers. Joyce Maynard is the daughter of Fredelle Bruser Maynard.

PHYLLIS MCGINLEY (1905-1978)

Phyllis McGinley was born in Oregon. She is well-known for her light verse and essays on modern suburban life, as well as for her children's books. She taught school in Utah and New York and later worked for an advertising agency. She also worked as a staff writer for *Town and Country* magazine. In 1961, she won the Pulitzer Prize for *Times Three: Selected Verse from Three Decades*, and her work has received numerous other awards.

WILLIAM ORMOND (W.O.) MITCHELL, (1914-)

W.O. Mitchell was born in Weyburn, Saskatchewan and has spent most of his life in the prairies, which provide the fictional setting for much of him best work. His novel *Who Has Seen the Wind*, which won him instant acclaim when it was published in 1947, is a sensitive portrayal of a boy growing up on the prairies and his attempts to understand the mysteries of life. Rural Saskatchewan is also the setting for the popular *Jake and the Kid* series which originated as short stories written for *Maclean's* and developed into a series of radio plays that ran weekly on CBC radio from 1950 to 1956. Mitchell's skill in creating colourful characters, using local dialect, and telling interesting stories made this series immensely popular. Among Mitchell's more recent novels are *The Vanishing Point* (1973), *How I Spent My Summer Holidays* (1981), and *Since Daisy Creek* (1984). Mitchell is known both as a novelist and a dramatist. An early novel, *The Kite*, was re-written as a full-length play, as were two early radio dramas, *The Devil's Instrument* and *The Black Bonspiel of Wullie MacCrimmon*. *Who Has Seen the Wind* has been produced as a feature film.

FARLEY MOWAT (1921-   )

One of Canada's most widely-read authors (his works have been translated into 23 languages and published in over 40 countries), Farley Mowat has been tremendously influential in attracting worldwide attention to the causes he has championed. His controversial first book, *People of the Deer* (1951), is a denunciation of Canada's treatment of the Inuit. *A Whale for the Killing* (1972), *Never Cry Wolf* (1963), and *Sea of Slaughter* (1984) are all concerned with humanity's need to learn to live in harmony with the other creatures on the planet. Through his work, he has raised public consciousness about the hazards of upsetting natural ecosystems by modern technology. He has also dispelled many misunderstandings about the people and animals of northern Canada and about survival in hostile environments. While Mowat is renowned as a superb storyteller, his books are basically non-fictional and often autobiographical. *The Dog Who Wouldn't Be* (1957) and *Owls in the Family* (1961) are recollections of his childhood in Saskatoon; *The Regiment* (1955) and *And No Birds Sang* (1979) are accounts of his World War II experiences; and *A Whale for the Killing*, *Sea of Slaughter*, and *The Boat Who Wouldn't Float* (1969) are based on his experiences during the eight years he lived in Burgeo, Newfoundland.

ALICE MUNRO (1931-   )

Although she has set some of her stories in British Columbia, Toronto, and other parts of Ontario, Alice Munro is most closely identified with rural southwestern Ontario, where she was born. She evokes the sense of small towns that resemble her birthplace of Wingham by incorporating remembered details that are, in her words, "not real but true." After leaving university to marry in 1951, Munro moved to Vancouver and then to Victoria to run a bookstore with her husband. While helping with the store and raising three daughters, Munro wrote short stories for magazines and the CBC program "Anthology." Her first published collection of stories, *Dance of the Happy Shades* (1968), was awarded the Governor General's Award. Her novel, *Lives of Girls and Women* (1971), received the Canadian Booksellers Award, and *Who Do You Think You Are?* (1978) and *The Progress of Love* (1986) also received Governor General's Awards. In her stories, Munro deals with the depth and complexity of emotional life. Her central characters, whether children or adults, are usually intelligent, very sensitive, and troubled. Her protagonists are often girls who feel that they are special or different from other people; often they aspire to be artists. These protagonists respond to the social pressures and expectations of others, especially their mothers. They know that they are "different," yet they desperately want to avoid mockery and humiliation, a desire that carries over to Munro's adult protagonists as well.

R.K. NARAYAN (1906-   )

Rasipuram Krishnaswami Narayan, who was born in Madras, India, is perhaps the best-known twentieth century East Indian writer. His books have met with favourable response from both readers and literary critics, and have been translated into all European languages. Narayan's novels and short stories are about his native land and its people. They are generally set in the fictional community of Malgudi, which is modelled after Mysore, the village where Narayan grew up. He presents his characters sympathetically and realistically, and is able to see the comic aspects of even the most serious situations. Among his popular short story collections are *An Astrologer's Day and Other Stories* (1947), *Gods, Demons and Others* (1965), and *A Horse and Two Goats and Other Stories* (1970).

ÉMILE NELLIGAN (1879-1941)

Émile Nelligan lived his entire life in Montréal and his poems are often regarded as the beginning of modern literature in French Canada. His almost legendary status in Québec literature and his reputation as a brilliant poet are based on poems that were all written between his sixteenth and his twentieth birthdays. Although he did not like school, he read widely and was deeply influenced by French poets such as Baudelaire and Verlaine. In 1897 he was admitted to a literary club of young writers known as the École littéraire de Montréal under whose auspices he gave several highly acclaimed readings of his poetry. Although his work is very melodic, much of it expresses a feeling of deep melancholy. He spent the last forty-two years of his life in mental hospitals, after sinking into a deep depression in 1899 from which he was never to emerge.

JOHN FREDERICK NIMS (1913-   )

John Frederick Nims was born in Michigan and educated at Notre Dame University, where he earned a doctorate and taught English and creative writing from 1939 to 1961. He then moved to the University of Illinois to continue his teaching and writing careers. His poetry has been collected in several volumes, including *The Iron Pastoral* (1947), *A Fountain in Kentucky* (1950), and *Knowledge of the Evening* (1960). Nims was one of the leaders in the reaction against the "modernism" of the 1940s. He was a pioneer in the postwar years of a new, highly urbane style. His poetry belongs to a tradition of grace and elegance and has an ease of tone which is deceptively simple.

ALDEN NOWLAN (1933-1983)

Born in Windsor, Nova Scotia, Alden Nowlan was largely self-educated. He left school in grade five and held various manual jobs, such as cutting pulpwood and working for the Nova Scotia Department of Highways, before becoming a journalist and editor with several New Brunswick newspapers. In 1968 he became writer-in-residence at the University of New Brunswick. Nowlan has published many collections of poetry, one of which, *Bread, Wine, and Salt*, won the Governor General's Award in 1967. In his poetry he frequently uses conversational rhythms and the idioms of local speech. His poetry reveals a sensibility and

affection for ordinary people and is often concerned with the effects of spiritual and cultural deprivation on their lives.

ATUKWEI OKAI (1941-   )

Atukwei (John) Okai was born in Accra, Ghana. His eclectic education has included studies both in Moscow, where he lived from 1961 to 1967 and completed a Master of Arts degree at the Gorky Institute, and London, where he earned a Master of Philosophy degree. He was awarded a Society of Arts Fellowship in 1968 for his studies in London. He published *Flowerfall* in 1969 and subsequently returned to Ghana, where he lectured in Russian at the University and became president of the Ghana Association of Writers. He gives many public readings of his poetry.

MICHAEL ONDAATJE (1943-   )

Poet, filmmaker, editor, and novelist, Michael Ondaatje was born in Ceylon (now Sri Lanka), lived in England from the age of eleven until he was nineteen, and came to Canada in 1962. He attended Bishop's University, the University of Toronto, and Queen's University, and is now teaching at York University in Toronto. Ondaatje has gained a reputation as one of Canada's most innovative and interesting contemporary poets. His work is strongly visual and makes use of cinematic techniques, sometimes resulting in surreal effects from the juxtaposition of real and imaginary voices and events. *The Collected Works of Billy the Kid*, which combines factual and fictional accounts of the western outlaw, won the 1970 Governor General's Award and has since been adapted for the stage and produced at Stratford, Toronto, and New York. His collection of poems, *There's a Trick with a Knife I'm Learning to Do*, won him a second Governor General's Award in 1979.

P.K. PAGE (1916-   )

Patricia Kathleen Page was born in England and came to Canada at the age of two. Raised and educated in Calgary, she studied art in Brazil and New York, before moving to Montréal in 1941, where she began to write poetry. From 1953 to 1964, she and her husband, the ambassador W.A. Irwin, lived in Australia, Brazil, and Mexico. Her early poems were of social protest and alienation, but Page also writes of innocence and experience, illusion and disillusion, childhood, dreams, love, fantasy, and terror. Her finely crafted poems often reflect the visual intensity one might expect from a poet who is also an accomplished painter. She is the author of a dozen books, including *The Metal and the Flower*, which won the 1954 Governor General's Award for poetry. Two more recent volumes, both published in 1985, are *Deaf-Mute in the Pear Tree* and *The Glass Air: Selected Poems*.

RALPH POMEROY (1926-   )

Ralph Pomeroy was born in Illinois, but since 1947 he has resided for long periods in Europe. In his varied career, he has worked as a magazine editor, an art gallery director, a stage manager, and a bartender. He was a painter until 1949 and then resumed painting in 1960. He makes his permanent home in San Francisco, California. His published books of verse include *Stills and Movies* (1961) and *In the Financial District* (1968).

ERIKA RITTER (1948-   )

Playwright, CBC radio host, and writer, Erika Ritter was born in Regina and educated at McGill and the Drama Centre at the University of Toronto. She has written a number of plays, including *Automatic Pilot* (1980), *The Passing Scene* (premiered Jan. 1, 1982), *The Splits* (1978), and *Moving Pictures* (1976). She has won ACTRA Awards for Best Radio Drama Writer (1982) and Best Radio Host (1986). She is also the author of two collections of humorous essays, *Urban Scrawl* (1984) and *Ritter in Residence* (1987), and many fiction and non-fiction pieces published in *Saturday Night*, the *Globe and Mail*, *Canadian Fiction*, and other magazines and newspapers. Both as a playwright and fiction writer she typically creates complex but zany characters, uses bright, witty dialogue, and turns everyday events into humorous situations.

SINCLAIR ROSS (1908-   )

Sinclair Ross, one of Canada's most highly respected novelists and short story writers, was born in Shellbrook, Saskatchewan and worked for the Royal Bank from the age of sixteen until his retirement in 1968. He then lived in Greece and Spain before returning to Canada in 1980. Ross's literary reputation rests primarily on his novel *As for Me and My House* (1941) and his short story collection *The Lamp at Noon and*

Other Stories (1968). The novel and most of the stories explore the theme of intellectual isolation in rural and small-town life on the prairies during the drought and depression of the 1930s. While the situations he portrays are frequently bleak, they include moments of humour and satire. The psychological penetration and the careful craftsmanship of his work have given Ross a prominent place in Canadian literature even though the quantity of his published work is relatively small.

ANDREAS SCHROEDER (1946-   )

Born in Germany, Schroeder immigrated to Canada with his family in 1951. He studied creative writing at the University of British Columbia, receiving his B.A. in 1969 and his M.A. in 1972. He has been an instructor of creative writing, a columnist for the Vancouver *Province*, chairman of the Writer's Union of Canada, and founder and editor of the journal, *Contemporary Literature in Translation*. Much of Schroeder's writing has been influenced by European surrealism. His strongest work is probably *The Late Man* (1972), a collection of short fiction, although he has also published several volumes of poetry.

DUNCAN CAMPBELL SCOTT (1862-1947)

Scott was born in Ottawa and had a long career in the Department of Indian Affairs, starting as a copy clerk in 1879 and rising to deputy superintendent, a post he held from 1923 until his retirement in 1932. An accomplished poet and short story writer, Scott found material for some of his best work in both genres through travels associated with his work with Canada's Native peoples. Frequently grouped with his contemporaries, Bliss Carman, Sir Charles G.D. Roberts, and Archibald Lampman, and considered predominantly a Romantic nature poet, Scott's literary reputation has remained high while the others' have diminished. His most anthologized poems today are descriptive narratives depicting some aspect of Indian experience. They frequently involve tragic irony and evoke a sense of both the harshness and beauty of nature.

RAYMOND SOUSTER (1921-   )

A native of Toronto, Raymond Souster has spent all his life in that city, with the exception of military service from 1941 to 1945. Souster is an urban poet. His poetry depicts the experiences of real people and uses the rhythms and vocabulary of everyday speech. More than two dozen collections of his poetry have been published, including *The Colour of the Times* (1964), which won the Governor General's Award for poetry. Souster has also been very influential in promoting the development of Canadian literature by encouraging young poets, editing literary magazines and anthologies, co-founding Contact Press, and serving as chairman of the League of Canadian Poets from 1967 to 1971.

MURIEL SPARK (1918-   )

Muriel Spark was born and educated in Edinburgh and spent several years in Central Africa. She returned to the United Kingdom during World War II and worked in the political intelligence department of the Foreign Office. She has gained international recognition for her fiction, which has been published in twenty different languages. Her most well-known novel, *The Prime of Miss Jean Brodie* (1961), about a remarkable Scottish schoolmistress, was adapted for both the stage and screen and enjoyed great success. In addition to writing more than a dozen novels, including *The Ballad of Peckham Rye* (1960), *The Bachelors* (1960), and *The Mandelbaum Gate* (1965), Muriel Spark has written numerous poems, plays, and short stories.

WILLIAM STAFFORD (1914-   )

Born in Kansas, William Stafford was a quiet, gentle religious youth, who, as a conscientious objector, did missionary work during World War II. Much of his adult life has been spent as a professor of English at Lewis and Clark College in Portland, Oregon. Stafford's poetry, like Wordsworth's, is rooted in the common world, and his poetic purpose is to make us see vividly the significance in ordinary events. He is such a keen observer of nature, and describes it so graphically, that when he writes "I could hear the wilderness listen," we are convinced of the truth of his words.

FRANK SULLIVAN (1892-1976)

Frank Sullivan, American humourist, was a member of the Algonquin Round Table, and a staff-member and writer for the New Yorker. His later works include *The Night the Old Nostalgia Burned Down* (1953), *A Moose in the Hoose* (1959), and *Frank Sullivan Through the Looking Glass* (1970).

DYLAN THOMAS (1914-1953)

The Welsh poet Dylan Thomas had an extraordinarily varied career during his unfortunately short life. His first two books were poetry, *Eighteen Poems* (1934) and *Twenty-five Poems* (1936), in which his strong sexual imagery and interest in metaphysical themes proclaimed a unique poetic vision. His third book, *The Map of Love* (1939), included stories and poems whose imagery sometimes included surreal elements. His subsequent writing included semi-autobiographical works. During the war years, Dylan Thomas's poetry looked through the eyes of his boyhood and reaffirmed his religious faith. During and after the war, he made films and broadcast frequently. With his rich Welsh voice, he was a superb reader of broadcast scripts and poetry, especially his own. He completed his last work, *Under Milk Wood*, a play for voices, a month before his death, but was still in the process of revising it for the stage and for publication. At the time of his death, Thomas had several unfinished works in progress, including a libretto for an opera to be composed by Stravinsky.

DENNIS TRUDELL (1938-   )

Dennis Trudell was born in Buffalo, New York, and educated at Denison University and the University of Iowa. He has taught English in colleges and universities in Wisconsin, Hawaii, and Pennsylvania. His poems have appeared in numerous anthologies including *New Voices in American Poetry*, *The Ardis Anthology of New American Poetry*, and *Quickly Aging Here: Some Poets of the Seventies*. His collections of poems include *The Guest* (1971), *Transient Tic* (1971), and *Avenues* (1972).

W.D. VALGARDSON (1939-   )

W.D. Valgardson grew up in Gimli, a primarily Icelandic settlement in the Interlake district of Manitoba. He was educated at the University of Manitoba and the University of Iowa. After teaching for some time in the United States, he returned to Canada and is currently head of the creative writing programme at the University of Victoria. He has published several volumes of short stories: *Bloodflowers* (1973), *God Is Not a Fish Inspector* (1975), and *Red Dust* (1978); a volume of poetry, *In the Gutting Shed* (1981);

and a novel, *Gentle Sinners*, which won the Books-in-Canada Award for the best first novel published in Canada in 1980. Most of Valgardson's fiction is set in small towns or isolated communities, such as the area in which he grew up. Many of his stories involve loneliness, isolation, and a struggle to survive and maintain human dignity in the face of poverty and a harsh environment.

E.B. WHITE (1899-1985)

Elwyn Brooks White, born in Mount Vernon, New York, is best known as a humourist who commented upon contemporary culture. After working on a newspaper, he became a contributing editor of the weekly magazine *The New Yorker*, writing the column "The Talk of the Town." Several of his books are compilations of these weekly columns. In addition to his essays on modern trends, urban and suburban life, governments, and New York, White also wrote poetry and two children's books which have become classics: *Stuart Little* (1945), a fantasy about a mouse in a human family, and *Charlotte's Web* (1942), about a girl's two pets, a pig and a spider. With his wife Katherine, White edited *A Subtreasury of American Humor* (1941). A brilliant stylist, he revised *The Elements of Style* (1959), a writing manual by his former professor, William Strunk, Jr.

WALT WHITMAN (1819-1892)

Walt Whitman was born on a farm on Long Island, and as a boy and young man was able to enjoy the natural countryside as well as the excitement of Manhattan. He spent his early professional years as a journalist and newspaper editor, getting involved in the politics and intellectual controversies of the day. He gave up newspaper work to concentrate on his great work, *Leaves of Grass*, which he published at his own expense in 1855. The work, with the exhuberance of its revolutionary new free-verse form and its celebration of the sensual world of experience, was far ahead of its time, and so it received little favourable attention from literary critics. However, the great Transcendentalist philosopher, Ralph Waldo Emerson, wrote to Whitman immediately after reading the book, "I greet you at the beginning of a great career." Slowly, European poets and critics came to appreciate Whitman's genius, but his fellow citizens still ignored him, and Whitman lived his life in poverty.

The poetry which some of his contemporaries termed "obscene" and later generations have hailed as daring and revolutionary reflects Whitman's love of the democratic spirit and the goodness of the common man. As one critic writes, Whitman "extolled the values of the common, the miracle of the mouse, the wholesome soundness of the calloused hand, the body's sweat." His use of rhythm in his verse was "symphonic," and his use of symbols and poetic figures was fresh and inspired by experience.

ELLEN WILLIS (1941-   )

Ellen Willis was born in New York city and attended a large high school in Queens. Her less-than-ideal high-school experiences form the basis for "Memoirs of a Non-Prom Queen," an essay written in response to Ralph Keyes's *Is There Life After High School?* After completing her secondary school education, Willis attended Barnard College and Berkeley, then became a journalist and rock music critic for *The New Yorker* and for *Rolling Stone*. She has also been an associate or contributing editor of *Cheetah*, *Us*, *Rolling Stone* and *Ms.* magazines. Her collection of twenty-eight essays, *Beginning to See the Light* (1981), encompasses a wide variety of topics, including rock music, film, politics, religion, and feminism. Her style is energetic, provocative, and frequently humorous.

WILLIAM WORDSWORTH (1770-1850)

Born in Cumberland, England, and educated at Cambridge University, Wordsworth lived for a time in France before returning to England and settling in Dorsetshire with his sister Dorothy. His friendship and collaboration with Dorothy and with Samuel Taylor Coleridge influenced his writing. Wordsworth concerned himself in his poetry with the life and language of the common person, rather than with the artificial diction of much eighteenth-century verse. He believed that excessive emphasis on the analytic, logical faculties of our minds led to a divorce of humankind from the natural world, and saw the imagination as a power which could unite the two. In many of his poems, natural scenes are described by a solitary observer to himself or to a close friend. Wordsworth was appointed Poet Laureate in 1843.

EVA-LIS WUORIO (1918-   )

Eva-Lis Wuorio was born in Finland, but is now a Canadian citizen. She has also lived in England, the United States, and Spain. Her published work includes adult mystery novels, young-adult books, and picture books for young children. Two of her more recent works are *Escape if You Can: Thirteen Tales of the Preternatural* (1977) and *Detour to Danger*.

DALE ZIEROTH (1946-   )

Dale Zieroth was born in Neepawa, Manitoba, a farming community where his German grandfather had settled. He attended local schools and the University of Manitoba before moving to Toronto, where he became involved in radio, publishing, and alternative education. In the early 1970s Zieroth moved to Invermere, B.C. and worked as a park ranger in the Banff-Kootenay region. His first collection of poetry, *Clearing: Poems from a Journey* (1973), begins with vivid, often grim memories of a prairie childhood, moves to a harsh depiction of life in the city, and concludes with a more hopeful, optimistic view of living close to nature in the Canadian Rockies. A second collection of poems, *Mid-River* (1981), is set primarily in the Rockies. Zieroth's best work, which is straightforward and deceptively simple in style, expresses thoughtful concern, and exhibits considerable power and intensity.

Index of Titles

Index of Authors

Index of Selections by Genre

Nonfiction

Short Stories

Poetry

Drama

Index of Selections by Theme

This index only lists those selections which the
editors feel best represent the given themes.

Adolescence

Childhood

Cultures

Death and Dying

Family

Humour and Satire

Love

Prejudice and Discrimination

Sports

Understanding and Knowledge

Index of Selections by Author's Nationality

Canadian

English

Irish

Scottish

Welsh

American

Credits

p.1 From *I Might Not Tell Everybody This* by Alden Nowlan. Toronto: Clark, Irwin & Co., 1982; p.2 From *A Book of Women Poets from Antiquity to Now*, edited by A. Barnstone and W. Barnstone. New York: Schocker Books, 1980. Reprinted by permission of the publisher; p.3 From *The Game of Our Lives*, by Peter Gzowski Used by permission of The Canadian Publishers, McClelland and Stewart, Toronto; p.8 From *Dance of the Happy Shades* by Alice Munro. Toronto: McGraw-Hill Ryerson, 1968. Reprinted by permission of the publisher; p.20 From *The Readers Digest*, 36:218 (June, 1940). Reprinted by permission; p.25 From *Collected Stories* by Graham Greene. London: Heinemann, and the Bodley Head, 1972. Reprinted by permission; p.28 Reprinted by permission of Lois Gould. © 1979 Lois Gould; p.38 From *Playback: Canadian Selections*, edited by J. David and M. Park. Toronto: The Canadian Publishers, McClelland and Stewart, 1978. Reprinted by permission; p.50 From *The Norton Sampler*, edited by Thomas Cooley. New York: Norton, 1979; p.53 "Me As My Grandmother" by Rosemary Aubert is reprinted from *Two Kinds of Honey* by permission of Oberon Press; p.54 From *The Burning Heart: Women Poets of Japan*. San Francisco: Leabury Press, 1977; p.55 From *Happy to Be Here* by Garrison Keillor. Markham, Ont.: Penguin, 1983; p.60 From *West of Fiction*, edited by L. Flater, A. van Herk and R. Wiebe. Edmonton: The West Press, 1983. Reprinted by permission of the author; p.69 From *A Choice of Dreams* by Joy Kogawa. Used by permission of The Canadian Publishers, McClelland and Stewart, Toronto; p.70 From *First People, First Voices*, edited by Penny Petrone. Toronto; University of Toronto Press, 1983. Reprinted by permission of the author; p.78 From *Poems New & Selected* by Patrick Lane. Toronto: Oxford University Press, 1978. Reprinted by permission of the author; p.80 "God Is Not A Fish Inspector" by W.D. Valgardson is reprinted from *God Is Not a Fish Inspector* by permission of Oberon Press; p.93 Copyright © 1972/77/79 by the New York Times Company. Reprinted by permission; p.96 Reprinted by permission of Faber and Faber Ltd. from *Collected* Poems *by W.H. Auden; p.98 from* Unto Dust *by Herman Charles Bosman. Capetown: Human & Rousseau, 1963. Reprinted by permission of the publisher; p.106 From* Quickly Aging Here: Some Poets of the 1970's, *edited by Geoff Hewitt. New York: Doubleday, 1969; p.107 From* Leaves of Grass, *edited by John Kouwenhoven. New York: The Modern Library. © 1950 Random House; p.108 Reprinted by permission of Don Congdon Associates, Inc. Copyright © 1950 by Ray Bradbury; Renewed 1978 by Ray Bradbury; p.121 From* Nobody Danced with Miss Rodes *by Sid Marty. Used by permission of The Canadian Publishers, McClelland and Stewart, Toronto; p.123 From* Ritter in Residence *by Erika Ritter. Used by permission of The Canadian Publishers, McClelland and Stewart, Toronto; p.131 "Lagoons, Hanlan's Point" is reprinted from* Collected Poems of Raymond Souster *by permission of Oberon Press; p.133 From* The Collected Stories of Hortense